Ad
Management,
and Society
A Business Point of View

Advertising, Management, and Society

A Business Point of View

Francesco M. Nicosia

Professor and Director, Consumer Research Program
Graduate School of Business Administration
University of California at Berkeley

A Project of the Consumer Research Program

McGRAW-HILL BOOK COMPANY

New York   St. Louis   San Francisco   Düsseldorf   Johannesburg
Kuala Lumpur   London   Mexico   Montreal   New Delhi   Panama
Paris   São Paulo   Singapore   Sydney   Tokyo   Toronto

ADVERTISING, MANAGEMENT, AND SOCIETY: A BUSINESS POINT OF VIEW

1234567890 MAMM 7987654

Library of Congress Cataloging in Publication Data

Nicosia, Francesco M
    Advertising, management, and society.

    A project of the Consumer Research Program, Graduate
School of Business Administration, University of California
at Berkeley.
    Based on testimony given before the Federal Trade
Commission in 1971 by members of the American Associa-
tion of Advertising Agencies and the Association of
National Advertisers.
    1. Advertising—United States. 2. Advertising.
I. California. University. Graduate School of
Business Administration. II. United States. Federal
Trade Commission. III. Title.
HF5813.U6N52   659.1'0973   74-2053
ISBN 0-07-046528-2
ISBN 0-07-046527-4 (pbk.)

This book was set in Press Roman by Allen Wayne Technical Corp. The editor was
Thomas H. Kothman; the designer was Allen Wayne Technical Corp.; the production
supervisor was Judi Frey.
The Maple Press Company was printer and binder.

To

A.F.,
D.M.,
M.E., and,
perhaps, x

Contents

Foreword

A foreword can sometimes be an opportunity to carry the theme of a book into a wider area of speculation. The theme of this book is that advertising needs to be better understood, both as a practice and an institution. As Spinoza would have put it, with understanding, our passions disappear. Those of us who become so irritated with the apparently inane "messages" of TV—those "pauses for a moment for station identification"—might pause for a moment ourselves to ask what "they" are trying to tell us and why they are trying. The word "appreciation" catches the spirit of the text; an appreciation is an honest appraisal and does not imply praise or blame, but rather a fine critical viewpoint.

To extend this appreciation of advertising a further step, I'd like to explore the viewpoint that advertising is one component of our culture's educational system. We educators often like to think of education as primarily the effort of the schools, from K to 12 to Bachelor to Master to Ph.D. However, in our more honest moments we must admit that education occurs everywhere, in the family, between friends, on the highway, in political speeches—everywhere, including advertising. Education is the process of learning; it should not be construed as merely knowledge acquisition, since it is a process of learning that enables us to make better decisions for ourselves and those we hold dear.

Educators are fond of dividing the educational system into faculty, students, administrators, and the public who pays. In the schools, we can do a reasonably good job of identifying these groups. But in advertising, the task of identifying the students becomes fantastically difficult. The teacher must stand on the corner, so to speak, delivering his lecture to all and sundry who pass by, some of whom are students, most of whom are not. Nor do most students attend his class for very long, and, therefore, his lecture must be very brief and to the point. No wonder there is such a vast amount of irrelevancy and redundancy in this school! Indeed, one begins to see why these two qualities, which exist in all educational programs, are really essential and valuable if they are properly designed into the system. In a school system where the student's interests are not well defined, as in liberal arts and advertising, the teacher must say a great deal that is irrelevant and/or redundant to many students.

I'd like to explore one very important feature of the educational process, especially as it appears in advertising; this is the pendulum that sweeps us from deception to enlightenment and back. Teachers often perceive their task as one of leading the student from ignorance-deception to the safe ground of basic understanding—of language, numbers, history, and nature. According to this view, once the student has learned his basics, he can begin to conquer other areas of ignorance-deception and thus gradually enlighten himself with the teacher's help.

The relevance of all this to advertising in a competitive economy is that, except for one area, advertising education has no basics, and its materials are taught in essentially a confusing manner. The one exceptional area discussed in the text concerns the measurements of size, weight, purity, etc., those matters that are important to the "school administrators" who work in the FDA and like offices. Beyond these basics lies confusion, which after all is the essence of education. Consider the matter of aspirin, We students go to various "classes," where the faculty tell us in no uncertain terms that all aspirin tablets are alike *and* that all aspirin tablets are *not* alike. What a school! But it is a school that enables each one of us to learn in our own individual way. And it is interesting to note that in the American system there is presently a strong trend away from teaching basic knowledge to the masses and toward teaching "competency" to the individual.

Is there any advantage to entertaining this speculation that advertising is a component of the educational system? I think so because I believe that this book should prove very valuable to those who are concerned with educational policy, just as I think that many of the innovations and methods of evaluation in education should prove useful to the advertising subsystem. The educators should be able to learn from the advertisers how to "teach" in areas of knowledge where there are no basics or agreed-upon doctrines, and the advertisers should be able to learn from the educators how to send much more informative and intellectually stimulating messages.

C. West Churchman
Professor and Research Philosopher
University of California, Berkeley

Preface

In both ancient and modern times, many societies have been able to go beyond fulfilling the need for survival. These societies have achieved material *abundance* in different ways, through different customs, laws, institutions, and technologies. Yet they have all utilized the same raw material: the physical, intellectual, and ethical energy inherent in all humans.

Along with material abundance comes the gradual increase in *discretion of choice;* consciously or unconsciously, a society and its members are involved in a stream of decisions defining what particular aspects of abundance they are interested in. They are making choices concerning *quality* rather than *quantity.* At this stage of development, the role of intellectual and ethical energy becomes greater relative to that of physical energy. *Affluence* is the opportunity to utilize intellectual and ethical energy in order to shape a future in which individuals are relieved from toil and can work toward achieving aesthetic and ethical goods.

At the same time, affluence poses an intellectual and ethical challenge, a challenge so difficult that most societies have failed to grasp its full meaning and potential. When they emerge from the long struggle to harness physical energies and attain material wealth, individuals and societies seem to be culturally unprepared to distinguish between quantity and quality. And failure to change one's own culture—i.e., one's norms, laws, institutions, and technologies—in order to deal with intellectual and ethical matters leads to a loss of historical momentum, to decay, and even to a loss of abundance.

Personal and *mass communication* have been key factors in shaping the long journey from survival to abundance and, eventually, to affluence and beyond. Modern, affluent societies have become particularly dependent on the existence of a *mass communication* system, for this system carries information about all possible individual and social choices—with regard to work, religion, politics, and so on. Affluent societies are now faced with the problem of managing this system: how can a mass communication system help society and its members make choices concerning the quality of individual and social life?

Advertising is only a part of a mass communication system, that part that deals with the exchange of economic information. But, as we shall see, this neat abstraction may hide the fact that each ad, as well as the entire advertising institution, is an integral part of a society's mass communication system and, ultimately, a product of its cultural ethos.

As a form of mass communication, advertising has been used since ancient times.

Its merits and demerits have been debated heatedly and repetitiously but, until recently, few efforts have been devoted to a systematic and detailed examination of what it actually does and why. *Why* do corporation executives use advertising, and how do they evaluate whether or not it works? How do advertising agencies operate? What active roles does the consumer play in the advertising institution? How does the advertising institution work and how does it relate to other social and economic institutions? What value criteria are appropriate for evaluating advertising as an institution? Is our knowledge of this institution sufficient to identify what changes are both desirable and feasible? According to what criteria?

Many groups are interested in advertising. We should thus expect to find a *multilogue*—a many-sided dialogue—taking place among them. In fact, however, it is the *critics* of advertising from whom we hear the most. Who has not heard of the views publicized by Packard and Galbraith? And what college student does not remember the negative evaluations of advertising by many (neoclassical) economists?

Consumers have played a much smaller role in this multilogue. One of the few comprehensive and imaginative studies of consumers' feelings, by Bauer and Greyser, has received curiously little attention. Occasionally we hear from consumers through complaints presented to courts or government agencies, but no foundation or government agency has undertaken any systematic monitoring or analysis of these complaints.

The *business community* has also remained relatively silent. As D. M. Kendall, chairman of the board of Pepsico, recently reiterated, "American advertising can sell many goods and services, but it has never found a way to sell itself." Until recently, there have been almost no systematic and comprehensive attempts made to communicate the why, what, and how of advertising from the points of view of business.

Nevertheless, an attempt was made to present a business point of view when the Federal Trade Commission held extensive hearings on modern advertising practices in the fall of 1971. Many witnesses submitted written testimonies. The Association of National Advertisers (ANA) and the American Association of Advertising Agencies (4As) organized and coordinated twenty-six written testimonies by corporate executives of member firms. The selection of practitioners satisfied a previously expressed desire by the Federal Trade Commission for evidence and experience rather than theory. (Exhibit A lists the names, positions, and firms of the witnesses, and Exhibit B gives a brief description of the two associations.)

THE CONTENT AND ORGANIZATION OF THE BOOK

The testimonies of corporate executives at the FTC hearings are the basic material of this book. They provide a new resource for the study of two major facets of adver-

EXHIBIT A

Alphabetical list of the Association of National Advertisers (ANA) and the American Association of Advertising Agencies (4As) witnesses, Federal Trade Commission (FTC) hearings, Fall 1971.[a]

ACHENBAUM, A. A., senior vice president, J. Walter Thompson Company

BANKS, S., vice president, Leo Burnett Company

CLAGGETT, W. M., vice president, Ralston Purina Company

COOK, S. W., chairman & chief executive officer, General Foods Corporation

COUSINS, N., former editor, *Saturday Review,* and editor, *World Review*

CRICHTON, J., president, American Association of Advertising Agencies

CUMMINGS, B. A., chairman, executive committee, Compton Advertising, Inc.

DEMSETZ, H., professor of economics, University of California at Los Angeles

DILLON, T., president & chief executive officer, Batten, Barton, Durstine & Osborn, Inc.

ENNIS, F. B., vice president, Booz, Allen & Hamilton, Inc.

GRAY, E. II, chairman of the finance committee, Whirlpool Corporation

HARDIN, D. K., president, Market Facts, Inc.

HEISKELL, A., chairman of the board, Time, Inc.

KENDALL, D. M., president & chief executive officer, Pepsico, Inc.

KRUGMAN, H. E., manager, public opinion research, General Electric Company

LIGHT, L., vice president, Batten, Barton, Durstine & Osborn, Inc.

LOEVINGER, L., attorney, Hogan & Hartson, and former FCC commissioner

MANELOVEG, H. D., executive vice president, McCann-Erickson, Inc.

MAYANS, F., vice president, Federated Department Stores, Inc.

OVERHOLSER, C. E., senior vice president, Young & Rubicam, Inc.

PERLMUTTER, M., president, Supermarkets General Corp.

SCHWARTZ, P. K., attorney, Davis, Gilbert, Levine & Schwartz

SEAMAN, A. J., president, SSC&B, Inc.

SKINNER, L. E., chairman of the board & chief executive officer, Skinner Macaroni Co.

THIELE, E. M., vice chairman, Leo Burnett Company

WEBBER, G., senior vice president, Benton & Bowles, Inc.

[a]This book also includes the written testimony of H. H. BELL, president, American Advertising Federation (AAF). The witnesses' affiliation is as of Fall 1971.

EXHIBIT B

From John Crighton, president, American Association of Advertising Agencies:
   pp. 2-3 of his presentation to the FTC Hearings, Fall 1971.

It may be appropriate at this point to explain the organizational auspices under which the material is submitted to the Commission. The Association of National Advertisers was founded in 1914; its membership of 500 companies is estimated to account for 75% of the national advertising in the country; while its members include the largest of American advertisers, it also includes many companies with relatively small advertising budgets—some 25% of its members spend less than $1 million in advertising in their annual budgets. It will from time to time be referred to as A.N.A.

The American Association of Advertising Agencies was founded in 1917; its membership of 363 agencies is estimated to account for about 75% of the national advertising placed through advertising agencies in this country. While most of the largest agencies in the United States are members, the median agency in the association bills about $1,750,000, and a number bill $300,000 or less. By billings we mean space and time ordered for advertising clients of which perhaps 15% would be agency gross income. That is to say, an agency with $2,000,000 in billings would be a company with about $300,000 of gross income, and the average net income is .6% or $12,000. It will be referred to from time to time as the Four As.

The only importance of this information here is that each organization is the only national organization of its kind, and that each represents a national cross-section—both large and small companies—throughout the country.

While these two organizations have not necessarily agreed on everything over the past half-century, they played a joint and combined role in the support of audited circulation, in the establishment and support of the Advertising Research Foundation, and in the establishment and support of the Advertising Council, which is our public service advertising organization.

As to why the two organizations elected to ask for a joint presentation: Simply that it seemed redundant to ask for the time to make two presentations, each of which would inevitably cover much of the same material.

tising: (1) advertising as a managerial function in business firms, and (2) advertising as an entire institution in society and the economy. They provide unique insights into *why* corporate managers consider advertising important at the managerial and the socioeconomic level. The presentations are candid and of immediate interest; more important, they include data that were previously unpublished or not readily available.

To make these testimonies accessible to interested audiences, it was necessary to shorten and rearrange them. Furthermore, extensive commentaries were inserted throughout the text for the following purposes: to furnish background information; to outline the main themes and give them continuity; to provide clarification by including additional points that emerged in the discussions between witnesses and commissioners; and to point toward the research necessary to describe and evaluate advertising at both the micromanagerial and macrosocial levels.

The commentaries are interpretations of the facts and views submitted by the witnesses. I based these interpretations on the growing number of theories and data in economics and the behavioral sciences that, in my opinion, underlie and explain the testimonies. I also tried to search for some of the still-elusive foundations—conceptual and empirical—that must precede individual and social action.

A unique aspect of the book's material is that it covers practically all the fundamental issues and criticisms that have dominated the literature for decades. (It was not an easy task to telescope so much into just one book.) Although comprehensive in its coverage of issues and criticisms, the book discusses advertising from the inside; thus, the resulting picture is one-sided. However unfashionable it may be, this choice of perspective is deliberate. There are two reasons for this: first, since most of the existing literature is *also* one-sided, by presenting the practitioners' responses, the book can contribute another side to the multilogue; and, second, I believe that it is in the interest of all parties to understand why practitioners act and feel the way they do. Understanding the facts, theories, and perspectives presented by the witnesses will help all who are concerned with identifying the parameters of the problems and thus increase their ability to work together toward satisfying individual and social needs. I am told that Oliver Wendell Holmes once said: "Many ideas grow better when transplanted into another mind than in the one where they sprang up." Let us hope that this will eventually be true of our subject.

The organization of this book was suggested by two of the most common meanings of the term *advertising.* The first is relatively narrow: it refers to what consumers see—an ad—and, by extension, to the activities that lead to it. Busy as we are with our daily lives, most of us consumers are unaware of the complexity of these activities, and have only a vague notion of what problems businesses attempt to solve.

Part 1 describes the problems advertisers and advertising agencies face in preparing, executing, and assessing an advertising campaign. It stresses the *why* of advertising management from the overall corporate perspective of one firm. Part 1 is essentially managerially, micro-oriented; it provides a picture of real-life problems and decision processes.

In its second meaning, the term advertising does not refer to a specific ad, to one advertiser or advertising agency, or to one mass medium. It refers to the *entire institution*—the set of all uses by all people and organizations of a society's mass communication system for economic purposes. Although most of the issues and criticisms in the literature ultimately concern advertising as an institution, our basic knowledge of this institution is extremely limited. This should not surprise us, for it is far more difficult to observe an institution than an individual, to study macro rather than micro phenomena. We share this problem with many other disciplines. (Let us recall that, in the 200 years of economic research preceding J. M. Keynes, there was no macroeconomics.)

Part 2 has a macro-orientation—that is, it focuses on the institution in its entirety, as a functional whole. It discusses theories and empirical evidence that may help us describe, and eventually explain, the internal structure of the advertising institution, its interactions with other institutions, and its possible roles in socioeconomic change. This macro approach is an attempt to answer a plea expressed a few years ago by Leo Bogart: ". . . the proper study of advertising research is the advertising system, and not of advertisements. . . . Why don't we start with the big picture, with a view of advertising as a tremendous institution which deserves study in its own right . . ." This macro approach is novel and thus naturally far from being conclusive, but it is essential to the comprehension and evaluation of the advertising institution.

By approaching Part 1 first, the reader gains the factual information at the firm level that may help him in considering the broad institutional problems examined in Part 2. Conversely, reading Part 2 first provides the overall perspective for the examination of the operations of advertisers and agencies presented in Part 1. Clearly, the two parts are interdependent, and the choice will depend on the reader's particular interest.

THE AUDIENCES OF THE BOOK

There are several groups of readers who may be interested in the data, viewpoints, and explanations presented in this book. The first group is made up of students and teachers interested in *why* advertising operates as it does. The book may be used in courses on advertising, marketing, and related topics. In view of the growing social concern with advertising, it should be very helpful in courses in Business and Society, Corporate Social Responsibility, and similar topics that are increasingly offered in many departments. The book's material is also relevant for courses in Consumer Behavior and Consumerism, for it provides much information about how consumers actually behave.

The second group of readers for whom this book is potentially of interest are those who work in advertising and other business areas. Many people working in accounting, finance, production, and personnel may seek a better understanding of the advertising function in their own firms. Some may have difficulty in explaining advertising to their friends and neighbors—and perhaps even to themselves. If they are unfamiliar with the advertising business, and given the popularity of the Packard and Galbraith views, they may even be ambivalent about advertising.[1] The facts reported in this book should have a special appeal to this audience.

Finally, the information in this book should also be useful to all who are interested in both the daily decisions made by advertisers and advertising agencies and their possible consequences on the economy and society.

ACKNOWLEDGEMENTS

It is always hard to remember one's own creditors. Strange as it may seem, I find it particularly difficult to remember those whose ideas are basic, for I tend to assimilate their ideas completely and then believe that they are mine. Among my creditors I should certainly list my students, from Ph.D.s to M.B.A.s to undergraduates. The latter have an especially uncanny ability to ask *enfant prodige* questions that have the effect of pulling the rug out from under me and making me rethink. Many of them will recognize in this book not only my lecture notes, but also the points that emerged in class because of their questions. Of the persons involved with the manuscript's development, I should name Mihir Bhattacharya, Robert Dunkle, Terry Kwan, Robert Mayer, Stephen Middlebrook, and Tyzoon Tyebjee.

Mary Oppenheimer made the mistake, once again, of volunteering her help. From the first to the final draft she guided my writing through the ineffable nuances and fluid grammar of English and, in her usual maieutic way, succeeded in also guiding my thinking. Her contributions were restricted only by my myopia and other, similar limitations, which I have in abundance (this, of course, is not my fault—I am told that humans are shaped entirely by the system and by genetics). But her contributions are all in the file; I thus sincerely hope that she will put them together in a manuscript that, I am certain, will provide healthy ecological competition for mine. Ellen McGibbon was supposed to just type all the drafts; caught up in the dialectical debate between Mary and me, she obviously ended up doing much more.

[1] Insights into this problem are to be found in two comparable studies of businessmen's opinions made in 1962 and 1971; see S. A. Greyser, "Businessmen re Advertising: Yes, But...," *Harvard Business Review*, May-June 1962; S. A. Greyser and B. B. Reece, "Businessmen Look Hard at Advertising," *Harvard Business Review*, May-June 1971; and S. A. Greyser and B. B. Reece, "Advertising Standards and Contents: Executives' Perspective," Working Paper, Marketing Science Institute, July 1972.

Several teachers and businessmen read parts of the manuscript, and I have tried to thank each one in the appropriate places. Paul Gerhold was especially generous with his time. Tom Carmody's belief in the original idea of this book was very helpful. A few colleagues tried their best to explain that I might commit academic suicide by limiting myself to presenting and interpreting a business point of view. But I am optimistic that we can turn the past unbalanced monologue into a constructive multi-logue. All in all, I am responsible for the content of this book, but I cannot take credit for its form.

The institutional climate provided by the Consumer Research Program, the Survey Research Center, the Institute of Business and Economic Research, and the Under-graduate and Graduate Schools of Business Administration, University of California, Berkeley, was very helpful. I appreciate this climate, for it is rare in a so-called state-supported institution, especially on a campus where "business" is not considered by many to be an academic discipline. Somehow, however, our foreman, R. H. Holton, still manages to bridge the widening gap between us on the firing line and the boards where strategy and priorities are set.

Last, but not least, I acknowledge the aid of the officers of the Association of National Advertisers and of the American Association of Advertising Agencies (especially John Crighton and Chet LaRoche). Without too much knowledge of what I had in mind, they helped me to gain direct access to more than 700 pages of typewritten testimonies, and literally volumes of other testimonies and questions and answers. I am also grateful to the witnesses for allowing me to omit many parts of their testimonies.

*Let everyone sweep in front of his own
door and the whole world will be clean.*

Goethe

Francesco M. Nicosia

Chapter 1

Introduction

OUTLINE

1 Social Groups and Mass Communication

2 Advertising in Society's Mass Communication System

3 The Components of the Advertising Institution
   3.1   Component 1: The Senders of Messages
   3.2   Component 2: The Seekers/Receivers of Messages
   3.3   Component 3: The Mass Media
   3.4   Component 4: The Advertising Agencies
   3.5   Component 5: Legislative and Regulatory Agencies
   3.6   Component 6: The Information Flow through the Institution

4 Summary

This chapter provides a background to both Part 1 and Part 2. We begin by considering mass communication within social groups; we then look at advertising as the use of a society's mass communication system for economic purposes; the chapter concludes with a brief sketch of the modern advertising institution and a description of its major components follow.

1 SOCIAL GROUPS AND MASS COMMUNICATION

Different life forms seem to prefer different life styles: some forms tend to live alone; others to live in groups. One necessary condition for living entities to form a group is the ability to communicate with one another. A group that can communicate effectively can get more things done than a group whose members cannot communicate as well. For communication to exist there must be a two-way interaction, at the very least. As a group increases in size and complexity, communication becomes a multi-way phenomenon.

     Humans excel in their potential to communicate. They communicate for many purposes—to express needs, hopes, moods, ideas, and so forth. They use communication

1

within the family, in schools, churches, theatres, political arenas, and the marketplace. As the size and complexity of a human group increases, the need for each member to communicate with many others increases in frequency and intensity. The need for *mass communication*—from one to the many—is ancient, as is the search for *means* of mass communication.

Facial expressions and bodily movements are somewhat limited means of mass communication. So man invented symbols—music, graphics, and languages—and added to the plain written and spoken word more precise, although limiting, languages such as geometry, calculus, algebra, and topology. The combination of a language and a powerful voice was one method of mass communication: thousands of years ago, central governments began to use criers to announce war victories, laws, religious ceremonies, and taxes; farmers and shopkeepers employed barkers to attract the attention of passers-by; army officers selected assistants with powerful voices to tell the soldiers what to do above the clamor of battle. Signs and then handbill messages also became means of mass communication.

But all this was still not enough. By accident or on purpose, through individual curiosity or government-sponsored research, new means for mass communication were discovered. These included print, the telephone, and then—in an increasing tempo— radio, television, coaxial cable, microfiche, and lasers, with each new discovery interacting with the others to create newer and more powerful vehicles for transmitting information, meanings, and, inevitably, influence.[1]

Mass communication is useful to society and must be nurtured. There are many ways to encourage a smoothly functioning system of mass communication. Thus, conventions, habits, mores, rules, and, finally, laws were developed thousands of years ago by many different societies. Improving the usefulness of these means is one of the most pressing tasks that face us today.

2 ADVERTISING IN SOCIETY'S MASS COMMUNICATION SYSTEM

Although "advertising" has many personal meanings, we can all agree that it refers to the use of a society's mass information system for economic purposes. Individually or in groups, men want access to society's mass information system in order to give or gain information and, eventually, to buy or sell a variety of things. As societies have become more complex, and as the technology of the mass communication system has improved, more and more individuals and groups have used mass communication for economic purposes, i.e., for buying or selling goods, personal services, and ideas. The absolute increase is staggering.

In modern society, there is hardly an individual who has not been engaged in advertising activities. The housewife wants to know the Thursday specials; her husband wants to know which car dealer offers the best year-end bargain. The young lady

---

[1] On the interaction among technology, information, and meaning, see G. Gerbner, "Communication and Social Environment," *Scientific American,* September 1972.

wonders whether the newest fashions shown in a magazine are available in local stores. While scanning a technical magazine, the eyes of the industrial purchasing manager are caught by a gorgeous model; his mind also registers that she is announcing the first error-free disk pack. The self-made steel distributor browses through a magazine at home, and the furniture ad makes him wonder if he should add a little extra touch to his new office.

The bright, young teacher has accepted a post at a different university and, although he condemns advertising as "manipulative," he prepared a classified ad to sell his house directly, thus avoiding the "useless" services of a real estate agent. (He may learn, however, how much time, skill, and knowledge are required, and that, to some callers, his ad seems misleading.) A church wants to hire a new minister or dispose of its obsolete pipe organ, a branch of the armed services wants to make it known that it now offers a three-year rather than the usual four-year program, and so on.

These examples help us realize why it is so difficult to understand and describe the advertising institution. *It is because advertising is used by everyone, not only by sellers of consumer goods.* Moreover, advertising is intrinsically related to the mass information system in cultural, economic, and technological ways. It interacts with all the other uses of the system and shares all the related problems—including the problem of regulation.

3 THE COMPONENTS OF THE ADVERTISING INSTITUTION

Our present knowledge of advertising is limited and uneven. At the managerial level, economic realities have forced each firm to search for ways to communicate economically with those consumers who might be interested in its product. In this sense, advertising has developed as a business function similar to production, finance, accounting, and so forth. We have some knowledge of how it contributes to the basic goals of any firm by matching the demands of some consumer group (which produces revenues) with the demands of labor, suppliers of material, capital, and public services (which produce costs). In particular, we understand reasonably well the problems faced by advertisers or advertising agencies and why managers approach such problems in particular ways. We shall develop an appreciation of the nature *and* the limitations of what we know about advertising as a business function from many of the testimonies reported in this book.

Our knowledge is far less satisfactory—perhaps completely inadequate—when we look at advertising as an institution, i.e., the set of all the people and activities concerned with the sending and the seeking or receiving of information for economic purposes. In recent decades, billions of dollars have been devoted to the study of such economic and social phenomena as production technology, labor, education, health, and poverty. Yet, in the field of advertising, government agencies and foundations have devoted very little time and money to the collection of appropriate data and appropriate analyses. We shall see that many of the federal statistics describing the advertising institution are, in fact, reprints of data collected by private advertising groups! Many discussions of public policy issues do not even seem aware that we lack concepts and data appropriate to the study of advertising as an institution, without which it is impossible to evaluate its macro roles in the economy and society.[1] In fact, the old mistake of confusing macro and micro approaches is still common in the literature.

Even though we are hindered by a lack of concepts and data, we can tentatively sketch the anatomy and physiology of the modern advertising institution. The overview of the institution and its major components that follows will also provide a perspective on the micromanagerial activities of advertisers and advertising agencies described in Part 1.

We group all the subjects and activities that make up the institution into six basic components and briefly describe what these components are, how they may interact among themselves, and what we know, or should know, about them. The components to be discussed are: the senders of messages; the seekers/receivers of messages; the mass media; the advertising agencies; legislative and regulatory agencies; and the entities being advertised.

3.1 COMPONENT 1: THE SENDERS OF MESSAGES

When asked, "Who advertises?", the typical American responds, "Why, business, of course!" As mentioned earlier, business firms are by no means the only ones that send economic messages through the mass media. Consumers, nonprofit organizations, and public agencies are also regular, often large-scale, advertisers. *Individual consumers* send messages in the form of classified ads in daily and weekly newspapers. On any day, millions of them may want access to the mass communication system for any number of reasons—to *sell* a used stove, a pedigreed dog, or a personal service, or to *buy* used furniture or the services of a baby-sitter.

Groups of consumers also use the advertising system for many economic purposes. Here, the most extensive users are cooperatives, agricultural or wholesale, supermarkets, and other retail operations. Credit and insurance "unions" and the well-known Consumers' Union are other examples of consumer groups that use the advertising system to buy or sell, to recruit personnel, or to increase their memberships.

Nonprofit organizations also advertise. Community hospitals, churches, civic groups, and educational systems use mass media to attract volunteers, sell tickets for charities or pancake breakfasts, or gain support for bond issues.

Last, but not least, *government agencies*—federal, state, and local—use the advertising system. The virtues of air mail or military service, notices of bids to be let or jobs to be filled, tourist promotions within the United States—these are only a few examples. In fact, recent figures show that "Uncle Sam . . . jumped from No. 100 among leading national advertisers in 1971 to No. 68 last year. . . ."[1]

---

[1] J. G. Myers, *Social Issues in Advertising,* A.A.A.A. Educational Foundation, Inc., New York, 1971.

[2] *Business Week,* June 23, 1973, p. 89.

Despite this, there are no strong data on the use of the advertising system by many of these groups. We do not know either the total number of messages they send or their total production and transmission costs. Nor do we know how the expenditures of these subjects are allocated to various media, such as newspapers, billboards, or the post office. Finally, we do not know how much of the production cost is paid directly to business firms and how much is absorbed by using internal production facilities, such as the U.S. Government Printing Office.

This lack of data leads to embarrassing gaps in our ability to describe and evaluate the use of the advertising system by all senders of messages. To anticipate some points to be discussed in Part 2, we believe that the fixed costs of a society's mass communication system should be allocated among the various uses, i.e., general, news, political, religious, cultural, and "economic." Further, fixed costs allocated to the advertising system should be divided among the various types of sender, i.e., business firms, consumers, nonprofit organizations, governments, and public agencies.

We need more information in order both to understand the advertising system and to reach "rational" conclusions concerning its regulation. Hopefully, someone, some-where, will begin to collect the simple descriptive data just mentioned. More appropriate information will eventually allows us to describe the cost aspect of the economics of the advertising institution and also the revenues and benefits associated with its uses.

Not surprisingly, *business firms* are the major senders of advertising messages. There are millions of them, and their variety is very great, ranging from the extractive, agricultural, fishery, and forestry sectors to manufacturing, wholesaling, retailing, transportation, communication, finance, and insurance. This variety increases with the evolution of technologies, the complexity of economic specialization, and newer socioeconomic demands. As an example, consider the recent explosion of new firms in the electronics industry and the impending boom in the water and air pollution sectors.

Firms use the advertising system for *various economic purposes* beyond selling goods. Many advertise to recruit labor and managerial personnel; they buy and sell information about financial events; and they send information to the general public for both legal and public relations purposes. Yet both public and private data about these uses are very scarce. For instance, a recent study wanted to determine how medium and large corporations go about hiring new graduate students; it was to include data on the use of mass media for such purposes. In a pretest it became clear that even the most cooperative firms did not know how much they spend in advertising through mass media, how they allocate funds among the media, or the number of messages in each media per recruiting period.[1]

Existing data are limited to one use of the advertising system by business firms: the *selling* of the firms' outputs. This narrow definition directs attention and data collection away from the many other users of the system, including consumers, government agencies, and nonprofit organizations. These and other uses and users also represent a

---

[1] J. E. Bryant and W. J. Derrig, *Marketing Potential of the MBA Resume Directory*, MBA Thesis, University of California, Berkeley, June 1972.

load on the communication system, with attendant costs and benefits. Yet as long as we think of the advertising institution as including only selling by business firms, we will lack even simple measures of the overall load on the communication system and of its total costs and total benefits. We shall return to the nature and limitations of available data in Part 2.

3.2 COMPONENT 2: THE SEEKERS/RECEIVERS OF MESSAGES

Any individual or group may make contact with a message either by *seeking out* messages that contain relevant information or by *receiving* messages. Hence the term *seekers/receivers* of messages.

Messages—political, educational, religious, economic, general news—are available from a variety of sources: mass media, face-to-face conversations, even mere observation. All the individuals and groups previously listed as potential senders of messages are also potential targets for mass media messages. At any given moment, the number of potential target-message combinations is astronomical; moreover, it is bound to increase as long as the technological and institutional complexity of our society increases. The number of advertising target-message combinations is probably only a small proportion of the whole.

Discussions of advertising often overlook the fact that individual consumers are not the only targets for ads. Further, these discussions rely on outdated stereotypes to describe how consumers make contacts with ads. First, consumers are seen as passive receivers; they are not granted the ability to search actively for information relevant to them. Second, consumers are seen as receiving messages through a "hypodermic needle." That is, mass media inject their messages directly into the mind of the consumer; there are no mediating entities in the consumer's mind nor can he create antibodies.

Do these two stereotypes describe how consumers actually behave? Research on this topic began in the 1940s; initially directed at political messages, it soon spread into the field of advertising. It found that human behavior and thought processes are vastly more complex than the stereotypes had indicated. First, individuals search actively for information that is important to them, and what they seek depends on previous predispositions. Thus, a committed Democrat is more likely to expose himself to pro-Democratic than to pro-Republican messages. Second, individuals are more likely to remember information that "fits" their preferences. Finally, an individual exposed to information that conflicts with his own predispositions is likely to ignore the message, to forget it more rapidly, or to rationalize away its content.

Thus, on any given day there are millions of individuals and organizations who deliberately seek access to the advertising system. It is misleading to refer to these users as "receivers." Even when they "receive" an ad, they actively manipulate its content in a variety of ways. Consequently, seekers/receivers of ads, like senders, are active participants in the advertising system. Matching sender-message-user depends on the activities—conscious or otherwise—of both advertisers and consumers.

In real life, both advertisers and consumers must do much sorting out to arrive at a "correct" match, i.e., one that makes sense to both parties. In Part 1 we shall learn how advertisers and advertising agencies attempt to obtain correct matches most economically. For society as a whole, much more knowledge is needed to describe fully how advertising messages are sought, received, and perceived. Agencies responsible for the regulation of our advertising system need new data in order to improve the system for both the senders and the seekers/receivers of mass media messages.

3.3 COMPONENT 3: THE MASS MEDIA

The matching of sender-message-user also depends on several other components of the advertising system, among them mass media—the core of a mass communication system. Mass media play a dual role in advertising: they provide a technological means of sending messages and take an active part in determining what messages are sent, by whom, to whom, and when.

Historically, mass media have made advertising more economical for both senders and users. Suppose we are living in a small English town during the reign of Elizabeth I and wish to know who is the new pope in Rome. Public announcements are usually made by a crier, hired by town authorities, who walks the streets crying out the news at certain hours. If we are in the fields working at those times, we may miss the news. Further, the town authorities may decide not to announce that there is a new pope. In either case, we must rely on word-of-mouth communication, with its attendant distortions. If we lived in the same town today, we could tune in to either public or private TV, to domestic and foreign radio stations, or read newspapers and magazines. As users, we have more sources of information. Senders also benefit from the diversity of mass media: If the pope wants to communicate with the faithful, he can choose from among many media.

Evolution in the number and kind of mass media must have been stimulated by the need of many individuals and organizations to communicate with one another. The variety of media making up society's present-day mass communication system is enormous:

- *Print:* from newspapers and magazines to weekly shopping guides and fliers.
- *Broadcast:* from television stations (national and local, commercial and public) to an increasing variety of radio stations—and, through technological developments, to new media that eventually may blur the current print-broadcast distinction.
- *Outdoor media:* posters, painted displays, and transit cards.
- *Direct mail:* with its ability to reach specific audiences.
- *Graphic Signs.*

But this list only skims the surface of the communication system. Directly or indirectly, other technologies and media must be included, too. Obvious though frequently overlooked examples are the country's *post office* and public or private *telegraph/telephone* systems. Finally, we must also include those organizations and individuals that provide necessary talents and technologies—the printing and electronic industries, the paper industry, craft unions, freelance artists, and the like.

The mass media are in a continuous state of flux. But the available aggregate statistics do not record the processes underlying change; they only record results such as costs, revenues, and employment. Thus we have little scientific understanding of change and must rely on hindsight.

The layman sees the regularity with which media deliver their messages and may think that an orderly process underlies it. But anyone who has ever walked into the editorial offices of a newspaper in the late evening may well have wondered how a paper could possibly emerge in a few hours from such frenetic chaos. Copy is missing, tempers flare, nothing seems possible except the imminent demise of the publication. Few researchers, critics, and regulators have first-hand experience of how the media work, and the professionals themselves lack scientific knowledge. Consider, for instance, how many media professionals fail in their own enterprises, or how many predicted several years ago the impending demise of radio! As researchers, we are tempted to think that so much "disorganization" is probably a very rational way to absorb the enormous uncertainty that derives from the impossibility of predicting changes in consumer preferences and subsequent reactions of advertisers.

In a relatively decentralized and affluent society, there is nothing predetermined about who can talk to whom about what. Senders and users of messages can gain access to mass media at either end of the communication equation at any time for any "legal" purpose. Given the diversity within both senders and users, the mass media have reacted in a classical illustration of cybernetics theory, i.e., by diversifying their own internal structure. Thus, historically, the number and kinds of media have increased tremendously. Each specialized medium develops in an attempt to cater to special groups of senders and users; each survives and prospers to the extent that it facilitates the coupling of correct sender-user pairs.

Yet we know very little about the economic and social processes through which the media achieve this goal. The economics of the mass media is especially difficult to disentangle because, in decentralized societies, the entire communications system as a whole is hopelessly entangled with that of its subsystems. For instance, in the United States the advertising subsystem supports most other uses of the mass media. In the case of traditional TV, it supports *all* other uses. Even though it may be premature to attempt to measure the benefits associated with each kind of use, we should begin some sort of accounting to disentangle the costs side of the economic equation. Such accounting would at least provide a rational yardstick to assess the costs and consequences of proposed changes in the mass media and the advertising system.

If we insist on using oversimplifications to explain how the advertising system works, we shall fail to regulate optimally and may even create more problems than we solve. After all, if we want to improve our car's engine, we must first learn how it operates. The same is true of the advertising institution.

Let us consider briefly a few illustrations of how action based on inadequate knowledge may be ineffective or counterproductive. Suppose we fear that the economic power of the national TV networks dominates the behavior of the local stations. To increase competition, the federal government grants local and cable TV stations the right to originate their own programs. But nothing happens: local and cable stations produce only a very few programs.[1] If we had understood the economics of TV, we would have avoided the costs of formulating and promulgating ineffective regulation.

Another example. Under strong pressures, TV networks agreed to give free time for anticigarette advertising. The effectiveness of a "two-sided presentation" is somewhat supported by laboratory findings in communication research. But then cigarette ads were ordered off the air entirely; anticigarette ads went also. And cigarette sales, which had been declining, began to climb again—another failure in social engineering. In fact, a violation of grandma's proverb: he who wants too much gets nothing.

A final example. Network self-regulation in the fields of alcohol and drugs has also been based on inadequate knowledge and has thus created a number of paradoxical situations. Hard liquor ads are not accepted, yet programs may favorably portray drinking. Further, beer and wine ads are accepted. On the other hand, with the blessing of friends and critics alike, media management produced excellent programs attacking the use of hard drugs. But they describe in detail how hard drugs can be obtained and used! Only recently have some researchers begun to ask whether the net effect of such "educational" programs is the one desired.

The use of society's mass communication system for economic purposes must be placed in its proper context, and we must begin with the collection and analysis of the necessary data. In fact, we must disentangle the basic paradox in which we are caught: the massive expenditure of funds and talent, both public and private, to argue about what regulation should be adopted for the "rational" well-being of the country, without "rational" efforts to gain information on the anatomy and physiology of the body to be regulated.

3.4 COMPONENT 4: THE ADVERTISING AGENCIES

Historically, advertising agencies are the youngest component of the modern advertising system. By and large, they perform two basic functions: creating an advertising message and selecting the media through which it is presented.

Even in face-to-face situations, it is difficult to create a message that makes sense to another person; it is much more difficult to communicate with large heterogeneous audiences via impersonal media. Agencies developed, in part, to supply manufacturers with the skill necessary to communicate via mass media. As we shall see, they work closely with advertisers to determine what to say about a product, brand, or service, and then proceed to suggest ways to say it. The "what" and "how" eventually emerge as a message—an ad.

But it makes no sense to construct a message without first deciding on its intended audience: a message attractive to one group may be meaningless to another and may antagonize a third. Thus, agencies also help advertisers determine their potential audiences.

---

[1] See, e.g., the analysis in R. G. Noll, M. J. Peck, and J. J. McGowan, *Economic Aspects of Television Regulation,* The Brookings Institution, Washington, D.C., 1973.

The creation of a message appropriate for a specific audience is a major step in correctly matching a sender and a user. But this matching also depends on selecting the correct media to carry each message, because different people use different mass media to gain information relevant to them. Thus, another basic function of advertising agencies is selecting the media that will bring the right message to the right audience.

To appreciate these two basic functions in a visual manner, let us describe the communication equation as:

senders–message/media–users

Agencies, therefore, intervene to increase the probability of matching senders and users. In this sense, they are intermediaries. In fact, in choosing media, they act as middlemen in the technical sense of the word, for they buy space and time on behalf of advertisers.

Despite the key role of agencies as a component of the advertising institution, we have little data that describe (1) the internal functioning of agencies and (2) their relationships with the other components of the advertising system. What is available is partly summarized by Mr. Crighton's testimony reproduced in Exhibit B in the preface. Note that if we measure size by amount of revenues, the average agency is very small (about $300,000 gross income per year), with the frequency distribution skewed toward medium- and small-sized firms.

The available data, however, do dispel some widely held stereotypes. First, average net income is less than one percent (.6)—hardly congruent with the popular image of advertising agencies. Even though Adam Smith noted centuries ago that middlemen (such as advertising agencies) perform economic activities, many people still believe that middlemen do nothing, yet receive profits higher than those in other economic sectors. Official data, however, have consistently shown that net profits, and, often, returns on investment, are the lowest in intermediary enterprises.

The second stereotype concerns the power of agencies to make people buy what they do not want. One must wonder about this power when it produces profits of less than 1 percent. As we shall see, agencies increasingly use psychology and other social sciences to discover consumer preferences and ways to communicate with consumers on their own terms.

In sum, with the increasing specialization and diversification in our society, advertisers have experienced an increasing need for specialists—middlemen who choose appropriate media and prepare appropriate messages. In an almost biological analogy, the response has been the birth of firms that fulfill this need. Although the number of agencies is small compared with the number of potential senders and users of mass media messages, their diversity is great. Agencies tend to be small and specialized. Some stress only creative activities; others specialize in one type of industry; some operate only locally; others operate only with regard to certain media. In later chapters we shall learn more about the birth and mutations of advertising agencies.

3.5 COMPONENT 5: LEGISLATIVE AND REGULATORY AGENCIES

Different members of a society may use mass communications for different purposes and, as long as we accept diversity among humans, the purposes of one group may conflict with those of another. This is where all societies have faced a knotty problem of regulation—a very difficult one to solve since it is, at the same time, both a cultural and an engineering problem.

We need to regulate the mass information system to get the most out of its technological potential within given economic constraints. That is, we need to devise an *efficient* system. However, an optimal regulation from the point of view of technology and economics may not be optimal for any one group in a society. Moreover, it may favor one group over another. In other words, an efficient solution may not be *effective* vis-à-vis the preferences of a society or of some group within society. As an example, it would be extremely efficient to publish only one general newspaper in the United States: plates would be produced in one central location and then flown to outlying regions. Yet such a system would not be effective in terms of our currently stated values of diversity and decentralization.

Finding an efficient mass communication system that is also effective is very difficult, especially since humans have some enduring and unpleasant qualities that have overrun many ideal social designs. For instance, we like to think that ancient Athens was one of the best civilizations that ever existed. But consider a simple case of a one-to-many communication: Socrates and those who wanted to listen to him. Athenian society gave Socrates a difficult choice—either stop communicating or be executed. (Today things have improved somewhat: some prefer to fire a teacher; others simply walk into the classroom and shove him off the podium.) During the bold blossoming of the so-called Renaissance, Giordano Bruno was burned in the middle of a Rome piazza. Galileo was merely ordered to recant and forced out of his position.

All of us will verbally agree that these are cases of poor regulation. Yet, in practice, access to a society's mass communication system may tempt each of us to use its potential power to "improve" society. Along with a historian, I used to watch colleagues address crowds through a megaphone during the Berkeley "Free Speech" Movement. We were both surprised how some of our colleagues had been transformed—from modest, gentle, careful teachers into forceful, dogmatic, true believers. How had this come about? Simple enough, the historian said. Remember that in each of us there is a small predisposition toward evangelism, perhaps even a bit of totalitarianism; give to each of us a means of mass communication—just a megaphone—and that predisposition may replace our best judgment. So regulation may be necessary to protect us from ourselves, to prevent us from abusing the potential power of mass communication.

All in all, then, regulation is here to stay. It helps a society's search for efficient types of mass communication systems, and it identifies the system that is believed to be relatively more effective at a particular time.

Throughout history, regulation of mass communication has covered all possible fields—cultural values, religion, politics, education, science. Economic areas, including advertising, have not escaped. In the United States, regulation of advertising has its roots in early attempts to guide economic activities, beginning with the creation of state public utilities commissions during the past century. Then, at the turn of the century, antitrust legislation began to develop, to be followed later by the creation of federal commissions (e.g., the Federal Trade Commission, the Federal Communication

Commission, the Federal Drug Administration, the Securities and Exchange Commission). More or less concurrently, the regulation of standards of measurement (weight, volume, etc.) grew out of the need to simplify commercial transactions and began, gradually, to protect the individual consumer.

Throughout the twentieth century, legislation and regulatory agencies have multiplied in an attempt to cover more and more economic activities. In fact, a single economic activity may be the object of several laws and fall in the domain of several regulatory agencies. Public utilities, for instance, may have to keep different accounting systems for city, county, state, and federal agencies.

Advertising activities have not escaped this trend. They are probably one of the most regulated economic activities. Yet data on the costs and benefits of regulating advertising are totally lacking. Hence, arguments on the need for and the effect of such regulation—like many other arguments—tend to be emotional.

In principle, regulating advertising is confronted with exactly the same problems faced in regulating the use of society's mass communication system for political, religious, educational, and other purposes. The historical repetitiousness of the debate over advertising largely reflects an underlying basic controversy over the ideal type of social organization. Advertising's history is part of the broader historical discourse about what man is, or what he should be, and its fortunes reflect the status of this discourse.

This linkage becomes clear when we consider the similarity of criticisms of advertising and political campaigning. Some argue that the amount spent on political campaigns should be limited in order to equalize the chances of rich and not-so-rich candidates. We find the same reasoning when some argue that advertising by large firms could give them a monopolistic advantage over small firms. The cry that politicians play on human emotions is echoed in the complaint that advertising appeals to irrational human qualities.

These and other similarities are both functionally and historically clear. Yet, especially in recent times, they are often ignored, as are the economic and technological interdependencies of advertising and other uses of society's mass communication system. Many explicitly prefer to treat the economic uses of mass communication as a category entirely different from political, religious, and other uses. We shall discuss later some of the reasons advanced for this differentiated, asymmetric treatment. For the moment, let us simply record some instances of differential, even discriminatory, treatment accorded to the advertising institution.

Regulation of deceitful or misleading statements, for example, should apply to any statement made through society's information system. In recent years, government agencies (such as the Federal Trade Commission, the Federal Communication Commission, the Food and Drug Administration, and the Securities and Exchange Commission) have progressively narrowed the range of permissible ad statements. Yet no equivalent concern has been focused on the use of mass communication by politicians or religious leaders.

A somewhat similar asymmetry applies to the cases of "persuasion" and "information." Although it is difficult to distinguish between these two cases on any basis other than personal feeling, many believe that politicians and religious leaders should be allowed to attempt persuasion while advertisers should not. Several years ago, car manufacturers were ordered to state publicly the retail price of new cars; consumer groups have advocated unit pricing in supermarkets and on packages. Yet candidates for the United States presidency are allowed to promise an entirely new social order without stating its price. The "full disclosure" doctrine is an emerging reality—but it applies only to consumer goods; that is, it is proposed only for those messages we call advertisements. The Federal Trade Commission has required advertisers to submit proof of advertising claims, but there is no law or rule that requires proof for the promises contained in political and religious messages. Thus, a firm must prove that its toothpaste does make teeth white, but a minister does not have to prove that following his precepts will open the gates of heaven.

All in all, advertising is only one use of a society's mass communication system, but it tends to be the object of different and more intense regulation than other uses. Do these differences tell us that economic matters are considered to be more important than political and religious ones? Or shall we infer that only in economic matters is there sufficient "engineering" knowledge to develop rational policies and regulations?

3.6 COMPONENT 6: THE INFORMATION FLOW THROUGH THE INSTITUTION

Information flow, the final component to be discussed, is the most difficult to define, yet it is central to objective descriptions and evaluations of an advertising system. Let us begin with an analogy. As a communication system, advertising can be thought of as a complex electrical circuit. At one end, stations feed electricity into the circuit; in the middle, lines carry electricity; and at the other end, stations either actively draw electricity from the circuit or receive it passively.

There is an intuitive correspondence between this electrical circuit and an advertising system. The input stations represent the senders of messages and the encoders of these messages (Components 1 and 4, respectively). The lines of the circuit are the mass media (Component 3), and the stations at the other end of the circuit are the seekers/receivers of messages (Component 2).

It is more difficult to find a correspondence for the electricity that flows through the circuit. In a very general way, we can think of the equivalent as *information*. But it is not easy to define information operationally. Does there exist an acceptable measure of information?[1] A gross unit of measurement could be a *message*. If we can standardize messages (e.g., transform the number of minutes for broadcast media into the equivalent

---

[1] Ultimately, a concept is that which we measure: that is, the things we measure and the operations we perform in measuring them together define the concept or variable we set out to measure. This may be a circular kind of thinking, but it cannot be avoided in any discipline. For applications to marketing of this methodological point, see F. M. Nicosia, D. L. MacLachlan and F. Schreier, *Marketing Research Methods: A Behavioral Approach,* Wadsworth, Belmont, Calif., forthcoming, Ch. 3.

number of inches for print media), then we can count the number of messages that flow through an advertising system per period of time.

There have been some attempts to count the number of messages, or ads, in the United States. It would seem, however, that these estimates were limited to consumer advertising and overlooked ads in the industrial, extractive, agricultural, service, and wholesale areas and messages sent by nonprofit and governmental agencies. Counting the number of advertising messages must be encouraged and the method of counting improved; this would at least give us a basis for detecting historical trends. Moreover, by relating the count to dollar advertising expenditures and number of users, we could gain some gross insights into the overall working of the system.

In the long run, we should also count nonadvertising messages concerning general news, politics, religion, etc. Counting these messages is essential, since advertising messages pay much of the cost of the entire mass communication system. If we have no such figures, the extensive jointness of costs and benefits will make it impossible to estimate the true cost of the advertising institution.

Even such counting and costing may not ultimately provide a usable picture of how the advertising system works, for two interdependent reasons. First, the number of messages sent is largely the result of activities in the overall economic and social system. At the very least, the number of ads must depend on the number of entities (products, brands, services, and ideas) that *can* be advertised. Second, counting advertising messages is not equivalent to measuring their content, the specific information in them. Unfortunately, the informational content of any message is a complex domain, difficult to measure. Let us discuss each of these points in turn.

The operation of an advertising system is affected not only by the number of messages it handles at any given time, but also—and more importantly—by the *number of entities that can be advertised.* As long as demands on the system by senders *and* users can vary substantially in a short time period, the potential, i.e., *capacity,* of the system to adapt economically poses a key economic question, which should be investigated. In the long run, furthermore, there may be a fundamental relationship between the number of messages processed and the number of entities that can be advertised. An economy with a very limited number of products, brands, services, and ideas would presumably have fewer messages to process through its advertising system. But if the number of these entities increases, how will the number of messages increase? Linearly?

At the moment, let us just note that the answer may depend not only on the number of entities, but also on such factors as the number of potential senders and users of ads; the kind and number of media needed to carry different types of ads; the kind and volume of work that advertising agencies must be ready and able to perform; and the nature of the regulation of the advertising system. The behavior of these components and their time rate of change can affect both the number of messages going through the system at any point in time and the content of these messages. At present, we lack clear measurable conceptualizations of these relationships; Chapter 11 does, however, examine data bearing on some aspects of the question.

The second problem involved in developing a map of the advertising institution is that of measuring the information that flows through the system. This is very important because much criticism of advertising focuses on the *content* of ads. But how do we measure the content?

In the profession, we distinguish consumer and industrial advertising; that is, the content of an ad is defined simply by the marketing nature of the entity being advertised. This definition of content has recently become problematic. During the 1971 FTC hearings on modern advertising practices, some commissioners insisted on defining the entity advertised in terms of its *physical and chemical characteristics,* as opposed to its possible *uses* or its *psychological attributes* as perceived by different consumers. Consider toothpaste. According to this view, if an ad describes chemical content, then the entity being advertised is the toothpaste. But if the ad describes how the toothpaste will improve the user's smile and social life, then some other "entity" is being advertised. From the FTC records, it is not clear what is being advertised in this latter case—is it aesthetics, sex, daydreaming?

We shall see that there are two major positions on this question. Professionals find that the content of an ad is inevitably defined by each consumer in terms of his perception of the entity being advertised. For example, one consumer may view a car as a means of transportation, while another sees it as a status symbol, and a third as something else altogether. Some critics, however, insist that a car is only a means of transportation. This view is also a perception, of course—that of someone who sees a car, or wants others to see it, only as a means of transportation.

The old concept of economic theory applies to both positions: a product is a bundle of potential qualities that are defined by the utility function—preferences—of each subject. But economic theory has never stated that all subjects have the same preferences. Further, the behavioral sciences tell us that perceptions of the same entity may vary enormously from subject to subject. In conclusion, both advertising professionals and critics define the entity being advertised as that which is perceived. They differ in the sense that professionals have learned that there are always multiple perceptions of any particular entity, while the critics insist that only one perception is possible (or acceptable).

The content of an ad is also difficult to define because of problems in measuring the *qualities of the information* in the ad. Among these qualities, truthfulness is paramount. If an advertiser says his brand will do a certain job, he is either telling the truth or lying. In principle, this is clear; in practice, however, it is naïve to assume that engineering or other sciences provide definitive answers, i.e., "the truth." In Chapter 13 we shall see that more often than we wish, several different "objective" criteria are available and can be used to evaluate the "technical" performance of a product. But who shall choose which objective criterion? What about those consumers who are not interested in technical performance? And what about those goods to which engineering notions cannot be applied?

It is also difficult to measure the popular qualitative distinction between information, defined as objective or rational, and persuasion, defined as subjective or emotional. The *information-persuasion distinction* seems to be ingrained in Western culture, but, on the basis of our current knowledge of consumer behavior, the distinction is unworkable. What is "objective" to one consumer is "emotional" to another. For example, it is often claimed that an ad stating only the price of a product is "information." Unfortunately, we know that different consumers will attribute different meanings to price, some of which are definitively subjective and equivalent to persuasion.[1]

In sum, the last component of an advertising system is the information that flows through it. Counting the number of ads is an approximate way of measuring the load on the system and its performance in different societies at different points in time. Eventually, we will have to also count the nonadvertising messages in order to study the jointness of costs and the benefits arising from advertising's roles in the total mass communication system. Further, we must consider how the number of messages relates to other factors and how the information content of ads may be measured.

To obtain data on the information component of an advertising system is critical because, in a sense, it summarizes the interaction among all the other components. In many ways it is the output of the system. Although there are conceptual problems involved in obtaining good data about this component, serious effort should be presently devoted to counting the number of messages flowing through the system. This will at least provide some index of the system's load and the basis for comparative performance in the same and in different societies at different points in time.

4 SUMMARY

As a society grows in size and in the complexity of its cultural and economic organization, its members—both individually and in groups—need to communicate more frequently with others. Technology has made possible an increase in the means of mass communication. Communication takes place only if there is a feedback from the receiver of a message to its original sender. This is true for both personal and mass communication. Feedbacks in mass communication tend to be slower than in personal communication and to have various forms. The interpretation of feedbacks by the sender of the original message is usually complex and costly.

The entire mass communication system is used for many purposes: political, religious, educational, and so on. The uses of this system for economic purposes comprehend and define the advertising institution. The mass communication system is used not only by business firms, but also by many other types of organizations, and by consumers. Historically, the economic uses of a society's mass communication system have been regulated and discussed on the basis of criteria not applied to other uses. The reasons for this difference in treatment are not clear; they are certainly not based on comprehensive knowledge of how the advertising institution works.

---

[1] Perhaps one way out of the present impasse is to invoke a distinction made in some branches of psychology—that of opinion versus attitude. We shall not pursue this since it would take us away from the main argument.

We have some knowledge of how each advertiser, advertising agency, and mass medium operates at the managerial level. As for consumers, their opinions of advertising appear relatively stable over time and, by and large, relatively favorable. It is also known that consumers actively search for information from a number of sources, including mass media; that they are selective in paying attention to different messages; and that they manipulate the messages' information through their own thought processes.

At the macro level, our knowledge is very sketchy; it suffers from lack of relevant concepts and data, and also lack of financial support from foundations, legislators, and regulatory agencies. At the moment, we suggest that the major components of any advertising institution are: senders of messages, seekers/receivers of messages, mass media, advertising agencies, legislative and regulatory agencies, and the information which flows through the institution.

The Advertising Business Function and Corporate Management

A Micro View:
The Nature and Roles of Advertising in a Firm

There is no such thing as a free lunch

Chapter 2

Advertising Management

An Introductory View

OUTLINE

1 Advertising Management as a Decision Process

2 The Role of Consumers in Advertising Management

3 **Advertising Management: A View from the Top** (excerpts from D. M. Kendall, chairman of the board and chief executive officer, Pepsico, Inc.)

Part 1 examines advertising as a decision process seen from the point of view of corporate management. In this chapter we first discuss the nature of this decision process (Section 1) and then present the criteria we have chosen to organize Part 1 (Section 2). The chapter concludes with a testimony that foreshadows many of the problems connected with the micromanagerial aspects of advertising (Section 3).

1 ADVERTISING MANAGEMENT AS A DECISION PROCESS

"Advertising" has many meanings. In Part 1, advertising refers to the activities and decisions of a would-be sender of ads: it is seen as an area of management decision making. On this micromanagerial level, advertising includes such questions as: Should a firm advertise at all? Are there alternative ways of communicating with others? Does the effort spent in advertising produce a larger return than an alternative investment— perhaps, changing the package design of a brand, hiring better salesmen, giving larger margins to retailers, increasing the R&D budget, or tightening up quality control at the the plant?

If a firm decides that some advertising is necessary and economic, then a host of other decisions must be made. What shall be said? Through which media? To which type of consumers? When and how often should a message be sent? And, finally, how can the firm assess whether its expectations were correct, i.e., whether it has reached the intended audiences and made sense to them, and whether advertising has produced more net revenues than some alternative actions might have done?

By plan or by default, each firm ultimately makes these decisions. Each firm

21

searches for a way to match optimally the sender-seeker/receiver pair in the communication equation. Its search consists of a stream of advertising decisions; the costs involved in these decisions and the results obtained determine the degree to which each firm is successful in its search for an optimal match.

The cost and the results of advertising decisions are also affected—usually to a very large extent—by the activities and decisions of other individuals and organizations. For example, consumers may seek different types of ads or may psychologically internalize the received ads in ways different from those intended by the firm. The media carrying the firm's ads may place them in the "wrong" context. The firm's competitors may come up with better ads, better prices, or even a better version of the product. Thus even at the micromanagerial level, the degree to which one firm optimizes the sender-seeker/receiver match depends on the decisions of many subjects. Finally, advertising decisions are also increasingly affected by the decisions of legislators, regulatory agencies, and courts.

All in all, the emphasis of Part 1 is on explaining the *entire decision process of advertising management* and its relationships with other management decisions. Ultimately, however, we must remember that one firm's decisions interact with, and thus depend on, all the other decisions and activities in a society. Advertising decisions are imbedded in a complex and changing socioeconomic milieu and are bound to reflect societal stresses often unrelated to economic events.

More importantly, advertising management is caught between two major sources of uncertainty. On one hand, technological change affects both the production of goods and the production of message flows. On the other, affluence (in terms of discretionary time and income available to consumers) not only permits an increasing differentiation in life styles, but also provides an opportunity for each consumer to change his own life style rapidly. The decisions of each advertiser, mass medium, and agency can be seen as attempts to decipher the uncertainties arising from technological developments and consumer affluence and to relate them in some economic manner to their own activities. Part 1 describes how corporate managers go about coping with these uncertainities.

2   THE ROLE OF CONSUMERS IN ADVERTISING MANAGEMENT

Two criteria have guided the order of our presentation of advertising as an area of managerial decision making. After a brief description of the ways in which advertisers and advertising agencies organize themselves (Chapter 3), we present the stream of advertising decisions in an almost *chronological* manner. But the sequence alone is not sufficient to illustrate the complexity of these decisions. We also need to spell out their locus, i.e., their common denominator and their common goal.

When firms advertise to sell their outputs, it is undoubtedly true that their goal is profit, "making a buck." Ads must ultimately help generate sufficient revenue to pay for their own costs *and* to contribute to the satisfaction of all the demands on a modern firm—from wages and salaries to payment to vendors of capital equipment and supplies, to taxes of various kinds, and finally to a competitive return on invested capital.

We could have stressed this goal as the second organizing criterion of the presentation. Instead, we have chosen to focus on the role of the *consumer*, since this approach is better able to capture the ways in which advertising management reflects the basic economic and cultural changes of recent decades.

As socioeconomic systems evolve from survival to affluence, each firm must face and resolve new problems. Compare the life of the average worker today and in the past. For instance, the coal miner of a century ago spent most of his life underground. Even the time left to him for consumption and for his inner life was minimal. Further, his wage provided only bare survival: he consumed just enough to be ready to work. He even lacked access to medicine to keep him working and to fringe benefits such as good housing. And he did not know whether there would be work on the following day.

Today the situation in this and many other occupations has reversed itself almost 180 degrees. In an affluent society, a rapidly increasing majority has an income that provides a life style well above the survival level. Even poverty may eventually become less a problem of survival than of social-psychological deprivation—e.g., deprivation of the opportunity to share with others the freedom to select how one would like to live. More important, in an affluent society, the majority has the time necessary to use income and other means to search for self-expression.

With an increasing portion of his time and income becoming discretionary, the affluent consumer tends to take the lead in setting the economic and cultural tempo of a society. The working of an industrial society has been essentially described by the mechanism "production causes consumption," but the reverse is now becoming true.[1]

Governments have recognized this in programs for the aged, social security, minimum wages, education, housing, and the like. Although these programs are still justified in the language of an industrial society—that is, in terms of the "right to work"—governments are gradually recognizing a new right intrinsic to postindustrial, affluent societies— the "right to consume."

The private business sector has done its best to adapt to these economic and cultural shifts. A key means of adaptation has been marketing decisions, which include advertising. In a recent award-granting ceremony, a researcher observed:

> . . . it took the Depression of the 1930s to underline once and for all that a key domestic problem of our economy was not how to produce goods but how to market them. At the same time, marketing came into play in an even more fundamental way—in the determination of consumer needs and the specification of what

---

[1] See F. M. Nicosia and Y. Wind, "Social Indicators: Toward a Sociology of Consumption," a paper presented to the International Congress of the Institute of Management Science, April 1972; F. M. Nicosia and C. Y. Glock, "Marketing and Affluence: A Research Prospectus," in R. L. King, ed., *Marketing and the New Science of Planning*, American Marketing Association, Chicago, Ill., 1968; C. Y. Glock and F. M. Nicosia, "Uses of Sociology in Studying 'Consumption' Behavior," *Journal of Marketing*, July 1964; and F. M. Nicosia, "The Role of Consumption in Economic Growth and Social Change," January 1966, mimeo. See also G. Katona, *The Mass Consumption Society*, McGraw-Hill, New York, 1964; and G. Katona, B. Strumpel, and E. Zahn, *Aspirations and Affluence*, McGraw-Hill, New York, 1971.

goods should be produced rather than simply how to sell goods produced on the basis of availability of materials and engineering efficiency . . .

This shift in the emphasis of marketing produced a major stimulus to the development of marketing research and especially to the growing attention being paid to the measurement of consumer needs and preference in the late 1930s. It is no accident that about this time the focus in marketing research began to shift increasingly from measuring ad effects, testing selling methods, and work on distribution channels to ascertaining the needs of the consumer.[1]

Our second criterion in organizing Part 1, then, is this need to ascertain consumer preference in planning, executing, and assessing advertising decisions (Chapters 4 through 7). In the communication equation, the interaction between sender and seeker/ receiver of an ad works both ways: each influences the other. The key historical fact is the change in the relative roles of the two parties.

In modern marketing and advertising it is progressively more economically useful to adapt to, rather than adapt, consumer needs. Only "idealized" monopolists can ignore this shift in the role of the consumer in setting the direction and pace of economic and cultural change. At least in decentralized societies, such monopolists cannot survive. Here it will suffice to remember the tragic history of United States passenger railroads. Both their managers and the Interstate Commerce Commission believed that railroads were monopolies, yet, as it turned out, the railroads monopolized only the rails and not the technological discoveries for moving people by road, water, and air. The failure of these firms to cater to consumer needs competitively has led to their decline.

Part 1 ends with testimonies that describe how advertising is used by corporate managers of several manufacturing firms, a department store, and a supermarket (Chapter 8). We conclude with some comments that sum up our main points (Chapter 9).

3 ADVERTISING MANAGEMENT: A VIEW FROM THE TOP *(excerpts from D. M. Kendall, chairman of the board and chief executive officer, Pepsico, Inc.[2])*

Before entering into a detailed examination of advertising decision processes, it will be useful to place these processes in the context of the overall organization of a business firm. The testimony of D. M. Kendall will give us an insight into the way corporate management views advertising as a business function.

I appreciate both the honor and the opportunity to talk with you today about advertising and the significant role it plays not only in the growth of my company,

---

[1] R. Ferber, "The Maturation of Marketing," *The Marketing News*, August 15, 1972, p. 3; a paper presented in acceptance of the Charles Coolidge Parlin Award. R. Ferber is Research Professor of Economics and Marketing, and Director of the Survey Research Laboratory, University of Illinois.

[2] The principal divisions of Pepsico, Inc. operate in the market of soft drinks (e.g., Pepsi-Cola, Diet Pepsi), snack food (e.g., Lay's Potato Chips, Fritos Corn Chips), and sporting goods (e.g., Wilson Sporting Goods), both domestically and internationally. The company is also active in the transportation and leasing business (e.g., North American Van Lines). In 1971, total sales were in excess of one billion dollars.

but in the continued health of our nation's economy. Speaking for myself—and, I believe, for all those whose testimony will follow mine—may I say that this chance to present the facts and dispel some of the fiction about advertising is most welcome. It has been said that American advertising can sell many goods and services, but it has never found a way to sell itself. I can't help but believe that these sessions will begin to correct that situation.

My remarks today will focus on the importance of consumer advertising in support of branded products. It is eminently fair to say that Pepsico brands . . . could not have entered the market, much less grown and survived in the market, without the aid of consumer advertising. Both Pepsi-Cola and Lay's Potato Chips, for example, were launched on a local basis with the limited, personal funds of the men who developed and named them. As consumers learned of these products, tried them and accepted them, sufficient profits were generated to increase the advertising and widen the markets. The process was slow and the progress was often unsure . . . and I think both took more patience than money. But somehow these products made it. And I often wonder: could they have made it—would they have made it—in an economic system other than our own?

Last year, Pepsico's total investment in consumer advertising was slightly more than 50 million dollars. I mention this figure mainly to indicate that advertising continues to play an important role in our company, but also to explain why I am seriously and personally concerned with what it says, how it works . . . and, often enough, why it doesn't work. . . .

As I see it, advertising is an inseparable part of the total marketing function. Essentially, the marketing function is one of identifying consumer wants . . . moving to fill those wants by developing products with appropriate qualities . . . packaging them for attractiveness and convenience . . . pricing them right . . . and ultimately getting them into good distribution.

Advertising's role in this function is to convey the news and the benefits of the products to consumers. . . . In the simplest phrase of all, this means selling the product. As the Commission knows, almost any kind of communication about a product— word-of-mouth, salesman-to-customer, the label itself—might be defined as advertising. Media advertising, which will be the subject of most of the following presentations, is only one way to do the selling job.

It is obvious, of course, that if marketing's first step is to identify a consumer want, advertising's assignment is to communicate how the product satisfies that want. A word, therefore, about consumer wants:

It is often said that "advertising sells people things they don't need." The best answer I've heard to that criticism was in a house ad run by the Young & Rubicam Agency. It went in part like this: "Yes, advertising does sell people things they don't need . . . things like television sets, radios, automobiles, catsup, mattresses, lipstick, and so on. People don't really need these things. They really don't need art or music or cathedrals . . . they don't absolutely need literature, newspapers or historians. All people really need is a cave, a piece of meat, and possibly a fire." . . . So when I'm told that people don't really need certain kinds of products—I have to agree very quickly. Marketing is a process that satisfies wants and desires most of which are not fundamental needs.

Let us pursue this "want" idea a little further. It's also been said that advertising *makes people want things they don't* really *want . . . or which they wouldn't have wanted if the advertiser hadn't somehow* manipulated *them. Indeed, advertising has been depicted as creating or inventing wants that did not, in fact, pre-exist.*

I want to be very clear on this point because I think it's very important. To the best of my *knowledge—and that of my business and advertising associates—*advertising has not and cannot invent a human want. *Advertising can and does cultivate or kindle* latent *or* dormant *or* previously unperceived *desires for certain products. But it cannot add* to *or subtract* from *the human senses or the characteristics placed in us by God and nature.*

Also in my experience, no amount of advertising can force any large number of people to buy things they don't want. *In support of this view, I urge that we look at the evidence . . . evidence which the business community has seldom pointed to for reasons that are embarrassingly obvious. This evidence consists of the myriad failures which American business encounters in its new-product ventures every year. You hear from businessmen—as you did from me a while back—mostly about the products that succeed. You don't hear too often that* most *of our new products* fail.

I cannot give you complete statistics on this because most product failures occur— as they should—in corporate Research and Development Laboratories where scientists continuously test new products or product improvements that might satisfy consumer wants more effectively. For my own company, let me admit that if one out of ten of our new-product ideas or product improvements *is considered worthy of test marketing, I'd count this a darn good batting average. [Emphasis added.]*

Even after this rigorous pre-screening process within the walls of corporate research centers, the bulk of what gets to the market-place ends up as a failure. I quote some statistics from a speech given in 1967 by Mr. Graf of the A. C. Nielsen Company: "Of 103 items on which the Nielsen Company did test-market measurements, 47, or 46% were withdrawn by the manufacturer after varying test-market intervals, because of poor performance. . . . Taking a separate look at the national picture, of the 1123 items which entered broadscale distribution during late 1965, only 649, or 58% of the total, remained in distribution one year later." That is, about half failed in test market, and almost half of the products which went national didn't even last a year.

Now up to this point I've been labeling as a "failure" any new or improved product which didn't meet the broad consumer acceptance. And looked at individually, *that's accurate—they* are *"failures." But if you step back a bit and look at the whole picture, something different emerges: a story of* success, *the successful functioning of an open, competitive, and* free *economy where consumers relentlessly weed out the products they don't want, and accept only those which serve some useful purpose to them. Right there is the reason for all these so-called "failures:" the fact that too few consumers really wanted what the businessman was offering. The products which fail each year do not lack for attractive product qualities, brand names, packaging, and strong advertising pressure, but they fail nonetheless because the consumer simply doesn't* want *them. To anyone who truly believes he can manipulate consumers, I would offer this humble advice: try it. And after you've had some failures let's get together and discuss "manipulation" again.*

A third criticism sometimes leveled against advertising is that it persuades people to "want" the "wrong things." These critics readily admit that advertising only sells people things which they really want, but they contend that people should not be left to choose by themselves because they'll end up wanting the wrong things. I have little to say about this criticism because it seems to me that either you accept freedom of choice, and a basically democratic procedure, or you don't. If we cannot rely on individuals to make good product choices based on their own judgment, what, may I ask, is the next choice we will deny them?

I mentioned a moment ago that media advertising is only one way to do the selling job. Some companies today still sell door-to-door. A greater number rely on dealers or store clerks to close the sale which advertising might have initiated. I don't intend here to criticize person-to-person selling. I might, however, remind all of us that the "advertising copy" delivered by the door-to-door salesman or even the sales clerk in the store is neither checked and double-checked by lawyers, scrutinized by Network Continuity Acceptance people, subject to the new 4-A's regulation plan, nor submitted in advance to the Federal Trade Commission. On the other hand, I think that few products in America are inspected as diligently and often as copy prepared for media advertising.

Of course, the basic reasons why companies such as mine prefer media advertising to other more personal forms of selling are economy and efficiency. There is literally no way to count how many salesmen at the front door it would take to reach the number of people who see and hear a television commercial. But even if such a massive sales force could be assembled, the costs of their salaries or commissions would raise product prices astronomically.

The use of media advertising, then, does not spring from some unexamined bias on the part of the manufacturer. Rather, it represents a conscious choice as to the most effective and efficient way to generate consumer demand. Where the product provides a wanted consumer benefit, advertising is a highly efficient way to generate a mass market for this product, lowering the costs of production and distribution. . . .

. . . I have no ax to grind, as an advertiser, in choosing any one set of advertising appeals instead of another—"factual," "emotional," or what have you. But I do feel an obligation to "inform" people about what matters to them—that is, the pleasure or enjoyment they can derive from using my product. I simply can't afford to be autocratic. My commitment is to give the consumer what she wants and, if her "wants" have an emotional component to them, it behooves me to recognize that fact. . . . Two more current complaints about advertising:

No. 1. "Advertising often is in poor taste." Agreed. There are many television commercials I find strident, abusive, insulting to my intelligence. I'm sure we all have entries for this category. But all too often, the commercials I find offensive are someone else's favorites. I think taste will always be best left to the marketplace where consumers can, if they choose, demonstrate their own discontent by refusing to buy the offending products. I also suggest—because it is my personal practice— that the chief executive of any advertising company exercise, if need be, the power to eliminate advertising which he or other responsible company officials—or the public itself—identify as dubious in taste.

No. 2. "Advertising inhibits competition by creating 'artificial' differences between products and thus sustaining 'monopolistic' market positions." I do not agree. On the contrary, advertising is a constant spur to competition since it provides the means to tell consumers rapidly about my new and improved products, and it gives my competitor the same opportunity to build business, a fact of which I must *be ever mindful. A word on this idea of "artificial differences." Most of the real advances in the quality of human life have been made in pretty small increments. Now for someone who is not directly involved and responsible, it's possible to belittle this kind of progress, to make fun of it, because we aren't aware of how hard it is to really "improve" on a product or process in a field where we're not expert.*

But let's not fall prey to this kind of thinking. Let's recognize that the deodorant toilet soap of today is indeed a much better product than the brown laundry soap of yesteryear, but we got there in small steps; that the refrigerators and the self-cleaning ovens and the dentifrices and typewriters of today are indeed better products than they ever were before. But we got there in small steps; and so forth. Let's let the consumer *judge whether the small steps we've taken are worthwhile to* her. *Because if for some strange reason we find ourselves legislating against these "small improvements," then I'm terribly afraid we may find that there are no improvements at all. If we only tolerate the "great leap forward," we may fall flat on our faces.*

In closing, let me restate a few key points. Advertising is an inseparable part of the marketing function. The effectiveness of advertising is amply witnessed by the growth of our economy and the high level of prosperity which our citizens enjoy. Indeed, advertising now is being criticized for being too *effective, for "manipulating" people to buy things they don't really want. If that were true, there'd be darn few of you drinking anything other than Pepsi-Cola. However, the facts tell a different story, a story in which consumers choose those products they* want *and ignore those products they* don't *want.*

On occasion, advertising appears which is misleading or deceptive. I do not kid myself that this is always accident . . . the unintentional result of human error or a breakdown in company-agency communications. But, I believe that remedies exist for this kind of problem. And I urge that those remedies be used vigorously when they are needed. However, to impose broad new restrictions on all of advertising— based even on the proven *and* intentional *deceit of a small portion of it—would be, in my opinion, a serious blow to free enterprise and a grave disservice to the very consumers we all hope to serve. . . . Thank you.*

Chapter 3

Advertisers and Advertising Agencies

OUTLINE

1 **The Internal Organization of a Firm's Advertising Department and an Advertising Agency** (excerpts from E. M. Thiele, vice chairman of the board, Leo Burnett Co., and chairman of the board, American Association of Advertising Agencies)

2 **The Organization of Advertising Activities**
   2.1 Factors Bearing on the Organization of Advertisers and Advertising Agencies
   2.2 A "Biological" History of the Advertising Agency

3 **Summary**

One of the least understood aspects of advertising is that even a single ad is the result of complex decision processes. When we see an ad, we are naturally tempted to think that it is the result of one decision. Yet, at the managerial level, *advertising is a stream of decisions* that imply a large number of activities. In one-man or one-family firms, all these decisions may be made by one person. In larger organizations, many people may participate: some may work for the advertiser; others for the advertising agency; still others for firms who specialize in printing, taping, lighting effects, and so on. Putting together the *right group of activities with the right group of people* is the organizational problem par excellence—and one that is all too often ignored.

Theoretically, the entire planning, executing, and assessing of an advertising campaign could be in the hands of the advertiser, or, at the other extreme, the advertising agency could carry total responsibility. In practice, the economics of overheads makes both extremes impractical. For example, few firms need a silk-screening or direct-mail specialist constantly. Thus, it is more rational for most firms to hire these specialists only when the need arises.

Several decades of experience have led to a standard allocation of activities between advertisers and agencies. Although there are many variations, both across different industries and within the same industry, for many firms this standard represents the best solution for (1) allocating advertising decisions to the two types of firms in an economical manner, and (2) retaining the necessary degree of coordination.

1 THE INTERNAL ORGANIZATION OF A FIRM'S ADVERTISING DEPARTMENT AND OF AN ADVERTISING AGENCY *(excerpts from E. M. Thiele, vice chairman of the board, Leo Burnett Co., and chairman of the board, American Association of Advertising Agencies)*[1]

Mr. Thiele's testimony illustrates the standard allocation of functions by describing the internal organization of a firm's advertising department and of an advertising agency. It shows who performs which activities and how the activities are coordinated within each firm and across the two firms.

> In this presentation I would like to give a broad overview of the . . . typical structure of an advertiser, its agency, and the working relationship that exists between them. . . . Advertising departments vary from one-man organizations to hundreds, depending on the size of the advertising budget, the importance of advertising to the company, and the industry within which it competes. It also relates to the amount of responsibility the advertiser delegates to its agency. A typical advertising department organization within a large company marketing consumer goods might resemble the following, with minor variations (Exhibit 3.1).
>
> In this simplified diagram we see the basic departmental structure of a corporation including such divisions of management as Finance, Manufacturing, Marketing, Industrial Relations, Quality Control, Research & Development, etc. The Marketing Director has reporting to him the Sales Manager with his staff, as well as the Advertising Manager and his staff, in addition to Sales Promotion and Merchandising personnel.
>
> The advertising staff might have as many as 100 people or more and might include specialists in research, copy, media, etc., in addition to people [the so-called product or brand managers] assigned directly against specific brands which the company markets.
>
> Now let's look at a typical advertising agency structure (Exhibit 3.2). Management must oversee the total operation of an advertising agency. It is they who are responsible to the stockholders for profit performance, the quality of the agency's total output, business development, quality of personnel, and all the other things that make for a successful business enterprise. Most large agencies have a review board to act as a quality control center for the output of the agency. This board will usually review all major marketing and advertising plans as well as specific executions on a regular basis.
>
> Reporting to the President are four main divisions: (a) Creative Services, which includes writers, artists, TV and print production people as well as traffic personnel; (b) Client Service people, which include account supervisors and executives; (c) Marketing Services, within which media, research, and sales promotion functions are performed; and (d) Administrative and Finance, which includes personnel, accounting, finance, etc. The functions of these divisions are as follows:

[1] Leo Burnett Co. is a very large advertising agency.

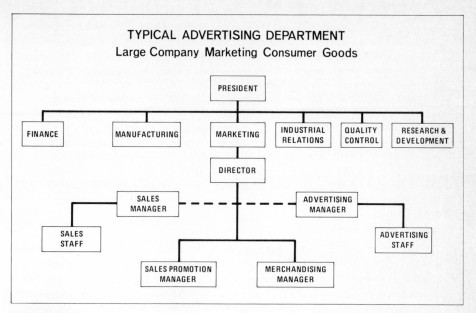

EXHIBIT 3.1

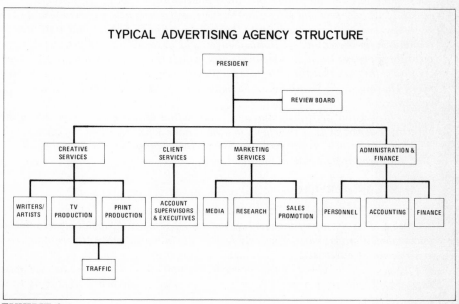

EXHIBIT 3.2

A. CREATIVE SERVICES

It is the job of the creative man to put into words and pictures a unique, attention-getting and persuasive positioning for the advertiser's product or service. The creative process is a highly cooperative one. Other agency departments supply information and objectives; writers and art directors work as a team to conceive, write, design, and produce commercials or print ads.

Production: *From the moment an ad is designed and written to the time it actually appears in magazines, newspapers, or on television, it is in the hands of the production people. They know what's practical for reproduction and work with the creative department in planning their work. They may purchase the graphic art services and materials and otherwise see assignments through to completion.*

Traffic: *It is the responsibility of this group to see that all production of the agency flows on a predetermined timetable. They also are responsible for the delivery of engravings, recordings, and films to publications, radio, and TV stations.*

B. CLIENT SERVICES

The key to the working relationship between the advertiser and its agency is in the account staff of the agency. In charge of each account is an account supervisor, *sometimes assisted by one or more account executives. These people are the basic coordinating point between the agency and the advertiser . . . [and are] responsible for interpreting the needs of an advertiser and communicating these needs to the staff people in the various departments of the agency. . . . [They] are usually responsible, in conjunction with the advertiser, for the development of marketing and advertising strategies also.*

It is the account staff which interprets these strategies to the copywriters, artists, media planners and buyers, researchers, and others in the agency who do the work of executing the strategies into finished advertising. The account staff is also responsible for presenting the finished advertising to the client's advertising department for approvals (including medical, legal, and policy considerations). After such approvals, they see that the advertising is placed in media according to the approved plan. Thus we see, in Exhibit 3.3, the important coordinating function of the account staff.

. . . the account staff maintains a two-way liaison between the key people in the advertising department of the client and the various departments of the agency. While various agency people may also contact the client personnel from time to time, the account staff acts as coordinator.

C. MARKETING SERVICES

These usually include media, research, and sales promotion.

Media: *It is the job of the media people to select from the many media vehicles the combination that most efficiently reaches the intended public for the product or service to be advertised. A good media person, in addition to having all the facts and figures, must be able to sense the environmental aspects of the media. He must choose a schedule from over 1,700 daily newspapers,[1] 3,000 magazines,[2] 6,000*

---

[1] *Editor and Publisher Yearbook,* 1971, p. 13.

[2] MPA Information Service, K. Powers by phone.

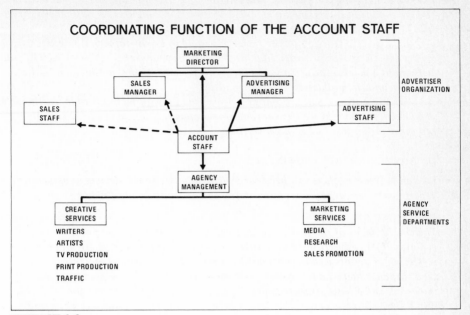

EXHIBIT 3.3

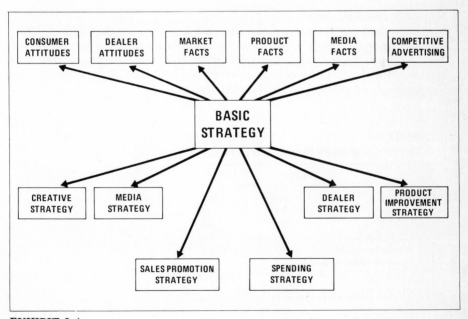

EXHIBIT 3.4

radio stations,[1] 600 TV stations, and innumerable outdoor and direct mail outlets. Today, in most agencies, media people call upon the computer to aid them in their task.

Research: *It is the job of the research people to be the information center of the agency. Research provides vital intelligence on who uses a product and why, the facts about a market, how consumers react to the advertising, product, and other elements, and the evaluation of creative ideas.*

Sales Promotion: *Sales promotion deals broadly with methods of increasing sales at point of purchase as well as coordinating premium offers, contests, couponing, and other promotions with the advertising.*

D. ADMINISTRATION AND FINANCE

Like all businesses, there is a need for general administrative services, a personnel department, clerical and secretarial staffs, and accounting and finance services. . . .

MARKETING STRATEGY

The development of the marketing strategy is obviously a critical point in the evolution of an advertising plan. Broadly speaking, this process is one of an extensive collection of data regarding consumer attitudes, demographic characteristics, market facts, product facts, facts regarding competition, etc. These are analyzed and discussed, and a basic strategy is developed jointly by the advertiser and the agency. This strategy then becomes the "grand plan" to which individual strategies must relate. Specific strategies for creative, media, sales promotion, etc. are then developed, and after client approval, are executed by the agency. Exhibit 3.4 will help in the understanding of a marketing strategy.

AGENCY COMPENSATION

Advertising agencies are compensated in a variety of ways for their services. This compensation includes fees from advertisers, but the great bulk of agency income is derived from commissions paid by media to the agency on advertising placed by the agency for a client. Historically, this commission has been 15% of the gross time or space cost of advertising placed. To illustrate:

EXHIBIT 3.5
AVERAGE 4–A AGENCY PROFIT EXPECTANCY

	Amount	%
Total billing	$1,000,000	100
Commission	150,000	15
Profit	6,600	.66

Source: 4–A's, *Ten-Year Record of Agencies' Costs and Profits,* August 1971.

[1]*1971 Broadcasting Yearbook,* p. 11.

For every $1,000,000 in billing placed by an agency, $150,000 is earned in commissions. The present rate of profit of 4-A agencies is .66% of billing, or $6,600 per million dollars of billing.

2 THE ORGANIZATION OF ADVERTISING ACTIVITIES

Mr. Thiele has sketched the major activities performed by advertisers and agencies and described how these activities are grouped and coordinated within each type of firm and between the two types of firms. We should not forget that many other activities are performed by mass media, research agencies, and trade associations. Variations on the basic organizational patterns illustrated by Mr. Thiele exist, however, and we will discuss some of the reasons for these variations.

2.1 FACTORS BEARING ON THE ORGANIZATION OF ADVERTISERS AND ADVERTISING AGENCIES

The specific division of activities between an advertiser and an agency varies within and across industries. In developing an organizational design for his mass communication efforts, any advertiser must consider a host of ever-changing factors: the number and types of potential buyers; the number of products and brands within each product line the firm markets; the number and type of competitors and the advertiser's relative position—not only in marketing, but also in production, finance, and other areas; the marketing channels used by the advertiser and his competitors; the technologies used in production and distribution; geographical and ecological conditions; and, of course, city, county, state, and federal legislation.

That these factors must be considered by each firm is intuitively clear. It is also clear that variations in these factors will lead otherwise similar firms to design different advertising departments. In many cases the results are not what the general public and scholars would expect. Consider, for example, the size of a firm. Common stereotypes imply that the smaller the firm, the less advertising it will do. Thus, its advertising department will be smaller and the nature of its decisions simpler.

This is a splendid example of misstating a crucial managerial problem. To begin with, the management question is not the *absolute amount* of advertising but the *percentage* of the total budget allocated to it. If a retailer operates only one suburban store, it would be foolish to spend an amount equal to that of a competitor who operates many stores throughout a metropolitan area. Yet, if local conditions warrant, the one-store retailer may find it useful to spend a much higher percentage of his budget on advertising! Second, and more important, the nature and complexity of a firm's advertising decisions, and thus of its advertising department, relate only indirectly to the size of its advertising expenditures. The one-store retailer may need to reach a small and relatively homogenous group of consumers: it may use expensive window displays, flashy neon signs, and elaborate leaflets placed frequently on the windshields of cars in nearby parking lots. The many-unit retailer must reach a broader and more heterogeneous group of consumers and may decide to use newspapers and radio. The complexity of the management problem—but not necessarily the size of the advertising budget—is greater in the second case; further, the amount of information needed to speak to different types of consumers is also higher. Both factors—complexity and high informational requirements—determine whether the large retailer must hire people to work full-time on advertising.

At what level of complexity and informational requirement does a firm find it convenient to delegate activities to outside firms? There are no simple and universal rules. One historical regularity does emerge, however. Through depressions and expansions, through war and peace, two sets of activities are usually delegated to the advertising agency: the invention and production of ads and the selection of the mass media through which to send the ads.

As we noted previously, the agency is a middleman in that it creates and places an ad on behal´ of the advertiser, its client. Here too, popular literature suggests that bypassing the advertising agency is a means of pocketing its profits. This reflects the medieval conception that producers and consumers are better off when middlemen are eliminated. But although one can eliminate the middleman, one cannot eliminate the activities he performs, nor the related costs. Small and medium-size retailers, for instance, tend to refrain from using advertising agencies because of strict economic calculations reflecting the nature of their operations. Yet they still must hire artists, bargain with local newspaper and radio salesmen, check the scheduling of the approved ads, and coordinate this schedule with window displays and with buyers to make sure that the advertised items are available on the right dates. Certain tasks must be performed whether or not an agency is hired; what varies is the allocation of tasks.

The advertiser is not the only one interested in determining which activities should be delegated to the advertising agency. Agency management also wants to know which activities can be performed at an acceptable rate of profitability.

Some agencies offer a "full line" menu; others limit themselves to specific activities. A talented artist and a skillful copywriter may form an agency and decide that their time is best spent in creating ads rather than in selecting media, testing advertisements, and developing promotional schemes. Or a man with extensive media experience may join forces with a management scientist to offer a computer-based media selection "shop." Another person with extensive experience in media sales and with good radio and newspaper contacts may become a "media broker" for either advertisers or agencies or both.

As these few examples indicate, advertising decisions involve many tasks and skills that can be organized in many ways—within and/or across firms. Theoretically, the combinations are infinite. In practice, cost and revenue considerations reduce the possibilities. Yet many alternative organizational designs do exist, and each agency searches for the internal structure that best serves its present clients. As clients' needs change, and as new clients are acquired and old ones depart, the very organization of the agency will also change.

Changes in the environment, in consumer preferences and purchasing behavior, in competitors' decisions, and in technologies also necessitate constant adaptations in the internal structure of agencies and advertisers. Thus there are no perfect organizational charts for advertisers and agencies. At this micromanagerial level, the rationality of advertising decisions cannot be based on the "perfect" organizational design. Rationality requires at least the ability to change, and at best an uncanny ability to foresee, plan, and implement changes before a competitor does.

The very process through which advertising agencies developed in the United States illustrates this constant pattern of adaptation—one in which trial and error on the micro individual level led gradually to the emergence of an entirely new institution.

2.2 A "BIOLOGICAL" HISTORY OF THE ADVERTISING AGENCY

The Madison Avenue stereotype has populatized an incorrect image of the nature and function of the advertising agency.[1] Stereotypes are part of any culture and have useful social psychological functions, but they are dangerous if adopted as the *sole* explanation of what goes on in a society and thus as the basis for public and private decisions. It will be useful to give a brief sketch of some of the changes in the United States that have led to the birth and evolution of the advertising agency since the mid-1850s. The sketch, of course, is only illustrative of how changes in economic, demographic, and social factors affect the structure of advertising activities within and across firms.

At the beginning of the last century, the United States population was small, and concentrated along the Atlantic seaboard. Illiteracy was high, industrialization limited, roads and rails embryonic; there were few newspapers and no telegraph or telephones. The United States was essentially an agrarian society. Production and demand were physically close: each family tended to produce enough for most of its needs, and the rest could be satisfied by contacting the producers directly. The need for mass communication is extremely low in a society of this kind.

Population grew exponentially and villages became cities. Industrialization created greater and greater specialization, and the direct contact between producers and consumers was lost. Gradually, the need for new means of mass communication grew, since word-of-mouth and town hall meetings could no longer provide sufficient information. The number of newspapers increased phenomenally, but the rate of publishing bankruptcies was also extremely high—it was not easy to find economically sound ways to meet the growing need for information. Competition increased and, in a search for revenues, newspapers' management turned to advertising. Salesmen were hired to visit manufacturers and to sell space for advertisements.

The appearance of the *space salesman* was probably the key factor in the eventual birth of the advertising agency. Consider his position. He would visit a manufacturer who had purchased space in a competing newspaper and, naturally, would fai¹ to make a sale. If he were turned down several times, he might have seen the handwriting on the wall—dismissal. An unpleasant thought at a time when unemployment compensation, social security, and other modern safeguards did not exist. What could he do to survive— to convince manufacturers to buy *his* newspaper's space next time?

---

[1] Many facts can be easily obtained by writing to the A.A.A.A., 200 Park Ave., New York. See also R. D. Peterson, "The Advertising Agency Industry: An Analysis of Market Structure Dimensions," abstract in *Western Economic Journal*, September 1971.

Some salesmen might have argued that their paper had a larger *circulation* and that buying from them would deliver more potential readers. We can imagine the confusion— and possibly deceit—that may have reigned, for at that time there were no services to audit circulation.

More important, other, more inventive salesmen might also have offered *services*— help in layout, design, and copywriting. Still others might have analyzed the readers of his and competing papers from the point of view of potential customers. For example, before visiting a toy manufacturer, a salesman might do some homework and learn that this manufacturer advertises in a paper read largely by young and unmarried people. If he could show that his paper had a larger circulation among people in the 25 to 45 age bracket, he had a point of interest to the toy manufacturer and might well have gained a sale.

We now come to a crucial moment. The salesman hired by one newspaper can sell its strengths but is limited by its weaknesses. (Note that neither strengths nor weaknesses are absolute; both are relative to the needs of specific advertisers.) A salesman's paper has a circulation (by sex, age, religion, education, income, etc.) that appeals to some advertisers but not to others. Further, more newspapers are now presenting socio-economic profiles of their own circulation to potential buyers of advertising space. In a sense, this competition among the media salesmen educates the advertisers, and they begin to press the salesman. Can he deliver the right kinds of readers?

Our salesman is faced with a classic situation: any competitive edge is a knife that cuts both ways. On the one hand, the socioeconomic profile of his paper assures him that a number of firms will buy from him, but it also disqualifies him from serving other firms. What is the answer?

Some salesmen approached the situation from the viewpoint of their potential clients. Manufacturers were attracted by mass production, with its promise of lower unit costs. But lower unit costs could only be achieved with a higher sales volume. Firms thus experienced an increasing need to advertise. Moreover, many firms were beginning to add product lines and increase the number of models, brands, and package sizes in each line. This further increased the manufacturers' need to advertise in order to reach different groups of potential buyers.

Those salesmen who understood this situation found an answer. In making a sales presentation, they had to be able to offer *choice* and *advice*, to say, for example, that for selling toys, those two papers were best; for haberdashery, those other two were better. But problems still existed. The salesman who wanted to give advertisers a choice could no longer work as a salesman for just one paper. Why should one paper pay salaries and commissions to salesmen who also sold space of its competitors?

Two solutions emerged. In the first, the salesman set himself up as a *broker*. He attempted to match the *demand* for space in specific papers with the *supply* of space in the required papers. This was a complex task because both the space needed and the space available were becoming increasingly heterogeneous. Different manufacturers wished to appeal to special audiences; at the same time, newspapers were beginning to differentiate their appeals to different audiences. Increasing heterogeneity of supply and demand inevitably creates a fundamental problem of social engineering: how can homogeneous supply/demand segments be found and matched? This is exactly the role of the brokerage function, one which certain salesmen proceeded to fulfill. (In any type of social organization—centralized or decentralized—as soon as a supply/demand heterogeneity appears, the function of searching and matching becomes necessary.)

Being a broker has certain advantages. First, the broker acquires no title, i.e., he does not buy space himself, and thus he avoids the risk of not selling it. This risk is absorbed by the newspapers. However, avoidance of this risk has a cost: the broker has no control over the price of the space being sold. More specifically, the broker has a limited opportunity to assess the needs of both seller and buyer, and he cannot directly influence the difference between the selling price acceptable to the newspaper and the buying price acceptable to the advertiser.

Some space salesmen and brokers began to experiment and found a second solution. They *bought* blocks of space from different papers and then went about selling their inventory to advertisers. Here we see the appearance of another classic form of middleman—the *merchant wholesaler*. In buying, he bargains on the purchase price; in selling, he bargains on the selling price. (Remember that price is only one element in a negotiation, and that it interacts with the number and kinds of services included in a negotiation—whether these are supplied gratuitously or on some additional cost basis.) The essential characteristics of this emerging new operation were: (a) in buying space from papers, our merchant assumed the risk that the space might remain unsold, and (b) he also bought the opportunity to do better than if he had remained the captive salesman of one newspaper.

By the mid-1850s then, there were three processes by which the different needs of advertisers and the different offers of media were sorted into homogeneous groups and eventually matched: the space salesman, the broker, and the merchant wholesaler.[1] Even today these three processes are available. However, a further "mutation" of the three operations finally led to the birth of the advertising agency as we know it today. Like other mutations, it developed because of the human desire to do better.

In negotiations with a space merchant wholesaler, an advertising manager might drive hard to lower prices. From his point of view, however, the manager was handicapped: he did not know the cost of space to the wholesaler or how low he could push the price. Consequently, he could not trust the wholesaler's advice. Suppose, for instance, that space in papers W and X permits the manager to reach the right readers but that he can also obtain much the same goal in papers Y and Z. Is it possible, the advertising manager wonders, that the wholesaler pushes paper X space because he bought it more cheaply than that in paper Z? If so, our manager would naturally like to buy the X space at a lower price.

---

[1] It is easy to see how outside observers may feel that the existence of three different processes is wasteful. However, as we have begun to see, the micro nature of this sorting and matching set of activities is too complex for us to describe, measure, and evaluate—even today. (See F. M. Nicosia, "Marketing and Alderson's Functionalism," *Journal of Business,* October 1962.) The factors, their combinations, and their rates of change, which influence the choice of a space salesman, broker, or merchant, are too numerous, and vary too much across firms and time. Nevertheless, as "engineers," we should not feel powerless; on the contrary, we acquire power when we recognize our limitations in influencing certain socioeconomic micro processes.

There must have been many advertising managers in the mid-1850s who thought this way. Some merchant wholesalers and brokers met this challenge by buying space on behalf of the advertiser (thus operating as agents) and letting him know the buying price. This became known as the *open contract*.

Technically, the new operation was not difficult to implement. The "agency" received a bill from a newspaper that stated the cost of the space bought and the commission to be retained by the agency. The agency then sent the bill to the advertiser, who paid the full amount to the agency. The latter retained the commission and sent the remainder to the newspaper. In principle, the advertiser has all the information he needs: he knows how much the agency makes and how much each medium costs, and can question the agency on why more expensive media are used.

Price of media is not the sole factor in any negotiation. As mentioned earlier, services also play a crucial role. Just as competition led newspapers to offer circulation profiles, agencies began to offer help in writing copy, preparing layouts, and the like. Increasingly, agencies stressed the creation and production of ads. Thus, even today, most agencies' activities focus on two major functions—media selection and the creation and production of ads.

3 SUMMARY

In this chapter we began to look closely at the host of activities and decisions that underlie the planning, execution, and assessment of an ad. Some of the activities we considered are those performed by advertisers and advertising agencies.

Mr. Thiele's testimony indicated the way in which some activities are allocated to the advertiser and others to the advertising agency. His testimony stressed that both sets of activities are coordinated toward the common goal of communicating information to selected consumers.

We have noted that the allocation of advertising activities to different firms is a problem of organizational design. This is a difficult problem, because a balance must be struck between two opposite and mutually exclusive goals. On the one hand, by allocating each activity to an expert, we gain the higher performance of each specialist. This is the advantage of any decentralization scheme. On the other hand, specialization is bought at a cost of a loss in coordination. Symmetrically, if we want more coordination, we get less specialization. In mechanical systems, it is usually relatively easy to approximate a satisfactory balance between specialization (decentralization) and coordination (centralization).

When this problem emerges in human systems, however, it is still practically impossible to conceptualize and compute solutions. Millions of advertisers have a wide choice of how to organize advertising activities. Computations of costs and benefits intrinsic to each firm can lead each to delegate a different set of activities to outside firms. Historically, however, it appears that a large number of advertisers has consistently found it convenient to delegate at least two basic tasks to agencies: the creation and production of ads and the selection of the media that have the highest probability of reaching the desired type(s) of audience(s).

Chapter 4

The Roles of the Consumer
in New Product Development

OUTLINE

1 **How Advertisers and Agencies Help Each Other Find New Products That Are Acceptable to Consumers** (excerpts from F. B. Ennis, vice president, Booz, Allen & Hamilton, Inc.)

2 **How Consumers Determine the Birth and Death of Products: Some Data** (excerpts from W. M. Claggett, vice president, Ralston Purina Co.)

3 **Summary**

A common and crucial criticism of advertising is that firms use it to force consumers to buy products that they do not really want. The chain of reasoning underlying this criticism is as follows. The firm begins with a set of resources—R&D findings, production and marketing expertise—and with the motivation to use these resources to maximize the difference between revenues and costs. If product X *appears* to be a high-profit product, then advertising is used to make consumers buy it—at prices as high as possible. Some critics actually begin by observing consumers' purchasing behavior, most of which they find unacceptable. They then assume that the observed behavior is caused by advertising and other promotional schemes. That is, what consumers do is caused by firms.

This reasoning assumes that demand is a function of supply alone. Yet in both micro- and macroeconomic theory, supply is also a function of demand. There are two conditions under which the latter relationship—or feedback—can be legitimately ignored. The first is monopoly. Monopolists can behave somewhat independently of demand, as can oligopolists engaged in collusion. Whether consumer goods firms fall into these two categories is, of course, a matter for empirical investigation. The influence of consumers on business firms can also be disregarded—and this is the second condition—if consumers can somehow be manipulated and convinced to do what they do not want to. Let us examine the actual relationship between consumers and firms.

Basic and applied consumer research—on both micro and societal levels—suggests that it is the consumer who tends to influence the firm, especially in affluent societies. As mentioned before, the affluent consumer has an increasing amount of discretionary time and income; thus, he is increasingly free to express his own values, to choose his own life style. Collectively, millions of daily consumer choices are more likely to set the tempo of conomic and cultural events than are the decisions of firms. There will always be an interaction between demand and supply, but some consumer literature stresses that the supply side—paramount in economies of survival—has become relatively less important in affluent societies.

It is increasingly evident, furthermore, that mass communication has limited power to change human thought and behavior, even consumer behavior. Consumers use information acquired through mass media, but there is no field or laboratory evidence to indicate that people act immediately on the basis of an advertising message or that their future behavior is based solely on mass media messages. In fact, the evidence points to the contrary; the major managerial problem advertisers face is learning not only whether an ad works, but if it works well enough to justify its own cost.

Professionals have become increasingly aware of the above knowledge. As reported earlier (Chapter 2, Section 2), an increasing number of firms have found that, to be successful, they must start with the identification of consumer needs and preferences. In this and the following chapters, we shall see how professionals attempt to apply this principle to advertising decisions.

Both readings in this chapter consider the case of a new product. They describe in detail, and with supporting data, how consumers influence the series of decisions that lead (1) to the formulation of a new product; (2) to its introduction; and, often, (3) to its abandonment following a negative judgment by consumers (as in the cases of the Ford Edsel and the GM Corvair—very expensive failures in an industry where only three firms have dominated about 80 percent of the supply for many years).

1 HOW ADVERTISERS AND AGENCIES HELP EACH OTHER FIND NEW PRODUCTS THAT ARE ACCEPTABLE TO CONSUMERS *(excerpts from F. B. Ennis, vice president, Booz, Allen & Hamilton, Inc.)*[1]

Identifying what different consumers feel, think, and do about an existing product, brand, or service is a difficult art; only in recent times has some help come from the emerging discipline of consumer research. Learning what consumers will feel, think, and do about a product that does not yet exist is far more difficult, requiring all the experience and technical expertise available to advertisers and agencies.

In the following testimony, F. B. Ennis describes the advertiser-agency interface as a process that attempts to find what consumer needs and preferences determine the probability of a new product's acceptance.

Since [the] interface and exchange of technical information between the advertiser and his agency is particularly critical in the area of new products, I'd like to describe how the process works and show how it might apply to a hypothetical new product. . . . [T]here are typically four stages. . . . These briefly are as follows:

[1] Booz, Allen & Hamilton is a management consulting firm operating both nationally and internationally.

A. THE CONCEPTUALIZATION STAGE

This is the point in the product's life at which it is only an idea. Based on an investigation of a market, it may have been determined that a possible need exists for a certain type of product not now being offered to consumers. The need to be fulfilled and the product attributes required are discussed in general terms; a rough estimate is made of the financial implications involved in developing and marketing the product; and the project is formally assigned to the company's R&D department for further investigation.

The agency is often called in at this time to obtain its opinions about the marketing potential of the proposed product, along with the performance and design features that would enhance its consumer acceptability. . . .

Case Illustration

Let's assume that a firm's marketing department . . . has determined that consumers would be interested in a new kind of ice cream product which does not have to be stored in refrigerators, such as a dry mix. The idea is reviewed with R&D technicians who state that it is conceivable to prepare an economical, freeze-dried product that will have the same if not superior tasting qualities than regular, store-bought ice cream. All the housewife would have to do is to add water or milk to the mix, beat it up and freeze it in the refrigerator just before serving it at the dinner meal.

The agency [people are] called in for their opinions on the product. They might point out that the product would have to come in a variety of flavors to satisfy the broad taste appeals of the consumer market, and that getting distribution in food stores with a multiplicity of flavored items would be very difficult until the product has proven itself. To solve this problem, it is agreed that R&D should work on the development of a "neutral" flavored product to which flavorings could be added by the housewife herself. . . .

B. THE PROTOCEPT STAGE

At this point, the technical feasibility of the product is established and a prototype model of the concept, or protocept, is developed. The purpose of the model is to give visual form to the concept; it is not necessarily a "working model" of it. . . .

The agency along with their counterparts in the client company are frequently invited to review this model and to make suggestions on its probable consumer appeal. Since the technical feasibility of the product has not been established and since this is when work on advertising and packaging traditionally begins, the agency is briefed on all the technical aspects of the product. . . .

Case Illustration

Going back to our freeze-dried ice cream mix, let's assume that R&D has now confirmed the technical feasibility of the product. . . . R&D has also determined that the dry mix should be packaged in vacuum-sealed, foil packets which will give the product a shelf life of up to six months before it begins to lose its taste qualities. A model of what the mix and its package will look like is prepared, reflecting the fact that each packet will contain a premeasured quantity of mix to provide a full pint of ice cream when reconstituted.

After listening to the R&D presentation . . . the agency might ask how rapidly the product's taste qualities deteriorate after six months. When told that the deterioration rate is significant, they could then point out that this may be a potential problem since many consumers might buy the product just for an emergency and store it in kitchen cabinets for longer than six months. They could advise their client, for example, that this is typically the case in powdered milk which is often purchased not as a substitute for whole milk but as an emergency replacement. . . .

It is therefore agreed to modify the product to endow it with a shelf life of at least one year. This is resolved by packing the mix in a thin, shell-like, edible material which contains a preservative . . . the product will now appear as an egg-shaped nugget which the consumer reconstitutes by placing the nugget in her blender, adding 4 oz. of milk and then beat and freeze. Eight of these nuggets will be packed in a cylindrical container, similar to the type regular ice cream cones come in, to provide the consumer with the capability of making a full gallon of reconstituted ice cream.

C. THE PROTOTYPE STAGE

This is the actual "working model" of the form in which the product will be offered to consumers. This is the most critical stage, since the manufacturer is very close to to the point at which he will "freeze" the product's design and specifications for production purposes. Generally speaking, this is the last opportunity the manufacturer has to reassess the product before going into mass production.

In this respect, the manufacturer will typically conduct two briefing sessions with his agency. The first takes place after the prototype of the model has undergone whatever laboratory tests are required to establish its performance capabilities, shelf stability, safety features, potential side effects, etc. . . .

Since this is the first time that the agency will have seen the actual product in its final form, this briefing session tends to be somewhat formal in content and is usually held at the client's R&D laboratories. R&D technicians will physically demonstrate the performance and usage characteristics of the product . . . A question and answer session is held in which the agency is free to query the technicians on all aspects of the product, including the general *nature of the claims that could be made in advertising.*

The second briefing takes place after consumer research has been conducted on the product. If it is clearly demonstrated as a result of consumer research that the product will, in fact, fulfill all the requirements for which it was designed, there may be no need, of course, for another briefing session with the technicians. It is not uncommon, however, to discover at this time that some consumers were dissatisfied with various features of the product, such as its color, or convenience, or taste, or utility, etc. In this case, the client and the agency will again be brought together to see what can or should be done to rectify these problems.

Since it is often difficult to satisfy all the demands of all consumers economically, the dispensable and indispensable characteristics of the product are reviewed to determine possible "trade-offs." For example, eliminating one feature of the product that might appeal to only a small consumer segment may substantially enhance the performance of another feature which might appeal to a large segment. . . . This is also the point where the agency will start to explore the specific *types of claims that can be made about the product.*

Case Illustration

Let's again look at what might happen in the case of our hypothetical freeze-dried ice cream mix. In the first briefing, a formal presentation is made to the agency in which R&D (a) reveals the product prototype and demonstrates how it is to be used; (b) invites the agency to reconstitute a batch of ice cream using the prototype nuggets, and to taste it; (c) explains that accelerated storage tests have been conducted in the lab and that the product will hold up under all types of environmental conditions; (d) states that taste tests have been conducted with a panel of home economic experts who preferred the taste of this product significantly over that of regular ice cream; and (e) reports that, based on a variety of toxicity and other tests, the product is safe for human consumption by all ages regardless of the life of the product, etc.

During the question and answer session that follows, the agency might ask questions of this nature:

- *Is this product more nutritional than regular ice cream? (No)*
- *Since the product will come in the form of an egg, could advertising refer to its "dairy richness"? (Yes, but because of its ingredients, not its form. Also, advertising should not imply that it is more "dairy rich" than regular ice cream.) . . .*
- *Is the product "fresher" than regular ice cream? (Yes, because the product's ingredients are freeze-dried in the plant whereas regular ice cream loses some of its freshness going through normal trade distribution channels.) . . .*
- *Is the end product smoother in texture than regular ice cream? (Against some, yes; against most, no.)*
- *Could a child make this product with an egg-beater instead of a blender? (Not easily; a blender should be used.)*
- *Since mothers are often afraid to have their young children use an electric blender, are you saying that the product should only be prepared by an adult? (Yes. For safety purposes, we will have to show on our label that the product is not intended to be prepared by children under 12 years of age.)*

As you can see, these are but a few of the questions that could be raised by the agency, and many of them can only be answered by technical experts. In effect, a formal briefing of this nature is essential in order to equip the agency with the basic information it will need to develop meaningful advertising.

Going on with our case illustrations, let's assume consumer research has now been conducted on the product and [the second] briefing is set up at the request of the agency. The types of issues that could be raised at this session might include these questions:

- *Many consumers reported adding maple syrup or butterscotch syrup to the mix to get a different flavoring, but that the product took longer to harden in the refrigerator than indicated by the directions. (Yes, we noticed this too and will have to change our directions on the label . . .)*
- *Many consumers also stated they did not like putting the egg-shaped nuggets in their blenders because the outer "shell" was like that of an egg itself and bits of this shell would remain in the product. Could this "shell" be made softer to overcome this concern? (No, because it would mean reducing the amount of preservatives contained in the shell and this would shorten the product's shelf life.) . . .*

- *Could we claim that the product "tastes like rich homemade ice cream"? (Yes, but that should probably be reviewed with the Legal Department since most people have never tried homemade ice cream.)*
- *How about the claim "now you can make any flavor you want at home for a price no greater than that of regular ice cream"? (No. By adding flavorings such as maple syrup along with the recommended 4 oz. of milk, a pint of the end product will actually cost the consumer a bit more than what she is now paying for a pint of regular ice cream.)*

Once again, the issues involved and the specific claims suggested can only be evaluated by technical experts, which makes a briefing of this nature virtually mandatory in the advertising development process.

D. THE PRE-MARKET STAGE

By definition, this is the last stage of both the advertising and product development process. The final specifications for the product have been established; a pilot run has been made in the plant to iron out any manufacturing problems; and the product is ready for mass production or test marketing. The agency has completed one or more specific advertising campaigns and a media spending program, which will be explained later by another speaker, and has submitted its recommendations to the client for final approval.

The advertising at this point is formally reviewed by the client's marketing personnel, the R&D technicians, the client's legal experts, and of course top management. . . . If approval is obtained by all parties concerned, the agency is then authorized to proceed with its final development.

Case Illustration

Returning to our freeze-dried ice cream mix which the manufacturer has decided to call "Scoop," this might be the reaction to three specific advertising claims submitted by the agency:

- Claim #1: *"Scoop contains a fantastic new quick-freeze ingredient that lets you make all your favorite flavors at home in only 60 minutes."* Reaction: *Disapproved by R&D since the claim implies that the product contains a special chemical that accelerates the freezing action, and this is not true.*
- Claim #2: *"Scoop is a new kind of ice cream that puts quality first."* Reaction: *Rejected by the Legal Department in its present form since Scoop does not meet FDA's "standards of identity" for ice cream.*
- Claim #3: *"Scoop can be stored in kitchen cabinets and makes up fresher than store-bought ice icream because it's homemade."* Reaction: *Approved by all concerned.*

In describing this briefing process, I do not imply that all companies do or should follow this procedure. I'm sure there are companies, for example, that do not assign advertising responsibility on a new product to an agency until after the technical feasibility of the product has been determined, or until an actual prototype of the product has been made . . . However, I know of no company that does not require that its technical experts provide the agency with a comprehensive briefing on a new product once the prototype has been developed.

As I see it, the purpose of this briefing and verification process is not only to ensure the substantiation of claims, but to ensure that the advertising is telling consumers exactly what the product can offer them. In the final analysis, the ultimate objective is to win over a satisfied customer, and not simply to avoid misleading the customer.

2   HOW CONSUMERS DETERMINE THE BIRTH AND DEATH OF PRODUCTS: SOME DATA *(excerpts from W. M. Claggett, vice president, Ralston Purina Co.)*

This testimony elaborates two main themes. First, Mr. Claggett presents data describing trends in consumer styles of life and notes the effects of these trends on the introduction and withdrawal of products. He then provides a detailed illustration of how some companies attempt to increase the probability of consumer acceptance of new products.

The argument underlying the testimony must be stressed. The decision process of a firm is a search for an optimal match between consumer needs and preferences and the skills and capacity of a firm. The firm's skills are essentially its capital equipment, its financial resources, and the talents of its personnel (from labor to top management). But these skills also act as constraints, especially in the short run.

To begin with, technology limits the kinds of products a firm can offer. For example, even if many consumers were willing to pay a very high price for a total security system that would enable them to walk through Central Park at night safely, there is no technology that could provide it. Or, even though it is possible to assure 100 percent quality control in assembling a car, there are not enough consumers willing to pay for it.

The firm's skills also act as constraints. Equipment, financial resources, and personnel are demands on the firm's operations. That is, a firm can exist if it meets not only the demand of its potential customers, but also the demands of those who supply capital equipment (vendors), money (stockholders, bondholders, and financial institutions), talents (from labor to management), and government services (taxes). Any privately or publicly held firm, even a hippie community, is engaged in matching many requirements; it survives only if this matching is acceptable to all concerned.

Mr. Claggett focuses on the way a firm goes about assuring this match. He shows that the firm begins by identifying consumer needs and preferences—the potential demand— and then matches them against the firm's skills—the potential supply. It is naïve to assume that a match is easily found. On the contrary, the decision process of the firm consists of a careful working back and forth between demand conditions and supply constraints, searching for a *specific need* of *specific consumers* that might be satisfied by a *specific product,* given the demands by labor and capital.

The acceptance of new products by the consuming public is certainly underscored by the fact that according to the Super Value Study, over 50% of the brands on their supermarket shelves weren't even present 10 years earlier (Exhibit 4.1). This was brought about by the fact that people's needs are shifting—life styles are changing, and today's consumer often wants different products than he did just a few short years ago.

EXHIBIT 4.1
SUPER VALUE STUDY

Items Handled in 1967 But Not Handled in 1957

Account for	55% of the items handled now
Contribute	52% of unit sales
Represent	52% of dollar sales
Earn	57% of dollar margin

These ever-changing needs also affect the stability of current products in the market. Occasionally some good products seem just right but are withdrawn after a period of time in the market place. . . . Most often the manufacturing companies are given credit for discovering new product ideas. In actuality, the people really thinking up new product ideas are the consumers themselves. They tell the manufacturer about their changing needs and give the manufacturer clues as to how he can best satisfy their ever-changing requirements.

In order to get specific, let's consider my company's own industry—the food industry—and picture what's been going on there for the past few years. Through a continuing study of consumer life styles, the MRCA (Marketing Research Corporation of America) Menu Census identified the fact that many people are moving away from three square meals a day (Exhibit 4.2).

EXHIBIT 4.2
MEALS PER HOUSEHOLD (In 2 Week Period)

July-December	1962	1967	Change
Average	54.6	54.6	No change
Morning	13.6	13.6	No change
Mid-day	10.8	10.4	−.4%
Evening	12.4	12.1	−.2
Carried Lunch	3.5	3.6	+.1
Snacks	14.3	14.9	+.6

Source: Market Research Corporation of America

Additionally, in many homes Papa no longer presides over the dining table, carving the roast (which Mama spent three hours cooking in the kitchen), serving up mashed potatoes and gravy (which Grandma spent an hour preparing) and offering homemade lemon meringue pie which the eldest daughter prepared from scratch. Formal family dinners seem to be disappearing in modern America.

Let's examine why this is happening. The housewife has additional things to do than stay in the kitchen; the kids are scattered to the four winds. . . . Furthermore, the family members want to do their own thing. Little Johnny doesn't want to have broccoli stuffed down his throat and Susie doesn't necessarily like lamb stew just because everybody else in the family likes it. . . . There appears to be a rising phenomenon of mini-meals scattered throughout the day, served at different times, with different choices for every member of the family. Consumers are clearly telling food manufacturers that they want a freedom of choice when it comes to menu selection.

Many consumers are also watching their weight. They are concerned about nutrition, and they are simply not gorging themselves with sweets and fattening foods like they used to. All of this tells food people that they'd better get on the ball and create new products which fulfill consumers' changing life styles.

Today, I would like to explain to you how food companies listen to consumers to find out what they desire . . . and how the companies must clearly communicate to consumers the attributes of new products they create. . . .

Also, you should be aware that, in spite of all of a company's sophisticated research, most firms have a rather high failure rate. Being an innovator of new products is risky, since the programs must be put to the toughest test of all—what consumers think about them. Booz, Allen & Hamilton reports that about 50% of new products fail before they even hit the market place. This same research study reveals that it takes nearly 60 ideas just to get one successful product line out of the other end of the spigot. Even after companies develop a good idea, this research reports that three out of four get weeded out by continuing testing in the research and development laboratory. Even after the company gets a viable product from the laboratory and goes through all the screening steps and all the consumer research, one out of every two of these products fail. Here are some reasons why this is so: inadequate product quality; poor concept/product match; inadequate product communication; inadequate advertising; poor distribution; poor merchandising support; poor product quality/price relationship; good repeat purchase rate, but inadequate frequency of repeat; poor package design; and timing of concept.

Another point absolutely vital to understand is the fact that product life cycles are a lot shorter than they ever were before. Many years ago, products used to be around for decades. Now A. C. Nielsen research indicates that nearly half of the food and drug products they measure have a life cycle of less than two years (Exhibit 4.3).

EXHIBIT 4.3
PRODUCT LIFE CYCLE (1961–1966)

Survival Time	% New Products
Over 3 years	15%
2–3 years	37%
2 years or less	48%

Source: A. C. Nielsen, New Items—
Problems and Opportunities

Consider the fine old products that are no more. You can no longer read the New York Herald Tribune, *climb in your Packard and run down to the corner store to buy such necessities as Post Cereals with Freez Dried Fruit, Choice Soap, Teel Toothpaste, and* Look *magazine. On the other hand, you could very well jump into your Maverick and wing down to the same store and buy Cool Whip, Close-Up Toothpaste and Teflon Cooking Ware.*

Since consumers are changing, . . . companies can't use the same old methods and develop the same old products. Instead of the traditional marketing set-up consisting of Assistant Product Managers, Product Managers, Product Group Directors, Marketing Directors, General Managers, and so on, many companies are setting up small, highly professional teams to develop new products. These "venture teams" usually consist of a Senior Marketing man who works in close concert with a Market Research Manager (who gathers information on consumer attitudes and trends) and with the R&D Technician who must deliver the finished product. This group spends at least one-third of its time analyzing consumer research data, listening to consumers and talking to consumers. . . .

In order to examine consumer attitudes in a professional way, most companies have a systematic new products development procedure. This system is generally broken down into six main categories, which are: Opportunity Analysis; Consumer Need Identification; Idea Generation; Idea Evaluation; R&D Product Work; and Test Marketing. Let's examine these one by one.

In the opportunity analysis *area, various product classifications are screened and in-depth analyses of product categories are conducted to determine where potential weaknesses are. . . . Opportunity analysis concerns, for example, industry/product class criteria; size of product category; trend/future outlook; competitive product mix; competitive new product activity; sales methods; and channels of distribution.*

Next, current family life styles are studied in great depth. An analysis is made of how today's consumer needs are changing and why. Members of the food industry are always striving for innovations in food technology, break-through packaging ideas, and other developments which will give them a competitive edge; but food manufacturers can't just stay within their own industry in this examination. They must even study what household appliances and cooking utensils are needed by Mrs. Housewife. For example, if we assume that the microwave oven will come into broad-scale usage in the relatively near future, then food manufacturers had better start working now *on new foods which consumers can prepare with this appliance.*

Next, the idea generation *stage is one which used to be called "brainstorming." But quite frankly, most companies don't depend upon new product ideas coming from within themselves or from creative types at their advertising agencies. The most effective brainstorming that is done in the food industry is with consumers through individual and group interviews. . . .*

After some feasible ideas are developed, we then create product concepts in the form of package protocepts and concept statements. They are shown to consumers so they can help the manufacturer more clearly communicate the product. . . . If all systems are still "go," most companies go to work on the product and design products to meet consumer specifications. A product prototype is then taste-tested with consumers. Most often it is a blind taste test where the consumers don't know in advance the brand name of the items they are helping to evaluate.

In other cases the company sometimes shows a consumer the advertising for a new product and then has him taste it so he can tell the company whether or not the product lives up to its advertising claims. After all of this, the company . . . actually places the product in a test market and advertises it. As a new product is being sold in the test market, the company assimilates a wide variety of consumer research data. *In order to measure sales, it conducts store audits, gathers data on warehouse withdrawals and factory shipments and it measures trade reaction. Advertising testing will also be taking place. Consumer diary panels are conducted and follow-up interviews with consumers are, too. If they don't buy the product, the company wants to find out why. It will specifically probe for ways in which the product can be improved. [Exhibit 4.4 shows one way in which a product is evaluated through research at each phase of the development cycle. A similar procedure applies to the development of advertising campaigns.]*

EXHIBIT 4.4
TESTING A NEW PRODUCT AT EACH DEVELOPMENT STAGE

1. CUTTING–Product Demonstration
   This is a laboratory demonstration of prototype product or competitive products.

2. TASTE PANEL TEST
   This is a taste test designed to give guidance to R&D in refinement of prototype product.

3. OUTSIDE TASTE TEST
   This is frequently a paired comparison test of our prototype product vs. a competitive product.

4. CENTRAL LOCATION TEST
   This is a test normally involving testing of both concept statement and prototype product designed to fulfill that concept statement.

5. IN-HOME USE TEST
   This is a test involving placement of product in homes of target consumers for about two weeks.

6. EXTENDED IN-HOME USE TEST
   Product and procedure is same as "In-Home Use Test" with the following exceptions:
   (a) duration of test will range from one to three months;
   (b) semi-finished or finished packaging may be used for part of the test;
   (c) respondents may be offered the opportunity to purchase the product to help determine if consumers would actually purchase the product in a market situation.

7. REAL-LIFE TEST MARKET
   A test market is a simulation of full national marketing effort for introduction of a new product. Everything is directed toward duplicating what would be done on a national basis. Test markets would normally encompass from 1 to 5 percent of U.S. population. Testing lasts at least nine months and could last a full year.

It may come as a mild surprise to some of you, but more often than not it costs more to conduct market research than it does to advertise a product in test markets. This is to say nothing of the product development research which often costs far more than both of these other expenses combined.

In spite of all this sophisticated research, products can and do fail. In many cases perhaps the company has misread the research or committed one of the other errors contributing to failure that were mentioned earlier. Sometimes all the research in the world can't predict consumer behavior. . . . For example, people told Bristol-Myers they wanted an analgesic antacid that could be taken without water; and extensive research told Ford Motor Company that consumers wanted to own a medium price Ford product in the late 1950's. But when Analoze and the Edsel were made available, not enough consumers actually bought them.

More often than not consumers reject a new product because it didn't have a meaningful point of difference. On the other hand, when a product difference results in a consumer benefit, new product advertising can be most effective. . . .

3 SUMMARY

In this chapter we have reported how advertisers and agencies go about finding ways to introduce successful new products. Success is measured simply by consumer acceptance high enough to recover costs—that is, the demands on the firm represented by suppliers of capital equipment, financial resources, personnel talents, and government services.

Both Mr. Ennis and Mr. Claggett exphasize that the consumer point of view is crucial: throughout the firm's decision process—from R&D decisions to the ultimate introduction—the consumers' basic predispositions are the crucial input. Essentially, the firm is trying to find ways to adapt its own resources so that the product introduced will satisfy enough consumer needs and preferences to satisfy the demands of its own factors of production.

Failure to meet consumer needs means the eventual failure of the product. This principle applies in the absolute; it is independent of any other factor. For instance, it is independent of whether a firm is large or small, or whether or not it operates in a situation of oligopoly. Examples of how large and oligopolistic firms can fail are numerous. The Edsel was a $400 million failure in a highly concentrated industry; the Ford Company could not sell the car to a sufficiently high number of consumers. And even DuPont finally had to accept the fact that, during the sixties, too many consumers did not like Corfam shoes.

This principle—the importance of satisfying consumer needs—seems to apply even in centralized economies, provided that these economies have gone beyond the stage of mere survival. To go to work without shoes is, at the very least, uncomfortable; for those who have been truly poor, owning a pair of shoes is a dream. With two pairs of shoes, one uses the old pair for work and the new one for dates. A third pair may be acceptable, especially if they look somewhat different from the other two pairs. Beyond that, one begins to experience the need for sandals, loafers, and ski boots. Finally, one simply has enough footwear. The individual may begin to trade footwear coupons for something else, with or without permission from the central planning committee. If this committee continues to invest natural resources in shoe production, there will be no "advertising" capable of convincing people to keep on buying shoes—the market will collapse. The more affluent the consumer, the more the central planning committee will have to study consumer needs and preferences if it wants to minimize the risk of misallocating national resources.

Yet the point of view that firms make people buy what they do not want is widely held. But empirical evidence indicates that a different situation is actually true. That is, *some* consumers may be dissatisfied if the productive sector does not offer them the products that fit *some* of their needs most accurately. Although some of them wanted a paid-TV option, in the early sixties Californians voted not to have it: apparently there were not enough consumers who shared this need and the alternative was thus economically unfeasible. On the other hand, there are so many types of cars and life insurance policies that the problem may become one of too many possible choices. As for advertising, an ad may influence some consumers positively—some may react by talking about the new product with friends; others may go to the dealer to look at it; perhaps some may even give the product a try. Other consumers, however, may not notice the ad at all, while still others may react negatively—perhaps very negatively.

At the micro level, then, there will always be some consumers who will not like a new product or the ads about it. But the problem for each firm is to find a sufficient number of consumers who will react favorably to both the new product and its ads. This number must be large enough to meet the demands of the suppliers of production inputs— capital equipment, financial resources, personnel, and government services. Given the high degree of heterogeneity among affluent consumers, the number cannot be equal to the United States population. Hence, there will always be some segments of the population that will be either unaffected or unsatisfied.

We may call this an impasse, a shortcoming, or a consequence of human hetero- geneity. Whatever one calls it, it is a problem faced by any form of social organization. One either has to accept heterogeneity among members of a society and develop institutions and regulations accordingly, or to eliminate the heterogeneity.

There is a final point concerning the testimonies of Mr. Ennis and Mr. Claggett. One may wonder whether the process they described is typical of United States firms: is it really true that firms work this way? Is it possible that some firms do know how to persuade people to do what they do not want? Although basic and applied research strongly suggests that no mass communication has such power, we shall keep these questions in mind as we proceed with other testimonies.

Chapter 5

The Roles of the Consumer in the Planning of Advertising

OUTLINE

The view that advertising manipulates the heart and mind of the consumer must presumably be based on some knowledge of advertising activities. In Chapter 4 we began sketching the evidence bearing on the validity of this and other views by investigating the role of the consumer in new product development and advertising. In this chapter we shall examine the role of the consumer in the planning of advertising.

The testimony in Section 1 gives a general view of how the creation of advertisements begins and ends with the consumer. Buying is seen as the result of a consumer's attempt to solve some problem, or satisfy some need. Based on the understanding of such problems, an ad is created that may suggest a possible solution. The two testimonies in Section 2 show how the planning of an entire advertising campaign is also based on understanding the nature of some consumer problem and on offering information that will help in its solution.

Creating an ad is only one of the main advertising decisions. It is also necessary to select media that have a high probability of reaching those consumers who experience the problem for which the product, and its ads, may be a solution. The testimony in Section 3 examines the corporate criteria concerning selection of media.

The physical creation of an ad involves another complex set of advertising activities. "Encoding" what one wants to say in a specific ad not only poses a number of semantic problems, but also requires handling a tremendous number of technological production problems. In recent years, many texts have deemphasized the treatment of this topic. Section 4 comprises six testimonies that provide an extensive managerial examination of the topic.

The testimonies are organized in a roughly chronological arrangement: we move from the planning of many advertising activities to their performance. At the same time, the presentations stress one factor common to all these activities: the role of the consumer in determining what information is necessary to create and send an ad that has a high probability of making some sense to at least some consumers.

1 THE ROLES OF THE CONSUMER IN THE CREATIVE PROCESS
(excerpts from T. Dillon, president, Batten, Barton, Durstin & Osborn, Inc.[1])

The question that T. Dillon asks goes to the very heart of advertising decision processes: How does one go about creating an ad or an entire advertising campaign? Although creation is a very basic human activity, we still are unable to understand it well, and we tend to accept is as an unexplainable event. Such terms as inspiration, luck, and curiosity are an open admission of ignorance.

Common sense, however, throws some light on creativity. First, a famous inventor—Thomas A. Edison—once stated that creativity is 99 percent perspiration and only 1 percent inspiration. For more average people, of course, perspiration, i.e., hard work, must play a much greater role. Second, hard work enables the accumulation of experience and, as one accumulates experience, regularities appear and can be used to guide creative efforts.

At least one regularity can guide advertising creativity: to satisfy a need, a consumer must solve some problems. The more we know about consumer problems and how different consumers go about solving them, the better the basis we have for creating advertisements that may help at least some consumers. This is the thesis Mr. Dillon emphasizes in the following passages of his testimony.

> *Usually the intent of advertising persuasion is to influence a brand decision. . . . I believe that virtually every consumer sees and hears advertising in the full knowledge of that intent. How are brand decisions influenced by advertising? As I shall*

---

[1] A very large advertising agency, also known as BBD&O.

demonstrate, the purchase of any brand is usually stimulated by the consumer's desire to resolve a problem or complex of problems. . . .

To understand the effect of the creative process on the brand decision, it is first necessary to visualize clearly how complicated the consumer's brand decision is. I should like to take for an example a simple brand decision that we will all probably make within a short time. That brand decision will be where to eat lunch. There are an estimated 1500 eating places in the city of Washington, D.C., and, providing each of us decides to eat lunch, we will each have to select one of them.

The simple fact of eating lunch springs from an elementary physical need . . . elementary needs are very few. The daily input requirements of survival in outer space or on a desert island can be listed as follows: about 2300 calories of balanced food intake; 3½ pounds of oxygen; 3 quarts of water; and a warm, dry place.

I suggest to you that all other purported human needs are culturally determined. They are not, in fact, physical needs, but they are satisfactions. The hierarchy of these satisfactions is determined by cultural patterns and by individual decision.

For example, virtually every man in this room is wearing a necktie. A necktie has no known physical function. . . . each tie has been chosen by some mental process from many thousands of necktie designs in the market. Not only that, but men do not commonly wear the same necktie two days in succession. They often maintain a substantial home inventory of various designs representing a large investment in what must be one of the most non-utilitarian articles of commerce.

In terms of basic human physical needs, this might be regarded as irrational. But in terms of providing human satisfactions, it evidently is not—else we are all irrational men. The rational economic man hypothesized by the economic textbook would never buy a necktie and certainly not go to a restaurant for lunch. Ever.

A purely rational economic decision would be to go to a food market and buy a stock of beef liver, potatoes, cabbage, carrots, white bread, margarine, dry milk and raisins. From these you could construct a 779–calorie lunch that would greatly exceed the recommended daily allowances for vitamins and minerals. One would not cook any of these, because is costs money and would probably diminish nutritional value. . . .

Let us take a homely national advertising product such as soap. Its utility is to clean, and the economic textbook man who looks for 779 calories at the lowest cost might well specify he wanted a glyceryl salt of a fatty acid at the lowest bulk price per pound. But people do not buy soap for itself; they buy it for the satisfactions that soap provides. To the housewife, who buys soap for her family, the decision process probably involves as many variables as the selection of a restaurant.

To be sure, if it is not your job to buy soap, you may consider that some of her considerations are trivial. But that may be simply because you are not a prime prospect for soap. On the other hand, to the average housewife, there may be no sense to the variety of fly rods in a sporting-goods shop. Yet to an avid fisherman, the length, weight and feel of a fly rod may be so critical that he will spend hours in a decision process.

Thus the housewife may have concerns as to the soap's scent, color, texture, shape, cleaning action, skin effects, deodorant quality, feel, price, packaging, lasting quality, sudsing and many other factors perceived by her as part of her satisfactions. To her husband, it is quite possible that these considerations are frivolous. That's because, of course, it's not his *problem.*

The first step, *then, of the creative process is to identify the prime prospect. Advertising is, after all, only a message, and a primary requirement in sending a message is identifying to whom it is to be sent. The prime prospect is defined as that group of individuals to whom the advertising should be directed. Usually they are high-frequency buyers who make the brand decision.*

There are statistical methods involved in developing a marketing strategy for a brand. From such research, an analysis, a picture of the prime prospect will emerge— usually in terms of demographics, purchasing patterns and attitudinal characteristics. A quite surprising phenomenon is frequently revealed by such studies. Most people have the notion that advertising tries to talk to everybody because everybody buys something. This is usually not so. In a large number of cases, the people who make the large proportion of brand decisions in any category are a relatively small proportion of the public (Exhibit 5.1).

EXHIBIT 5.1
IDENTIFICATION OF HEAVY USERS

Instant Coffee: 7.7% of total female heads used 5 or more cups of instant coffee a day, and they accounted for 53.5% of total product usage.

Regular Cola: 20.4% of total adult females drank 5 or more glasses of regular cola a week, and they accounted for 71.5% of total product usage.

Instant Potatoes: 6.2% of total female heads used 6 or more packages of instant potatoes a month, and they accounted for 60.2% of total product usage.

Spray Starch: 6.9% of total female heads used 4 or more cans of spray starch a month, and they accounted for 48.0% of total product usage.

Fabric Softeners: 5.7% of total female heads used fabric softeners in 8 or more washloads, a week, and they accounted for 44.7% of total product usage.

Regular Shampoo: 20.1% of total adult females used regular shampoo 2 or more times a week, and they accounted for 69.1% of total product usage.

Hair Shampoo—Dandruff: 15% of total adult men used dandruff shampoo 2 or more times a week, and they accounted for 81% of total product usage.

Movie Film: 5% of total adult males used 4 or more rolls of movie film in the past year, and they accounted for 82% of total product usage.

Books—Hard Cover: 4% of total adult men bought 10 or more hard-cover books in the past year, and they accounted for 54% of total hard-cover book purchases.

Regular Beer: 25% of total adult men drank 5 or more glasses of regular beer a day, and they accounted for 85% of total product usage.

Source: W. R. Simmons, 1971

The second step *of the creative process is to determine what problems the prime prospect has in the category under consideration. To illustrate this and subsequent steps . . . I have picked paper towels as an example because they lie somewhere between the utility of calories and the non-utility of neckties, and represent a quite characteristic nationally advertised consumer product. They are, of course, not a basic human need. People mopped up and dried things with rags for centuries, and it is unlikely that they dreamed of paper towels. . . .*

To an average man, no doubt, all paper towels look alike. With male logic, it may be hard for him to see why paper towels should not be solely on a price and quantity basis. But, to a mother of three subteen children who have a dog, the prospect of a washload of rags every day is not inviting. To her a paper towel is a necessity, and she has quite firm personal opinions about what characteristics that paper towel should have. Men who write economic textbooks generally have the chauvinism not to place any economic value on the time and effort involved in a woman's housework.

The heavy paper-towel user is defined as one who uses an average of eight rolls a month. Among female heads of household, the 15.4% who purchase at this rate represent 41.2% of the paper-towel usage. Typically, she will be a housewife, 25 or over, with children, living in A and B counties and having a high-school education or better.

A customary step in finding out the problems of this prime prospect is to invite her to attend what are known as focus groups. These are essentially group discussions of eight to ten housewives with a discussion leader to keep them on the subject—in this case, paper towels. You might not think that a group of ten women could talk about paper towels for a couple of hours, but I assure you they can. They have bought and tried many brands; they have a very accurate estimate of their prices and a knowledge of their physical characteristics as revealed in their daily use.

Advertising creative people attend these meetings and . . . [the] attitudes and concepts that are derived from such interviews then become the basis for more quantitatively accurate interviews with large samples of prime prospects. If the work is properly done, the advertising creative man will have available to him a very rich source of data on the decision process of housewives in making the brand selection.

Normally, you find that the prime prospects have quite differing hierarchies of satisfactions that they are seeking. These may cluster into groups. Some will be most concerned with the strength of the paper towels. Some will have more concerns for absorbency. . . . Some may believe that cost outweighs any other characteristic.

The third step *in the creative process is to examine the product or service in the light of what has been learned about the prime prospect and the problems involved in his decision process. This usually requires the creative man having to personally involve himself with every detail of a manufactured product. . . . What he will try to do is visualize that product through the eyes of the prime prospect—not through the eyes of the technicians who make it. It is an important difference. The assignment is to match up some set of the decision problems of the prime prospects with the characteristics of that product or service which will most likely lead to brand trial.*

At this point in our process, we will have developed what is called a copy concept. In simpler terms, this is a statement of what you hope the prime prospect will carry in his memory about your brand. It must be relevant to her decision. And yet it cannot be too complicated. The human mind is not designed to carry away a ream of engineering specifications that are irrelevant to the decision process. No doubt your necktie can be described accurately in terms of its net weight and threads per inch— but you are not likely to care and certainly not likely to remember.

Suppose that you are developing a copy concept for a paper towel. Having examined the prime prospect's notions about paper towels, you have observed that a great number of them are concerned about the ability of the towel to sop things up that are spilled. This matches with the fact that from a laboratory standpoint, your brand will absorb so many grams of water per square inch per second. You are aware, however, that the prime prospect's experience suggests that in order to get absorbency, she may have to put up with a towel that comes apart when it gets wet. Actually, the lab tests indicate that in this respect you are materially better than your leading competitor. If this is substantiated by testing the idea on prime prospects, you have a copy concept which will communicate that the brand has a very high degree of absorbency and yet is strong when wet.

The fourth step *is the execution of this copy strategy by executing, shall we suppose, a thirty-second TV commercial. In order to do this successfully, the commercial you prepare must accomplish the following: it must get the attention of the prime prospect; it must identify the domain of her decision; it must register the memory of your brand in this domain; it must register in her memory the content of the copy concept; and it must link the concept to the brand.*

This is not easy to do. Advertising has to work hard to be looked at to begin with, and harder to be remembered for more than a brief moment. For example, if you ask people the next morning what commercials they saw the night before, they have very little recall. If you probe them about specific commercials, they can with some effort remember the category. Of those who remember the category, a fraction will remember the brand. And of those who remember the brand, a fraction will be able to repeat the content of the concept.

The answer to this is some form of dramatization designed to communicate all of the above factors. The form of dramatization is usually dictated to some degree by the subject matter. If we wish to demonstrate the absorbency of a paper towel, it is probable that we shall show an actual demonstration. On the other hand, if it is softness we wish to demonstrate, it may better be accomplished by association.

What the creator has in his mind is a large amount of information about what has interested people in the past. He knows that people would rather watch people than things. They are more attracted by the unusual than the ordinary. Mostly his knowledge is a compendium of all the visual and auditory effects that people are most likely to pay attention to and remember. In this he must remember, however, that the prime prospect's behavior is not representative of all people, and what is attention-getting and memorable to them may be unique.

It is probably impossible for me to give instructions that would apply to the construction of every commercial, but it is not because they are so very subtle. The technique that newspapermen use to get your attention with a headline may be combined with the stage techniques of telling a story and the memory techniques of a jingle. The restrictions are severe. You have thirty seconds, and the more time you waste on getting attention, the less time you have to register the brand and copy concept. If you dwell too long on the copy concept, the attention and brand name may be reduced.

Ultimately, the commercial is written in a form called storyboards—a sequence of still pictures with the voice and sound effects typed underneath. From perhaps a dozen initial storyboards, the process of approval within the agency and client organization will whittle these down to a few to be decided on by the client top management. Before this is done, they must, of course, pass through a sieve of inspection by client and agency attorneys, product technicians, consumer testing panels, network acceptance committees and other checks and balances that will be best described by others.

Another step of the creative process is the study of competing advertising, and these films are provided by an organization that takes them directly off the air. This transfer process does not give high-quality photography, but does make it possible to observe what competing brands are doing in various markets.

Once the commercial is on the air, the prime prospects for these products may pay some attention to them, remember some brand names and remember perhaps something about the product satisfactions each one offered. When she next approaches her brand decisions, she will retain some fragments of this. She will also retain quite strongly her previous brand experiences and the brand experience of those she has talked to. She will also, through retail food-store advertising, have been bombarded with price information. In the store she will be affected by the amount of shelf stock, point-of-sale displays and the current pricing structure in that store for both advertised and non-advertised brands. She will, then, reach out and deftly remove a package of paper towels from the shelf. She will probably do the right things in terms of maximizing her satisfactions.

I must tell you that every year people in marketing make the mistake of thinking that the lady in the food store doesn't really know what she is doing. Every year hundreds of new products are launched into test markets with very adequate advertising budgets. Yet, the failure rate is estimated at at least 80%—and since people tend to hide failures, that is probably low.

What happens is that the new brand spends enough to get awareness of its existence—which is not too hard. But if the concept doesn't make sense to Mrs. America, she doesn't try it even once. If it does make sense, she tries it once. Then if she is disappointed, she goes right back to her previous brands.

2 THE ROLES OF THE CONSUMER IN THE FORMULATION OF ADVERTISING STRATEGY *(excerpts from A. A. Achenbaum, senior vice president and director of marketing services, J. Walter Thompson; and from C. E. Overholser, senior vice president and director of marketing research, Young & Rubicam[1])*

The basic guideline in the *creation* of advertisements is understanding what different consumers feel, think, and do. The specific strategic and tactical decisions that implement the guideline vary a great deal. The next two testimonies illustrate how two different firms go about *implementation*. We begin with a selection from the testimony of A. A. Achenbaum.

---

[1] J. Walter Thompson is one of the oldest and largest advertising agencies; Young & Rubicam is a major advertising agency in the United States and abroad.

A. THE ROLE OF STRATEGY

To begin with . . . strategy is the communications' objectives—based on knowledge of the consumers in the market place. It specifically recounts: who [the advertiser] wants to reach—the market target; *what brands he wishes to compete against—the* competitive posture; *what he wants to sell—the* buying incentive *he is offering that the product will support; and how he wants to present or describe it—the* communications environment. . . .

The strategic input is made up of three elements—market information, analysis, and judgment (Exhibit 5.2). The market information is sometimes guesswork—most often fact. The analysis is sometimes done systematically, sometimes intuitively. It is a rare major advertiser who sticks to guesswork and intuition alone. . . . For example, at the agency I just left—Grey Advertising—they did almost 50 major strategic studies for its clients in the last 8 years. Bear in mind that this is only what the agency did. Most clients do their own work. Moreover, recognize that these studies cost in the neighborhood of $35,000 to $150,000 to do. . . . Obviously, these clients take [consumers'] feedback seriously.

It is difficult to describe all the specific information that is obtained in any one of these studies and the amount of analysis that is done. But let me give you one

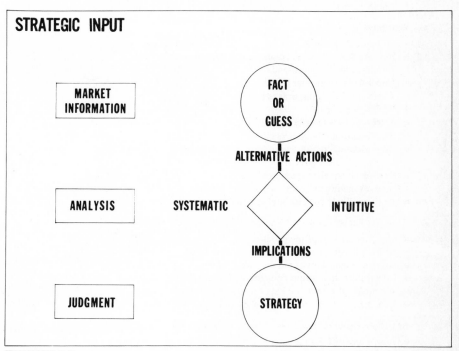

EXHIBIT 5.2

example. In a study of the men's after shave and cologne market, the questionnaire used was 23 pages long. Let me just quickly show you a list of some of the information that was obtained and used in the analysis (Exhibit 5.3).

EXHIBIT 5.3
QUESTION AREAS COVERED IN MAJOR MARKET STUDY OF AFTER SHAVE LOTIONS AND COLOGNES

A. Who Uses After Shaves and Colognes
   - How many men used these products in the past six months.
   - What types of products do they use.
   - How much of an overlap is there in use of after shave, colognes, and all purpose lotion.
   - How often do men use these products.
   - What are the user's demographic profiles.

B. What Types and Brands Do They Use
   - How do people classify brands.
   - What are the main types.
   - What types do they use.
   - What brands do they use.
   - How often do men use each type.
   - Where do they apply each type.

C. Who Buys These Products
   - Do people buy these products as gifts or for regular use.
   - How much of the total volume do gift brands account for.
   - Who buys the regular brands.
   - Who selects the regular brands.
   - Where are the regular brands bought.
   - Who buys the gifts.
   - What types are bought as gifts.
   - What brands are bought as gifts.
   - What product combinations are bought as gifts.
   - Do women select gifts in the store.
   - How often are gift brands used.
   - How often are gift types used.
   - Are users likely to start buying brands they've received as gifts.

D. What Are People Looking for in After Shaves and Colognes
   - What dimensions of the product are people concerned with.
   - Which after shave dimensions are most important.
   - Which cologne dimensions are most important.
   - How do the dimensions compare in importance.
   - Are men and women looking for the same things.
   - How different are after shaves and colognes.

E. Are These Different Groups of People Looking for Different Things
   - How many different groups of people are there.
   - What is the description of each group.
   - How do females fit into these groups.

Let me also show you what the study framework looked like in schematic form (Exhibit 5.4). If you would study this schematic, you will realize to what lengths major advertisers go to understand their customers and to attempt to please them. Moreover, these advertisers are not solely interested in what the average man wants. They try to learn whether there are separate [consumer] segments that require special products.

The methods used in getting this data are all above board. The consumers volunteer the information, often spending over an hour answering questions. They also recognize the purpose for which it is obtained. There is nothing subtle or manipulative about it.

While all this information is useful, perhaps the most useful is that concerned with what people are looking for in the product. It is this information which the consumer considers most salient. Since revelation of the specific data could be useful to competitors, let me show it to you in somewhat masked form (Exhibit 5.5a and b). As you can see, some of the product qualities desired are not ingredients or functional benefits. So-called emotional benefits play a role in what people get out of a product. Status, brand reputation, sex appeal, and masculinity are things people are interested in.

B. THE COMPETITIVE WEDGE

The strategy the advertiser chooses must take into consideration his competition. . . . Schematically, the advertiser visualizes the problem as wedging his product, price, and promotional effort between his prospective consumers and his competitors' price, product, and promotional effort (Exhibit 5.6). . . .

To the degree that each competitor attempts to wedge himself into the consumers' minds to move his brand and to the degree that each uses that information he thinks is most relevant to his market, the consumers will obtain a variety of viewpoints about the competitive products being sold. While some of us may not appreciate the form of the communication or for that matter disagree with what is said, this competition of ideas is a key and economical means by which consumers seek information.

C. THE ADVERTISING EXECUTION

The advertising execution is the outgrowth of the advertising strategy—it is made up of the copy, the media, and the money spent. To develop the copy or the message takes a creative spark—a feeling about how a product when presented in print or over the air waves will in fact persuade a consumer to act. It is probably in the execution where the persuasion is built into the advertising (Exhibit 5.7).

Yet no one knows exactly what kind of execution will truly convince people on an a priori basis. While experience plays a big role, there are no general rules on how it is done. It, therefore, has become the job of copy research or testing to tell the advertisers whether an execution is effective—whether it communicates the strategy and whether it persuades the consumer.

D. COPY TESTING

There is hardly a major advertiser or advertising agency not involved in some kind of copy testing or evaluation. Last year, Grey alone did over half a million dollars worth

SCHEMATIC OF THE MARKET RESEARCH METHOD FOR CONDUCTING MARKET TARGET-BUYING INCENTIVE STUDIES

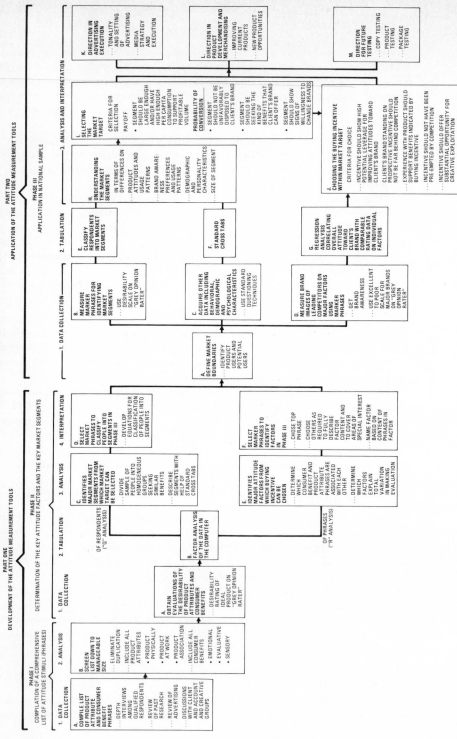

EXHIBIT 5.4

ATTRIBUTES OF IDEAL BRAND: MEN'S TOILETRY

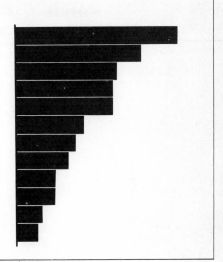

PLEASANT TO USE EVERYDAY
MASCULINE IMAGE
SEX APPEAL
POST USE THERAPY
MULTIPLE USE
GIFT APPEAL
PRODUCT REPUTATION
CONDITIONS _____
HIGH STATUS
USED BY SOPHISTICATED PEOPLE
PACKAGE APPEARANCE
EXPENSIVE

EXHIBIT 5.5a

ATTRIBUTES OF IDEAL BRAND: AUTOMOBILE PRODUCT

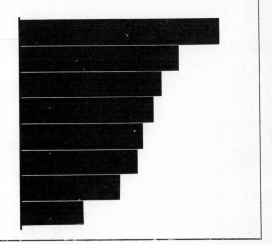

PRODUCT PERFORMANCE
CONVENIENT LOCATION
PERSONAL REASSURANCE
FRIENDLY SERVICE PEOPLE
CLEAN OUTLETS
GOOD REPAIRMEN
WELL KNOWN BRAND
CONSCIENTIOUS SERVICE

EXHIBIT 5.5b

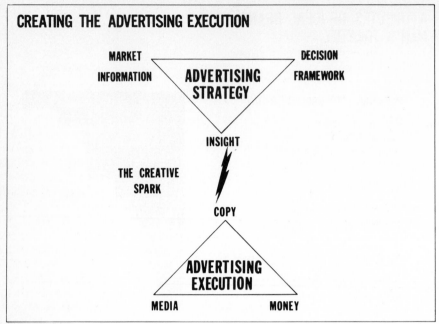

EXHIBIT 5.6

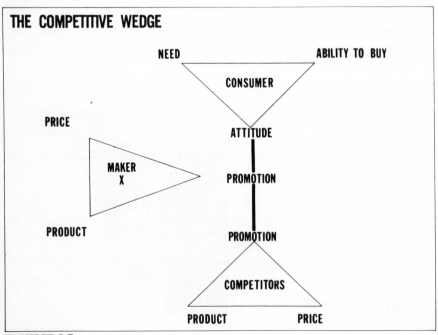

EXHIBIT 5.7

of copy testing for its clients. J. Walter Thompson spent an even larger sum on this function. . . . The results leave a great deal to be desired. There is little agreement on how to best test advertising. . . . Many different techniques are used but there is a great controversy over which, if any, works best.

But this is certainly not a situation where manipulation can run rampant. To the degree that researchers represent the scientists in the advertising business, they are hardly the all-powerful manipulators that Vance Packard described.

E. PRODUCT EVALUATION AND SUPPORT

It is both a cliché and an axiom in the advertising business that advertising cannot sell a bad product. And it is a rare national advertiser who tries to. In fact, most of the sophisticated clients do extensive product research to find out not only whether the product satisfies prospective consumers, but also whether it can support advertising claims. Perhaps not enough is done. But there are often cost reasons involved. . . .

Again using my experience at Grey, in the last 8 years alone, it did almost 50 product or package tests for its clients. Many a product has been killed or revised on the basis of this research. And many an advertising campaign scrapped as a result. This is hardly a picture of not caring what the consumer thinks, of manipulation.

It should be clear from even this limited perspective of a few agencies that the advertiser and his agency . . . intent is not to manipulate [consumer] behavior to their own ends. To the contrary, in practice, the major advertiser seeks market information so that he can hopefully satisfy his prospects' needs and desires more effectively than his competitors. And as I indicated, they do this openly and without compulsion. This can hardly be described as unfair methods of competition or deceptive trade practices. . . .

We continue with another illustration of how a firm uses the basic concept that successful communication relies on knowledge of what different consumers feel, think, and do. The testimony is by C. E. Overholser.

There are three basic steps in shaping advertising strategy, and consumer research is essential in helping us to make intelligent decisions at each. The three steps are: Product Class Definition; Prospect Group Selection; and Message Element Selection.

A. PRODUCT CLASS DEFINITION

Why should the definition of our brand's product class be any problem? Isn't it perfectly obvious? A cigar competes with cigars. . . . But do Tiparillos . . . compete in the consumer's mind with cigarettes as well? Do White Owls compete with all other cigars, or are they seen as an appropriate alternative only to the smokers of certain other cigars, which comprise a discrete subsegment of the cigar market?

I submit that the answers to these kinds of questions are by no means self-evident. . . . Traditional definitions of product classes as used in the trade are often arbitrary or obsolete . . . bearing little relationship to the alternatives consumers face up to in their own minds when making a purchase decision. Increasingly as new products proliferate, brands compete across traditional product class lines or are specialized so as to compete primarily within a narrow segment of a traditional product class.

The first decision our advertising strategist must make is whether to compete broadly within the conventional product class, to compete only with some segment of the conventional product class, or whether to attempt to expand demand for the brand as an alternative for some other product class. This so-called positioning decision guides the selection of prospect groups and the selection of message elements to be communicated.

How does research help us to position a brand? Measurement of consumer attitudes and behavior are directed at answering two key questions: Is the "conventional" product class expandable? And, is the "conventional" product class segmented? Or segmentable?

For example, in the case of a product class like beer, a survey might indicate (I say might, because I am only hypothesizing here, not reporting findings) that most consumers seldom consider beer as a good substitute for other beverages. . . . Moreover, analysis of cultural trends, and long-term beverage drinking trend data might indicate what appears to be a gradual secular decline in beer drinking. We would conclude then that the "conventional" product class for beer was not readily expandable. In Exhibit 5.8, the dots representing competing entities on our symbolic map of the beer market are all within the circle representing the conventional product class.

A study of dessert consumption behavior, on the other hand, might indicate that flavored gelatin desserts were considered appropriate for many occasions when some other dessert was actually served, implying an obvious possible opportunity to expand the conventional product class—by suggesting increased usage. For gelatin desserts, some of the dots might represent other products like ice cream, fresh fruit, or cookies.

Beer is similar to gelatin desserts on our other key criterion, however. In both cases, there is not very important segmentation within the product class. Every beer is different, and consumers perceive difference in quality; but with a few fairly minor exceptions, beers are not seen as being different in character. By and large, most beer drinkers expect the same benefits and seek to satisfy the same general wants regardless of which beer they prefer. We have the same situaiton with gelatin desserts. We call this an unsegmented market.

Cigarettes, however, are an example of a segmented product class. . . . Twenty years ago all major brands of American cigarettes were 87 mm long, without filters, made of nearly identical blends of Kentucky burley tobacco without special flavor additives and packed in soft, paper packets of 20. . . . Today the following distinctly different segments can be listed: non-filter straight (the 1930s standard); flavor filters; hi-filtration filters; menthol flavored; 100 millimeter; and feminine design. Those lines in the chart (Exhibit 5.8) . . . symbolize this segmentation. And, of course, there are all sorts of degrees and combinations of the above as various differentiated brands have been developed to satisfy the spectrum of wants which have evolved in this market. At the same time, for obvious reasons, there is no role for advertising in expanding the overall demand for cigarettes. No dots fall outside the circle.

The most complex of our cases is represented by the electric shaver market. There research might indicate that the product class is both expandable (as men may be converted from wet shaving) and segmented as men have developed varying value systems in respect to the relative benefits of closeness versus comfort or preferences for various features. The shaver may symbolize both segmentation and expandability.

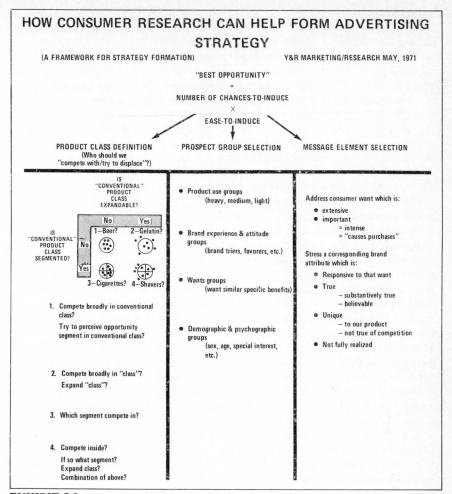

EXHIBIT 5.8

Each of these four represents a prototype, although none of the actual examples fit that prototype precisely. Each of these prototypical situations raises different questions. In situation 1, the beer case, we must decide whether to: compete broadly in the conventional class, or try to perceive an opportunity segment in the conventional class. (As might be done in the case of beer by estimating the opportunity for increasing the number of that small minority who prefer a dark beer.)

In situation 2, typified by gelatin desserts, we have a different choice [of] whether to: compete broadly in the conventional class; try to perceive an opportunity segment in the conventional class; or try to expand the class. For markets in situation 3, segmented but not expandable, the problem is more simply stated: which segment to compete in. Finally, the most complex situation, 4, a market which is both expandable and segmented. Here we must answer a series of questions: shall we compete within the conventional class? If so, in which segment? Shall we try to expand the class or adopt a combination strategy?

Sometimes the answers to these questions come easily . . . many answers are dictated by the physical and objective characteristics of the brand in question. But in many instances, particularly during the development stages of a new product, a very careful evaluation based on the best possible research of consumer value systems, perceptions, and behavior is required, if we are to decide wisely.

We use consumer research to help us select among alternative product class definitions on the basis of what we call the "best opportunity" concept. . . . We define the best opportunity as the product of "the number of chances for advertising to induce" behavior or attitudes favorable to our client's objectives times *the ease with which such behavior or attitudes can be induced. In other words, how many people may be interested in what we have to say and what are our chances of inducing a change among these people?*

Research cannot provide us neat, precise numbers to substitute into our equation. In particular, estimating the ease with which prospects can be induced to respond to an advertising strategy is a judgmental process. But research can *tell us how many people eat dessert and how often . . . [or] how many people are primarily interested in closeness in shaving versus those who value comfort more, or speed and convenience. These kinds of data help us to estimate the number of chances various product class positioning strategies will provide. Secondly, research is used to estimate the ease to induce factor. For example, we can measure the relative extent of dissatisfaction with various competitive brands, indicating where trial of our brand might be relatively easy to induce. We can estimate the degree to which consumers consider our brand to be an appropriate substitute for other products. . . .*

Each alternative positioning is reviewed and a choice is made on the basis of our research-based judgment as to which alternative will yield the largest multiplied product of numbers and ease. I want to stress the phrase research-based judgment. The research rarely dictates the best decision. . . . Unfortunately, marketing research is, like all the other applied social sciences, an inexact discipline more akin to the process of gathering and evaluating evidence in a judicial procedure than to the precise series of mathematical proofs and laboratory experiments which typically underlie engineering decisions.

B. PROSPECT GROUP SELECTION

Having made a tentative decision on the nature of the product class, we move on to consider a more precise definition of who will be the best prospects for our advertising. The best prospects for the advertising are not necessarily the best prospects for the brand itself. There may be no need to preach to the firmly converted. Now, of course, the very act of selecting a competitive frame provides a first rough cut at defining prospects, [e.g.] if we define our product class as cigars, we pretty much exclude non-cigar smokers from our prospect group. . . .

We use research to define prospects more specifically. Not all users of our product class are equally good prospects for our advertising. There are four major orders of classification which are widely used to help pinpoint the target of advertising.

First we are always interested in knowing how product usage patterns vary within the population. It may seem equally obvious that we would select heavy users as our best prospects since they, by definition, represent the largest number of chances we have to induce a purchase. But this is not always the case. Often heavy users are the most difficult to induce. They tend to be already well informed. They are likely to have very strong opinions based on extensive product experimentation, and they are likely to be very habituated in their purchase behavior. Hence, many advertisers may choose the lighter user as the best prospect for an advertising effort. . . .

We also pay close attention to brand experience and attitude groups. We want to know how many people are aware of our brand, how many have tried it, on what occasions do they use it, what are their satisfactions, dissatisfactions with our brands and with competitive brands. All of this sort of information is used to help guide us as to whether to direct our advertising, for example, at consumers who have already tried us in the hopes of increasing their frequency of use or to concentrate on inducing trial among those who have not tried us.

. . . we often find through attitude research that a significant number of consumers have a badly mistaken opinion about our product. For example, many people believe that decaffeinated coffee has inferior flavor, and yet in blind product test after blind product test this myth is disproved. Clearly, there is a good opportunity to induce trial of a decaffeinated coffee if we can persuasively inform this group that decaffeinated coffee is equal in flavor to other brands. Thus, we may choose a specific "attitude group" as our prime advertising prospects. Suppose that research discloses that many users of competitive brands perceive it as weak in some important attribute —certain hair grooming preparations may be seen as too greasy. If we can determine how many and what sorts of consumers hold this attitude, they may become the prime prospect group for a brand which is, indeed, superior in the attribute in question, for example, a grease-free hair grooming product.

The most important research input to the process of defining prospect groups is the study of "wants groups." Advances in consumer research methodology have enabled advertisers to gain a much clearer idea of the configuration of consumer wants. That is, progress has been made in classifying consumers according to the relative value they place on specific benefits which a product may offer. An over-simplified example: dentifrice users tend to fall into several distinct benefit-seeking segments. Group I seeks maximum cavity prevention. Group II seek maximum whitening and brightening. Group III seeks maximum mouth and breath freshening. Group IV seeks maximum flavor satisfaction. . . .

. . . if research can distinguish such benefit-seeking segments, characterize them in terms of their dominant wants, count their members, provide a detailed account of their characteristics, and finally tell use how our brand is rated by each of the groups, if we then match our knowledge of the true attributes of our brand to our knowledge of the consumer want structure, then we have a powerful tool by which to judge the best relative opportunity presented by each of these segments.

Working with one or more of the orders of classification I have discussed, and employing our "best opportunity" index, we develop a prospect group definition. The decisions involved are seldom easy. In the first place, the research base is never as complete as we wish it were. Often major factors have to be estimated because they *have not [been] or cannot, without great expense, be measured. A more intractable problem remains, however, for the advertising strategist. There is a tendency which might even be dubbed the "iron law of market segmentation" for research to present us not with a pat solution but with a dilemma. As size of opportunity goes up—ease to induce goes down. The logic is fairly obvious: if wants are diverse, and they seem to be getting more so every day, the larger the number of people one tries to satisfy with a single appeal, the poorer the fit will be. Conversely, if one attempts to "be all things to all people" by stressing a broad spectrum of product benefits, one may wind up being everyone's second choice. Moreover, the larger the prospect group, the more likely it is that competition is already strongly entrenched with good products designed to fill that segment's wants structure. Thus, when we look at the larger prospect groups, they almost invariably look harder to induce than the smaller ones ones. . . .*

A word about demographics and the latest buzz word, "psychographics." Such statistics merely tell us about the characteristics of various groups of people. Things like age, income, education level, sex, family size, and geographical location are commonly called demographics. Things like how leisure time is spent, social and political attitudes, cultural interests, and personality traits like aggressiveness or venturesomeness are now generally called "psychographics." We use such information about prospect groups to help us decide on media and to guide the tone of advertising copy. We can use descriptive data on media audiences to match the demographic characteristics of the viewers of our advertising to that of our prospects. If our prospects tend to be young, copywriters are likely to use somewhat different vocabulary and visual imagery than they would if they were trying to communicate with people over 40. If the prospect tends to have a special set of leisure interests, like sports or workshop hobbies, both the message and the medium may be affected.

By this time I'm sure you will have realized that the issues of product class definition, prospect group selection, and message element, which we come to now, are all highly interrelated. In a sense the questions represent different aspects of the same basic question—the question of finding the best opportunity to inform persuasively and thus induce a change in attitude or behavior.

C. MESSAGE ELEMENT SELECTION

To make the final set of strategic decisions, those in respect to the content of the advertising message itself, we first of all need to study the technical product research which tells us how the product performs in the laboratory. Secondly, we need to know how our product and competitive products perform in natural use when tested among consumers under blind conditions, i.e., under conditions where is it not possible for the consumer to know what brand she is using, hence it is not possible that she be influenced by reputation or imputation of quality from price, package, etc. Third, we need to know what users and non-users of various brands think of those brands when they are identified—that is, when all imputed virtues or faults are allowed to play their role in affecting attitude. Finally, of course, we need once again to study the expressed wants of various groups of consumers. All of this information, much of which I have already discussed in connection with prospect group selection, must then be evaluated once again to help us to select message elements which will give us the best opportunity to induce response.

This process starts by identifying and selecting for address a consumer want which is reasonably intense and hopefully is crucial in causing a purchase to be made. . . . The prospects will be relatively easy to induce . . . if we can select an attribute of our brand to stress which is responsive to that want. . . . We try also to select an attribute to stress in which our brand has an advantage over competition. Ideally an attribute which is not only important, but unique.

This again generally raises the problem I discussed earlier, a corollary of the iron law of marketing segmentation. The more important an attribute is to a large number of consumers, the less likely it is that any brand in a highly competitive free economy will have a unique advantage. The strategist must often face a difficult choice between emphasis on an important but generic quality or on a somewhat less important but differentiating quality.

. . . we try to select an attribute for stress in our message which is not only responsive to an important want, true and unique, but one which is not fully realized by the consumer. . . . We search for opportunities to correct falsely-based, negative opinions about our brands or to inform people of positive virtues which have not previously been well communicated. We concentrate, of course, on information which we have reason to believe will be of real interest to our prospects. A thirty-second commercial is not a patent application or even a catalog specifications sheet. If we are to succeed in communicating any information within that time frame, we must limit ourselves to one or two key points.

The consumer will pay attention or not, gain information or not, be persuaded or not, depending upon her particular set of wants and the prior level of her information and, of course, depending on our skill in communicating. In the long run, she will choose the brand whose good points and bad points best conform to her personal value system.

Case Illustration

Let me spend the remainder of my time showing you how the development of a recent Young & Rubicam campaign was guided by such research. I've already mentioned that a cigar is not just a cigar, that there is a real question as to what product class definition is most appropriate for any one brand. The White Owl Cigar is a full-size, 10 to 15¢ cigar manufactured in a variety of shapes. Should it be advertised as an alternative to all other smoking products, to all cigars, or should we limit our competitive effort to the large cigar field or perhaps to the even narrower subsegment, 10 to 15¢ cigars?

All of these product class definitions were considered in the light of facts developed through analysis of sales data and consumer research. The long-term trend in the cigar market has been downward for large cigars and upward for the smaller, slimmer shapes. Over the past 10 or 15 years, dozens of new brands responsive to this change in consumer preference have been introduced. Our client, the General Cigar Company, makers of White Owl Cigars, has been in the forefront with brands like Tiparillo Cigars, on which we are the agency, and Tiajuana Smalls Cigars. Tiparillo Cigars and Tiajuana Smalls Cigars, like competitive small cigars, tend to appeal to younger smokers and very significantly are positioned competitively as alternatives to cigarettes as well as to other cigars. But White Owl Cigars, as a traditional full-size cigar, is at a disadvantage competing for this new product. Although the total potential, or number of chances, to induce for large cigars is relatively smaller than it is for all smoking products, the ease to induce factor is much more likely to be favorable for White Owl Cigars in the smaller, large-cigar market. Research also indicates that large-cigar smokers tend to stay within certain rather rigid price lines. A two-for-a-quarter smoker is a very poor prospect for a 25¢ cigar and vice versa. Again, on the grounds of relative ease to induce, the decision was made that White Owl Cigars should compete narrowly within its own particular subsegment of the market rather than attempt to build new demand for large inexpensive cigars at the expense of other tobacco products. It follows that the prime prospect for White Owl advertising should be defined as the regular smoker of large 10 to 15¢ cigars.

The findings from a blind product test of White Owl Cigars against a leading competitor, Brand X, gave further guidance to our strategy. Two samples of smokers were recruited to take part in this test. The samples were statistically matched in every respect except that one sample were regular White Owl smokers and the others were Brand X smokers. Each sample of consumers were given two packages of cigars which were distinguished only by code numbers and asked to indicate which code they preferred after they had smoked both packs. The two test cigars were, of course, White Owl Cigars and Brand X.

The key findings are shown in Exhibit 5.9. It is not surprising that the White Owl smokers tended to prefer their own brand by a margin to 59% to 28%, even though the White Owls were not identified as such. What was surprising and very important to us was that Brand X smokers also tended to prefer White Owl Cigars by a margin of 51% to 38%. It was apparent that Brand X smokers were good prospects for White Owl if they could be induced to try White Owl.

We also were able to guide our media and copy people as to the character of the large-cigar smokers who comprised our prospect group. The index numbers in Exhibit 5.10 indicate that large-cigar smokers are predominantly in older age groups and are spread evenly across income groups. Of course, for a lower-price cigar like White Owl, the low-income segment is particularly important.

BLIND PRODUCT TEST FINDINGS

	Smoke White Owl	Smoke Brand X
Prefer White Owl	59	51
Prefer Brand X	28	38
No Preference	13	11

EXHIBIT 5.9

```
LARGE CIGAR – REGULAR
SMOKER PROFILE
                                 FREQUENCY
            ┌  18 – 24              70
            │  25 – 34              57
     AGE   ┤   35 – 49             105
            │  50 – 64             122
            └  65 & OVER           154

            ┌  10,000 OVER         104
  INCOME  ┤   5,000 – 9,900         91
            └  UNDER 5,000         111
```

EXHIBIT 5.10

```
PERCEPTION OF BRANDS

 •  Although White Owl rated better on blind test:

 •  Brand X rated better in consumer perceptions:

    –  Value
    –  For man who knows cigars
    –  Real tobacco flavor

 •  Brand X seen as more appropriate for common man

      White Owl for          Brand X for

      Doctors                Truck Drivers
      Lawyers

 Yet no difference in actual occupations of brand smokers
```

EXHIBIT 5.11

*In addition to the blind product test data and the demographic data, we had
information from still another survey source that, despite White Owl's strong
performance under blind test conditions, Brand X had a better general reputation
among cigar smokers (Exhibit 5.11). It rated better in consumer perceptions of value
"for a man who knows cigars" and for "real tobacco flavor." Moreover, White
Owls were thought of as being more appropriate for upper-class smokers like doctors
and lawyers; Brand X for truck drivers—this despite the fact that there was no
difference in the occupational patterns of actual smokers of the two brands.*

*This information reinforced our tentative decision to concentrate our advertising
effort upon informing smokers of directly competitive large cigars that White Owl was*

a better-tasting, high-quality cigar. Knowing that we had to overcome considerable prejudice, we decided to change the tone of our advertising to make it more down to earth, more plebian in manner. The strategic recommendations which flowed from the research were: compete narrowly in low-price, large-cigar market; maximize effort against older man in broad income range; induce trial in order to close product quality/perception gap; present product on "human" common-man-to-common-man basis.

2.1 THE COMMUNICATION EQUATION AND THE MANAGERIAL SEARCH FOR A SOLUTION

Let us consider the implications of the Dillon, Achenbaum, and Overholser testimonies. At the micromanagerial level, advertising is a function within a firm: it is performed in an attempt to communicate to one specific group of consumers, and it consists of a stream of advertising decisions. In the preceding sections we began spelling out the nature of these decisions—namely, what problems they attempt to solve.

The testimonies indicate that management problem solving begins with finding what consumer needs and preferences exist. But all their needs and preferences may not be met by attributes of a product that a firm can economically develop, produce, and distribute. Diagrammatically, the problem may be stated as follows:

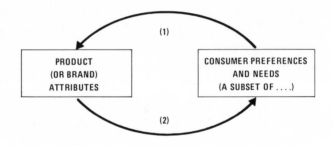

We must understand the nature of this problem and how the professionals go about solving it. Note that the original communication equation "sender-seekers/receivers" of an ad was a bit too general. We now see that, to solve the communication equation, we must first solve for the two problems indicated by arrows (1) and (2). Ideally, the solutions of the two problems should be arrived at simultaneously; in practice, as we saw in the testimonies, they are reached by successive approximations.

In the problem indicated by arrow (1), we begin with consumer needs and preferences, and search within the firm for the product or brand whose attributes fit some of these needs and preferences most closely. In some sense—as signified by the direction of the arrow—we can say that the former (consumer needs) determine the later (product attributes). The former is the independent variable; the latter the dependent variable.

The world is not that simple, however. To begin with, since no firm can possibly try to satisfy all consumer needs and preferences, a manager must have some initial idea about which subset of needs and preferences his firm may be able to satisfy. Although arrow (1) implies that this subset is known, in practice we must search for it. This search is initially guided by the resources and talents a firm has or may acquire. Such resources and talents provide a basis for at least guessing what set of attributes can be developed in the form of a product. Arrow (2) indicates this problem: given a potential set of attributes, determine whether there exists some subset of consumer needs and preferences that may be satisfied by such attributes.

Solving the communication equation begins with solving the interaction between the two arrows. The firm must find the set of product attributes and the subset of consumer needs and preferences that fit best. Yet the best fit is not only difficult to find, but also, once found, rapidly becomes obsolete because of continuous change in both the supply and demand sides of the communication equation. Continuous technological developments and economic competition undercut a firm's position, as does the increasing instability of preferences and needs, a consequence of the growing amount of discretionary time and income available to an increasing number of consumers.

We should also observe the emergence in the three testimonies of a theme that will turn out to be crucial in the following chapters. What do we mean by product (or brand) attributes? There is no doubt that the professionals so far have one, and only one, answer: those attributes that are perceived by some consumers. The expression "a car is a car is a car" has very little meaning in affluent societies. A car is not a simple set of engineering specifications—torque curve; brake horsepower curve; rear end suspension geometry; weight distribution and its changes under acceleration, braking, and cornering; ratios of transmission gears to differential gear, to wheel diameter; and the like. Further, even if we agreed to describe a car in these terms, we would know little about its performance unless we also knew its intended uses. For instance, the optimal combination of the above attributes is different for city or highway driving. The different uses—actual or intended—of a product by different consumers, determine which attributes are relevant to which consumer.

Presumably, the consumer is the one who chooses the set of attributes of interest to him. Let us remember a particularly famous case in which management forgot the users' point of view. In the late 1950s, the Ford Motor Company decided that the attribute "safety" would give it a differential advantage over its competitors. Accordingly, seat belts were purchased and distributed to dealers, and salesmen were trained to emphasize their availability—a substantial investment. When the new car models were introduced, advertising began emphasizing the theme of safety. The reasoning underlying this investment in seat belts and advertising was as follows: there must be a large number of consumers with a need for safety; we shall inform them that our cars have an attribute, seat belts, that satisfies this need.

Perhaps there was such a need for safety. But human perception and mental processes must also be taken into account. In the late fifties, the perception of seat belts turned out to be very negative. Salesmen and dealers noticed that the mention of seat belts scared people; seat belts evoked the dangerous rather than pleasurable aspects of driving, and people began to walk out of the Ford dealers' showrooms. Within a few months dealers rebelled. They stopped mentioning seat belts and demanded that the Ford Company stop using that theme in its advertisements. A flop. Irrational consumers? Perhaps. Yet, just a few years later, after publication of Nader's *Unsafe at Any Speed*, seat belts began to be accepted. Note, however, that this acceptability seems to be limited to perception, since recent statistics reveal that relatively few people use seat belts and, of these, probably even fewer wear them correctly.

According to our witnesses, a product is what consumers perceive it to be. Any business—or public agency serving consumers—must try to find a fit between consumer needs and preferences and product attributes *as perceived by consumers*. If it does not make the attempt, it will not meet the needs and preferences of consumers, nor will it generate revenues, and it will consequently fail to meet the demands of labor, capital, and government (i.e., taxes).

The advertising problem must be solved in this context of matching attributes with needs. *The content of an ad,* therefore, is determined by the kind of match anticipated. For example, if sports car drivers feel the need for protection in case their car rolls over, and our car has a built-in roll bar, then our advertising information must try to facilitate this specific attribute-need pairing.

3　THE ROLES OF THE CONSUMER IN THE CHOICE OF MASS MEDIA
(*excerpts from H. D. Maneloveg, executive vice president, McCann-Erickson* [1])

Media are the vehicles that carry ads, and the choice of one medium rather than another will have a strong impact on the solution of the communication equation. As in the case of ad content, the first factor to be considered here is the match between media attributes and consumer preferences regarding media. However, this matching is complicated by the diversity of consumer media preferences and by the technological features of different media.

Media, like any product, can be differentiated in terms of attributes. Consumers do, in fact, differentiate among media; even more important, different consumers perceive and use media differently. As noted in Chapter 1, Section 3.3, the key problem for the manager of any medium is adapting his medium's attributes to changing consumer needs and preferences. The result—different media appeal to different consumers—is a given for the advertiser. He and his agency must choose the subset of media-consumer pairs that facilitates his communication program. Note, again, the role of the consumer: the advertiser will reach the right type of consumer only if he knows the media this consumer prefers.

---

[1] McCann-Erickson is one of the largest advertising agencies in the United States and abroad.

The selection of the right media must deal not only with consumer media preferences but also with the technological features of different media. In principle, the choice of an ad's content *and* the choice of how to encode this content in some particular "symbol" (language, design, music, etc.) are determined by what we know about the consumers to whom we want to communicate. But radio does not carry written copy; print media do not carry sound; and some papers do not allow a choice of colors. Basically, we are usually confronted by one of two problems. We may have found the right combination of symbols for the right type of consumer, but the media that reach this consumer type cannot technologically (or for cost reasons) carry such optimal symbols. Or we may have the right combination of symbols and media, but the consumer type we want to talk to does not make use of such media.

With this background firmly in mind, we can now move to the discussion of media selection by H. D. Maneloveg.

One of the two basic components of an advertising effort [is] to create a compelling sales message; that's the function of copy. The second is to determine who the prime customers might be and then to select vehicles in [such] a way that the best prospects are reached enough times to foster awareness of the copy claim. That's the function of media. . . .

Now what are the factors that go into determining a sound media proposal? There are basically six: the communication requirement; emphasis on the prime prospect; geographic sales analysis; efficiency/effective balance; the pressure of competition; and the budget. By discussing each and citing examples you may be able to see how all need to be balanced in order to make each specific plan work. . . .

A. THE COMMUNICATION REQUIREMENT

Here we have what is normally the most important factor in choosing the various media for our sales message. . . . If we are required to show demonstration or visually compare one brand with the other, television becomes the most logical contender. If an articulation of sales points is required, print—magazines and newspapers—comes to the forefront. If mood through music lends credence to the sales points, then radio holds promise. If all we require is package identification and a short sales idea, then outdoor makes sense. The selection of media is always tied to the message (and while this may be contrary to Marshall McLuhan, it remains a fact of marketing life). Thus, before a media planner starts building his proposal, it's essential that he knows what the copywriter is trying to say and in what media form it can best be said. . . .

B. EMPHASIS ON THE PRIME PROSPECT

Here is where the media man must do his best work. . . . Here he becomes a market expert rather than just a media man. Before a planner develops his proposal, he must secure a fund of knowledge about who buys the product or service being advertised. . . . Through client and agency consumer research studies, brand rating index, Simmons Research data, audits and surveys, and others, the media planner learns who the heaviest users of the products are and he explores media to determine which will deliver these prospects. For insurance he may be trying to key against young males,

18-34. For a European airline, men and women, upper educated, higher income groups from 18-49 years of age. For a soap or detergent, women only, with primary emphasis on ages 18-49. . . . Each product has a demographic profile that pinpoints the best customer. . . . And the data we have on media is geared to the market profile information. Thus, if we're aiming at men and women and have decided that television does the best job, we go for prime time television 8:00-11:00 in the evening. But this makes sense only if our budget permits the cost of prime time national television (more about this later).

Now within these top viewing hours—when 55-65% of the homes of the nation are tuned in—the demographic requirements of the brand determine our selection of specific media vehicles available through the networks. (It must always be remembered that the networks in almost all cases determine the programs to be put on the air; we select from these; we, like shoppers, buy from the available stock.) A program such as the Lucy Show is oriented more towards the middle and older age groups and products with that kind of skew purchase there. A program like the Lawrence Welk show was a natural for a denture cream because most of its audience [was] over 45 years of age. Room 222 and the Partridge Family speak best to the teenage audience. . . . Daytime serials aim at the younger housewife, quiz shows at the older.

The media man must pore over all the demographic data supplied by A. C. Nielsen and other syndicated sources and select properties that target in on his specific audience. He does the same when analyzing print as well.

C. GEOGRAPHIC SALES ANALYSIS

Here he decides where to place his "weight." Across the nation or regionally. Often he chooses a thin layer of national weight and then supplies additional units where he has favorable sales conditions. It is in this area that he decides whether he should be on network television, which covers the nation with a hook-up of 150-200 stations, or utilize spots in ten or twenty more markets. If he should use national magazines or regional editions of same. If newspapers in selected markets make more sense than a national Sunday supplement. Here is where demography (target audience), geography, and the budget mesh together.

Take magazines for example. A media planner considers Life[1] *magazine, but a four-color page cost is $54,000. That seems too high for the budget so he has the alternative of buying* Life *regionally to go specifically against his best sales territories, or he can review his demographic data and if the product is bought by higher income people and the message is oriented to a higher educational plane, he can buy three times as many insertions by picking* Sports Illustrated, U.S. News, Saturday Review,[2] Atlantic, or Harpers. *If the plan is frequency-oriented, the latter may be the best way to go. . . .*

In determining vehicles the planner must always keep in mind how the public

---

[1] About a year after this testimony, *Life* ceased publication.

[2] Also defunct.

spend its time with media. There is much criticism about the advertiser's idolatry of television and the attendant fostering of clutter. But there's a reason for that. The people spend their time there. Look how men divide their hours of the week with the major media (Exhibit 5.12). And women (Exhibit 5.13). As advertisers we must logically go where the people are. And the people are with the electronic media, the

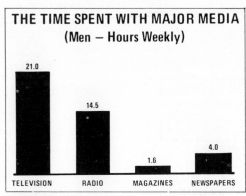

EXHIBIT 5.12

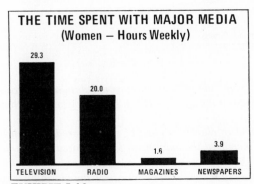

EXHIBIT 5.13

mass electronic media. People will argue that we are missing a good bet by not supporting educational television. It certainly warrants support, but the public doesn't seem to gravitate to these types of programs. Here is the latest A. C. Nielsen data on viewer use of educational television (Exhibit 5.14).

The vital ingredient is to be where the sales are. And often the majority of sales fall into a few major markets (Exhibit 5.15). View how this product's sales position is in the major markets of the country. As a consequence we tend mostly to place our weight there. But some could choose to cover territories where they are weak. Most

A. C. NIELSEN RATINGS FOR EDUCATIONAL TELEVISION

	WK. OF SEP. 20	WK. OF SEP. 27	# OF STATIONS
7:30 – 11 PM MON.-SAT.	0.6	0.7	150+
9 AM – 12 NOON SAT.	0.2	0.1	39

EXHIBIT 5.14

SALES BY TELEVISION MARKETS

	"TOP" 3	"NEXT" 7	"NEXT" 18	"NEXT" 30	"BALANCE" 164
PERCENT OF POPULATION	20%	20	20	20	20
PERCENT OF CLIENT SALES	28%	31	16	15	10

EXHIBIT 5.15

MINUTES OF COMMERCIAL TIME PER HOUR
Prime Time

	NETWORK	LOCAL	COMBINED
PRE 1965	6	1:20	7:20
1965–69	6	1:20	7:20
1969–PRESENT	6	2:00	8:00

EXHIBIT 5.16

marketers, however, follow the "place the money where your sales are" approach. Thus we normally end up with greater message weight in the major markets than in smaller.

Touching lightly on the subject of clutter, it must be remembered that television networks and stations have not increased the amount of time devoted to commercials. The time has remained relatively the same (Exhibit 5.16). But what has happened is that advertisers have embraced the 30-second commercial over the old minute route and today we have more messages going to the public than before. Interestingly, while there is much concern over the subject, it has not affected the recall of commercials by the public to any great extent. And in an era of rising costs the need for efficiency dictates the wisdom of the 30-second unit at this period of time. Now this brings us to the next subject.

D. EFFICIENCY/EFFECTIVENESS BALANCE

When exploring various media alternatives we must take unit costs and attendant efficiencies into account. In the past we measured cost value in relation to homes delivered. But today, in an age of market segmentation and product proliferation as

MEDIA EFFICIENCY

	WOMEN 18-49 (000)	COST PER UNIT	CPM FEMALES 18-49
30 sec. annc., CBS Thursday Night Movie	6,300	21,400	3.40
30 sec. annc., NBC daytime "Concentration"	1,530	1,900	1.24
20 sec. prime time break in Top 50 markets	4,000	23,000	5.76
1000 line newspaper ad in Top 50 markets	17,450	82,000	4.70
1 page 4 color in LH Journal	9,420	37,400	3.97
1 page 4 color in Life	10,390	54,000	5.20
1 page 4 color in Parade	10,375	69,300	6.68

EXHIBIT 5.17

we concentrate on specific target audiences, we now view media vehicles in relation to the cost of delivering our prime customers. Our criterion is cost per thousand prospects delivered. Here is a comparison of how various alternatives perform (Exhibit 5.17). As you can see, the prices vary dramatically. And on the surface it would appear that the lowest cost property should get most of our advertising dollars. But here again one must weigh the communication requirement and the geography of the brand to decide which vehicle is best for a specific effort.

All this, whether it be network, spot, print, or newspapers is where we as media people end up. After the planning stage we must go out and buy. Our purchases, hopefully, conform to the statistics of the plan, yet as we buy in each market it is the medium that tells us what they have available and what the going price is for each item. The selection from all availabilities should be equal to the efficiency goals set by the plan.

And while efficiency—especially if the budget allows for adequate frequency—is a major factor, it is not necessarily synonymous with effectiveness. There are many times when we are willing to buy high-cost specials over minutes in movies; spreads in magazines over single pages; or an eight-page insert in Sunday newspapers rather than a number of insertions in the daily newspaper. Marketing requirements of certain products—beyond just audience goals—often dictate a change in strategy and a desire to be "big" at one moment in time to support a promotion, a new product introduction, or a support for distribution. While the popular belief is that we worship the rating and only purchase the lower cost properties, that is not always the case.

E. THE PRESSURE OF COMPETITION

In our competitive economic system we must position our brand or service so that it talks as often as our competitors to our key customers. Before a media plan is developed, we examine the delivery of our own previous efforts as well as that of competition—and weigh both against usage information. In this manner we decide where best to apply pressure in the upcoming plan. Coverage and frequency patterns vis-à-vis competition form a framework for many media decisions. And all this must be measured in relation to the dollars allocated to advertising—the budget.

F. THE BUDGET

Advertising budgets are determined within the framework of the overall marketing expenditures. Sales promotion, merchandising, packaging, point-of-sale material and the like blend into the total cost of selling a product. Advertising is but one factor. And the media man, given his budget, must work within the constraints of that dollar figure to deliver maximum pressure but effective pressure as well.

There is a belief that most advertising budgets are large and that the message weight is such that the population is bombarded dozens of times a week with a sales message. This is not so. On two counts. First, most budgets for individual products or brands are not large for the job at hand. And, two, people are not overwhelmed by messages as one might expect. The cost of sending one letter to all sixty million homes now comes to $4.8 million. Few national advertising campaigns for individual brands come in at this figure. My own agency's breakdown is shown in Exhibit 5.18.

EXHIBIT 5.18
BREAKDOWN OF BILLINGS

Number of accounts over $5 million	6
$2.5 to $5.0 million	6
$1.0 to $2.5 million	23
Under $1 million	73

And what kind of overall message pressure does a large account produce? Take a grocery manufacturer with a healthy expenditure of over fifteen million dollars. . . . Our messages only talk to our total public a little over twice a week. Certainly in the peak selling season the frequency goes up but not as much as expected. In the case of a furniture product with a budget somewhat over $1.5 million the picture is the same. . . .

Within the electronic media the way of buying is shifting somewhat. Take television. While the networks still control most of the programming that's put on the air, advertisers attempting to be more selective in their audience requirements are moving to more varied types of programming. Entertainment will, of course, continue to fill 70–80 percent of the time but many astute advertisers are buying differently than they have in the past. Specials which were expected to drop this year because of the new three-hour rule have not, and there are as many if not more than there were in years past. Advertisers in my own agency (still needing a base of low cost frequency against prime audiences and going that route) are now willing to pay more for programs of stature. For one client we are continuing the highly successful Charlie Brown specials. Another stays with the charming Dr. Seuss specials for children. A major corporation tells its story on the nightly network newscasts; another one of our clients is trying to mount a special on the new Kennedy Center, CBS Sixty Minutes, and Meet the Press. Still another is looking at the Young People's Concerts. Elsewhere companies like GE with its Monogram Series, Xerox and Civilization, and even P&G last year in National Geographic are heavily into cultural, high caliber programming.

The cycle of media planning is a never-ending one. It goes something like this (Exhibit 5.19). Computers, new technology, and more sophisticated research lend information to make better media plans. But with it all remains the judgment of the media man and his intimate knowledge of the brand's requirements. The new science has only led us a part of the way in our media knowledge. . . . We still do not know how to measure perception nor the direct relation of sales.

THE MEDIA PLANNING CYCLE

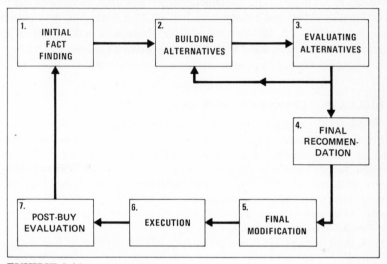

EXHIBIT 5.19

4   THE ROLES OF THE CONSUMER IN TV AND PRINT PRODUCTION

(excerpts from G. Webber, senior vice president and manager of creative services, Benton & Bowles; R. Fearon, president, Friedlich, Fearon & Strohmeier; H. Edel, president, Herman Edel Associates; G. Gould, president, Teletronics International; P. Kohl, assistant director, General Foods Kitchens; and L. Hartman, assistant in charge of home economics, General Foods Corp.[1])

An increasing number of Americans spend their time and income on leisure activities: the sale of picture and movie cameras is growing exponentially; college extension courses—once taken exclusively "to get ahead"—now include more and more courses in music appreciation, play writing, pottery, and silk screening. As a consequence, many

---

[1] Benton & Bowles, and Friedlich, Fearson and Strohmeier are advertising agencies; Herman Edel Associates ia a producer of music for advertising; and Teletronics International is a TV production company.

Americans may know something about the technologies available for making ads. Yet the physical and technical processes involved in translating advertising into graphics, sound, and film are enormously complex.

In this section we shall touch on this complexity, stressing as usual the ways in which the consumers' viewpoints bear upon the making of commercials. The presentation below was actually made in a studio to which the FTC Commissioners moved. For simplicity, we shall not report the visual aspects of the presentation, and we cannot report the sound portion. However, the text below does capture the major points made. The presentation was coordinated by G. Webber, and contained four parts: a brief overview of the basic tools and techniques of film and TV and how they are used in advertising; a discussion of food photography, with a live demonstration before TV cameras; a discussion of special production procedures in print and TV; and, finally, two case histories illustrating procedures used in the filming of product demonstrations in commercials.

A. TOOLS AND TECHNIQUES OF FILM AND TV: AN OVERVIEW

(Mr. Webber) Let us begin with the tools and techniques of the film craft and its close relative, videotape. It should be borne in mind that these tools and techniques, which you will see illustrated, were not invented by advertising itself. They have been borrowed, for the most part, from more than a half century of film technology and practice. McLaren did a film using human animation 25 years before Gulf Oil used the same technique. The great Russian director, Eisenstein, used quick-cuts for interest and impact 50 years before the Pepsi Generation. And D. W. Griffith, not Kraft Foods, invented the close-up.

Film, in all its manifold forms, is basically a representation *of reality . . . not reality itself. The moment you step into a studio you step into a world of artifice, an "unreal" realm of cameras, sets, props, lights, sound equipment, and technical crews. . . . The very act of recording an event on film, of imposing a technical and artistic medium between the subject and the audience, moves it one step away from reality.*

The producers of advertising film have three obligations: to communicate the advertising message clearly; *to communicate it* accurately *and* honestly; *to communicate it with* interest *and* impact. *. . . If you want a man to listen, you have to get his attention first. The use of various film techniques to get the viewer's attention is entirely valid and central to the job of communicating advertising ideas.*

Let's look at some of these tools and techniques in the context of commercials. First, various **camera lenses** *and how they are used. [Long shot: helicopter view] A bird's eye view, shot from a helicopter. A lens and camera angle that gives the big picture. [Close-up: Crisco "Holiday Pies"] Close-up for appetite appeal. Television, with its small screen, is essentially a close-up medium. [Snorkle: Cascade "Perfect Table"] To get really close—the snorkle lens, that snakes in and out and around the subject. [Microphotography: Ants and transistors] An ant's eye view that makes a tiny transistor look as big as a barn door. [Black leader] And there's a special lens called the fisheye which can create a world of fantasy.*

Lighting. *An essential and critical element in film-making. Essential to the clear delineation of the subject being photographed. Critical to the atmosphere and aesthetic feeling of the picture. [Single source: Del Monte] A landscape. Early morning. [Night scene: GE] Absence of light can be effective, too. [Cosmetics] Bright exterior lighting to evoke a sense of beauty. [Documentary: Detroit police] Black-and-white documentary. Appropriate to the seriousness of the subject.*

Makeup. *An artifice that's been around as long as man looked upon woman and found her fair. The camera sees its subject with a single eye, without the stereopticon effect of human vision. It flattens out people's features. Makeup gives the face a more rounded look, makes it look more like a face looks to the human eye. Let's see exactly what makeup does. [Model before makeup] Here's how this man looks just as he walked in off the street. No makeup. Shadows under the eyes, stubbly whiskers, forehead shiny. [Same model made up, split screen] Here he is with makeup on. The shadows eliminated, the beard smoothed away, shiny areas eliminated. A more modeled, rounded look to the features. [Clear split screen, move in on made-up man] Everyone from the lowliest bit player to the President himself knows that the magic of makeup can make a world of difference. In this next spot, you will see how makeup lets us span a generation in a family. The young people in the snapshots are the same people who play the middle-aged mother and father [Kodak "Yesterdays"].*

There's an old saying in film: a picture is made in the cutting room. Editing, *the putting together of the various scenes of a film in their proper sequence, is a critical component of production. Good editing is essential to the clarity and understanding of a commerical . . . can also contribute to the vitality and interest of a film . . . also a way of synthesizing and compressing experience. Two examples, in which editing compresses the essence of two highly dissimilar experiences into a few seconds: a day in the life of a short-order cook, and the excitement of a polo match [AGA: "Short-order Cook"; polo sequence].*

Optics. *Another essential tool of film-making. Things that are done to film in an optical laboratory after it leaves the camera and the editing room for the purpose of adding information (such as a title surprinted over a scene) and creating interest [RCA "Many Faces"; AT&T "Yellow Pages"; Burlington Mills logo].*

Slow motion. *Another familiar technique. Largely used for aesthetic effect, or to heighten interest and attention [Hartford Insurance "Falling Man"]. At the opposite end of the spectrum—*speed-up action, *a technique as old as the Keystone Cops. In this spot, it is used for comic exaggeration and to emphasize a copy point, that Midas does only one job and does it well and fast [Midas Muffler "Installation"].*

Animation—*another film technique that has great usefulness as an advertising medium, for at least two reasons: it's a good way to tell a complex story, and it can be done with humor and style. Long a favorite film form of children, it is also effective in communicating with adults [3M "Chameleon Man"].*

Hyperbole *and* **metaphor** *are ancient art forms that have intrigued creative man since the days of Greek mythology. They have also intrigued the creators of commercials who use these visual figures of speech to create interest and* *memorability in TV advertising [Gulf "Human Animation"; Plymouth "1/2 Car"; Cracker Jack; Ortho "Fantastic Voyage"].*

(Mr. Edel) **Music** *serves many purposes in advertising. It can help underline the mood of a commercial—whether it is sad, warm, longing, youthful, conservative, or far out. It can emphasize a product benefit or difference, highlight action, or underscore a selling phrase. But above all, the prime purpose of music in television advertising is to* get the viewer's ear. . . .

I have selected four commercials where music is a vital ingredient. In each case the music makes a different contribution to the spot. In the case of the first one you will hear—a spot for Almond Joy—you have an opportunity to take a unique product difference and play upon it—in a light, refreshing way. The lyrics here are all important—they set up the problem all of us have had—sharing that favority candy bar. But with Almond Joy—you can give away half but still have a whole. Musically, our melody is light, orchestrated to appeal to the young people who are potential buyers of the product [Almond Joy "You Can Share Half and Still Have a Whole"].

The next spot is for Whirlpool Washing Machines, called "Lint Pickers." Here we use classical music to highlight the dramatic action of the commercial. The music is overstated, over-obvious, with the intent of humorously involving the viewer. The ultra-grand manner of the finale and the deliberately overdone orchestration is obviously tongue-in-cheek and does much to highlight the visual [Whirlpool "Lint Picker"].

Next, again a very broadly played situation—where the music is very menacing, foreboding and action-motivating. This is a Hollywood film in :60 with a score of traditional scope—telegraphing by sound what the visual is compressing into the short commercial span [Foster Grant "The Coup"].

Finally, a melody, with real meaning in the lyrics and a situation that everyone has experienced in their own way. Musically, we catch the importance of these moments in an orchestral setting that not only complements the visual but also appeals to the potential buyer [Kodak "Green Grass of Home"].

These four are examples of what we try to do in all our music. Talk straight (musically) to the viewer in a way that is interesting and compelling. Being aware of the market we are trying to reach and writing up to that target. If we have done our job successfully, the viewer should not have been aware of the music but rather should have felt it as part of a total experience.

B. FOOD PHOTOGRAPHY

(Ms. Kohl) One responsibility assigned to the [General Foods] Kitchens since 1928 is to test the recipes and prepare the food used in General Foods product advertising —first for print and more recently for TV as well. In our department of 90 we have about 40 home economists. At the demonstration area directly before me is Ms. Hartman. While I am talking, Ms. Hartman will assemble, frost, and decorate a cake just as it was done a few weeks ago to be photographed for a Christmas season print ad.

You'll be most welcome to taste the cake because the food photographed for our advertising is always edible. We never use anything on or in the food which a homemaker could not serve her family. Of course, there was a time when I couldn't have made that statement. There was a long period when we had to use all sorts of unusual techniques and ingredients in order to have recipes survive photography sessions and look realistic in finished print ads and commercials. I'm talking about the period in advertising history before air-conditioned studios—the period before studios were equipped with working refrigerators and freezers and ovens. At that time there were no strobe lights—all lights were unmercifully hot. Film was inferior. . . . Some color film tinged everything yellow; that of another manufacturer turned everything slightly blue—which is not a good color for most foods. . . .

Last month the Wall Street Journal *ran a feature on food photography which caused some smiles of nostalgia in my own department. The article reported on such advertising photo techniques as stuffing a turkey with cotton to make it plump; bolstering a collapsing soufflé with dry cereal; shoring up a tired cheesecake with mashed potatoes; using three times the amount of gelatin called for in the recipe in order to make the molded gelatin dessert stand up for the camera. Contrary to this report in the* Wall Street Journal, *it has been our experience that with the tremendous improvements in refrigeration, air conditioning, lights, film, and cameras, it is now possible to photograph most foods exactly as they are prepared in the home kitchen.*

I qualified that by saying most foods because every now and then there is a great-tasting recipe which is downright ugly in an honest photograph. Beef Stroganoff, for example, is a highly popular recipe which is a failure in front of the camera. The mushrooms blend into the sour cream sauce which hides the existence of beef strips. The camera flattens this gorgeous tasting dish into a blah beige mess. We cannot follow the recipe and get an appetizing photograph of Beef Stroganoff. So we resolved the problem by not photographing it at all even though it is one of the most popular combinations to serve with one of our rice products. . . .

Just as a casting director narrows down the field of actors, the art director eliminates the less photogenic recipes. Days in advance of the shooting of a print ad or filming of a commercial, the recipe finalists are prepared in our photography kitchens for what we call an advertising showing—a meeting at which the recipes are studied in the framework of the print ad layout or television storyboard. The photographer and art director decide on background color. Much time is devoted to the selection of serving dishes. These should have style and be of interest to the consumer, but cannot mislead her. A demitasse spoon, for example, can make a sherbet glass seem larger than it is. During this same meeting, the photographer and our home economists discuss how the food chosen can be expected to react under lights—or during the action called for in the commercial.

From this comes the decision of how many duplicates of the recipe will be needed. For instead of adding cotton or mashed potatoes or any other extraneous ingredients to support a wilting or melting food subject, we keep feeding the camera a fresh subject. For example, we recently did a whipped topping commercial for which we baked 40 cake layers—or enough for 20 peach shortcakes. We needed this kind of backup because the commercial called for a great deal of action and everytime there was a retake, we had to start off with a fresh shortcake.

. . . Ms. Hartman is preparing a cake before us just as she would in the studio. Under ordinary circumstances we would have come to the studio with one already finished cake to be used as a stand-in during the period when the photographer is

adjusting lights and camera and the actors are walking through the action. Meanwhile, our home economist would be working on one to twenty final subjects. In this case, the cakes would be baked in our kitchens and brought to the studio along with everything needed to complete the recipe. In the case of a subject as sensitive to transportation as a souffle—all subjects would be baked in the studio. . . .

Ms. Hartman has been making a Christmas tree cut-up cake which was photographed for the ad shown on the screen. This ad will run in the December issue of Good Housekeeping, Better Homes & Gardens, *and* Family Circle. . . . *and now if we may turn on the television cameras, we can see how Ms. Harman's cake matches the Christmas tree in the ad.*

What Ms. Hartman has demonstrated is what we hope will go on in many home kitchens throughout the holiday season: that by following the recipe in the ad any homemaker can duplicate the very real cake in our ad. It is our opinion it would be a disservice to the consumer and plain bad business judgment to show the lady a cake she can't achieve.

C. SPECIAL PRODUCTION PROCEDURES IN PRINT AND TV

(Mr. Fearon) In defining advertising some fundamentalists strip it to the bone and call it nothing more than communications. It is that, of course, but more besides. . . . A good deal of the effectiveness of ads with beautiful models is the association of the reader with beauty. And isn't that what the product is for? Cosmetics, fashions—all relate the reader to the ideal to which they aspire. Mental attitude is a key element. But an interesting thing has been happening in advertising. It's become more and more natural. Real, everyday people. Look at this ad for a hair spray [Slide: Pssst ad]. The models used were girls on the staff of the agency. And here's an ad for Volkswagen [Slide: VW ad]. They are real people who actually did buy the car to replace the mule when it died. The advertising agency heard about it after the fact and took this photograph. They didn't even clean up the car.

Let me now talk specifically about one of the techniques used in the production of print— **retouching** *of still photographs, and why it is done. This photograph was taken at Trinity College, Dublin, for an Irish Tourist Board advertisement [Slide: Irish Tourist Board]. Note the woman in the pink dress in the background, just off the shoulder of the model on the left. She is a distraction. So for a cosmetic effect, we take her out [Slide: Irish Tourist ad]. Here's the final ad without her. Here's another photograph for the Irish Tourist Board [Slide: Irish Tourist Board]. Note the [tree's] dead branches reaching down to the turret. A simple retouch took out part of the branch and made a less confusing picture. . . . In all these cases the retouching is for cosmetic effect and to simplify the picture. Nothing has been done that alters the content of the visual message. In all the preceding cases it might have been possible to get everyone together and reshoot. But only at great cost and a delay in time which is often critical. So these "cosmetic" bits of retouching are economical as well as helpful to readers in clarifying and simplifying the ads.*

Another technique of print production is the use of **composite photographs:** *putting together two or more photographs to make one. Some subjects are difficult to photograph in one piece. For instance, these coins [Slide: Coins]. And this still* *life in a Birdseye ad [Slide: Birdseye ad]. They were shot separately so that each could be in sharp focus. The depth of field of a camera often will not allow all elements of a photograph to be equally sharp.*

Here is a dramatic shot of a gambling casino [Slide: Gambling casino]. This retouched photo [Slide] shows the lamps lowered just slightly to increase the dramatic effect and balance the visual elements better. Also, the name of the casino was removed. The local government didn't want to favor just one business establishment. . . . Here is another example of composite photography. This photograph [Slide] of a group of animals would have been impossible. Can you imagine the chaos if all these animals had been actually brought together? So they were photographed separately [Slides–run through] and put together by our retoucher and here is our final ad [Slide], a part of a campaign done through the Advertising Council for Muscular Dystrophy.

The slides you have seen are some examples of how we employ certain production techniques to improve the visual effectiveness of an advertisement. The techniques are not used to distort or misrepresent information about products and services presented in the advertising. They are used for the purpose of clarifying and simplifying graphic elements, for aesthetic and artistic reasons, and for enhancing the visual interest and impact of the advertising. That's the purpose of all the artistic effort.

(Mr. Gould)   There are two facts of **television** *life that make it necessary to treat colors in a special way in order to reproduce them accurately on the home screen. The first is that of the 90 million television sets in American homes, 60 million . . . present our color pictures only in shades of grey and black and white. The other factor is the difference in response to color between the human eye and the complex electronic mechanism we call television. The eye is perfect. Our man-made system is not.*

Let's examine the first problem and its solutions. I've created this girl to illustrate what can happen to a colorful young lady in the world of the black and white television receiver [Girl demo]. What you've seen illustrates the difference between color and grey scale shading. Grey scale is the different degrees of grey between white and black. Two different colors, for example, pink and light blue, may reproduce perfectly on the color TV screen. However, on the black and white TV screen, only their grey scale shading is reproduced and they appear identical and undistinguishable from each other.

Prior to color television, we concerned ourselves only in monochrome reproduction of scenery and props, costumes, lettering, and titling. The same was true of the advertisers' products and their packages. We used a standard grey scale, such as this one, as our guide and it was a relatively simple matter to make sure that the lettering on a package, for example, was at least two or three of these grey scale steps away from its background to make it clearly legible over the average TV receiver.

Today, in color, we attempt to reproduce the natural colors accurately, because of artistic considerations in the case of scenery, clothing, etc., and because of the importance of package identification, in the case of an advertiser's product. However, many traditional packages were designed before the advent of color television. But even those that are more contemporary are designed basically for the consumer's eye and not for the TV tube. In packaging, therefore, we confront not only the problem of color vs. grey scale, but also the problem that arises from the differential in perception between the eye and the TV camera. I have several packages here that will demonstrate this point [Package demo].

I trust that these illustrate the color vs. monochrome problem that exists in today's television broadcasting. The approach in scenery and clothing is merely to design the colors of these elements within the parameters that have evolved since color TV began. Where such flexibility does not exist, such as in product packaging, the color correction techniques demonstrated here have been successful in achieving reasonably accurate reproduction on both the color and monochrome screens.

(Mr. Webber)   As Mr. Gould has shown you, the television medium has certain technical characteristics—actually limitations—that require corrective measures to insure a clear, accurate portrayal of the information on the home screen.

One such characteristic is the limitation of film and the television system to record highly reflective surfaces without "blooms" or "flares" which mar the picture. If these flares are too intense, thus overloading the television system, they can ruin a $2,000 cathode tube. Here is the problem as recorded on videotape. The object, a chromium-plated electric iron, when properly lighted, appears like this [Videotape of electric iron]. To correct this condition on reflective surfaces such as this electric iron and the brightwork of automobiles, the surface is sometimes sprayed with a substance that dulls the finish [Hand enters picture, sprays hot spot]. . . .

Another situation in film-making that requires a special technique is the problem of photographing distant objects when the camera cannot be placed close to the object. For instance, a head-on shot of automobiles on a freeway. Or race horses breaking from the starting gate. In these cases, a telephoto lens is used [Telephoto shot of horse race].

One limitation that constantly faces the commercial film-maker is time. How to tell a meaningful story in 60, 30, 20, or even 10 seconds. A few years ago the normal commercial length was one minute. Now a majority of spots are 30 seconds. . . . How, for instance, do you show a man aging twenty years in the space of 30 seconds? In this case, it was done by two techniques: makeup and the lap dissolve [Rockefeller for Governor "Convict"]. Another challenge: How do you convey the fact that a food manufacturer such as Del Monte sells not only green beans but a large and varied number of other canned vegetables? In the short span of 5 seconds? [Del Monte "Green Beans"].

And, finally, there is the problem of multiple takes. Film-making would be vastly more simple and less costly if the need to do a scene over and over again could be eliminated. Unfortunately, everything that can go wrong in film usually does. The shadow of the sound boom falls across the actor's face. The camera jiggles on its dolly tracks. The actress smiles too much or not enough. A 747 goes over the studio and ruins a sound take. The dog falls asleep instead of eating his bowl of food. And the actor blows his lines. Not once, but eight times [Adam-12 sequence].

D. TWO CASE HISTORIES OF PRODUCT DEMONSTRATION

The final part of this presentation has to do with standard procedures currently followed to insure accuracy and honesty in product demonstrations. During the past

8 years a substantial body of policies and procedures governing the portrayal of products and their use in television advertising has been developed and put into practice by advertisers, their agencies, the NAB and the networks. . . .

Say the item featured in a commercial is a boy's T-shirt and the point of the commercial is that the advertised product gets out really tough dirt in a before and after situation. Because several takes of a given scene are usually necessary in order to get one where the lines, the action, the lighting, etc. are all correct at one time, the agency brings several clean T-shirts to the shooting. One of the shirts is put on the boy, and he's directed to play in the mud, spill food, climb a tree or whatever. . . . The dirt, in short, is not a laboratory concoction; rather, it's exactly what it appears to be—mud from a playground, soil from spilled food, dirt from climbing a tree, or whatever.

Let's say it's necessary to shoot the scene five different times with five different T-shirts. Each shirt is carefully tagged and identified so the agency knows the take in which it was used—for example, Shirt A was used in Take 1; Shirt B was used in Take 2, etc. Then the five shirts are placed in a conventional washing machine and washed with the advertised product according to package directions. Finally, in the "after" scene, where the little boy is shown wearing a clean T-shirt washed in the advertised product, the shirt used in each take of the "after" scene is likewise identified, and when the commercial is finally edited together, care is taken to insure that the shirt used in the "after" scene is the same one used in the dirtying scene shown earlier in the commercial.

The point is that regardless of how many takes were shot, what the viewer sees on her home television screen is visually intact and shows, with the same identical garment, a chronological story of how that shirt got dirty and how that same shirt looked after it was washed. To the viewer watching the commercial on her home television screen, it makes no difference whether the "before" and "after" shirts match up. . . . But in an attempt to be totally accurate in presenting evidence of the product's cleaning ability, the agency elected to take the extra care and precautions I've just outlined.

I could spend the rest of the day giving you examples . . . but I think two examples will suffice. . . . Although the degree of scrupulous care and documentation is impressive, it is by no means uncommon in the industry. The first product is Joy, a liquid dishwashing detergent manufactured and sold by Procter & Gamble. Here is a commercial from the current campaign making use of a reflectance demonstration— that is, someone seeing their reflection in a china plate [Joy: A 30-second commercial]. Here is what was done to insure that the degree *of reflection shown in the commercial was as honest and accurate and realistic as the agency and advertiser could possibly make it.*

The agency engaged a film studio and did several hours of experimental shooting photographing reflections on a wide variety of plates and chinaware under a wide variety of lighting conditions. After considerable experimentation, a series of five different 8 × 10 still photographs were produced of a woman's reflection on a given plate under five different lighting conditions. Basically, the intensity of the light was varied to produce different degrees of reflectance. These photographs were then turned over to an independent market research organization..They called on homes and found housewives who had a china dinner plate without a pattern in the center. Each of these women was then given a bottle of Joy and asked to wash one of her china dinner plates. After the dinner plate was washed and dried, the housewife was asked to take the plate to the dining area of her home, look for her reflection in the plate, and was then asked which of the five photographs, each showing a different degree of reflection, most closely resembled the degree of reflection she could see in her own dinner plate. While some of the 150 women interviewed selected each of the five photographs, one was selected far and away more than any of the others, and from that time on the degree of reflectance evident in that photograph was used as the standard against which all future shooting of this sequence in subsequent Joy commercials was matched. The cameraman literally had the photograph on the set and was instructed to light and shoot the scene in such a way as to duplicate the degree of reflectance shown in that photograph. Naturally, the takes were selected with the same objective in mind and the finished film was also required to conform to the reflectance evident in the photograph.

The second product is Royal Plus 6 Golf Balls, made by Uniroyal, which features a distance demonstration between Royal Plus 6 and Acushnet Titleist, the leading golf ball in the country. Here is the commercial [Royal Plus 6]. And here is the documentation:

1. *A detailed description of how the test featured in the film was conducted. This includes these facts: (a) Royal Balls were selected at random by Dr. Nicolaides from two dozen balls shipped from the Uniroyal plant where they were, in turn, picked at random from current production; (b) Titleists were picked at random by Dr. Nicolaides from four dozen balls bought at three different pro shops in the New York area; (c) detailed description of the launching technique; (d) flights of the golf balls were laid out with the aid of an engineer's compass to insure accurate measurement from launching gun to point of ball impact.*
2. *Shooting record detailing data on 18 pairs of balls fired. One item is of special interest in this record: Pair #9 which shows that the Royal carried 60 feet farther than the Titleist was eliminated because it was such an obvious fluke in favor of Royal. The average distance advantage of Royal over Acushnet in the tests—with Pair #9 eliminated—was just over 6 yards.*
3. *Affidavit from the agency producer, certifying that the test was performed as described and noting that the men spotting the ball impact were pre-doctoral graduate students in the Aerospace Department at Notre Dame.*

Demonstrations of superior attributes or performance are quite understandable and, legitimately, very useful to a manufacturer seeking a strong sales position in a competitive market. News of a product's superior performance is also of legitimate interest to consumers, as well. . . .

5 SUMMARY. THE BASICS OF ADVERTISING MANAGEMENT DECISION PROCESSES

We began Part 1 by stating that the problem faced by an advertiser is solving the communication equation sender-seeker/receiver. Searching for this solution requires solving a complex of problems, some of which have been illustrated by the testimonies reported in this and previous chapters.

These problems and their interdependencies are illustrated in Exhibit 5.20. The overall solution begins with the firm and the consumers. The firm's technological,

ADVERTISING MANAGEMENT DECISION PROCESSES

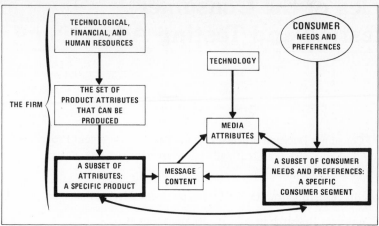

EXHIBIT 5.20

financial, and human resources make it possible to consider the production of some product (or brand, or service, or idea), which may be described by a set of attributes. At the same time, consumers have needs and preferences, and some may have needs and preferences such that the set of attributes of the firm's product become relevant to them. The first step toward establishing a two-way communication between the firm and these consumers is to find a match between product attributes and consumer needs. This means (a) finding a technologically and economically feasible subset of product attributes that matches a subset of consumer needs, *and* (b) finding a subset of consumer needs that matches some of those product attributes that can be obtained economically.

The second step in establishing communication builds upon the solution found in the first step. Given a match "product attributes-consumer needs," find (a) a message whose content makes sense to the group of consumers identified in the first step; (b) the media that reach this group of consumers; and (c) a way to encode the message's content that is technologically and economically feasible for the media that reach such a group of consumers.

All this, of course, only sketches the main problems faced by advertisers and advertising agencies, and the reasoning underlying the approach of these firms in solving such problems. Among the many issues not considered, we might mention the specification of roles within a family. In many product classes, the buyer may not be the user, e.g., a housewife may purchase beer for her husband. Or the reader/viewer (e.g., the child) of a bicycle ad may not be the buyer (e.g., one parent) who, in turn, may not be the "financial authority" approving the expenditure (e.g., the other parent). Whose needs and preferences should an advertiser consider? Not an easy question to answer, for the various roles change across families. Even within a family, they may change across different product classes.

So far, we have described only the planning of advertising decisions. In the following chapter we shall turn to the execution and assessment of these decisions.

Chapter 6

The Roles of the Consumer in Pretesting and Testing Advertising

OUTLINE

1 **The Stages of Consumer Decision Processes: Some Basic Measurement Procedures** (excerpts from L. Light, vice president and senior research associate, Batten, Barton, Durstine & Osborn, Inc.)

2 **Measuring Results** (excerpts from D. K. Hardin, president, Market Facts, Inc.)

3 **The Role of Consumer Research in Advertising Management**

4 **Summary**

In planning any advertisement, a manager must not only define his goals and assumptions about the problem to be solved but also must select the activities needed to reach his goals. In addition, he must decide how to assess whether he has achieved his goals satisfactorily. Decision making implies coordination among goal selection, execution, and assessment.

Ultimately, advertising must contribute to the generation of revenues large enough to cover its own cost and at least some part of overhead. (Ideally, it should contribute more to overhead than would other, alternative efforts.) Yet our evolving knowledge of consumer behavior makes clear that advertising stimuli do not and cannot generate purchases—directly. Complex social and psychological processes intervene between any stimulus (the ad—whatever its nature and whatever medium carries it) and any act of behavior (purchase). Thus generating sales cannot be a *direct* purpose of advertising. The direct purposes depend on which parts or stages of the consumer decision process the firm wants to affect.

These remarks illustrate the complexity of the "message content-consumer needs and preferences" link contained in Exhibit 5.20 and the ensuing problems involved in matching the content of the message with a subset of consumer needs and preferences. As we take a closer look at this problem, we see that a good match requires a deep understanding of consumer decision processes. Such understanding helps us (a) understand how ads may indirectly affect behavior, (b) choose the stage of a decision process at which we want to apply our stimuli, and thus, ultimately, (c) choose the specific goal or goals that can be reached directly by an ad.[1]

---

[1] For a detailed treatment see, e.g., D. A. Aaker and J. G. Myers, *Advertising Management*, Prentice-Hall, Englewood Cliffs, N. J., 1975.

In this chapter we present testimonies that discuss the goals, execution, and assessment of advertising plans (Sections 1 and 2). Then we spell out some of the ways current knowledge of consumer behavior affects all advertising management decisions, from planning to execution and assessment (Section 3).

1 THE STAGES OF CONSUMER DECISION PROCESSES: SOME BASIC MEASUREMENT PROCEDURES (*excerpts from L. Light, vice president and senior research associate, Batten, Barton, Durstine & Osborn, Inc.)*

The testimony by L. Light begins with a sketch of known stages of consumer decision processes and of the main goals that may accordingly be assigned to ads. Mr. Light then discusses the major factors that determine whether an ad has reached its direct goals, and he reviews some of the most popular testing procedures for measuring the extent to which a goal has been achieved.

In my opinion, the best way to win a brand decision from a consumer is to communicate *to that consumer that a product or service solves a problem that he or she already has. . . . What is important is that only* after *identifying this prime prospect, only* after *discovering his or her problem, and only* after *determining what attributes of the product solve this* already existing problem, *do we turn to the advertising. The purpose of the advertising is to* communicate effectively *to prime prospects that a particular brand is a better solution to a particular problem. It is the job of advertising researchers to evaluate whether a commercial or advertisement is likely to accomplish this difficult assignment. . . .*

A question that immediately arises concerns the selection of a measurement criterion. The use of sales as the criterion for advertising effectiveness is clearly most desirable from a management point of view. But sales is not *directly feasible as a criterion because advertising is only a partial determinant of sales. As a result, researchers often use other measures of advertising effectiveness. These alternative measures . . . usually focus on awareness and/or attitudes.*

There seems to be agreement among consumer researchers that the following model, or one similar to this, is representative of consumer behavior. This model indicates that consumers move through a sequence of stages. It is very important to remember that advertising is only one part, a small part, of all the stimuli impinging upon the consumer. But, in today's discussion I am paying attention only to the subject of measuring the effects of the advertising stimulus. This hopefully leads to brand awareness and also communicates a benefit associated with the advertised brand. This awareness combined with the many complementary and competing stimuli may then lead to some change in attitude toward available brands. This attitude change may result in arousing sufficient interest so that the consumer will try the product. If the product does, in fact, deliver the benefit that interested the consumer to try in the first place, then the consumer is likely to be satisfied and is likely to re-purchase the brand. While researchers do differ as to the number and the nature of the stages in the model, they seem to agree with the general flow (Exhibit 6.1).

It is not surprising then to discover that most measures of advertising effectiveness

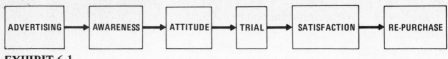

EXHIBIT 6.1

focus on evaluating awareness and/or attitude. These are the two stages closest to the advertising input. By awareness *I mean the memorability of the advertising and what it communicates about the advertised brand. By* attitude *I mean changes in brand preference toward the advertised brand.*

Proponents of the above consumer model believe that awareness is a necessary condition for effective advertising. *For this reason, measures of awareness have enjoyed a great deal of popularity. The measurement criterion is: did the advertising communicate the intended concept in a memorable way? . . . Fortunately, [this] is measurable. Some researchers maintain that an adequate evaluation of advertising effectiveness must include attitude change. Here the measurement criterion is: did an exposure to an advertisement or commercial bring about a favorable change in attitude toward the advertised brand? Unfortunatley, experience indicates that a single commercial exposure is unlikely to produce reliable changes in attitudes toward a brand. Furthermore, the psychological literature on attitude change is still somewhat ambiguous as to how attitude change may be appropriately measured.*

What are the ways researchers measure either awareness or attitude change due to a commercial or advertisement? There are in fact many available . . . procedures [which] vary primarily on three dimensions.

The first dimension may be termed the exposure conditions. *Some researchers believe that advertising must be evaluated under* realistic *conditions. This means that a television commercial must actually run on the air to be tested; a print ad must actually run in a magazine or newspaper to be evaluated. But along with realistic exposures come the many uncontrollable variables of the real world. Therefore, other researchers profess that the best way to measure advertising effectiveness is to use a* controlled environment *such as a theater or a laboratory. This permits the researcher to control many of the variables that might otherwise contaminate his study. But the artificiality of the exposure conditions sometimes creates questions about the generalizability of the results.*

The next dimension concerns the execution *itself. All researchers agree that it is best to measure a* finished *commercial or a* finished *advertisement. Unfortunately, this is often too expensive and too time consuming. As a result, researchers are turning to measuring* pre-finished *executions as a surrogate for the finished commercial or advertisement. But, here too, I have some questions about the validity of these results.*

Most advertising researchers prefer to use quantitative *information to evaluate an advertising execution. But some prefer* qualitative *data such as the kind obtained by depth interviews. They claim that this kind of information provides greater insights into the advertising. But the qualitative data are open to question since the conclusions are subject to the varying viewpoints of the interpreter.*

Each of the various positions has its proponents. Each can be criticized. None is perfect. The Marketing Science Institute prepared a review of many of the various techniques used in advertising measurement. The conclusion in this review was that none of the procedures provide what was described as an "ideal measurement procedure." Since there isn't an ideal system, what I will do is review for you each of the more popular communications testing procedures.

MEASUREMENT PROCEDURES: AN OVERVIEW

Let us begin with TV testing. On-air testing *provides a quantitative evaluation of finsihed commercials under realistic exposure conditions. To conduct an on-air test we run a commercial in a program in a few selected markets. Then we telephone a random sample of households trying first to identify program viewers and then to identify commercial viewers. Once we have a sample of 150 program viewers we determine what brands they recall having seen advertised on the program. And among those who do recall the brand, we ask them to report, if they can, what was said and shown in commercials. . . . as you can see, the "A" commercial is the better one (Exhibit 6.2). It communicates the basic product concept more effectively to more people.*

EXHIBIT 6.2

	A	B
Brand Name Registration	30%	18%
Proven Viewership	11	6
Dry/Not Wet Claim	82	82
Aerosol	44	36
Keeps Hair Natural	24	9

I would like to mention a few amazing *statistics that come out of on-air testing. In order to get only 150 qualified viewers of a prime time television program we have to call about 3,000 homes. That's on a good show. Now, unfortunately, these 150 program viewers do not pay attention to the commercials. Just 24 hours after having viewed the program, the odds are that only 3 of the 150 program viewers will spontaneously recall having seen a commercial for your brand. If we ask the remaining 147 people, "did you see a commercial for (name the brand)?", two out of three of these 147 people will still say* No. *I mention these statistics because it points out how difficult it is to make an advertising impression of any kind at all.*

Because of this very difficulty, and because of the many uncontrollable variables associated with on-air testing, some advertisers have turned to the use of theater testing. *By theater testing, I mean inviting about 200 people into a theater to view a half-hour television program. Commercials are inserted into this program. The usual kind of communication information is obtained. . . .*

How about print ad testing? *One method is called a mock-up or "dummy" magazine test. Print ads are tested by inserting a test advertisement into a magazine and then placing this magazine with a sample of respondents. Respondents are interviewed after having read the magazine at their own leisurely pace. They are then asked a series of questions similar to those obtained in television testing.*

A technique known as a portfolio test is sometimes used to evaluate print advertising. About 10 or 12 advertisements are put together in a booklet form; one of these is the test ad. Respondents are asked to examine each of the ads and then tell us what is being communicated by each.

Another method is to simply show commercials or advertisements to people and ask them to discuss in depth what they saw and heard. From this we obtain insights telling us what the commercial communicates. . . . The information obtained from this procedure is not quantitative but it provides us with some clues and indications about a commercial's or an advertisement's performance. The group interview is quite popular. This involves inviting about 8–10 people into a room to discuss a variety of topics. They are told that they are being recorded and viewed. We show them a commercial or advertisement. A trained moderator directs the discussion. We try to learn what the advertising communicates, what consumers like and dislike about it. . . .

RELIABILITY

A question still remains. Are these different testing systems reliable? Suppose you tested a commercial using any of these various systems. And then you tested it again under similar circumstances. How different from the first score would the second score be? This is what we mean by reliability. *Certainly, any measurement system must be reliable if it is to be useful. Several years ago I had the opportunity to examine a very large volume of data to determine the reliability of communications testing procedures. We found that available techniques had quite a* large amount of unreliability. *This doesn't mean that these techniques should be discarded. But it does mean that they should be used with this unreliability in mind. We concluded that about 50% of the time a test result is likely to be inconclusive in telling us whether a given commercial is a "good" one or a "poor" one. Either judgment or further research is indicated under such circumstances. . . .*

There is no agreement as to which of many alternative approaches is best. But the objective of all the systems is the same. We want to see if an execution of all the systems is the same. We want to see if an execution is likely to be effective *or* ineffective. *We want to learn if there are any* miscommunications. *We want to see if there are any* negative attitudes *associated with a commercial. We want to make sure that the advertising communicates* honestly, completely, and effectively. . . .

If, as a result of the above discussion, you have the impression that advertising research is far from an exact science, *then you have the right impression. We can do a reasonable job of determining what the advertising communicates. But the only way we can maximize the odds that our advertising is effective is to be sure that what we have to communicate about a product solves a consumer problem. This is best determined* before *the advertising is created, not after.*

Appropriate use of these systems will help insure that advertising does effectively communicate the given concept as intended. Communications testing should be viewed as insurance. *The purpose is to avoid running an ineffective commercial or advertisement* before it appears in full-scale media. *It is this kind of insurance that communications tests provide.*

2 MEASURING RESULTS (*excerpts from D. K. Hardin, president, Market Facts, Inc.*[1])

Mr. Light's testimony indicates the complexity of one of the problems advertisers must solve: matching message content with the needs and preferences of some group or groups of consumers. This complexity stems from the fact that consumers are not stimulus-response automatons; complicated psychological and social mechanisms intervene between any stimulus and possible response (e.g., a purchase). It follows that, although the *indirect* goal of any ad is to create sales, its *direct* goal is to influence a particular moment or stage in consumer decision processes.

Since we know that there are several critical stages in these processes, more than one goal may be assigned to an ad or a series of ads. Usually these goals are: to attract attention; to generate awareness; to create specific knowledge of the attributes of the advertised product, brand, or service; to make such attributes appealing so that, eventually, the probability of trying out the advertised product is increased; or to reinforce positive experiences with the purchased product in order to increase the probability of repurchase, and thus the formation of brand loyalty.

At the firm level, managers must distinguish among the many goals that may be assigned to different ads or campaigns. Although the overall goal of advertising is its contribution to profit (or at least to overhead), this contribution can be measured only if we first know an ad's specific objective, the degree to which it has attained that objective, and the way the objective indirectly contributes to reaching the firm's overall goal. All conversations about advertising—at the micro and macro level—are meaningless without the specificity implied by these remarks. Without this specificity, any conversation about advertising is, at best, a means to enliven cocktail parties or other social events. These points are elaborated in the testimony of D. K. Hardin.

> . . . . *Measuring advertising results is a major part of our business. During the last 12 months, we have evaluated advertising results for approximately 60 product/service lines or corporate advertising campaigns.*
>
> *I should like to start out by talking about the criteria we use for measuring advertising effectiveness. Basically, the criteria depend entirely on the objectives of the advertising. Thus, the initial stage in advertising effectiveness studies typically involves reaching agreement with the advertiser on the changes or effects he wishes to achieve with his advertising. The most obvious and logical of these is the generation of sales or purchases. On the other hand, it is often discovered that the role of the advertising is not actually to generate sales, but rather to create certain conditions which have to precede the execution of the sale. . . .*
>
> *Let me start with new products which provide a somewhat less complex medium for measuring advertising effectiveness, since no advertising of any kind has preceded the introductory effort on which the new product is launched. Because of the very high cost of launching new products today, and because the major manufacturers*

---

[1] Market Facts, Inc. is a publicly owned marketing research firm and is probably the largest survey company in the United States.

have learned that they have to risk a very large fraction of their total advertising dollars in the first few months of the launch if they are to achieve and retain distribution while the product is getting started, we have become increasingly involved in attempts to program the right amount of advertising dollars and apply the right advertising theme in launching the new product. As a result, a substantial amount of marketing research on advertising themes and copy appeals precedes any new product launch.

We are very involved in the test marketing of new grocery and drug products. For example, we have approximately 24 new grocery and drug products that we are test marketing today. The evaluation of advertising themes and particularly spending levels [the so-called advertising weights] is usually a critical part of this test marketing. In a limited survey we conducted among a sample of the 100 largest advertisers, among other things we asked them to describe their most recent test marketing experience. We also asked them to tell us whether or not they evaluated advertising spending in the test marketing experience. Better than half—58 percent— said that their most recent test marketing experiences had included testing of advertising weights.

Now, how are advertising weights tested for new product launches? Basically, what we try to find out is whether the effect of additional advertising dollars can be translated into sales dollars. The criterion of effectiveness is the extent that the marginal profitability of the sales produced by the advertising exceeds the cost of the advertising. One must also consider the difference in final buyer purchases generated by one's spending level vs. another, or one campaign vs. another. . . .

The major use of effectiveness research lies in determining the correct allocation of marketing resources. *In other words, how much should be spent and how should it be spent? Our testing often involves marketing options that go beyond advertising (i.e. sampling, couponing, and point-of-sale displays). Thus, we attempt to measure shares of market under alternative spending levels and develop an estimate of optimal promotional spending. This type of experimentation is not restricted to print and electronic media. The same measurement concepts can be utilized with coupon promotion or various forms of direct mail where the sales results can be directly measured and compared with the promotional cost to come up with an optimum marketing level.*

Often in test markets, sales measures are not enough because it is recognized that advertising effects may precede the sales action by a substantial period of time. In other words, attitudes may change well in advance of the new product purchase. This is particularly true of products with long purchase cycles. Some of the more common measurement approaches are as follows:

1. For new products, multiple waves of household interviews may be conducted in the test market at more or less equal intervals, say, three months. *These interviews may measure awareness of the brands in a product class, attitudes toward these brands, purchase preferences and plans. They will also measure current purchase behavior and repeat buying patterns. The goal of new product launches is not only to develop a high trial use for the new product, but also to develop regular repeat buying. This, too, can be considered the role of the advertising dollars.*

2. For existing products, the measurement of advertising may be a more or less continuous activity. *For a number of companies, we conduct studies which may*

monitor effects over three or four years. The basic formula for these studies is to measure the changes which take place in consumer awareness, attitudes, and purchase behavior and contrast this with the advertising inputs for the client's advertising and competitive advertising (Exhibit 6.3).

EXHIBIT 6.3
TYPICAL MULTI-WAVE DATA

	March 1970	September 1970	March 1971
Aware of Brand A	71%	77%	79%
Prefer Brand A	27	28	34
Have purchased Brand A in past year	37	38	42
Last purchased Brand A	24	27	32
Share of promotional dollars spent	28	30	29

Technically, these studies may involve a nationally representative sample of interviews conducted at regular intervals. This interval is usually every six or twelve months. The method of conducting these studies may involve a national panel of households where the studies can be conducted by mail, or a national probability sample of telephone households, or a national sample of personal interviews.

The interviews are always with the person to whom the advertising is directed. For example, we would interview only women to measure the effects of cake mix advertising, while a combination of men and women would be used for beer or automobile advertising. These studies typically use fairly substantial samples ranging from 500 to several thousand interviews in each wave. The basic evaluation is again in terms of the results achieved in contrast to the funds expended (Exhibit 6.4).

3. Some new devices have been developed for measuring advertising effectiveness. *One of the more interesting ones is the split-cable CATV system of which there are several in existence, including one operated by Market Facts.*

The split-cable is a system for campaign testing in a single market. The client's national advertising effort, which comes into the cable over the air waves, may be cut out of half the homes and a new commercial substituted in its place. This may be done for a period of several months so that, in effect, half of the households in a market have seen only the current campaign and half have seen only the new one.

Simultaneous with these alternate campaigns, we measure awareness, attitudes, and purchases of the client's product before, during, and after these two campaigns are broadcast. In this way, it is possible to determine which campaign is generating the higher sales volume.

The use of these various measures of advertising effectiveness is quite widespread, and the selection of a particular approach is a function of the risk level involved and the overall advertising expenditure level. Also, advertising evaluation tends to take place

EXHIBIT 6.4
SALES CONVERSION CREATED BY ADVERTISING EXPOSURES

	Brand A	Brand B	Brand C
Switched to brand after exposure	12.3%	15.1%	18.7%
Switched away from brand after exposure	10.4%	10.8%	11.1%
A. Net gain in users	+ 1.9%	+ 4.3%	+ 7.6%
B. Estimated value of user (marginal profit on all purchases)	$ .251	$ .351	$ .204
Profit value of 100 complete advertising exposures (A × B)	$ 4.77	$15.05	$15.50
Cost of 1000 complete advertising exposures	$11.45	$11.45	$11.45
Gross profit contribution (deficit) per 1000 exposures	(− $6.68)	$ 3.60	$ 4.05

where there is some level of uncertainty about the effectiveness of the advertising or the need for it.

Some advertising is also done for the purpose of helping to get distribution, especially for new products. For example, combining an intensive advertising campaign with substantial couponing to consumers may be extremely helpful in getting the grocery trade to stock the product at the start. This is an effect which is a more subtle measurement. Our measurements have tended to focus on the ultimate consumer—the purchaser herself.

Our role in these evaluations requires a high level of objectivity. We emphasize this by not allowing any of our executives to become financially involved with any other operation. Nor are our executives allowed to become board members of other companies, or to otherwise participate in any other business. . . .

I would estimate that the measurement of advertising effectiveness is a signficiant part of the total market research scene today—perhaps as much as half the dollars spent are related to measuring promotional effectiveness.

3   THE ROLE OF CONSUMER RESEARCH IN ADVERTISING MANAGEMENT

All advertising decisions rely directly or indirectly on some knowledge of how consumers feel, think, and act. In the preceding chapters we have seen how professionals use this knowledge—from planning to executing and assessing advertising. But we have been looking at consumer behavior secondhand. Before proceeding further, we must look at consumer research firsthand to appreciate our knowledge and its applications to advertising.[1]

By the end of the 1950s, it had become clear that consumer behavior is a multivariate phenomenon. A turning point was the publication in 1958 of Morgan's review of the many factors found to be relevant to understanding consumer behavior.[2] Morgan's list provided an exhaustive "anatomy" of both internal components, such as psychological variables, and external components, such as economic, demographic, and social variables, of consumer decision processes.

The next step—one especially relevant to both managerial *and* governmental action— was determining how all these components might fit together. That is, it was necessary to construct the "physiology" of consumer behavior. One of the first statements concerning the need to study the possible maps of interactions among the components of consumer decision processes appeared in 1960.[3] This need to map consumer decision processes became recognized very rapidly in both applied and basic research quarters. A survey of 1,500 firms in the United States and Canada (by the Conference Board, 1962) revealed that advertisers, advertising agencies, and research firms were abandoning the naïve idea that advertising impinges on the consumer in a stimulus-response fashion: they were beginning to distinguish some of the major psychological stages that mediate between a stimulus and its possible effects on a response. The psychological states most often considered were awareness, recall, and changes in "opinion," or even "attitude," toward the advertised product, brand, or service.[4]

These intervening psychological processes were not new to the marketing community: salesmanship literature had already recognized them, and they had been encapsulated into the acronym AIDA (Attention, Interest, Desire, and Action) in the 1920s! The work of the Conference Board was rapidly followed by other associations more intimately concerned with the advertising business: DAGMAR and other acronyms were invented to express the importance of psychological processes in advertising decisions. From the mid-sixties to the present time, advertising textbooks have gradually codified the views incorporated by concepts such as AIDA and DAGMAR.

In the meantime, basic research on the consumer was continuing. The goal was to obtain more detailed, and thus more useful, maps of consumer decision processes,

[1] For a more detailed discussion, see F. M. Nicosia, "Research in Consumer Behavior: Problems and Perspectives," *Journal of Consumer Affairs,* Summer 1969. For a more advanced review, see F. M. Nicosia, "Brand Choice: Toward Behavioristic-Behavioral Models," a paper presented to the Symposium on Management Sciences and Behavioral Sciences, sponsored by the University of Chicago and the Institute of Management Science, July 1969.

[2] J. N. Morgan, "A Review of Recent Research on Consumer Behavior," in L. H. Clark (ed.), *Consumer Behavior: Research on Consumer Reactions,* Harper, New York, 1969.

[3] F. M. Nicosia, "Forecasting Trends in Styling," *Proceedings,* American Statistical Association, Stanford, California, August 1960.

[4] H. D. Wolfe, J. K. Brown, and G. C. Thompson, *Measuring Advertising Results,* National Industrial Conference Board, New York, 1962.

especially the psychological ones. The first part of the sixties saw the emergence of at least three main directions of research.

In the first of these directions, the researcher approaches the study of psychological processes (especially learning) by directly measuring their *overall* effects on behavior. These efforts have produced a stream of results and advertising applications by Kuehn, Massy, Frank, Montgomery, Morrison, Haines, Ehrenberg, Aaker, and many others. In contrast, the other two research directions attempt to measure *in detail* how ads and other stimuli are internalized and manipulated by consumer thought processes.

One of these directions relies essentially on a branch of social psychology usually called "gestaltist." This approach was proposed in a dissertation at the University of California, January 1962, and a subsequent summary article.[1] Several elaborations of the approach followed.[2] Later work incorporated not only the point of view of gestalt, but also of sign-gestalt (Tolman), problem solving (H. Simon), and communication research (especially findings from the laboratory work by the Hovland group and findings from survey work by the Lazarsfeld group).[3]

The other direction is rooted in other schools of psychological theory, especially modern learning theory. The first elaborations by Howard[4] appeared in 1963. The work of Sheth[5] led this research to full maturity a few years later with the incorporation of key concepts from attitude research.

As a result of these and other approaches advertising decisions have come to be based more and more on knowledge of consumer needs and preferences.[6] The complex maps of decision processes that have emerged from consumer research are extremely useful in planning, executing, and assessing advertising efforts. They bring to the attention of management the fact that ads may work differently depending on the particular stage of the decision process at which they are aimed, and that the overall effect of an ad will vary according to the stage at which that ad reaches a consumer.

Consider the very simplified map of consumer decision processes in Exhibit 6.5a. In the case of a new product, or for a group of consumers who know nothing about an existing product, the content of the ad will interact only with general psychological

---

[1] F. M. Nicosia, "Toward a Model of Consumer Decision Processes," *Proceedings,* American Marketing Association, December 1962.

[2] For instance, during the 1963 Ford Foundation summer workshop at the University of California, Andreasen attempted to develop, in detail, a crucial phase of the thought processes under investigation. A. R. Andreasen, "Attitudes and Customer Behavior: A Decision Model," Working Paper, Institute of Business and Economic Research, University of California, Berkeley, 1964.

[3] F. M. Nicosia, *Consumer Decision Processes: Marketing and Advertising Implications,* Prentice-Hall, Englewood Cliffs, N.J., 1966.

[4] J. A. Howard, *Marketing: Executive and Buyer Behavior,* Columbia University Press, New York, 1963; and *Marketing Management, Analysis, and Planning,* Irwin, Homewood, Ill., 1963.

[5] J. A. Howard and J. Sheth, *The Theory of Buyer Behavior,* Wiley, New York, 1969.

[6] In the sixties, an increasing number of basic and applied researchers contributed considerably, among them: Bauer, D. Cox, Engle-Kollat-Blackwell, Kassarjan, Lipstein, Myers, Robertson, and Venkatesan.

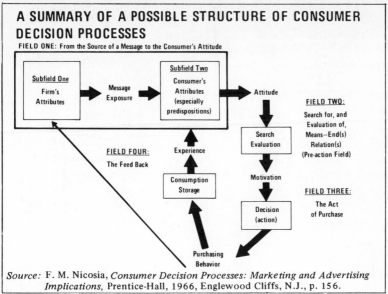

A SUMMARY OF A POSSIBLE STRUCTURE OF CONSUMER DECISION PROCESSES

FIELD ONE: From the Source of a Message to the Consumer's Attitude

Source: F. M. Nicosia, *Consumer Decision Processes: Marketing and Advertising Implications,* Prentice-Hall, 1966, Englewood Cliffs, N.J., p. 156.

EXHIBIT 6.5a

predispositions (see Field One in the exhibit). The best this ad can do is to catch the attention of some consumer and linger in his memory in some detail for a short period of time. But if we are dealing with a brand familiar to a consumer group, and if the ad reaches this group at the point of purchase (see Field Three), the content of the ad will interact with a rather specific and psychologically clear set of preferences concerning the brands available in the store. Or, if the ad reaches a consumer after he has bought the advertised brand, the ad's content will interact with the information the consumer has acquired from the direct use of that brand. A more detailed description of the stages of decision making that may be the target of an ad is in Exhibit 6.5b.

The principle is clear. The same ad content may convey different meanings and possibly evoke different reactions. Therefore, the goals of an ad, and thus its content, should vary according to the stage of decision making at which a firm wants to reach a group of consumers. The important point is that maps of the decision processes offer a basis for more exact measurement of how advertising works and what its effects are. Once these maps are translated into mathematical models, both planning and evaluation of advertising will be on an even firmer foundation than that described in the preceding testimony.[1]

---

[1] One of the very first illustrations of work in this direction is in B. Lipstein, "A Mathematical Model of Consumer Behavior," *Journal of Marketing Research,* August 1965. For advanced applications of mathematical models in assessing how marketing stimuli affect consumers differentially, see J. M. Arbuckle, "The Role of Mathematical Models in Statistical Models," MBA thesis, University of California, Berkeley, June 1970; and F. M. Nicosia and B. Rosenberg, "Substantive Modelling in Consumer Attitude Research: Some Practical Uses," in R. I. Haley (ed.), *Attitude Research in Transition,* American Marketing Association, Chicago, Ill., November 1971.

THE MAIN STAGES OF CONSUMER DECISION PROCESSES

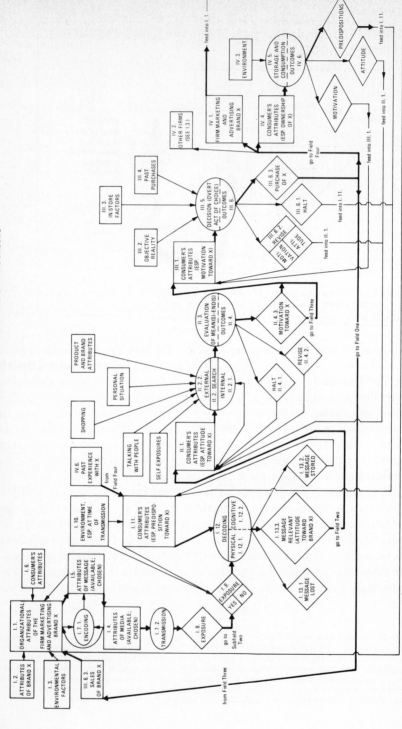

Source: F. M. Nicosia, *op. cit.*

EXHIBIT 6.5b

One of the main themes that has emerged from the testimonies presented so far is the impact of the consumer on advertising management decisions. Gone are the days when it was believed that mass media stimuli could condition or manipulate consumer responses. The creation of an advertising campaign or a single ad—from planning to execution and assessment—depends on understanding consumers; differentiating among them in terms of the needs a firm may satisfy; and realizing that only an appreciation of the complexity of decision processes can offer a sound basis on which to articulate different ads for different purposes and to measure their results.

4 SUMMARY

In this chapter we have seen how professionals go about making advertising decisions and assessing their impact. Matching the content of an ad to the needs and preferences of a specific group of consumers is not easy. Needs and preferences evolve according to complex social, economic, and psychological processes. Further, different ads may be appropriate at different stages of decision making. Accordingly, if an advertiser wants to reach consumers who are not aware of his product, he must tailor the content of his ads with that in mind. If, on the other hand, he wants to counteract the influence of a new competitor on his customers, he must choose a different message content.

In all cases, the objective of the ad must be specified. But this cannot be done without some knowledge of consumer decision processes. The more we know about these processes, the easier it is to specify objectives for advertising stimuli and to compute their contribution to the generation of revenues necessary to meet the demands of the factors of production.

This, in a nutshell, is the engineering of advertising management. The search for a solution to the communication equation begins with the search for consumer needs and preferences that will match the capabilities of a firm, and vice versa. This matching implies a number of other necessary interactions with consumers. The final interaction considered in this chapter was that of matching different stages of consumer decision processes with different purposes of advertising messages.

The reasoning of our professionals can be summarized as follows: adjust a firm's capabilities so that it can meet the specific needs of a number of consumers to an extent great enough to pay for the factors of production. In this sense, firms adapt to consumers, and thus advertising decisions are affected by consumer's decisions.

At this stage of our presentation, a different argument could be made. For instance, it might be asserted that firms try to gain knowledge of consumer behavior, not in order to adapt to it, but to manipulate it. That is, the consumers are induced to adapt themselves to the demands of production factors—i.e., the demands by labor, capital, and governments. In particular, it could be argued that the consumers are made to adapt to the demand of one factor—the profit or, more appropriately, the returns-to-capital factor. This mode of thinking assumes that consumers can in fact be manipulated. It is too early in our presentation to discuss this assumption, but we shall return to it in Part 2, Chapter 13.

Chapter 7

The Lawyers at Work

Values, standards, norms, sanctions, rewards: all these are necessary for humans to work together. Some are unspoken; others are verbal; still others are written down in forms of procedural codes, rules of conduct, and laws. The world of legal order is complex, for it attempts to capture not only what is functional but also—and ultimately—what a certain social group considers ethical.

Not all procedures, rules, and laws are created by legislators. Courts make law as they resolve cases presented to them. Public agencies such as federal and state commissions establish rules that are, in many ways, equivalent to positive law. They do this by regulating industries (e.g., public utilities) and economic activities (e.g., issuing stocks or hiring labor). Finally, the executive branch of the government itself—from federal to city levels—can set forth further rules of behavior.

Dealing with laws and regulations at the micromanagerial level is extremely complex. One cause of complexity is the large number of agencies entitled to make rules. Further, a law or rule must be interpreted: how does a given rule—which is, of necessity, general— apply to the specific problem and action of one firm? Even more important, constant changes in cultural values and technology call for new interpretations of extant laws and often for totally new laws. The very principles underlying lawmaking, interpretation, and enforcement are changing—in degree and kind. Not only is the number of regulated economic activities increasing almost exponentially, but the spirit of legislation and regulation has also changed dramatically. For example, although a buyer was once believed to be fully capable of assuming responsibility for entering into a contract, recent legislation has attempted to protect him. And while earlier laws were almost exclusively limited to stating which actions were illegal and *could not* be performed, there is now a strong tendency toward developing rules that state what a firm *must do*—they are of the "do" type.

We shall return to these and other trends in Chapter 15. Here let us note that few of us appreciate how many laws and regulations progressively envelop business decisions. Even fewer realize how many of the advertising decisions discussed so far are subject to laws and rules.

1   CLEARANCE PROCEDURES AND SAFEGUARDS (*excerpts from P. K. Schwartz, of Davis, Gilbert, Levine & Schwartz*[1])

The testimony by P. Schwartz indicates how laws and rules may be applied to one or another advertising decision. It is, of course, only a sketch and far from exhaustive.

The general subject of Clearance Procedures and Safeguards encompasses various facets, . . . I will start by talking about the people who administer the system.

First of all, of course, there are the lawyers, at both the agency and the client [advertiser]. They are trained in the requirements of the Federal Trade Commission, Federal Drug Administration, Federal Communication Commission, and other regulatory bodies; they have special knowledge of marketing and commercial advertising production. . . . In addition, there are . . . medical and other scientific or technical experts . . . who give guidance to the lawyers when necessary for them to clear copy. Such experts are also engaged by the networks and NAB [National Association of Broadcasters]. . . . Finally, there are the various laymen whose function is essential to the administration of the clearance system. . . .

In the agency the clearance procedure is generally established as a staff function, with the individual in charge having direct lines of communication to and with account supervisors, creative directors, production studios, and, when necessary, to the chief executive officer or other executive officers of the agency. At all the networks there is a Broadcast Standards Department, sometimes referred to as the Continuity Clearance Department, headed up by lay people who are highly skilled in clearing copy. . . .

Before going into the details of the clearance procedures, let me say a few words about the significance of the source of an advertising claim to the clearance procedure. Obviously there are various sources. First of all, naturally, there is the client. . . . Then there is the agency itself. . . . Another common source is research conducted by the client, often by outside independent laboratories or experts . . . engaged to study or test the attributes or possible attributes of a particular product. Then there are . . . ideas such as those sent in by the public, or those brought to mind by competitive claims. Finally, conferences in the agency, or between the agency and client, with respect to ideas, product performance, consumer needs, substantiation, or methods of production, frequently give rise to other ideas and product claims. . . .

---

[1] A law firm specializing for almost forty years in representing advertisers and advertising agencies.

Now I'd like to turn specifically to the clearance procedure itself. The clearance procedure involves various steps: there is the Initial Clearance; the Final Clearance; and the various stages of approvals in between, depending upon the policies of the particular advertiser and agency, or on the legal problems involved.

When an idea is first reduced to writing or visualization, it is placed in the clearance system. The system itself usually starts before the client has seen the advertisement in concrete form. The proposed advertisement is submitted to the lawyers for review, usually in early copy form, or rough layout form, or storyboard form. The legal review obviously includes the basic copy claims, the words used, the art and photography used, and the production techniques intended to be used. However, legal review also covers just about any other legal matter. . . . For example, proper labeling; pricing problems; Robinson-Patman problems; questions of state regulations, such as for alcoholic beverages and lotteries; . . . wording of guarantees; and so on ad infinitum.

The legal review also includes a careful checking of the proposed advertisement against the various media rules and regulations, as well as the rules and regulations of NAB and sometimes other associations such as the Better Business Bureau. Legal review involves a recognition of special product problems such as acne products, mood drugs, toys, personal hygiene products, and so on. Substantiation from medical experts and testing organizations is requested when appropriate. . . . The relevancy or significance of particular claims is checked. For example, if a claim is made that a product has a particular ingredient, it is required that there be enough of that ingredient present to have a recognized and significant meaning or benefit to the consumer. The lawyer's comments, questions and discussions are reported back to the agency and the client. . . . When necessary, liaison meetings between the lawyers, account groups, creative groups and the client are held . . . to be resolved to the satisfaction of the lawyers. . . .

Furthermore, before an advertisement is produced, the method of production is additionally cleared by the lawyers. For example, with regard to a radio commercial, the voices used may have to be checked; with regard to a print ad, the varying print sizes might have to be checked to make sure that no misleading benefits are implied; with regard to television, there are any number of items that have to be checked, such as the use of studio or special lighting, use of mock-ups, and the showing of time lapses.

Substantially all responsible agencies also have some kind of pre-production clearance reporting system, principally for television commercials. This is handled by phone or by meetings, or by the use of printed forms (see Exhibit 7.1). The printed form shows in rather simple manner how it is intended to produce the commercial. The form is filled out and submitted to the lawyers. . . . [This] gives the lawyers the opportunity to make sure that the actual product is being used, and, if not, that there is an appropriate disclaimer or explanation; if a super is going to be used, it gives the lawyers an opportunity to make sure that the wording is legible, is on the screen long enough, and is in proper size.

As one example of the extent of the checking by the lawyers, let me describe the basic ground rules which they check into before a testimonial may be used. The method of the initial contact with the testifier, as well as the relationship of the

EXHIBIT 7.1

TELEVISION COMMERCIAL TECHNIQUE CLEARANCE

DATE: _____

CLIENT _____ PRODUCT _____ JOB NO. _____

PRODUCTION HOUSE _____ FILMING DATE _____

The following questions with respect to the production of the above commercial(s) are to be answered by the agency producer, and the form signed by him and copies sent to:

1. _____

2. _____

3. _____

1. WILL MOCK-UPS BE USED?
   If yes, describe:
2. WILL ANY SPECIAL PROPS OR DEVICES BE USED?
   If yes, describe:
3. WILL ANY SPECIAL LIGHTING BE USED?
   If yes, describe:
4. WILL PRODUCT AND/OR PACKAGE BE COLOR CORRECTED?
   If yes, describe:
5. WILL PRODUCT BE STORED OR PREPARED FOR USE IN ANY WAY OTHER THAN IT WOULD BE BY CONSUMER?
   If yes, describe:
6. WILL THE PRODUCT BE PHOTOGRAPHED IN USE IN ANY WAY DIFFERENT THAN THAT USED BY CONSUMER?
   If yes, describe:
7. WILL A DEMONSTRATION, TEST, OR COMPARISON WITH OTHER PRODUCT BE USED?
8. (a) If yes, describe:
   (b) If yes, has such demonstration, test or comparison been incorporated into the commercial to be telecast?

Signed: _____
(Producer)

NOTE: TO BE SUBMITTED AFTER THE PRE-PRODUCTION MEETING BUT IN ALL CASES PRIOR TO ACTUAL SHOOTING. If the techniques outlined above are modified or changed substantially during the production session an appropriate amendment is to be filed.

testifier to the advertiser, are both ascertained; the question of whether the testifier is a current user, or has used the product for a reasonable period of time, is verified. Normally, he must be testifying about his own personal experience with the product and his statement must be truthful not only with respect to his own personal experience, but also with respect to the claims that may be made for that product by the advertiser. Normally, the testifier is required to sign a written statement verifying all of these facts, but whether in writing or not, there is always some kind of verification required from the testifier. . . .

With regard to final clearance, first as to print advertising, once type has been set there is normally no further need for clearance. . . . However, with regard to television, after the commercial is produced, the film or tape, in rough stage, is shown to the lawyers for review. At that time, a further legal check is made to determine if the finished commercial deviates from the approved script or the approved production report. . . . The commercial is also checked to make sure that the results that appear are not different from the script, regardless of whether or not there were unintentional deviations. . . . A special check is made to make sure that the transition of the commercial from storyboard to film does not add, or result in, any implication that could not be seen on the storyboard. . . . Radio tapes are subject to legal review similar to that applied to television, but on a less regular basis, because legal problems for radio are not as complicated as the legal problems for television.

At this point I would like to refer to the supplemental function of the media in this entire clearance procedure. All broadcasters exercise a review of advertising (as well as of program material). This is handled by a department at each network, referred to as the Broadcast Standards Department. . . . This separate, independent review . . . includes an inquiry into the basic truth of claims, an examination of the substantiation necessary to support the claims, a determination as to whether or not the produced advertisement conforms with the NAB policies as to legalities and NAB advertising standards; a determination as to whether or not any state or federal regulations may require special language or disclaimers (such as sweepstakes, beer or alcohol advertising, etc.), and finally, a check of the advertising as against the particular broadcaster's advertising and taste policies (such as advertising of women's personal products).

If the Broadcast Standards Department is not fully satisfied with the proposed advertisement, the agency or the client then has the burden of proof of satisfying that Department and furnishing the necessary substantiation. The network itself frequently uses outside experts in whatever field it deems necessary, depending upon the advertising involved. . . .

Another aspect of the involvement of media in legal clearance is the National Association of Broadcasters. The NAB not only requires that all advertisements appearing on its members' stations comply with all legal requirements, but it also establishes its own basic advertising standards, which frequently go beyond purely legal requirements. For example, NAB standards prohibit advertising of fortune telling, or some women's personal products, or hemorrhoid preparations, or certain degrees of sex in ads. It has special rules regarding advertising of weight reduction products, arthritis products, gambling, hard liquor, mood drugs, acne. It has special rules regarding advertising to children. And it has an extensive panel of outside experts to assist it in determining whether or not an advertisement complies with legal requirements as well as with its own standards.

From time to time, and continuing for as long as it feels such requirement is warranted in a particular field, NAB requires presubmission to it of advertisements in that field. As of today this applies to advertisements relating to toys, mood drugs and feminine hygiene products. In situations where presubmission to NAB is not required, NAB will nevertheless still act on specific advertisements brought to its attention . . . by subscribers, or by the general public, or by its own staff, or by competitive advertisers. Occasionally, where a Broadcast Standards Department and an advertiser cannot agree on whether or not an advertisement is legally acceptable, the advertisement might be referred to NAB for an opinion; however, normally each network makes its own decisions and is careful to preserve its independent right to do so. . . . Actually, NAB's "jurisdiction" is only over its subscriber stations, but since they include the major stations in the major markets, NAB approval is very important to advertisers and agencies.

As I mentioned earlier, there is really no limit to the kinds of legal problems that are checked or that might arise in connection with a particular advertisement. I referred to the use of guarantees, pricing representations, and others. There are also problems involving the use of names, pictures, money, stamps, flags, disclaimers, etc., etc. Some of these items are rather simple to check; others call for a more careful legal review. For example, with regard to drugs, claims made on behalf of over-the-counter drug products are checked against reliable information available about those drugs. Questions are raised as to whether or not the supporting information appeared in a reputable text, such as Goodman and Gillman, or in scientific published papers, and so on. Frequently, special tests are run to provide, obtain or support claims; in addition, physicians, pharmacologists, or scientists might be retained to advise with regard to specific drug claims.

Advertising directed to children is another example. The special responsibility involved in connection with an advertisement directed to children is understood by everybody—the advertiser, the agency, the media. . . . Frequently, words which would be perfectly proper when used with regard to adults are not approved solely because the advertisement is directed to children. I might mention, at this point, that the use of fantasy in advertisements directed to children raises particular problems, still unresolved. For example, everybody knows that children live in a world of fantasy and if that were to be eliminated completely, conceivably an advertisement that shows Santa Claus would be prohibited; . . . possibly a showing of Walt Disney characters might be prohibited. Nevertheless, it is clearly understood that, from a legal point of view, there must be some permissible mix of responsibility and fantasy so that children can be talked to in their own language, but will not be misled.

Another example of a legal problem that requires special consideration, particularly under today's revised rules, is the matter of endorsements. May a Mickey Mantle say in an advertisement that he eats a certain breakfast cereal, assuming that it is truthful that he does, or is that going to unfairly mislead a child into believing that that child is going to become a great baseball player, or grow up big and strong; or will it only mislead little boys and not little girls? . . . It seems that today, suddenly and without any prior announcement by legal authorities, a new standard *is being applied which would require a person endorsing a product to have special expertise with respect to the particular product he is endorsing. If that is the test, then a movie star could not say that he wears certain suits because that might be a representation that he believes that suit to be of good quality and probably he knows nothing at all about sewing, weaving or textiles. In any event, as far as endorsements are concerned, legal clearance procedures today require that such a person be qualified with respect to the particular claim involved, that the statement he makes is based upon his own personal knowledge or experience, that he actually uses or tested the product, and, of course, that the statement is truthful not only as to him, but also with respect to the product itself.*

Legal clearance for contests also requires more than simple legal approval. The contest rules have to be checked out; various state regulations and Post Office regulations have to be checked; value of prizes must be verified; and so on.

Now, just one last word for the . . . lawyers. They do their best to keep current, but they are continually faced with the difficult task of trying to project what FTC and other governmental agencies will think about a particular advertising claim or product. And, of course, today, we lawyers always have to be prepared for announcements of new rules or conditions, such as the current new rules regarding contests requiring that all prizes be awarded and requiring a statement as to the odds of winning; or such as the current new rule regarding testimonials, arising out of the toy racing car cases, where a racing car driver is considered as not being a proper person to endorse a toy racing car; or the current new principle in the Un-burn case, where it is claimed that an advertiser must have in its possession adequate and well controlled tests which substantiate the efficacy of its product before the advertisement appears, regardless of how many years the ingredients of that product had been used and accepted by the public and the medical profession.

However, we do our best, and I must say that our job is really made easier by virtue of the degree of cooperation from agency and client, regardless of which one we actually represent. There is no doubt that the infinitesimally small number of advertisements that are found to be legally objectionable, as compared with the hundreds of thousands of advertisements that are produced in just one year, is the result of one essential factor: a sincere desire on the part of these agencies and advertisers to produce and present truly legal advertisements. . . .

2   REGULATING THE MEANINGS OF ONE AD

The preceding testimony lists an impressive array of activities that individual firms—advertisers, agencies, and media—perform to ensure that an ad complies with the word and spirit of laws and regulations. A number of questions come to mind, however. How many firms follow the procedures described in the testimony? How strictly are they implemented? Can these procedures indeed satisfy laws and regulations, or are improvements—or even basic changes—necessary? These and other questions ultimately concern the entire advertising institution, and thus we shall consider them in Part 2.

The effects of regulation on management action must be appreciated. One effect, for instance, is cost: the procedures reported are expensive to implement. The resulting benefits, however, may be high: protection of the three organizations—advertiser, agency, and media—that share in the creation and dissemination of an ad. And the need for such protection increases as laws and rules on advertising decisions grow.

Note that the testimony discussed only one set of laws and rules—those that bear upon the content of an ad. (Other laws and rules, such as those concerning the possible economic effects of the advertising institution on competition, will be treated in Part 2.) We have already mentioned (Chapter 1, Section 3.6) the problems inherent in defining and assessing the content of an ad. Let us now see how these problems apply to regulation.

Extreme cases of false ads are easily disposed of. For instance, "miraculous" waters were once advertised as a matter of course. The number of such untruthful ads has decreased enormously, although the dockets of the Federal Trade Commission and of local Better Business Bureaus show that, unfortunately, a number of untruthful ads are still around. The question here is clear: how and why were such ads allowed to enter the society's mass communication system? Was it because there were no clearance and safeguard procedures in the advertiser's and/or his agency's officer? Was it because their procedures had loopholes? Or was the medium that carried the ad at fault? In general, it is possible for management to trace the path of an untruthful ad and thus take corrective action. And it should be relatively easy to enforce corrective action, especially by severe sanctions imposed by the industry itself, by regulatory agencies or by courts.

But most of the ads inserted into the mass communication system are not false. Consider, for example, the so-called misleading ad, which may mislead some, though not all, consumers. As we shall show in Chapter 13, the psychological meaning of the content of an ad depends partly on who examines that ad. Suppose that a TV ad shows how, after using one brand of toothpaste, a girl's teeth are whiter and her social life better. Some girls may believe that using this toothpaste will turn them into "belles of the ball." In this sense, they have been misled. But the problem is not whether, in fact, these girls have been misled. The underlying issue is: who is responsible for their believing that changing a mere toothpaste brand will assure social success? Are the girls themselves responsible or is the advertiser? Or society?

Someone may argue that the ad should explain that the brand may help a girl's aspirations by making her teeth a bit whiter. Another may add that the commercial should also point out that whiter teeth are obtained by adding abrasive substances to the toothpaste, thus potentially endangering the teeth's resistance to cavities.

If one were to follow this reasoning ad absurdum, one might reach the rather simplistic solution that ads should state only the chemical, physical, and mechanical properties of a product or brand. At this point, every girl who wanted whiter teeth— for social or other reasons—would have to take courses in chemistry, dentistry, and the like in order to make a choice. Accordingly, this implies that the ads are not informative for people who have not taken such courses.

What could management do if a law were to say that only such "truthful" and uninformative ads were legal? Should it stop advertising—with unknown consequences to its brand's cost structure and eventually its final retail price? Or should it start a promotional campaign—in mass media or by brochures—giving brief courses in chemistry, dentistry, and so forth?

The current trend toward regulation of ad contents may create further managerial problems. Different groups of people may perceive the same ad as misleading, but for entirely different reasons. During the question and answer period at the hearing of the Federal Trade Commission, some Commissioners seemed to argue that a toothpaste should be viewed purely as a means of preventing cavities, not as a means for achieving whiter teeth or a more successful social life. Presumably, consumers who have the latter needs are irrational.

The principle underlying these observations should be clear by now. When we examine an ad's content, we are really discussing the meaning of an ad in terms of the needs and preferences of one or another group of people—not in terms of its physical, chemical, or "engineering" properties. *As long as people tend to have different needs and preferences, the content of any ad will tend to have different meanings.* We shall return to this principle in Chapter 13. At this point, note that it applies not only to consumers but also to managers. Examples of how managers give different meanings to the content of ads are easy to observe: managers of the national television networks have decided that ads for liquor will not be accepted, although wine ads will. Some print media will not accept ads for products designed to prevent venereal diseases. For some firms, an "integrated" ad is still inconceivable.

There is no way for advertising managers to escape this situation of relative meanings: it is typical of heterogeneous and decentralized societies. Nor can managers escape the consequences of the interaction between two opposing facts of life: the heterogeneity of members within a social group, and the cultural homogeneity of the entire social group. On the one hand, each advertiser attempts to identify the existing differentiation of the social group into subgroups, and to relate to one or more subgroups on the basis of their specific needs. On the other hand, legislators and public servants attempt to identify some general norm that applies to the public interest at large—a reasonable activity, since they are indeed charged with the responsibility of watching over all of society.

But since both the overall cultural orientations of a society and the particular values held by specific groups change, it is impossible to reconcile, once and for all, the different points of view of individual advertisers and public regulators. Clearance procedures and safeguards are merely a way to ensure that, as both sides change, some working compromise is maintained.

The extent to which a satisfactory compromise can be reached depends on how the private and public sector operate. On the public side, we can ask how legislators and regulators can keep in touch with the prevailing cultural values. The election process provides a partial answer by keeping legislators responsive to their constituencies. Further, as long as the legislative process is one of bargaining, the prevailing "majority" values will be reflected in new legislation and changes in the old.

It is not clear, however, whether regulators can be made responsive to the interest of society *and* of specific subgroups. As a minimum first step, it is necessary to increase the quantity and quality of public agency staffs if the public interest is to be properly identified and measured, since better staffs would help to avoid the misspecification of the public interest. A classical example of misspecification is provided by the past regulation of passenger railroads. By not urging the railroads to spend funds on R&D, by compelling them to offer progressively uneconomical services, by not realizing that the concepts of competition and monopoly in real life are different from those in traditional textbooks, by not observing that consumers were increasingly turning to other modes of transportation—regulation resulted in a failure not only to meet the need for long-distance traveling, but also to meet the newer need for urban mass transit.

Yet even if regulators could rely on staffs qualified in the study of consumer behavior in specific product classes, they would still need to know more about the social context within which the affluent consumer operates. Regulatory agencies will have to measure changes in consumer life styles and other related social indicators—a responsibility of legislators who, so far, seem interested only in the areas of consumer protection and safety.

In addition, a workable compromise will depend on whether there are safeguard mechanisms that prevent public regulators from imposing their own meanings and perceptions of what is acceptable and/or desirable on the heterogeneous members of society.

The extent to which a workable compromise can be achieved also depends on what each advertiser, agency, and medium does in the area of clearance procedures and safeguards. There is no doubt that each firm will derive long-run benefits from formulating and applying good procedures and standards. Management cannot escape this responsibility to its own stockholders, to labor and other factors of production, to its own consumers, and, ultimately, to the public at large. Nor can a firm escape its responsibility to ensure that other firms also develop clearance and safeguard procedures through which the possible conflicts we have discussed can be resolved economically and ethically.

3 SUMMARY

Many advertising decisions relate directly or indirectly to a society's verbal and written norms, regulations, and laws. Many activities must be performed to ensure that advertising decisions satisfy existing rules and laws. The importance of this is very great, so great that each organization—advertiser, agency, and media—tends to check the legality of its decisions by developing its own internal, specialized, legal staff. Another sign of the importance of laws is media management insistence that it has the right to review ads to ensure their compliance with existing laws and rules.

There are many laws and regulations that bear on advertising decision processes, such as those concerning libel and the effects on competition. The testimony presented here stressed laws and rules that deal with the content of an ad. Is it truthful? Are the claims in the ad supported by some scientific evidence? Does the person endorsing the advertised product have relevant expertise? And the testimony has sketched the outline of procedures that good firms usually apply to their operations.

The management of each firm satisfies its own immediate interests by developing and implementing good clearance procedures. The cost of these procedures is essentially an insurance premium, because they decrease the possibility of making mistakes that might be costly in terms of monetary penalties and negative public reaction. Further, evidence of the use of good procedures may indicate that a possible violation was only an unintentional mistake.

Management of each firm should also find long-run advantages in the development and application of clearance and safeguard procedures. These may be viewed as a bridge between the firm's point of view and that of public agencies. A firm is necessarily concerned with the needs and preferences of a specific group of consumers, whereas the public agencies must, by law, be concerned with the broader and more general values prevailing throughout society. Differences and conflicts among a number of possible micro views and a more general macro view are unavoidable, especially in pluralistic and decentralized societies. Both micro and macro views, furthermore, tend to change, especially in affluent societies. Thus, clearance procedures become instruments for interpreting existing laws and rules; they provide a basis on which managers and regulators can discuss ways to solve potential conflicts.

Perhaps even more important, the widespread use of such procedures may become the basis for establishing self-regulation, that is, norms and procedures to which *all firms* may voluntarily subscribe and against which they may measure the behavior of deviant firms (see Chapter 15, Section 2) and apply sanctions against them.

Clearance and safeguard procedures will always be difficult to develop and formulate, especially when they concern the content of advertisements. The problem is not one of determining whether an ad contains an outright lie, but whether the information in an ad concerns actual product attributes. Since the same attributes may be perceived differently by different people, it is difficult to establish an absolute meaning for any attribute. For example, advertising the high price of a brand may satisfy some critics of advertising. Yet in consumer research we can make the case that such an ad may mislead those consumers who perceive high price as an indicator—sometimes the only available indicator—of high quality!

Nor can idealism be satisfied by resorting to "objective" information of an engineering type. Different engineering attributes may or may not be relevant to specific performance or use criteria: if users differ with respect to the problem they want to solve through the purchase of the product, there is no unique solution to be found in any list of engineering properties. Furthermore, research tells us that man, when acting as a consumer, knows only his own reality. Thus, some subjects will consider "objective" information completely irrelevant; others will manipulate such information through known psychological processes until they find some meaning that fits their initial predispositions. And so on with a large number of psychologically healthy processes that will always reduce any "objective" reality to meaningful subjective reality.

Chapter 8

Corporate Managers Look at Advertising

OUTLINE

The preceding chapters have examined the major classes of advertising decisions and illustrated the problems advertisers and advertising agencies must solve daily. Ultimately, the responsibility for advertising lies in the hands of corporate management; it is management who decides on the amount and kind of advertising needed to reach corporate objectives. The data available to corporate management and, above all, management philosophy, determine the role of the advertising function in the entire organization.

The testimonies in this chapter show us how four corporate managers look at the advertising function in the context of their own firms. One speaker is a relatively small manufacturer who describes his own advertising philosophy, as well as that of two other small manufacturers. The other speakers represent a large consumer durable goods manufacturer, a nationwide group of department stores, and a medium-sized regional supermarket chain.

1   THE USE OF ADVERTISING BY SMALL MANUFACTURERS: THREE EXAMPLES (*excerpts from L. E. Skinner, president, Skinner Macaroni Co.*[1])

Our first testimony is by L. E. Skinner, whose philosophy on the use of advertising comes through loud and clear. At the end of his presentation, Mr. Skinner also comments on the use of advertising by Winnebago Motor Homes, a recreational vehicle manufacturer, and by Morton House Kitchens, producer of a full line of quality canned meats and baked beans.

Advertising is an integral part of my business. I have been in the business world for almost four decades. In my early years with the Skinner Macaroni Co., I worked in every department prior to becoming the firm's Chief Executive Officer almost 20 years ago. . . . What good does advertising do? Let me illustrate.

The macaroni industry is very diverse in terms of company size, management philosophy, and marketing techniques. Our industry is composed of about 75 companies, some fairly large (three times my size), and some very small, and some in between. . . . Because of the nature of our industry, there are no one or two firms which dominate the industry on a national basis. Instead we have many strong regional brands. . . .

We are quite proud of our plant in Omaha, Nebraska. . . . We have invested more than 3-1/2 million dollars in this plant because we want to produce top quality pasta. We use only 100% semolina in our macaroni products. Pasta requires skillful and knowledgeable manufacturing, but in terms of raw materials, it is nothing more than wheat, water, and enrichment. The better the wheat, the better the macaroni . . . we use . . . the highest grade of durum available—100% semolina, the most costly grade of wheat. . . . This gives my product many advantages over most competitors. My product looks better, it cooks better, and it tastes better. . . .

I invest many thousands of dollars each year in my own system of distribution centers throughout my marketing areas in the midwest, southwest, southeast, and far west. These give me another advantage of a readily available product that is fresher . . . our costs force us to be priced a penny or two more on the shelf.

. . . none of these advantages can be of any benefit to the consumer unless she knows about it and buys the product. How do we tell her? . . . Our product costs her more. She is not going to take it off the shelf without a very good reason. We are in the mighty tough position on that shelf unless we have some way of communicating with her about our product. With 7000 items in a supermarket, each one gets 1/5 of a second of the shopper's viewing time (29 minutes). If we don't tell the consumer, no one else will.

That's why we must have advertising. How do we separate ourselves from our competitors? Those who sell for less . . . those who do not use prime ingredients . . . who do not match my production facilities . . . who do not have as fine a product? The answer is advertising.

Advertising also is one of the only ways a small company like ours can compete with the giant brands for a share of the shopper's dollar simply because no one has

---

[1] The Skinner Macaroni Co. is a producer of high-priced, high-quality "pasta" products.

a corner on creativity. With a much smaller budget, it is difficult *but certainly possible for the creative, inventive manufacturer to compete with much larger corporations. . . .*

At Skinner we use advertising for a number of purposes. To explain our quality story is only one purpose. We also use advertising to help the consumer with a tested recipe, to offer money-saving coupons, to explain a new product, and, of course, to introduce our product and company to a city we have just entered. Another consideration, of course, is that due to the great mobility of our population, we must continue to tell people about our product even where it has been well accepted for years—simply because of the great influx of people into that city from other areas of the nation [SLIDES ARE SHOWN NEXT].

[PUT THIS IN YOUR CASSEROLE AND COOK IT] This is an attempt in straightforward language to explain to the consumer why Skinner is a better macaroni product. At the same time, the ad contains an offer for a cookbook which we published. The cookbook has recipes and much other information which is helpful to any homemaker.

[SAVE MONEY—SAVE CALORIES WITH ROMA MACARONI MEALS] Roma is a brand name we recently purchased in the San Francisco Bay Area. This ad illustrates one of the means we have of combating misconceptions about our product. It is possible—very possible—to use macaroni, spaghetti, and egg noodles in low calorie meals. This ad gives two specific low calorie recipes. It also gives a 10¢ coupon. . . .

[SAVE MONEY—SAVE CALORIES] A recipe folder—this is an extension of our media advertising—a recipe folder offered free to the consumer at the grocery shelf. [WE'RE PUTTING OUR MONEY WHERE YOUR MOUTH IS] . . . we believe in our product strongly enough that we only ask the consumer to try it, in a situation where she cannot lose: If she does not like it for some reason, she sends one of the two coupons back to us and gets a full refund of the purchase price. If she does like it, she sends the other coupon to us and receives a coupon good for the next package free. . . .

The Skinner Company is more than half a century old. It is still a small company, in the area of 10–11 million dollars in sales, spending less than 2% of its sales volume in direct advertising to the consumer. But we feel it is a pretty mighty 2%. . . . So advertising has been good for us. And advertising has been good for the consumers of our product, too, because it introduced them to a quality macaroni product that they continue to re-purchase year after year.

I would also like to tell you about two other smaller firms from my area because their stories, too, reflect "the good that advertising does." One is Winnebago Motor Homes of Forest City, Iowa. The other is Morton House Kitchens of Nebraska City, Nebraska. Advertising has played—and continues to play—a vital role in the success of these two remarkable growth stores. . . .

Winnebago is a recreational vehicle company located in Forest City, Iowa. This company has grown from 4-1/2 million dollar sales in 1966 to more than 70-1/2 million in 1971. This success has been a result of recognizing a trend in the industry, filling a need of the consumer, and aggressively advertising. From a meager beginning the company today employs more than 1,700 people in a community of 3,841 population. This represents a remarkable thrust for the economy of Northeastern

Iowa. With the farms and farmer population steadily decreasing, the growth of Winnebago in Forest City has added greatly to the employment of the area, making it possible for people to live in a rural environment and to halt to some degree the migration to the metropolitan center. . . .

Winnebago advertises in three media: (1) To owners of present recreational vehicles through an ad such as this [SLIDE SHOWN]. (2) To the general public with ads in Time, Reader's Digest, Better Homes and Gardens *and other media like this [SLIDE SHOWN]. (3) As the industry leader, they are now employing television to provide greater penetration of the mass market. The Winnebago success story would not have been written without a quality product and consumer advertising.*

Morton House Kitchens, a producer of a full line of quality canned meats and baked beans, is located in Nebraska City, Nebraska. In 1961, sales totaled 4 million dollars. By 1968, gross sales reached 13-1/2 million dollars at which time the company was acquired by Lipton Tea. This growth was accomplished through selective advertising and good sales effort.

Advertising was employed to communicate the Morton House story: A good-tasting, quality product, priced competitively. National women's magazines, local hometown newspapers and radio—both local and national—have been used. Arthur Godfrey for several years was the primary spokesman for the Morton House story. Not only did he carry the message on his national radio program, but he was employed in magazine and newspaper advertising and in point-of-sale.

To effectively communicate the appetite appeal, on a small advertising budget, national women's magazines were employed. Through this medium, honest reproduction can be accomplished showing the quality and the promise of good taste. Here are several examples of magazine advertising which told of Morton House's economy, quality, and good taste [SLIDES SHOWN].

Morton House has grown phenomenally because it was able to advertise, to tell its story, to compete with the giants. The result—a successful company employing more than 300 persons in a rural community of 7,600 population. Without the opportunity to advertise, to talk directly to the consumer, Morton House would not have grown nor prospered.

2 THE USE OF ADVERTISING BY A LARGE MANUFACTURER (*excerpts from E. Gray II, chairman of the finance committee, Whirlpool Corp.*[1])

We now move to a firm—Whirlpool Corp.—with 1970 sales of more than one billion dollars. The witness, E. Gray II, states:

My purpose is to discuss with you the practical good that advertising does for a business, speaking not from the viewpoint of a professional advertising man, but rather as a plain, garden variety businessman who uses advertising because it is one of the essential links in the series of managerial functions all of which must be

---

[1] Whirlpool Corp. is a manufacturer of TV sets and major home appliances; it is a principal supplier to Sears, Roebuck and Co., which sells Whirlpool products under its own brand name, and it also sells products under its own name.

*performed well if a product is to be supplied successfully to the American market. . . .
I will discuss just two points. First, as a practical matter, what good does advertising
do—and second, what can the business community do to protect and enhance the
integrity and thus the effectiveness of advertising?*

*Since I am not a theoretician, nor for that matter particularly competent in the
field of advertising per se, I can make my points more clear, I believe, if I stick to the
viewpoint of a corporate officer with final responsibility for the success or failure
of the company and, as such, a person concerned with the proper place in the whole
setting of his business that advertising occupies. I hope to make clear that while
advertising is absolutely essential to the growth of a company and the introduction
of new products or brand names, advertising itself cannot generate growth nor insure
the success of a new product.*

*Since our own company is a typical one, and the only one I really know much
about, I hope you will permit me to use examples from my experience there.
Immediately after the war, in 1946, our company did about $13 million dollars of
annual business making only wringer washers and ironers and selling over ninety
percent of its output to Sears. It seemed clear to us that this was not a viable formula
for the long run, so we set about broadening the base of our business in two ways:
first, by broadening our customer list—second, by broadening our product line.*

*Accomplishing the latter involved a specific series of critical moves. Over-
simplified, it involved: 1. design of the new product; 2. prototype testing; 3. tooling;
4. pilot production; 5. engineering testing; 6. market testing with this limited
quantity; and 7. (assuming all signals were go up to here) the beginning of regular
manufacture in quantities commensurate with our hopes for the product line. Over
the years, this procedure has required anywhere from five years and about $1-1/2
million on our original automatic washer, to three years and three million dollars on
our latest household appliance, the residential trash compactor.*

*At this point, we have no customers and no sales. Not even a waiting public.
They have never even heard of our product. Our job now is to inform the customer
of the merits of our product so that in considering the purchase of such an appliance,
she will know we have one that she might want to consider. So, the 8th step in the
series is advertising and the related functions of sales promotion. This is a completely
separate step and an absolute prerequisite to the whole plan in the first place. . . .*

*Advertising costs in the appliance business may run as high as 12 to 15 percent
at start-up, but eventually must be reduced to 5 percent or less. I'm not going to
say that advertising is the most important step in the journey from idea to success in
the market. That would be like saying the right front wheel on your car is the most
important one. They are all necessary, of course, including advertising. . . .*

*This process, repeated time and time again, has brought our company from one
plant employing 1200 people in 1946 and 200,000 wringer washers a year, to a
company employing 28,000 people in 17 plants that will ship this year almost eight
million major appliances to American homes. Of that, two and one-half million will
have been sold through distributors and dealers under the brand name "Whirlpool"—
a brand name that didn't exist twenty-five years ago. It has taken its place in
appliances right along with great names you all know, such as General Electric,
Frigidaire, Westinghouse, and Maytag.*

Of course, we are only one of many competitors in this field. I daresay this business is one of the most competitive in the country (although that subjective opinion may be biased by the scars of competitive battle—the thinning hair and the wrinkled brow). However, one basic statistic I think bears out this contention rather dramatically. Because of the large volumes this competition has produced, appliances are selling today at 95.2% of the 1957–59 Consumer Price Index versus 142.3% for all items, and 104.6% of the 1967 index versus 122.4% for all items. Products like the automatic washer and the dryer, which were considered luxuries when introduced in the early fifties, are now classified as necessities. Through their use, many, many millions of housewives have over the years been freed of much of the drudgery of unglamorous household chores and, even more importantly, have been able to make their homes more comfortable and healthful for the whole family. Without advertising, this emancipation would have taken generations; would probably have been the achievement of only one or two firms and would have cost a great deal more.

Let me conclude this first part of my presentation by applying the foregoing reasoning to two products, one of which has finally "arrived" as a viable product, while the other is just getting started.

The first is our automatic ice maker, a very popular item on our refrigerators. This has become a profitable product over its 13 years of existence. We certainly would not have invested nearly 2 million dollars in improvements to bring it to its current state had we not had advertising to help us tell its story to the public. One satisfied user telling another is, of course, essential to the continued life on the market of any product; but when starting from scratch, the process would be so slow and the costs, therefore, so great that it would be a commercially impossible undertaking.

Now I want to show you a product in the "hopeful" state—the residential trash compactor I mentioned earlier. We expect it to become a useful addition to millions of households. But I ask you, how could we get the customer to understand it without imaginative advertising? I assure you, we wouldn't have even tried to bring this product to market if advertising had not been available or was unduly circum-scribed. Development costs and a brand new plant in Danville, Kentucky, which already employs 700 people, represent about a 9 million dollar investment. With luck, we will get the product in the black in 1972, and get back our investment 10 years after first designing it.

If, however, the consumer doesn't think it will be useful to her—or worth the price, you can be sure she won't buy it and we will have lost our bet on it. I repeat, the function of advertising is to inform—the customer will decide.

Last year, while our industry sold some 29 million labor saving appliances to American consumers, we didn't sell them any ironers. We sold them very, very few appliances that wash and dry their clothes in the same machine (in spite of enormous investments made to bring it to market), and we sold them no machines to dry clean their clothes at home automatically. I don't know why not. I believe that such appliances would aid American housewives—would give them more time, save their money, make them happier. But they don't think so—and apparently our advertising can't persuade them into thinking so.

It is the consumer, not the advertiser, who defines what is necessary and what is not. . . .

Now, my concluding point. If advertising in its many forms is not effective, then the process I have described will break down and the forward march of new and better products and more and better jobs will cease. You have seen recent opinion surveys that clearly show a growing disbelief in advertising messages. I believe them. This means that our selling efforts are being discounted by our customers. . . .

It behooves us all, and businessmen in particular, to use this tool in such a way that its credibility is repaired if not completely restored. (Although I don't suppose that condition will ever be realized.) The F.T.C., of course, has the statutory assignment of regulating the verity of advertising claims. I believe business has the moral and social responsibility to do its best to discipline its own actions in this regard also. . . .

3 THE USE OF ADVERTISING BY RETAILERS

In the next two readings, we turn to the use of advertising by retailers. The testimonies underline several key points which illuminate both the differentiation and complementarity between national and local advertising.

3.1 The Use of Advertising by a Department Store (*excerpts from F. Mayans, vice president, Federated Department Stores, Inc.*[1])

We begin with the managerial role of the advertising in a department store:

As a one-time executive with Young & Rubicam, I saw something of the workings of national advertising. As an officer of a retail merchandising organization, I now see something of the workings of local advertising. I see local advertising primarily as an aid to well-trained sales personnel. It is one of many such aids; certainly, good lighting and imaginative window displays, attractice merchandise presentations, and special events like fashion shows, and gourmet cooking classes are others. All of us are customers at one time or another; and as a customer, I regard department store advertising as service—like credit and delivery and the right of returning unsatisfactory merchandise. The retailer is my agent in the marketplace; his advertising gives me information on the wares he has accumulated and in which I might be interested. It should tell me what options he can offer—brands, pricelines, sizes, colors, fabrics— the pertinent information to enable me to decide if I want to buy a specific product at his store now.

Local department store advertising, then, is essentially a communication of information. In my view, our kind of advertising does very little to create a demand for either goods or services that do not fulfill an already existing physical or psychic desire. Nor can our advertising foist off on an unwilling public fashions the customer does not really want.

If you doubt this, ask women about the midi. They told us, very succinctly at the cash register, that the midi skirt was not going to be a success no matter who was

[1] Federated is a national organization with 180 department stores in 16 states, including such well-known establishments as Filene's in Boston, Sanger-Harris in Dallas, Shillito's in Cincinnati, and Lazarus in Columbus.

plugging it. So we offered other options as quickly as we could; pants suits, for example. Merchants who were sensitive to their customers' wishes and who could move rapidly enough to provide attractive choices did not take such a bath on the midi. . . . The fashion world could not create a demand where none existed. It is interesting to me—although I don't pretend to understand all of the social implications—that, at roughly the same time large numbers of American women declared their fashion independence, American men abandoned a generation of grey flannel coloration and, almost gleefully, began their own fashion revolution. Some say this phenomenon grew out of new subcultures and lifestyles. National advertising helped give impetus to these new fashions, stimulated a desire to wear them, and did a lot of pre-selling for us. Locally our challenge was to determine what was going to be good in Columbus and in Milwaukee and in Houston, to get the goods, and to advertise that we had it [SLIDE]. For example, "polyester double-knit slacks. . . . wide belt loop style with Ban-Rol waistband, non catch nylon zipper, easy flare leg . . . machine washable . . . black, camel, chocolate brown and navy . . . $13." With this ad we include size chart, telephone shopping number, stores in which the slacks were available and shopping hours.

I suspect these new men's fashions do fill some psychic need; certainly the blue serge and the grey flannel serve the same utilitarian function as the double breasted, brass-buttoned Bill Blass jacket and the flare-bottomed double-knit slacks. But, if our 50-year-old, size-44 assistant controller is happier with his new image, that's really his business. And if my wife prefers an avocado refrigerator to a white one, I've learned that is her business.

Let me cite two other specific examples of our customers' capacity for making up their own minds. Several years ago, DuPont, which has developed scores of successful new products, introduced a new synthetic—Corfam—destined to become the Edsel of the shoe industry. It was, by most testimony, an excellent product with many utilitarian advantages over natural leather. It was introduced only after the most sophisticated market research and supported by national and local advertising. Initially, our sales of Corfam shoes were pretty good; but in a short period of time, customers stopped buying Corfam shoes. None of us knows quite why; but since people didn't buy them, we don't have them any more.

On the other hand, within the past few months a seemingly spontaneous and overwhelming demand for ten-speed bicycles has sprung up through much of the country. I talked with a salesman in Shillito's sporting goods department two weeks ago when that store received its first sizable shipment of ten-speed bikes. He told me customer inquiries about such bikes came almost entirely from adults and began to build in Cincinnati in mid-summer. These customers knew specifically what they wanted; they were unwilling to settle for anything else.

What are the origins of this customer preference? Certainly, I have not been aware of any massive, nation-wide advertising campaign for ten-speed bikes. Perhaps this new interest is related to concern about pollution and impossible traffic snarls. Perhaps it was sparked by Dr. Paul Dudley White's counsel, that bicycling is a greater exerciser and conditioner for the middle-aged. At any rate, a full-blown customer demand is here. It may be fragile and temporary or it may continue for years. Our task as local merchants is to get the product as promptly as we can and to let our customers know we have it. Advertising is our quickest, most efficient means of *doing this. Here is a dummy of an ad to run in Cincinnati newspapers on Sunday, October 31 [SLIDE]. It is informative and specific—"496 bikes ... 10 speed ... centerpull clapper brakes ... metal pedals ... aluminum fenders ... clay wall tires ... $99."...*

Indeed, many newspaper readers, in those instances when a city-wide newspaper strike occurs, say they miss the daily ads about as much as they miss news coverage. In 1950, Pittsburgh's three daily papers were strikebound for seven weeks. A post-strike study showed that 74.1% of the women interviewed said they missed local store advertising—second only to the 79.0% who mentioned missing local news. ... *In the ninth week of the 1963 New York City newspaper strike, Batten, Barton, Durstine & Osborn, Inc. took a similar survey.* Advertising was the most missed feature. *In 1971, the* Pittsburgh Press *was strikebound for 129 days. Most of the* Press *readers (53.5%) said they missed local and state news, while 52% said they missed sales advertisements in a survey by Guide-Post Research, Inc. ...*

Sometimes, of course, we goof; and then we hear promptly and clearly from our customers. For example, in Cincinnati last spring, Shillito's ran TV, radio and newspaper ads on a raincoat sale—in each instance, stating that the raincoats were available downtown and at all branches. Through some logistical foul-up, the raincoats did not arrive on time at one branch; but lots of customers did. Some of the business generated by those ads was lost forever. Since competitors in the same center had raincoats for sale, we probably did something to increase their volume that day. We took some orders for coats, but believe me we would rather have had the coats on hand.

Our main concern, of course, is earning and keeping customer loyalty. One classic story concerning our Lazarus store in Columbus, Ohio, may illustrate. Some of you might recall that when ball-point pens first reached the market about 25 years ago, they were relatively expensive—about $15, I believe. Eventually a reputable manufacturer introduced a ball-point to retail at about $7.50. The stationery department at Lazarus sold about 700 of these pens; and, when the pens failed to write without skipping as the points picked up grease and dirt, Lazarus began refunding money on the 700 pens. Of the 700 sold, 2,000 were returned. ...

Local advertising generates economies of size and volume which make it feasible to accumulate in one location a volume and variety of merchandise at the time and price that suits the customer best. We feel advertising reduces *the cost of mass distribution of merchandise and, therefore, is a productive element of our economic system. Now let us return to our ten-speed bicycle ad. We first received about 70 of these bikes in early October. Our first 70 sold to walk-in customers at $120. They were* not *advertised because there was insufficient volume to afford it. Now, when we have 496 bikes to sell, our competitors also have bikes and the going price is not $120 but $99. We can sell at the lower mark-up and earn a profit because advertising probably will enable us to sell out in a single day. At least, we hope so. In a business in which the very best operators earn less than a nickel on each dollar of sales, we are acutely aware of the cost of services. We must be able to justify these costs to our shareholders and to our customers.*

Last year our advertising expenditures in relation to sales were slightly higher than they were in the past several years because our merchants felt we needed a stronger promotional effort during an uncertain economic period. Still, for the sake of some general comparisons, Federated's advertising costs, in its department store divisions, ranged from less than 1% of sales to more than 4%; but averaged less than one-fourth the cost of selling payroll alone and were not much greater than our delivery costs.

Now let me cite an unrelated cost of doing business, but one which concerns us far more than our advertising expense, one which costs both customers and share-holders money, and which certainly is destructive rather than productive. Our inventory shortages last year—a significant portion of which is due to theft, internal and external—amounted to almost twice our advertising budget. And, I daresay, our record probably is better than that of most of our competitors. In a number of cities we are joining with other retailers and the media in an effort to use advertising as a tool to combat this economic and moral problem [SLIDE].

I have, perhaps, oversimplified the mechanics of local retail advertising. To appreciate the difficulties a department store ad manager faces, you should recognize that department stores are no longer monolithic in character nor in the merchandise they stock. Shillito's in Cincinnati is different than Shillito's in Louisville, and different in Louisville than in Lexington. Indeed, a branch store on the west side of town may differ substantially from one on the east side. With a growing diversity of life styles, with increasing affluence, with greater freedom of shopping choice, advertising becomes a more important and more complex communications channel. . . .

I don't know to what degree national and local advertising affect public taste and behavior, but the combination of the two certainly has helped popularize everything from brushing your teeth regularly to joining a book club. Our job, as local merchants, is not to direct the nation's cultural progress, but to serve as our customers' advocate in the marketplace. We have to be sensitive daily to shifts in customer desires and to feed that information to the thousands of manufacturers throughout the world who supply us with goods for our customers. Our advertising, I think, identifies us and what we stand for in our market. . . . We know at the close of each business day if our advertising has communicated with our customers.

3.2 The Use of Advertising by a Supermarket Chain (*excerpts from M. Perlmutter, president, Supermarket General Corp.*)

When we move from department stores to supermarkets, do we see advertising from a different perspective? The answer given by the following testimony says no. Although the specifics vary a great deal from department stores to food stores, the witness elaborates many of the same points made in the preceding presentation; he also introduces other perspectives and data on the use of advertising by corporate management.

Note that the retail food business is often thought to be dominated by very large corporations whose power allows small "Mama and Papa" stores to survive. Yet Supermarket General Corp. was formed in 1958, when three small independent food retailers joined to open a large supermarket. Within ten years, it had become one of the fifteen largest retail food chains in the United States. Operating ninety Pathmark supermarkets in a five-state region in the northeast, this firm had 1971 sales of more than $750 million.

My assignment today, as I see it, is to tell you something about the conduct of our business, about how we use advertising in that business, and about the role we think that advertising plays for us. . . . As one of the representatives of retailing on this program, I think it is not amiss to point out that retailers are necessarily consumer-oriented in their thinking . . . we talk to the customer, we listen to the consumer, spend our working days with the consumer, and we rely on the consumer for our success just as the consumer relies on us to meet his everyday needs. If we do our job well, we find out the consumer's needs and wants, his or her preferences and idiosyncrasies. The slightest customer reaction—to the merchandise we offer, the prices we charge, the service we provide—should trigger an immediate response from us.

In this very pragmatic sense, we are experts on the consumer. Neither the government consumer agencies nor the various consumer groups nor even so famous a consumer advocate as Ralph Nader really knows the consumer as well as we do, and none of them has to. . . . [but] we get the response at the cash registers.

Just like our customers, we tend to be critical about the things we buy. So as a consumer of advertising, rather than a seller or a practitioner of the craft, we like to feel that we are getting our money's worth. And for our purposes, we find that advertising serves four basic functions: (1) it helps us achieve the kind of merchandise turnover we need; (2) it helps us move the special or featured items; (3) it is a channel of communication with our employees; and (4) it offers a medium of communication with our customers about many subjects other than prices.

Let me spell these out one at a time. Any supermarket organization, and ours in particular, must rely on the interrelated principles of high volume, low markup, and fast turnover. That is our magic formula, and it enables us to offer our customers the lowest food prices in the world.

It may sound simple, but it is anything but simple in this operation. At Pathmark, we turn over our grocery warehouse merchandise at the average rate of 45 times a year, which most retailers would probably describe as phenomenal. It means that our products, many of them assembled from all over the country and various parts of the world, stay in the warehouse for an average of less than ten days. To keep from running out of stock, we have to order as much as 30 days ahead, and we must make many more good guesses than bad about future consumer demand. There has to be a steady flow into and out of our warehouses. . . .

We use both print and broadcast media. We also publish a weekly bulletin that we call the Value Planner, *and we distribute copies at the checkout counters of our stores. The* Value Planner *might be described as a short course in home economics, featuring items that are attractively priced, recommending seasonal budget-stretchers and offering nutritional information. . . . In any given week, we endeavor to promote the sale of a large number of grocery and food market items in our ads. That means that we pack into our print advertising a lot of information that our customers want to have. And that, of course, is critically important in helping us achieve high turnover. . . . In a sense, we owe a debt to national product advertising, which has helped presell our merchandise by describing its qualities and, through brand names, identifying it in a way that is important to many of our customers.*

Now for the second function of advertising—moving featured items. Typically, these are new products or special buys or a product whose price has been cut by the manufacturer, perhaps because of a price drop in the raw commodity. . . . In these cases, . . . advertising becomes all the more necessary. . . .

A special case of this kind involves the movement of surplus commodities. Here advertising is often able to add a dramatic dimension. Our stores cooperate with both the government and with producers' groups in avoiding catastrophic market gluts through extraordinary efforts to dispose of products in temporary oversupply. The benefits extend all the way from the farmer, who is saved from taking a loss or even from dumping merchandise, to the consumer, who gets some real bargains.

The U.S. Department of Agriculture advises retailers, on a monthly basis, of what foods are expected to be in overabundant supply, through its Plentiful Foods program. This information comes to us four to six weeks in advance, so that we can plan campaigns for promoting these foods. They are usually perishables that would otherwise go to waste, but they may also be goods canned at the height of the season. Customers learn about these items when we feature them in our regular advertising, tell about them in our Value Planner, *or carry special signs on our shelves with the U.S.D.A.'s Plentiful Goods program logo.*

Pathmark also cooperates with the voluntary program of three farm organizations— the National Council of Farm Cooperatives, the Farm Bureau Federation, and the National Grange—in disposing of surplus food. Retailers learn of the surpluses through the National Association of Food Chains or directly from the producers, and then pass on the information to their customers through extra advertising and displays. The special push on these items may last a month or more, often with the assistance of such organizations as the Lamb Council, Sunkist oranges or other producer groups. . . .

I mentioned communication with our own employees as the third function that advertising serves for us. There are of course other and more direct ways to communicate with employees, but we have found that the advertising directed at our customers is one of the most effective. . . .

Finally, we use advertising for other than price information. We put on television commercials, for example, that explain our pricing policy, which we think is peculiar to our own stores. We believe in having a large number of low-priced items, rather than a few dramatic <u>loss leaders</u> *that are meant to lure the customer into the store. Indeed, we have been trying to get rid of the "come-on" specials completely, although surplus items sometimes fall into this class.*

We have also used this informative kind of advertising to throw light on some of the lesser known aspects of shopping, such as private labels. Or "single unit" pricing, which has been given some special attention in recent months. Well, we use that kind of unit pricing—that is, we show the price per ounce, per pound, per pint, per 100 sheets, or in terms of whatever unit makes sense for the given item. And we find that perhaps half *of our customers are aware of this kind of unit pricing—and that* a *smaller proportion will actually use it, although most will tell you they are in favor of it [emphasis added].*

But about two and a half years ago, we instituted something we call "single unit" pricing—that is, giving prices of only single cans or bottles or pounds. We felt that such multiples in pricing as six cans for $1.35 or twelve jars for $.89 had reached the point where they were confusing to both the customer and the cashiers. The tendency of the customer is to buy the multiple, both because of this confusion and because he felt that he might miss out on a bargain if he bought just one or two or whatever he really needed. So we dropped all such multiple prices, and expressed all our prices in terms of the single unit.

When we did that, the immediate effect was to hurt us in two ways. First, we eliminated fractions of a penny in favor of the customer, and since we operate on a very narrow profit margin, anyway, there was a noticeable effect on our earnings for a while. And second, we lost out on sales. . . . We will never know for certain, of course, but it is our feeling that over the long term we have gained—both in our volume of business and in that very intangible but very precious asset for any retailer, the confidence of his customers. We used advertising to explain what we were doing with single unit pricing, and why, and I think that our customers understood that it was in their interest. Perhaps it is for reasons like these that Pathmark is able to boast that our average sale is at least double the national average.

Because our stores have been so successful, we have tried to explore the reasons for it, so that we would not get caught short if things ever began to go wrong. . . . We recently commissioned a study which involved depth interviews with 895 shoppers, divided about equally in three different regions. A total of 585, or 65 percent, said they usually checked newspaper ads for food prices before going shopping. Of those 585, there were 456 who compare the ads of several stores, while only 127 looked just at the ads of their favorite stores. . . .

These results have been corroborated in a national study conducted by Burgoyne Index, Inc. of Cincinnati, which has found in each of the last eight years that around 75 percent of shoppers interviewed in eight cities will read newspaper food ads before shopping, and that they would read an average of almost three ads apiece. Another study reported by the trade magazine, Progressive Grocer, showed that peak sales of specially-priced items in A. & P. stores would coincide with the appearance of advertising, and that the peaks would be as much as 200 percent higher than the low point of the week. This survey also said something about the shopper's own feelings about the validity of advertising. A product would sell 65 percent better when it was flagged with an "As Advertised" sign than when it was unmarked.

Because of our belief in advertising as a force for good, we have used space in our ads to call for blood donors when requested to do so by the Blood Bank program. And we have publicized a pamphlet we have had printed in English and in Spanish to explain the Food Stamp program to the poor—a service that even the government did not perform on a bilingual basis at the time.

I suppose it might almost be said that we had better believe in advertising. When we open a new store, it usually includes drug, bakery, delicatessen and other departments not found in most supermarkets. And it represents a major commitment in time, money and talent—at least $1 million in land and building, $500,000 in equipment, $250,000 in minimum inventory, a staff of 150 employees, a share in warehousing, purchasing and distribution costs and in the backup of general management capability. To justify that kind of investment, the store must reach its full operating rate from a standstill start in a very short time. I simply know of no way this can be done without advertising—not just advertising that says we are now in town, but advertising that tells what kind of institution we are.

This is no blind faith on our part. As businessmen and merchants, we like to know what will work and what will not. We have experimented, for example, with dropping *all advertising for one group of our stores for periods of up to three months. For the first week or two, there was some drop in sales, but no startling change. But then the sales decline grew cumulatively worse. In-store promotions could not make up the difference. If there was an alternative to advertising, we could not find it.*

In terms of total sales, our advertising costs are not high—less than 1 percent, even including the costs of publishing the Value Planner *and our various public service advertising activities. But advertising is an essential link in our communication with our customers. Without it, we know that sales volume suffers. And our ability to deliver lower prices to customers depends on high volume. A drop in volume would inevitably mean higher prices, within the limits of what the competitive situation allowed. And if we can't stay within those limits, the alternative is having our business disappear. That would be harmful to the advertising media, to our suppliers, to our employees or to our customers. So, my vote has to go to the kind of partnership we have created among producers, distributors, consumers and the advertising that helps them all work together.*

3.3 NATIONAL VERSUS LOCAL ADVERTISING: DIFFERENTIATION AND COMPLEMENTARITY

In the preceding two testimonies, we turned to the use of advertising by retailers and examined several key questions which had not yet been considered explicitly. For example, should any one ad contain all the information about the product being advertised? This question is important to advertisers and consumers, as well as to critics, who complain that many ads are not sufficiently informative.

There are certainly many ads that say relatively little about the many attributes of their product. For instance, in humorous ads, such as those for Volkswagen, the information content of each ad is usually limited to one product attribute. The two testimonies reported here, however, indicate a general difference between the information content of national (manufacturer) and local (retailer) ads.

National ads tend to stress the overall image of a product, or one or two attributes—those believed to be most important in differentiating a brand from its competitors. Thus, ads that promote bus travel stress the fatigue of driving one's own car; they do not specify rates, schedules, connections, or reservations. Or national ads introducing a new canned tomato paste may stress only flavor or ease of preparation, omitting details of price, calories, and nutritional content.

Additional information, often more specific, tends to appear in local retail ads, labels, and in package designs. Thus, supermarkets handling the new tomato paste may advertise the price and can size, while the package will describe its chemical components and directions for use, and possibly offer one or more recipes illustrating the ease of preparation.

The managerial implications of these observations should be clear. Any advertiser must decide *how to allocate the total information* he wants to supply to consumers among the various media—local, national, and even on the package itself. In this context, the retailer is essentially an alternative medium available to the manufacturer of consumer goods.

The retailer, in fact, provides access to a number of media. First, he can use local mass media, and the advertiser will frequently attempt to foster such use by assuming part of the retailer's advertising costs. Second, the retailer provides salespeople as another channel of information. We know from consumer research that personal, word-of-mouth channels are far more effective than mass media. Thus, in several industries, manufacturers offer special promotional literature and training for the retailer's sales personnel.

All in all, the problem is conceptually clear. To transmit information relevant to the consumer, the advertiser must know both the best combination of media (personal, mass national, mass local) to use, and which specific information to send through which medium. While our present ability to compute the optimal allocation of information to media is limited, advertisers seem, in practice, to favor providing more specific information on the local-retailer level than on the national level. The information content assigned to packages and labels, and to sales personnel, becomes still more specific.

This general rule makes sense for at least two reasons. First, time and cost constraints make it difficult to be specific when using mass media, especially TV. Further, the consumer pays little attention to details in his daily exposures to mass media such as TV and billboards. However, the same consumer often scans the local newspaper carefully before deciding where to shop: at this moment he or she is motivated to read much more specific information. Thus in a sixty-second commercial we can hope to communicate that the consumer "should leave the driving to us," while at bus terminals and at travel agents we may provide extensive material on schedules and prices.

Another key point stressed in the testimonies was the effect of advertising expenditures on sales, turnover (the time rate at which goods are sold), and net profits. The figures supplied by the last two witnesses should be considered carefully, particularly the relationship between advertising and turnover: although advertising increases costs, the expense may be more than offset by the speed with which goods are sold. Our witnesses state specifically that they use advertising to sell high volumes at low margins.

There is nothing compulsory about such managerial behavior: one can make just as much net profit by selling fewer goods with a larger margin on each sale. The emphasis on selling high volumes at thin margins—and using advertising to reach this goal—is in many ways a characteristic of United States management. Another characteristic is management aggressiveness. The history of United States management differs sharply from that of other countries in that, in practically every industry, there have always been managers who want to do better. They break with traditions, take on the "big boys," and declare war. They do this by spending more on R&D, by sticking their necks out to introduce new products (as an example, reread the account in the preceding section on the risks taken and the failures encountered by Whirlpool), by changing packages, by cutting prices (how many times were resale maintenance laws defeated, not by laws or critics, but by competitors?), and by advertising and other marketing methods.

The two witnesses from the retailing field reaffirmed the point made most explicitly by Mr. Gray of Whirlpool: advertising cannot make people buy what they do not want!

As an example, advertising and other promotional devices tried by *all* the firms involved in producing and selling midiskirts (from producers of fibers to textile firms, from fashion designers to retailers) did not succeed in getting this style accepted. The witnesses also asserted that affluent consumers behaved as if their purchases were aimed at satisfying psychological and social needs as well as physical needs connected with hunger, climate. and fear. As we shall see in Part 2, this assertion raises crucial issues: what is meant by social psychological need? Should advertisers appeal to only one subgroup of social psychological needs? And who is going to choose this subgroup?

4 SUMMARY

In this chapter, we heard witnesses who ultimately decide whether to use advertising as one of the means to meet the demands on the firm by various interest groups—vendors of equipment and materials, labor, capital, and government services. We heard from both large and small manufacturers and from retailers. Although it is difficult to compute the exact returns on advertising expenditures, experience strongly suggests that advertising helps the operations of these firms.

The witnesses believe, first, that advertising is a means of implementing the aggressive management philosophy of many United States firms. To sell at low prices, and thus at lower margins, it is necessary to sell a high volume. Whether it introduces new products or simply reminds consumers of an existing product's attributes, advertising may stimulate demand and, thus, total sales of a firm. To the extent that advertising succeeds, it indirectly contributes to lower prices.

But the witnesses also pointed out that advertising is only *one* of the tools used by corporate managers: a firm's total sales cannot depend on advertising alone. Many factors influence consumer acceptance and thus sales. A product or a brand may fail to meet consumer needs and preferences; its quality may be unacceptable; its price may be out of line with the intensity of the consumers' needs; middlemen and retailers may favor a competitor's product; competitors may have lower prices or introduce more satisfactory products, thanks to heavy investment in R&D. Any one of these or other factors can reduce consumer acceptance of a firm's brand, and no amount of advertising, however good, can make up for the loss.

If a firm does a good job in all other areas of decision making, advertising will help: it will help a small firm to grow and a large firm to remain large. But what is a good job? Meeting the needs and preferences of some consumers was the answer given by our four corporate managers, who thus re-emphasized the importance of the consumer illustrated in earlier chapters.

The speakers also provided perspective on what types of consumer preferences a firm should fulfill. Should each firm in the business sector attempt to meet every kind of need and preference? Should a firm limit itself to meeting nonpsychological needs and thus advertise only the physical and chemical properties of its products? The questions are complex, for purchases often fulfill different needs for different buyers.

Some may buy a bicycle for transportation; others because the doctor ordered more exercise. For still others, a bike may be the means of joining a social club, of enjoying a Sunday morning ride through a nearby park, or of giving a Christmas gift to their children or grandchildren.

Yet, which of these needs is psychological, and which nonpsychological? Since our parks and wildlife are endangered by an enormous increase in the number of visitors, should they be protected by a decree forbidding Winnebago Company from advertising its vacation motor home vehicles? Ultimately, and more importantly, is the distinction between psychological and nonpsychological needs readily recognized by each of us or is it relative to our personal views of the world?

The speakers' answers to these questions was clear: business firms exist only insofar as they can meet the needs of *some group* of consumers. They cannot pass judgment on what is good or bad for the consumer—nor is it their moral responsibility to do so. At any given time, societies have political and legal mechanisms for judging what is good or bad behavior. Although Ford Motor Company could not persuade enough consumers to pay for optional seat belts and roll bars fifteen years ago, lawmakers did find the political courage to force car manufacturers to install seat belts and force consumers to buy them.

Another major point in the presentations concerned the allocation problem we began discussing in Chapter 3. There the key question was how to allocate different advertising activities to different firms and to departments within each firm. The question examined here was how to allocate information to different channels of communication. We have seen that national ads tend to supply rather general information. At the local level, ads become more specific, while the information delivered by sales personnel is still more detailed. This allocation seems to be the result of two commonsense factors: the cost of national mass media, and the state of the consumer decision process. The closer a consumer is to the actual point of making a purchase, the more likely he is to need increasingly more detailed information about a large number of product or brand attributes.

Chapter 9

Some Concluding Remarks

OUTLINE

This chapter summarizes what we have learned about the managerial aspects of advertising. It also begins the transition to Part 2, i.e., to testimonies that look beyond advertising management to advertising as an institution and as a part of both the economy and the society as a whole.

1 THE NEED FOR A MASS COMMUNICATION SYSTEM

To work and live together, humans need to communicate with one another. As the size and complexity of a social group increases, the need for mass media also increases. Individually and in groups, man uses mass communication to send or seek information about news, politics, religion, and many other matters.

Man has always sought to exchange information about economic matters, but the modes and intensity of this exchange have changed over time. In ancient rural societies, each family produced most of the goods it needed and its remaining needs could usually be satisfied by direct purchases from local producers. In such societies, information could also be exchanged directly. But the structure and function of our society have changed drastically. Size, technological development, and specialization have increased enormously and, in the process, have complicated the exchange of information. No longer does each family produce most of what it needs; instead, it produces (or receives) income with which it can buy goods. Further, these goods usually cannot be purchased directly from producers.

138

An astronomical number of activities and enterprises now separate consumers and producers. The need to communicate has increased for both groups and mass media have gradually complemented the more limited face-to-face channels of communication. The birth and evolution of advertising management and of the advertising institution reflect this need for consumers and producers to exchange information. Moreover, in any modern society, the advertising institution is embedded in the entire mass communication system—structurally, functionally, and in terms of both benefits and costs.

Another event—the rise of affluence—has also affected the nature of advertising management and of the advertising institution. Affluence does not merely mean abundance, for industrialization already achieved the production of large *quantities* of goods. Rather, affluence means that more and more members of society have an increasing amount of discretionary income *and* time. Indirectly, but dramatically, the micromanagerial and macrosocioeconomic aspects of advertising have been influenced by this development.

Some social scientists have already observed that the amount of discretionary income and time available is probably the most powerful indicator of social change, especially of basic changes in cultural values, norms, rewards, and sanctions. Consumption patterns used to reflect the uniform need of most of society's members to buy goods in order to survive and to be ready to work the following day. In this historical context, the quantity of goods bought was a reasonable measure of the quality of life. But in affluent societies the "right to work" is gradually being replaced by the "right to consume." Each person is freer to choose the kind of life he wants to live and then select the basket of goods he needs and the type of work, if any, he needs to do in order to buy such goods. Consumption patterns are becoming differentiated and are reflecting *individual definitions of the quality of life.* These patterns are the most accurate indicators of what a society is and, probably, of its ethical fiber.

The consequences of the growth of affluence are just beginning to be felt. More consumers are free to search for the satisfaction of needs other than survival and mere abundance. Their search extends to means for satisfying *needs intrinsic to each person.* These needs, wants, wishes, and desires are essentially aesthetic and ethical, and thus necessarily individualistic, whether they be shared by few or many other people.

In his search for satisfaction, the individual is confronted by the complexity of his environment and the impossibility of establishing direct contact with all the producers of the goods that might offer what he or she wants. Each consumer needs information to satisfy his own goals effectively. Thus, the information flowing through the advertising system cannot be homogeneous, for different persons need different information. Each retailer attempts to satisfy some of these information requirements by bringing a wide assortment of choices to consumers and by sending information about these choices via local mass media. Additional information is available to each consumer from a variety of other channels: word-of-mouth, salespeople, and, of course, ads in mass media.

The same factors that cause consumers to need more information also influence the producers of consumer goods. Firms do not know where their potential buyers may be, what they might specifically like, in what quantities, at what times, and at what prices.

Each firm tries to reach some potential market through middlemen, salespeople, and mass media. Each firm must at least guess which consumers want what products for what reasons; each can attempt to tell consumers what needs its own product will fulfill.

Given the task of the advertising institution as a facilitator of contacts between firms and consumers, a key question concerns the optimal way to organize people and activities to perform this task. Traditionally, in decentralized societies, each individual consumer, mass medium, advertiser, or advertising agency sends or seeks information in its own ways and in its own interest—within a framework set forth by laws and regulations. Thus, the performance of this institution is essentially the result of individual decisions and of trial and error. But how do these decisions interact? And, even more basic, what do we know about them, i.e., how do individual consumers, media, advertisers, and advertising agencies go about making decisions concerning the exchange of information via mass communication?

Part 1 outlined the decision processes of advertisers and agencies. Contrary to popular belief, advertising management is not solely concerned with the problem of sending information to consumers; nor is this problem a simple one. Each firm is part of a complex environment that reflects the drastic changes brought about by the transition from industrialization to affluence.

The management of a firm's advertising function is deeply affected by the ambiguities and uncertainties that surround this transition. In an industrialized society, advertising management had the relatively easy task of helping the firm obtain lower unit costs by stimulating consumption. But in a postindustrial affluent society, advertising management is learning that it is the affluent consumer who calls the tune with his desire to fulfill needs that are highly qualitative and individualistic, and thus very difficult for a firm to identify and satisfy.

2   THE MAJOR CLASSES OF ADVERTISING
MANAGEMENT DECISIONS: A SUMMARY

At the managerial level, the problem of finding appropriate advertiser-consumer pairs is very complex. Firms cannot solve the communication equation simply by trying to contact as many people as possible via mass media. In fact, they have been compelled by market realities to abandon this stereotyped strategy; unfortunately, certain interest groups do not realize how obsolete and dangerous this stereotype is for all concerned.

At the managerial level, each firm is faced with consumers searching for information about increasingly different needs and preferences, which, furthermore, are in a continuous state of flux. Advertising management has realized that, to solve the communication equation, it first needs information about the consumer. Advertising, then, is a complex decision process of first *acquiring need-preference information from consumers* and then *disseminating product information to them.*

The nature of this decision process and the conditions bearing upon it are governed by basic economics or, to use more fashionable terms, by subtle but powerful rules of ecological *balance between inputs and outputs.* On the one hand, management is bound by the demands of the factors of production—labor, supplies of equipment and materials, suppliers of financial means, and suppliers of public services. Moreover, these resources limit a firm to producing certain goods only: at any particular time, a firm can offer only one set of product attributes. On the other, any one set of product attributes cannot possibly satisfy all consumer preferences, for in an affluent society these are too many and too differentiated.

Matching supply with demand at the managerial level is extremely complex in an affluent society. To assess the probability of creating revenues sufficient *to satisfy the demands of the factors of production,* a firm must search among consumers to discover whether a sufficiently large number have needs that can be matched by the firm's product attributes.

We have seen that this problem is critical in the introduction of new products. But all the testimonies show that the same problem also applies to existing products and brands. This is so because a product attributes-consumer needs match that was satisfactory at one point in time may rapidly become obsolete. A raw material may no longer be available or may become too expensive. Competitors may cut prices, offer more services, improve the attributes of their own products, or adopt new technologies, thereby reducing their production and distribution costs. And those consumers who were previously satisfied with the firm's product attributes may change the priorities of their preferences or may experience new needs altogether.

All in all, then, the first major class of advertising decisions involves *matching product attributes with the needs of some consumer group(s)* in a way that makes economic sense, i.e., in a way that balances the demands of input factors with the demands of those groups. Further, such decisions must be monitored continuously. No advertising management can afford to rest on its laurels, for success does not depend on the amount of past and future advertising expenditures but on the correct reading of trends and on the matching of product attributes with ever changing consumer needs and preferences.

The choice of any particular product attributes-consumer needs match has two consequences for advertising management. First, since each attribute is presumably relevant to some consumer need, the selected product attributes define the possible content of future advertising messages. Second, the advertiser has also defined the people to whom the future possible ads must be directed.

Another class of decisions now follows. To begin with, economic considerations prohibit advertising each and every possible attribute-preference pair. Furthermore, *the content of each ad* must vary according to the specific goals of each ad. Given the desired consumer reaction—awareness, understanding, liking, or satisfaction with a brand—management must select the pair that has the highest probability of triggering the desired reaction. Finally, management must choose the *form* in which to express the content of each ad. For example, a group of consumers may consciously or subconsciously see the purchase of a waterbed as a means of satisfying sensual needs. Here the potential attribute-need match is clear, but it is not at all clear how best to evoke this association. Some consumers may react to a hint of sex, while a reference to warm, tropical seas might be preferable for others.

The choice of the content and form of an ad is governed strictly by *economic considerations* of costs and results. Yet there are other constraints on these management decisions. Some are legal and others are related to the *technological possibilities* of mass media. As an extreme case of the latter type of restriction, we may recall that General Foods decided not to advertise Beef Stroganoff because it was technically impossible to photograph it in an appetizing manner. Only recent—but expensive—technological innovations have made it possible for management to consider a wider choice of form and content in constructing ads.

The next class of advertising decisions concerns the selection of a specific *combination of mass media.* As pointed out in Chapter 1, the mass media have continuously adapted themselves to the increasing heterogeneity of consumer preferences. Contrary to popular belief, even television is not a homogeneous, monolithic medium: there are three national networks, many local networks, and a growing number of cable TV systems, as well as the noncommercial public broadcasting stations. And even though the national networks undoubtedly dominate the choice of programs—from general news to all other subjects—within each network there is an almost frantic search for differentiation of programs during the day and throughout the week in an attempt to reach different viewers.

Consumers have different *patterns of media preferences* and different patterns of topic preferences. Thus the choice of the best media mix is dictated by the choice of the consumers a firm wants to reach and their media-topic preferences. We have seen that media choice is not simply a question of minimizing cost, because this strategy may reach consumers who are not interested in the firm's product. We further learned that the form and content of an ad that was "best" with respect to a particular group of consumers might not, because of technological limitations, be best suited to the particular media that reached that consumer group.

We also saw how the *degree of use of certain media* might vary according to the specific goals assigned to different ads and the overall marketing strategies. We learned, for instance, that a different media mix and a different intensity of use will be chosen depending on whether a firm wants to maximize frequency (the number of times the firm wants to reach the same consumers); to develop a generic image of its brand; or to give specific information about the brand's availability at the retail level.

The next class of decisions we examined was how the advertiser organizes the many activities implied by all these decisions. Here we saw that the problem was essentially one of *allocating activities and decisions* within the advertiser's firm and across other firms, especially such firms as advertising agencies. This is clearly a problem of organizational design, and we found that its parameters were fluid. Advertisers and agencies continuously assess which firm should do what as the many relevant market factors shift in number and relative importance.

A similar allocation problem turned out to be the *assignment of different types and amounts of information to different ads.* Some ads merely attempt to create awareness;

some want to communicate specific product attributes; others try to remind the consumer of prior information at the point of purchase; still others try to reinforce positive past experience with a brand. More importantly, we saw that this allocation is often intertwined with the allocation to the advertiser or the retailer of the type of ad best generated by one or the other firms.

3   THE ROLES OF THE CONSUMER IN ADVERTISING DECISIONS

As we spelled out the major classes of advertising decisions, we observed the ubiquitous roles of consumers. Management needs information from the consumer to solve each of these decisions—which consumers have which needs; which ones may be interested in which product attributes; what will be said to them in what form; which media and topics they prefer; and when and how often shall one say what. We recognized that the more a firm knows about consumer decision processes, the more effectively it can relate to consumers in terms of their personal perferences and in terms of the firm's resources.

If each firm operated in a world of plenty, each one could do a better job of gathering and using information about consumers' preferences and behaviors. But this information is expensive, and often time consuming to collect, and it is not always available when needed. More important, our witnesses—even those who had vested interests in consumer research—stressed that consumer research is often unable to deliver reliable and valid information.

And there is an ultimate limit to the degree to which a firm, private or public, can attempt to satisfy each consumer, a limit mercilessly established by the demands of the factors of production—from labor to government taxes. To satisfy these demands constitutes not only a legal and moral constraint on management, but also on economic necessity. To meet the demands of both production factors and consumers is the condition for a firm's survival; it is also the primary social responsibility of any firm— either privately or publicly owned.

At the managerial level, then, a firm can exist only if it satisfies both these demands. And in an affluent society, the tempo and direction of management action are increasingly determined by the consumer. The many examples of product failures by very large firms, even of some who operate in classical situations of oligopoly, are the often-tragic evidence supporting this fact. In affluent societies, corporate and advertising management must adapt to both the proliferating number of consumer life styles and the rapid changes within them.

To the extent to which each firm adapts to consumer trends, the nature of the advertising decisions examined in Part 1, and in many more technical discussions, is clarified. Understanding how a firm can initiate and continue a dialogue with some consumers, including a dialogue via mass communication, is the prerequisite for making better advertising decisions and, presumably, for increased satisfaction of those consumers who prefer such discourse with a firm.

Understanding these managerial decision processes is also a prerequisite for effective legislation and regulation: Legislators and regulators also must understand the ubiquitous and growing role of the consumer. They must become aware that affluent consumers have new rights and needs that challenge the creativity of social management. Although legislation and regulation were touched upon explicitly by only one of the testimonies reported in this part, many other points discussed were concerned with the relationships between society and its individual members, operating as firms and/or consumers.

4 A FIRM, ITS CONSUMERS, AND THE PUBLIC INTEREST

The regulation of economic activities begain in the second half of the last century with the creation of public utility commissions by several states, and the writing of the first federal antitrust legislation. In the 1910s, the tempo began to accelerate with the creation of federal regulatory commissions. The Great Depression witnessed a further increase in public regulatory agencies and laws. As the United States began to move beyond abundance during the fifties, laws and rules continued to proliferate. By some counts, today there are at least 200 bills concerning the limited domain of marketing and advertising activities.

Throughout Part 1, we saw that advertising decisions are affected by laws and rules. We familiarized ourselves especially with those that impinge directly on decisions concerned with content (Chapter 7) and form (Chapter 5, Section 4) of ads. Part 2 will consider many more laws and rules affecting other managerial aspects of advertising, and the subject will become considerably more complex. To avoid possible confusion, we should organize what we have learned so far about the *interface between the public interest and the interest of private parties,* such as single firms and single consumers.

This interface causes natural stresses and conflicts between private and public interests that affect corporate and advertising management. To understand these conflicts and to search for their possible solutions, we must consider (a) the meaning of the term *public interest,* and (b) the role of uncertainty in corporate decision processes.

THE PUBLIC INTEREST

The first factor affecting corporate management is the general meaning of public interest. In principle, Western cultures have equated the public interest with that of society. The public here includes all individuals and all of their public and private organizations (e.g., clubs, partnerships, corporations, churches, political parties, and nonprofit organizations). Laws and regulations make it easy for each member of society to transact business, any business. Defining rights and duties enhances the *public* interest in the sense that *each and every* member can reasonably plan and pursue individual goals.

For our purposes, an important feature of the meaning of public interest is that basic legislation and regulation are generally addressed to all members of a society, not to specific individuals or publics. Society states that if any person wants to enter into any social transactions with any other person, a set of rights, responsibilities, and constraints guide his choices. Within these rules of conduct, each person and organization is free to act according to its own interests. These laws and rules may be characterized as *prohibitory:* in order to protect *and* enhance the interest of all, they place a screen of "thou shall nots" on and around social action.

Other laws and rules are *prescriptive:* they tell the subject "thou shall." Thus, they are actively involved in the subject's decision process. Throughout history, society has often found it necessary to set specific norms concerning decisions about the production and distribution of goods deemed to be of a public nature (e.g., transportation and electricity), or those concerning labor. Corporate management of public utilities, for example, is told very specifically how it ought to compute the rate of return, how to compute and allocate fixed costs to different products and periods, and what specific prices can be charged.

By and large, rules that state what management ought to do—rules that become an integral part of management decision making—find their economic justification in the supply and demand characteristics of public utility operations. It is the economics of the situation that make it useful for society to deprive any potential buyer or seller of the freedom to negotiate certain parts of a transaction; thus, neither a utility nor a consumer can ordinarily negotiate the price or the voltage of a kilowatt. It is the structure of costs and revenues that explains why the interest of *all* publics is best protected by limiting the freedom to negotiate by *any* public—any consumer and any firm.

In recent decades, similar laws and rules have affected an increasing number of decision-making areas. They have affected specific publics (e.g., farmers and labor) and specific types of economic activities (e.g., the sale and purchase of securities, the design of automobiles, and the writing of loan agreements). Recent history, our testimonies and records of the FTC hearings, and current public policy statements all offer strong evidence that there is a clear tendency to formulate laws and rules that are specifically directed toward advertising management as well.

Corporate managers take a negative stance on this "interference" with their decisions. From their viewpoint, the social transaction implied by the sending and seeking/receiving of a message is a transaction between two private parties—a firm and a consumer. As long as the attempt to establish contact by either party respects general laws, and as long as the content of the message is legally and ethically acceptable (e.g., no false statements are made), our witnesses do not see why society should intervene further.

Recent laws, regulations, and FTC policy statements reflect a different point of view. From this perspective, it is in the public interest—i.e., of society as a whole—to establish *the* meaning of an ad: e.g., to establish whether an ad is selling a car, a daydream, or sex. It is in the interest of all consumers to establish whether an athlete who presents a brand of beer is really a beer expert. Or, it is asserted that all society will be better off if regulation establishes that some human motives are rational and others are irrational—for all consumers.

We shall devote an entire chapter (Chapter 13) to examining the substance of these points. For the moment, note that if society were to establish a list of rational human motives, management would have to choose only those advertising themes on the rational list. Or, if society were to insist upon the use of experts, advertising management would have to choose only nutrition experts to present the qualities of a particular breakfast cereal. But what of consumers who may relate to a product on an irrational basis? For instance, what would be the consequences for consumers who may wish to relate to foods through criteria other than nutritional content?

The characteristic feature of this trend in public regulation is that the *public* interest and the *consumer* interest are assumed to be identical. But our witnesses indicated that this is not the case in practice; different consumers have different interests. The witnesses recognized that some interests, such as safety and truthfulness, are common to all consumers, and that laws and rules concerning them are therefore in the public interest, i.e., in the interest of all consumers. But beyond this, the witnesses found it impossible to equate the public interest with the specific interests of different types, or publics, of consumers. A firm can match costs with revenues only if it recognizes that any one product tends to have private meanings that vary from public to public, from one market segment to another.

Current trends in legislation and regulation, however, assert that consumers share more than the need for safety and truthfulness. All consumers, it is stated, share—or ought to share—the same rational motives. All consumers buy—or ought to buy—a car only for its functional attributes as a means of transportation; therefore, it is contrary to the interests of all consumers to advertise and produce cars that differ in nonfunctional attributes such as color, design, and many other nonfunctional, but very popular, notions.

In sum, one source of conflict in the interface between society and its members comes from the different meanings attributed to "public" in the phrase "public interest." From the business perspective, public and consumer interests are the same only for health, safety, and truthfulness. Beyond that, there are many types of consumers with different interests, and the content of the communication between a firm and any one consumer type is a private affair. Only these two parties—not society—can judge and decide what is in their interest. Current regulatory trends, however, assume a sameness in consumers' interests with regard to product attributes and motivations. If one accepts this premise, it is perfectly logical to require firms to introduce such considerations into their advertising decision making.

At first glance, one might conclude that there is no possible solution to the conflict between the two points of view. Yet the dynamics of the situation suggest that many social managers believe there is only one solution. That is, legislators and regulators have the legal power to intervene in management decision making. Thus, just as they have the power to declare the production and sale of certain drugs unlawful, they could also prescribe to advertising management that cars can be referred to in ads only as means of transportation. Or, as one of the witnesses reminded the FTC commissioners, since ties fill no known functional need, lawmakers thus might decide to declare the advertising and production of ties unlawful.

Corporate managers will resist these attempts at intervention in choice making by firms and by individual consumers. Nevertheless, at least in the short run, the extent to which society believes that consumers feel and think alike—or even the extent to which society believes that consumers ought to feel and think alike—is largely determined by the makers of laws and regulations themselves.

In principle, limiting the choices of corporate management also implies limiting the consumers' choices. In practice, the extent to which consumers may resent this limitation is difficult to assess. The oft-quoted fact that consumers are ill-equipped to bargain with the private sector applies even more to their inability to influence legislators and regulators, at least in the short run.

DECISION MAKING UNDER UNCERTAINTY

Although management considers its communication with potential buyers a private dialogue, within general rules of conduct, regulators want to participate actively and transform the dialogue into a three-way communication. Several testimonies in this and the following part argue that such intervention essentially erodes the principle of freedom of choice and thus the political ideology of the country.

In addition a consideration of an intrinsic managerial nature underlies the business point of view. The testimonies repeatedly underscore that further legislation and regulation of advertising decisions will create a higher degree of uncertainty than that faced at present. And management, understandably, abhors uncertainty.

The major source of uncertainty for those who make advertising and corporate decisions is the same one that affects any firm operating in a postindustrial, affluent society. This overall uncertainty is caused by two interdependent factors. First, any entity must somehow find a balance between inputs and outputs if it is to survive. It should be enough here to recall Alchian's or Penrose's early biological analogies, Wiener's cybernetic notions, or Boulding's and Churchman's system ideas: the need for ecological balance between inputs (costs) and outputs (revenues) applies to human organizations also, including private and public firms. Second, the conditions affecting the behavior of costs (inputs) differ drastically from those affecting revenues (outputs). And the differences increase as a society becomes more affluent.

On the *cost* side, corporate management faces increasingly limited options in decision making. More and more costs are fixed—not only traditional plant and equipment costs, but also labor and government services. Materials, supplies, and inventories are fixed costs too, because they are needed to produce outputs which, *if* sold, provide the revenues needed to meet expenses. The demands of input factors on the firm—be it private or public—are there at the end of each month or quarter. They must be met sooner or later by revenues or tax subsidies. This ecological balance is elementary in theory but difficult to achieve in business practice.

Then we have another cost: *technology.* Improved technology can lead to lower cost —*if* one can sell more.[1] Lower unit costs are obtained through the investment in new and

---

[1] Unsold output is a waste of resources. In a decentralized economy, the cost of such mistakes is mostly borne by private groups and, at the total economy level, it may be compensated to the extent that other firms made the right decisions. In a centralized economy, the mistake of producing unwanted goods tends to be borne more directly by the entire society and has a lower probability of being compensated by other decisions.

larger "quantities" of technology, which means higher fixed costs. In this sense, technology affects management in the same way as the other input factors.

But the rate of technological change must increase in order to meet the demands of affluent consumers. Thus, today's new technology, with its attendant fixed costs, may be obsolete tomorrow because a competitor has adopted a still newer technology. In a word, technology means both the certainty of high fixed costs and the uncertainty of being able to meet such costs tomorrow. It hits management both ways.

Let us now turn to *revenues*. Unlike costs, revenues are not fixed. At the managerial level, the most impressive characteristic of an affluent society is the increasing difficulty of predicting how consumers will behave.

Increasing amounts of discretionary income *and* time allow each consumer to try out various styles of life: trials are more within the reach of each consumer, and errors are less costly. Strong empirical evidence of the volatility of the affluent consumer was presented in this part and more will be given in the next. For each firm, this means that it is increasingly difficult to make plans and to know where revenues will come from. The amount of revenues each firm can count on tomorrow to meet the continuing demands of fixed costs is very uncertain indeed.

Each firm is caught in this dilemma: costs are fixed and must be met, but revenues are neither fixed nor certain. Consumer research, marketing, and, of course, advertising become the instruments to reduce uncertainty on the revenue side. They are means of adaptation based on understanding consumers and their differences, relating to some consumers, and anticipating, if possible, their sudden changes in preferences.

But fixed costs, technological change, and affluent consumers are no longer the only sources of uncertainty that affect corporate management decision making. Increasingly, *legislation and regulation* are also becoming a new and powerful source of uncertainty.

In most cases, as we shall see in Part 2, attempts to regulate the content of ads are based on value judgments and thus on subjective criteria. Since there can be as many criteria as there are government officials, advertisers and agencies cannot at any given time know which ad is permissible. The costly uncertainty of determining which government official will interpret which ad in which way is now added to the difficulty of knowing which consumer will interpret which ad in which way. And, beyond falseness, regulation of ads' content cannot help affluent consumers either. At best, such regulation will help those of us in the consumer research profession to chase down all the possible meanings of an ad under scrutiny—and then to disagree among ourselves on methodology.

Because of the role they must play, government officials tend to be unaware of the uncertainties faced by different firms and the ensuing problems of balancing costs and revenues. The very nature of their mandate—to protect the public interest in general— tends to make them insensitive to the increasing differentiation among affluent consumers. To satisfy their mandate, these officials find it useful to perceive a sameness among consumers that goes beyond considerations of safety and health to include aspirations and predispositions.

Nor can we ignore that government officials, trapped in the growing subculture of an ever-increasing population of regulatory agencies, necessarily tend to invest their limited resources into more visible activities. Swayed by political winds and faced with the realities of obtaining budget approvals, their priorities tend to switch from emphasis on health, safety, and similar problems common to all consumers to issues that are more apt to endanger an agency's survival. Almost imperceptibly, regulators and their staffs tend to become slowly but inexorably insulated from the varied interests of different consumers.

As we have seen, no one firm can address itself to all consumers. It can merely attempt to establish a successful dialogue with one or more specific consumer groups. But legislators and regulators must often relate to all consumers—to the general public rather than to some specific public. This difference in perspective necessarily leads to stress and conflict between firms and government officials. The officials search for solutions by simplifying the nature of affluent consumers, and by postulating the existence of an average consumer characterized by a typical rationality and a broad spectrum of identical needs. To the extent that uniformity of aspirations and behavior decreases in affluent societies, laws and rules are bound to be based on shifting ground. Thus, neither the interpretation and application of extant laws and rules nor the promulgation of new ones can be predicted by management.

5 SUMMARY

In Chapter 1 we began with a description of the major components of the advertising institution, i.e., the milieu in which advertisers and agencies operate. The testimonies and commentaries in Part 1 identified the ways in which corporate management visualizes the role of a firm's advertising function. We spelled out the major phases of advertising decision processes and showed how such processes are a part of the overall corporate problem of balancing costs and revenues. In particular, we noted the ubiquitous presence of the consumer in everything from planning to execution, control, and evaluation of advertising decisions.

We also noted the ubiquitous role of legislation and regulation, for they bear on decision making by both individual firms and individual consumers. Anticipating the discussion of many themes in Part 2, we sketched the basic tension between individual and social decisions. As more laws and rules are inserted into the dialogue between a firm and a group of potential customers, the tension continues to increase.

From the perspective of corporate management, there are at least two major factors creating stress. First, while a firm attempts to communicate with specific publics or segments of consumers, legislators and regulators relate to all publics and to the general public. Second, laws and rules ask management to address itself to the needs of an average consumer just at the time in history when consumers are becoming more differentiated. At the same time, it is becoming increasingly difficult to interpret current laws and rules or to predict possible new ones. Thus legislation and regulation become additional sources of uncertainty impinging upon corporate and advertising management.

In principle, it is reasonable to assume that private and public managers have some common goals. At the very least, both must resolve the tension between the interests of individual firms and individual consumers, on the one hand, and the interests of the public at large—i.e., society—on the other. What do we need to know to come up with improvements in the current situation? To find possible solutions to the conflict between the individual and society?

We shall search for such knowledge in Part 2. Equipped with an understanding of advertising as a business function, we are ready to raise the level of our study in order to gain an understanding of advertising as an institution and of its roles in the economy and in society. Although our study will be more complex and arduous, it will lead us to a clearer and more useful conceptualization of the interface between individual and social interests as they apply to the exchange of economic information via mass media.

Part Two

The Advertising Institution and Society

A Macro View:

The Nature and Roles of Advertising in a Socioeconomic System

*I do not seek to know all
the answers, I seek to
understand the questions*

Chapter 10

The Advertising Institution

Introductory Comments

OUTLINE

1 The Study of the Advertising Institution: Problems and Challenges

2 Organization of Part 2

After sketching the complexity of the entire advertising institution in Chapter 1, we focused on the activities of the advertiser and the advertising agency. In Part 1 our approach was micromanagerial, examining advertising decision making at the level of the individual firm. In Part 2 we move from micro to macro problems. Our examination will now be focused on the entire advertising institution and its roles in a socioeconomic system. In this introductory chapter we begin to familiarize ourselves with the nature, purposes, and challenges of a macro study of advertising.

1 THE STUDY OF THE ADVERTISING INSTITUTION: PROBLEMS AND CHALLENGES

The advertising institution was earlier defined as the set of all activities of individuals and organizations as they relate to the sending and the seeking/receiving of "economic" information via mass media. The institution thus includes such *classes* of subjects as the senders of ads; the advertising agencies; the mass media; the seekers/receivers of messages; legislators, regulatory agencies, and courts; and the messages that flow throughout the institution. Note that the advertising institution is only one part of a society's mass communication system, i.e., the system that provides for the flow of information concerning human events in politics, religion, education, and so on.

There are several reasons why it is imperative that society understand the advertising institution as a whole—that is, approach the study of advertising at the macro level. The primary reasons are economic and social. From the very beginning of this book we noted that every social group relies increasingly upon a system of mass communication as its size grows and as it becomes more dependent on specialized technologies. It is almost a truism to assert that the well-being of any such group is affected by the organization of its mass communication system. Each possible form of organization

153

implies a different combination of costs and benefits. Costs and benefits can be evaluated in terms of a society's preferences as well as in strict economic terms. Ultimately, a social choice of one type of advertising institution over another is bound to reflect both economic and social criteria.

In fact, much of the debate about advertising concerns the institution as a whole. Even criticisms of a single ad or TV program may rest upon and ultimately reinforce conclusions about the entire institution. Similarly, legislation is directly or indirectly concerned with such questions as: Does advertising hurt small business? Create drug dependence? Provide accurate information? All these involve the socioeconomic roles of the institution and its overall costs and benefits. Finally, administrative and judicial decisions—even when ostensibly concerned with determining the truthfulness of a particular ad or granting a license to a particular radio station—are also attempts to improve advertising's contributions to society. None of these macro issues can be resolved without understanding how the institution actually works and how it interacts with other parts of society.

If it is true that any social group needs to assure itself of optimal performance from its mass communication system—which includes advertising—it is also true that this goal can be attained only on the basis of facts. Two types of facts are essential: first, we need to know the social, political, and cultural preferences of a society; second, we must also know the costs and benefits inherent in the different organizational forms the advertising institution may take.

FACTS CONCERNING SOCIETY'S PREFERENCES

Legislators, regulatory agencies, and courts need to know a society's preferences since these determine the kinds of decisions they make about advertising. In a highly centralized political system, for instance, industrial advertising may take the form of bulletins, circulars, trade meetings, and other forms of "acceptable" mass communication. In a politically open and decentralized system, however, exchange of information can also occur through personal salesmen, direct mail, trade magazines, shows, and the like. Similarly, the cultural preferences of a group will affect the content of ads. Thus, contraceptives can be advertised in some societies but not in others.

Identifying these social, political, and cultural preferences is a difficult task. In principle, democratic societies have a system that should make the task relatively easy: voters' preferences are expressed by elected legislators in the form of laws, which, in turn, are interpreted and implemented by regulatory agencies and courts. Changes in voters' preferences are reflected by changes in elected representatives, laws, and interpretations of laws.

In practice, it is more complicated. Changes may come about slowly because of built-in rigidities. In our country, for instance, United States representatives are elected for two years, presidents for four years, and United States senators for six years. Thus, changes in social preferences cannot be reflected by immediate changes in the law. Further, elected officials may misread the voters' preferences. Finally, regulatory agencies and the courts themselves may, openly or unknowingly, incorporate their own social preferences into their decisions.

An even more important complication is the existence of multiple and differing values and institutions within the same society. In a pluralistic society, no advertising institution is likely to please everyone. And proposed changes, also, will please some and displease others.

While we shall not discuss what United States preferences are, we shall discover again and again that much of the contemporary debate about the advertising institution is founded in disagreements about what society does or should prefer. And we shall often conclude our analyses with a plea for clarification of such preferences by legislators, regulators, and the courts.

The present ambiguities in laws and regulations inevitably hamper the economic performance of advertising. Such a state of affairs also makes it difficult to identify and assess the costs and benefits of the present advertising institution, thus depriving the public of the knowledge necessary to plan and implement improvements.

FACTS CONCERNING THE ECONOMICS OF THE ADVERTISING INSTITUTION

To achieve optimal performance of the advertising institution it is also necessary to know how its components interact; the costs and benefits of differing modes of organizing the institution; and its socioeconomic roles. The testimonies and commentaries in Part 2 stress the search for, and evaluation of, facts that describe the technical features of the advertising institution.

In this part we wish to establish specific facts that describe, and hopefully explain, the exchange of economic information via the mass communication system. But, as we shall see, the task is a difficult one.

Let us briefly discuss why this is so. To begin with, stereotypes of advertising sometimes hinder rational consideration of existing data. The distortions that stereotypes impose on facts are not, of course, limited to advertising. In a classic experiment in the 1920s, Lasker gave children a silent reading test in which one item was:

> Aladin was the son of a poor tailor. He lived in Peking, the capital city of China. He was always idle and lazy and liked to play better than to work. What kind of a boy was he: Indian; Negro; Chinese; French; or Dutch?[1]

The most common answer was "Negro."

But although we have become increasingly aware of the influence of racial, religious, and ethnic stereotypes, there is almost no acknowledgement that stereotypes about advertising may also interfere with the ability to deal rationally with existing data.

Many people, for example, believe that there is more advertising at present than in the "good old days." In reality, advertising expenditures as a percentage of both gross national product and personal consumption expenditures have decreased from 3.3 percent and 4.4 percent, respectively, in 1929 to 1.9 percent and 3.1 percent, respectively, in 1971. It is generally believed also that the institution *causes* economic changes, but all available data suggest that, to a large extent, the institution tends to follow—i.e., adapt to—economic changes.

[1] B. Lasker, *Race Attitudes in Children*, Holt, New York, 1929, p. 237.

A third example: TV is generally considered the major vehicle for advertising addressed to consumers. But, after the initial growth period, TV achieved a substantial equilibrium in its relationships with other mass media. In fact, total TV advertising expenditures have been hovering around 60 percent of total newspaper advertising expenditures for some time (about $4.1 billion for TV and $7.0 billion for newspapers in 1972).

Ignoring known facts affects not only cocktail party conversations but also, and more importantly, legislation and regulation. The greatest weakness of the historical debate about advertising is that it is filled with value judgments about the institution, even though it is rarely clear which facts are being evaluated. The multilogue referred to in the preface will be possible and bear fruit only if we have relevant facts. Only when these are available, and rationally considered, can we proceed to ask whether the existing situation is good or bad with respect to social goals. Then we will be better able to suggest directions for legislative and regulatory action, i.e., criteria for allocation of public funds. To illustrate this critical point, let us anticipate some of the cases to be discussed later.

First, there is some evidence that relatively few consumer complaints received by government agencies concern advertising. And, of these complaints, most are directed at local rather than national advertising. Yet, at present, the majority of federal agencies' efforts are directed toward the regulation and policing of national rather than local advertising.

Second, substantial funds are devoted to assessing and reducing the possible effects of violence in TV programs directed to children. But no public agency seems to have noticed that the amount of time children between the ages of two and five are *allowed* to spend in front of a TV set *after 5:00 PM* equals 47 percent of their total TV viewing time. For children between six and eleven, this amount increases to 67 percent of their total TV viewing time. It is thus doubtful that we can reach any satisfactory solution to this problem if we ignore the engineering nature of the phenomenon, i.e., the intervening social process represented by the roles of parents.

Basic and applied evidence in the behavioral sciences documents the impossibility of defining objectively the meaning of a message—i.e., its informational content— independently of the point of view of the receiver. Nevertheless, federal agencies are devoting much of their energies to a search for "objective information," thus diverting their scarce resources from the task of seeking out false advertising in the areas of consumer health and safety.

Finally, it is generally believed that the reduction or abolition of national TV advertising would reduce prices and thus consumer expenditures. However, since national network TV advertising expenditures in 1971 were $2.7 billion and personal consumption expenditures were $665 billion, abolition of these expenditures would amount to a very small potential per capita saving. Furthermore, in order to conclude that this would, in fact, yield a saving, other facts would have to be established. For instance, we would have to establish that all TV national advertising had absolutely no informational value for any consumer; if it did have, then this value would have to be subtracted from the "saving." And since national TV programs are supported by advertising, the saving would also have to be reduced by the cost of providing consumers with alternative sources of general news and entertainment. And so on. Consideration of simple facts at least establishes the magnitude of the problems and provides the direction for reaching solutions that will satisfy the public interest.

The interplay between stereotypes of advertising and existing knowledge is one of the factors that will make the task of Part 2 difficult and challenging. Because of the current gaps in our knowledge and the influence of stereotypes, an unbelievably high number of assumptions are accepted and communicated as facts. Let us quote from a most authoritative journal in scientific disciplines:

> .... Yet we proceeded to fumble our way toward a system under which advertising and its *influence,* while not *drowning* the media, certainly *dominated* its development, preempted its time, and *controlled* its programming. ... Now in the 1970s, we see television showered with time-consuming, obtrusive, and sometimes dishonest commercials endeavoring to sell a *captive* audience products that the viewers often *do not need*—or that may be useless or downright harmful—and at *artificially elevated* prices.[1]

The terms that we have italicized indicate only a few of the assumptions presented as known facts. As our analysis unfolds, we shall see that some of these assumptions are wrong, others are untested, and still others have been explored with very conflicting results. We should not be surprised, of course, that such things can happen even in scientific media. Scientists are also human,[2] and they are susceptible to the emotional involvement that triggers most conversations dealing with advertising and its socioeconomic roles. But the prevailing mixture of emotion and fact will make it difficult for us to separate one from the other.

And what about the facts that are known? How numerous, how basic, and how robust are they? Unfortunately, the quantity and quality of current knowledge about the advertising institution are primitive. In Part 2 we shall learn that the available data cover only a limited number of the institution's properties and are, at best, rough approximations of the information needed for public policy decisions. More importantly, it will become clear that we have not yet developed the concepts that are necessary in order to study advertising at the macro level. It has become relatively easy in recent times to create "numbers," but, without clear concepts, data are not valid measures of relevant facts and cannot provide legislators, regulators, or courts with a basis on which to optimize the performance of the institution.

---

[1] From *Science* 13:1263–64, quoted in J. G. Myers, "The Structure of an Advertising Message," *Journal of Advertising*, Spring 1974. Italics are ours.

[2] The subjectivity of science and scientists has recently become the object of empirical evidence; see, e.g., I. I. Mitroff, "The Myth of Objectivity or Why Science Needs a New Psychology of Science," *Management Science*, June 1972.

THE MACRO APPROACH

The final difficulty—and challenge—we shall meet in Part 2 stems from the novelty of a macro approach to the study of advertising. With very few exceptions,[1] advertising has always been studied as a management function. The approach has always been micro-managerial, even though private and public judgments, as well as legislation and regulation, concern the entire institution. But to use knowledge about micro phenomena to describe and evaluate macro phenomena is often misleading.

Other disciplines have acknowledged the necessity for distinguishing between micro and macro approaches in studying human and physical events. In economics, for example, the study of individual firms or consumers provided a limited basis for understanding and regulating the entire economic system. Thus, a macroeconomic approach had to be invented. If we study a system of interaction among subjects, we cannot understand the behavior of the group merely by adding together what we know of each subject. In an interactive system, the sum of the parts often differs form the whole.

A major feature of Part 2 is a systematic inquiry into how we can conceptualize advertising as an institution, as a macro entity embedded in the larger system of economic interactions, which, in turn are only part of our society. To do this, we use the theories, facts, and methods of basic and applied disciplines, especially economics, psychology, and sociology.

The facts and views of the witnesses reported in Part 2 are cast in this macro approach. Their meaning and limitations and, ultimately, the pros and cons of advertising, become clearer. More important, as we interpret and clarify the conceptual and empirical content of the testimonies from the point of view of business, we identify some of the knowledge society needs in order to regulate its advertising institution optimally.

All in all, Part 2 is more complex and challenging than Part 1. Fewer facts are available, and we must also struggle with the necessity for conceptualizing an institution which, by its very nature, is not perceivable by our senses in the same way as ads, newspapers, and TV shows are. Finally, we shall discuss topics that are often loaded with emotional content, and here it will be hard to appreciate theories and points of view that may contradict instinctive feelings. But if we succeed in understanding the technical reasons supporting the business point of view, we can develop a better understanding of other points of view, of the workings of the advertising institution, and hopefully of the changes that can be made to satisfy social goals.[2]

---

[1] See, especially, some of the questions raised by J. Simon in his *Issues in the Economics of Advertising*, University of Illinois Press, Urbana, Ill., 1970, Ch. 7, and R. Schmalensee, *The Economics of Advertising*, North-Holland Publishing Co., Amsterdam, Holland, 1972. The macro approach presented in the following chapters is an attempt to respond systematically to L. Bogart's invitation "Why don't we start with the big picture, with a view of advertising as a tremendous institution which deserves study in its own right?" (From "Where Does Advertising Research Go From Here?" *Journal of Advertising Research,* March 1969, p. 10.)

[2] In practically all cases, the testimonies are addressed to other points of view and are thus bound to cover most of the fundamental issues concerning advertising and society. The arguments used to explain the business view reflect, of course, the dialectical nature of current attempts to understand advertising—in this sense, as in any other debate in the political arena or in front of a court, the arguments are naturally biased.

2 THE ORGANIZATION OF PART 2

The systematic review of what is known about the advertising institution begins with a testimony that gathers most of the relevant and available macro data in concise form (Chapter 11). These data and the concepts underlying them are examined in the commentaries. The examination then continues by exploring differences across countries and across time, possible interaction between advertising and the economy, and the structural relationships that may have governed growth of both the advertising and economic systems during the past forty years.

In Chapter 11 we study the advertising institution and its socioeconomic roles at the maximum macro level, but in Chapter 12 we focus on the more specific roles the institution may play. The first role relates to the ways in which the institution interacts with the mass communication system as a whole. The testimonies of two publishers discuss (a) the extent to which the advertising institution pays for the cost of the entire communication system, and (b) the extent to which the institution helps to maintain a "press" free from governmental control and other pressures and open to diverse viewpoints in politics, religion, and other areas of social life.

Chapter 12 continues with a testimony that introduces the relatively new and controversial topic known as the economics of information. Going beyond more traditional economic theory, new developments in this area stress that information is not free, that humans do not—and cannot—have perfect information. The advertising institution is therefore seen as an industry that both produces information and competes with other means of communication such as word-of-mouth, personal selling, labels, and package and product design. The commentaries sketch the lively debate between the new and the more traditional viewpoints. They also show how the conceptual debate influences the measurement of the effects advertising may have at the industry level; on prices, profits, and industry concentration; and on other economic yardsticks.

The examination of the macro roles of advertising in Chapters 11 and 12 relies, by and large, on economic considerations. Chapters 13 and 14 broaden the scope of the study and systematically introduce concepts and findings from the behavioral sciences. The kinds of effects to be identified and assessed are behavioral and of direct concern to the consumer.

We proceed in two steps. In Chapter 13 we ask whether messages flowing through mass media—including ads—can affect the seekers/receivers; what kinds of effects have been observed in basic research; and under what kinds of conditions. The first part of the chapter reviews basic literature in social psychology and communication research. With this background, we turn to the discussion of the term *information*. While this term has a reasonably clear meaning within the economic theories used in the previous chapters, the behavioral science perspective leads us to a fundamental distinction between information (that which is in the message) and communication (that which is perceived by a seeker/receiver of a message).

We shall find that the interpretation of the information content of a message varies from person to person. Thus, although there are ways to measure information objectively, its interpretation is bound to be subjective. This basic knowledge allows us to search for the qualities that may make information manipulative. The search here is for operational definitions of manipulative information; only these definitions can be used objectively by legislators, regulators, and courts in their attempts to pinpoint socially undesirable effects of advertising and to prevent manipulative information from flowing through the advertising institution.

After having studied whether and when the advertising institution *can* manipulate consumers, we turn to the question of whether it *does* do this in Chapter 14. One of the testimonies discusses, from a humanistic perspective, whether words do manipulate consumers. The other turns to a large set of previously unpublished data to explore whether there is evidence of manipulation in consumer buying and attitudes. The last two testimonies discuss the institution's possible effects on children and its possible relationships with the use of illegal drugs.

Chapters 11 through 14 develop the concepts necessary for a macro study of advertising, gather and evaluate pertinent data, and introduce new data. Equipped with this knowledge, and aware of its limitations, we turn in Chapter 15 to the problems of regulation that are at the core of much of the historical debate about advertising. The business point of view is presented by two testimonies. One forcefully examines trends in public regulation, especially by the Federal Trade Commission. The other describes a recent and comprehensive new system of self-regulation devised and implemented by advertisers and advertising agencies, and reports the activities and results of the first year of the system's operations.

Chapter 11

The Macro Roles of the Advertising Institution

In this chapter we begin a systematic review of what we know and do not know about the possible macro relationships between the advertising institution and the economy and society. While our knowledge of this topic is extremely elementary, the social and economic questions are crucial, and the problems are challenging.

Section 1 reproduces a testimony that gives a quantitative picture of the advertising institution and its relationships with the economy and the household sector, i.e., consumers. The concepts and measures on which this picture is based are limited in several important ways. These limitations and the ensuing problems are discussed at length in Section 2.

In Section 3 we discuss ways to overcome the current limitations in concepts and data and examine analytical procedures that can yield the kind of knowledge policy makers need to provide an efficient and effective mass communication system. For example, it may be useful to compare different countries at one point in time and through time. We especially examine two most crucial questions: (1) How can we discover the effects of the advertising institution on the economy as a whole, and vice versa? and (2) using available data, can we determine the structural relationships between the economic and advertising systems that may have governed the growth of these systems during the past forty years?

1   THE ADVERTISING INSTITUTION: SOME BASIC FACTS
(excerpts from E. M. Thiele, vice chairman, Leo Burnett Co.)

This part of Mr. Thiele's testimony brings together data concerning the general nature of the institution. Although these data have long been available, they have rarely been put together in such an accessible and informative manner.

Mr. Thiele's presentation is very matter-of-fact, as if he had purposely avoided drawing inferences, reaching conclusions of fact, or making value judgments. It is indeed difficult to interpret such seemingly straightforward data: the commentaries will examine these difficulties and point to ways to overcome them.

> *In this presentation I would like to give a broad overview of the size and scope of the advertising industry, with some emphasis on how advertisers and advertising agencies are organized and how they work together. . . .*
>
> *The advertising business in the U.S. represents an expenditure by American industry of an estimated $19,715,000,000 in 1970. This is 2% of the gross national product, and that percentage has remained virtually constant since 1940 (Exhibit 11.1). The advertising industry represents the country's largest service industry, working for over 17,000 companies.[1]*

EXHIBIT 11.1

	Total Advertising Volume	Gross National Product	Ad Volume As % of GNP
	(Billions of $)	(Billions of $)	
1940	2.08	99.7	2.09%
1950	5.71	284.8	2.00
1960	11.93	503.8	2.37
1970	19.80	976.1	2.03

Source: Handbook of Basic Economic Statistics, July 1971, p. 225, and Marketing/Communications, July 1971.

[1] "Advertising–Today–Yesterday–Tomorrow," Section 1, "The Growth of Advertising," *Printer's Ink,* June 14, 1963, *Standard Directory of Advertising,* 1971.

According to the Department of Commerce, an advertising volume of over $18 billion in 1968 placed advertising in the top 20 industrial group categories and ahead of such industries as mining, tobacco, leather, lumber, furniture, air transportation, hotels, and motion pictures (Exhibit 11.2).

EXHIBIT 11.2

Industry	1968 Sales (MM)
Retail	$237,092
Wholesale	205,418
Food	86,342
Contract Construction	70,831
Petroleum	63,436
Automobiles	57,988
Chemicals	51,081
Machinery	48,782
Electrical Machinery	46,362
Primary Metals	43,564
Fabricated Metals	36,429
Transportation Equipment	34,872
Telephone & Telegraph	23,486
Apparel	22,661
Textiles	20,822
ADVERTISING	18,127
Motor Freight	16,984
Stone, Clay and Glass	14,228
Mining	13,795
Instruments	12,432

Source: Survey of Current Business, July 1971, p. 40.

The percentage of sales spent in advertising in 1968 was an average of 1.17% for all industrial groups. The range was from a low of 0.14 advertising to sales ratio for mining industries to a high of 3.30% advertising to sales ratio for nondurables. It is important to note also that almost every major industry spends some money in advertising (Exhibit 11.3). Within these major industrial groups there are several important subgroupings which should be mentioned, such as drugs, food, automobiles, and clothing (Exhibit 11.4). The percentage of advertising to sales for all industries has remained stable since 1954 (Exhibit 11.5).

The total advertising expenditures by American industry is about 3% of all personal consumption expenditures. This ratio too has remained [relatively] stable since 1940 (Exhibit 11.6). The current rate of advertising of $19.8 billion amounts to just under $100 for each person in the United States.[1]

[1] *Handbook of Basic Economic Statistics,* July 1971, p. 225, *Marketing/Communications,* June 10, 1971.

EXHIBIT 11.3

Industry Group	Advertising As % of Sales
Nondurable Goods	3.30%
Durable Goods	2.07
Services	1.79
Wholesale and Retail	1.03
Communication	0.71
Transportation	0.65
Agriculture, Fisheries, Forestry	0.48
Contract Construction	0.19
Mining	0.14
Total Average	1.17%

EXHIBIT 11.4

Industry Subgroup	Advertising As % of Sales
Drugs	9.54%
Food	2.52
Automobiles	1.14
Clothing	0.82

EXHIBIT 11.5

Year	Advertising As % of Sales
1954	1.09%
1956	1.07
1958	1.13
1960	1.16
1962	1.16
1964	1.18
1966	1.19
1968	1.17

Source: Advertising Age, January 25, 1971, p. 77. Data taken from Internal Revenue Service files.

EXHIBIT 11.6

Year	Total Advertising Volume	Personal Consumption Expenditures	Total Advertising As % of P.C.E.
	(Billions of $)	(Billions of $)	
1940	2.08	70.8	2.94%
1950	5.71	191.0	2.99
1960	11.93	325.2	3.67
1970	19.80	616.7	3.21

Source: Marketing Communications, July 1971, pp. 50-51.

The total advertising expenditure by American industry each year involves many diverse elements which comprise the advertising industry. These are: Advertising departments of companies; advertising agencies; publishing (newspapers and magazines); broadcasting (TV and radio); direct mail; graphic arts; outdoor and car card; premium and sales promotion; research films; and specialty and novelty. It is estimated that the industry employs over 1,000,000 people, with commercial printing and broadcasting alone accounting for some 489,000 employees.[1]

As we have seen, the advertising appropriations that pass through this system in order to sell goods and services to the American consumers are substantial. The great bulk of these expenditures are paid to the media which carry the advertisements. A look at the expenditures in 1970 by media dramatizes the diversity of communicational channels in American society and the substantial support of a free press and electronic entertainment by advertising (Exhibit 11.7). Among the media, newspapers enjoy the greatest support, followed by television, magazines, and radio (Exhibit 11.8).

EXHIBIT 11.7

Media	Amount (MM) 1970	% of Total
Publications, Newspapers	$ 7,140	36.2%
Broadcast (TV and Radio)	4,938	25.0
Direct Mail	2,736	13.9
Business Papers	714	3.6
Outdoor	237	1.2
Farm Publications	63	0.3
Miscellaneous (Point of Purchase, Car Cards, Weekly Newspapers)	3,887	19.8
Total	$19,715	100.0%

EXHIBIT 11.8

Mass Media	Amount (MM) 1970	% of All Media
Newspapers	$ 5,745	29.1%
Television	3,665	18.6
Magazines	1,323	6.7
Radio	1,278	6.5
Total	$12,011	60.9%

Source: Marketing Communications, July 1971, pp. 50–51.

[1] *Employment and Earnings, August 1971.*

It is important to make a distinction between national and local advertising. They may be defined as follows. National advertising is advertising by manufacturers or sellers of service who market on a broad geographic basis (either regional or national) and whose advertising contains little or no local reference. Local advertising is advertising which is directed to a limited geographic area, in large part by local merchants usually indicating at what price a product or service is available. In 1971, 59% of advertising was national; 41% was local.[1]

Advertising dollars that go to the various media are allocated and spent either directly by advertisers or through advertising agencies. Of the total advertising expenditure in 1970, the 4,000 advertising agencies in America placed less than half.[2] *Generally speaking, advertising agencies are most often used by national advertisers, while department stores and other large, local merchants maintain their own advertising departments for preparation and placement of their advertising. Smaller advertisers depend on the various local media for assistance in the mechanical production of their advertising.*

In Summary: The advertising industry in the United States is a large and important industry—among the top 20 industries in the country. The industry represents an expenditure of over 2% of the gross national product. It employs directly over 1,000,000 people, and it affects the business lives of millions more indirectly. The growth of the advertising industry parallels directly the growth of all business in the nation. About 40% of all advertising is "local" advertising and is placed by retail merchants. About 60% is "national" advertising by advertisers whose products are sold on a broad, geographic basis. Much of this advertising revenue is placed through advertising agencies.

[1] *Marketing/Communications,* July 1971, pp. 50–51.

[2] U.S. Census of Business.

2 UNDERSTANDING THE SOCIOECONOMIC ROLES OF THE ADVERTISING INSTITUTION: CONCEPTS AND DATA[1]

It is human to assume that "facts speak for themselves." Yet, like any other stimulus, facts (e.g., data) are also perceived via perceptual processes and are ultimately interpreted subjectively (see Chapter 13, Section 2). Let us illustrate this point, for it is crucial to the analysis that follows.

One person may feel that the increase in total advertising expenditures since 1950 is "enormous" (see Exhibit 11.1), a proof that our society indeed spends "too much" on advertising. Another may conclude that since advertising expenditures, as a percentage

[1] I want to thank R. Artle, M. Etgar, R. Ferber, P. Gerhold, A. Reza, B. Roberts, R. Schmalensee, and Y. Wind for several helpful suggestions. I owe much to the challenges and contributions of my undergraduate and graduate students over a number of years. I also learned from the reactions of R. Holton, S. Magee, and S. P. Sethi when I presented some of the ideas in the text in one of their seminars a few years ago.

of gross national product, have remained constant for thirty years, our society has not become more advertising-oriented. A third may argue that because more pressing social needs have emerged, part of the resources allocated to advertising should have been directed elsewhere. A fourth may counter that if advertising expenditures had not increased, economic growth would have been lower. Still others may simply dismiss much of the above data, noting that advertising expenditures and gross national product are not valid measures of the roles of advertising in the economic system. In all these cases, different perceptions—of social goals and economic means of attaining them—create different interpretations of the very same "facts."

Even with agreement on goals, the same data may lead to different interpretations if we lack engineering knowledge of how an institution works. Consider a husband and wife driving along a highway. Their engine starts to emit strange noises, and they begin to argue about whether the car can make it to their destination. If both are ignorant about what is under the hood, they are wasting their time. Only a knowledgeable mechanic can judge whether the car is likely to get them to their goal and, if it is not likely to do so, what action is advisable.

These remarks set the stage for the discussion below. Over the centuries, *both* a lack of engineering knowledge *and* disagreement on goals have hindered our ability to assess the advertising institution. On one hand, we have no engineering base on which to judge whether it is *efficient* for a society to allocate 2 or 3 or 4 percent of its gross national product to advertising in order to achieve certain economic and social goals. On the other, a society may have goals other than economic efficiency. Thus it is possible to have an efficient advertising institution that is not *effective* because it conflicts with social goals such as freedom of political thought or a change in the distribution of income and wealth. Unfortunately, we do not have a list of our society's goals, nor of their relative importance. Even if we did, we could not compute the loss (or gain) of efficiency needed to make the institution more effective, for we do not know the efficiency of present or alternative advertising institutions.

Both efficiency and effectiveness must be considered in order to understand the socioeconomic roles of advertising. The following section defines the concepts of efficiency and effectiveness and indicates their value in our analysis.[1]

---

[1] Our examination is both a simplification and a limited application of welfare economics. For example, we treat the social choice of an optimal advertising institution only in an ex-ante planning context and only barely touch upon the question of costs inherent in change from one type of institution to another. For the roles of welfare economics concerning the choice or evaluation of an advertising institution, see R. Schmalensee, "Advertising and Economic Welfare," in S. Divita (ed.), *Advertising and the Public Interest*, American Marketing Association, Chicago, Ill., 1974. In limiting our examination to the traditional concepts of efficiency and effectiveness, we are particularly overlooking some of the insights gained by recent literature that also considers the concept of *equity* (e.g., considerations of real-income distribution, quality of life, number of options available to each member of a social group in choosing a life style, and rate of utilization of natural resources) and the concept of *public good* (e.g., communication systems like the telephone that are characterized by the "access–no access" property). On the concept of equity, see, e.g., P. Varaiya and R. Artle, "Locational Implications of Transaction Costs," *The Swedish Journal of Economics*, vol. 74, 1972, and R. Artle, "Urbanization and Economic Growth in Venezuela," reprint from Vol. XXVII, Papers, Regional Science Association, n.d. For the concept of *public good*, see, e.g., R. Artle and C. Avernous, "The Telephone System as a Public Good: Static and Dynamic Aspects," *Bell Journal of Economics and Management Science*, Spring 1973.

2.1 THE CONCEPTS OF EFFICIENCY AND EFFECTIVENESS

In order to examine the possible roles of the advertising institution, it is necessary to understand the basic distinction between effectiveness and efficiency. Unless this distinction is clear, and unless it is also clear that without some measure of efficiency we cannot constructively examine ways to improve effectiveness, random thinking and random action will prevail at both managerial and public policy levels.

Efficiency has several meanings; here we shall adopt that of the engineering sciences. Efficiency is the ratio between input and output. If inputs and outputs can be measured, the value of this ratio can be computed. Higher values of this ratio indicate higher efficiency.[1]

Suppose, for example, that we want to choose between two different advertisements (A_1, A_2). The output we want to obtain is readership; the input is cost. In a pretest, we can compute the readership and the costs of the two ads, (R_1, R_2) and (C_1, C_2) respectively. We can thus compute the efficiency ratios,

$$E_1 = \frac{R_1}{C_1} \quad ; \quad E_2 = \frac{R_2}{C_1}$$

and thus identify which ad is more efficient.

This engineering reasoning also applies at the macro level. Suppose that the output is gross national product and the inputs are two different advertising institutions, whose costs are measured in dollars. As before, two efficiency ratios can be computed and the more efficient institution can be identified. In both cases, efficiency is the only criterion for choice.

While efficiency deals with economic facts, *effectiveness* deals with the preferences (values) of a decision maker, a firm, or a society. Suppose that, in the above example, the more efficient advertising institution uses mass media that are privately owned, whereas the other one uses publicly owned media. If society values public ownership more than private, it may choose the less efficient institution since it is more effective with respect to society's values. Society is involved in a trade-off between engineering efficiency and effectiveness. Its choice is based not only on the criterion of efficiency but also on other value criteria.

AN ADVANCED, AND MORE USEFUL, DEFINITION

Welfare economics can be used to illustrate in more depth the distinction between efficiency and effectiveness, and their interdependence in analysis and decision making at the public policy level. Exhibit 11.9 represents the problem faced by a society interested in finding (1) the most efficient use of its resources (capital and labor) and (2) the most effective use of these resources.

Let us begin with efficiency. Engineering knowledge of the available technological processes that transform resources (or inputs) into products and services (or outputs)

---

[1] The definition given in the text includes several familiar variations, among them: (1) given a desired level of output, choose the alternative with the minimum cost; and (2) given a number of alternatives with the same cost, choose the one that yields the maximum output.

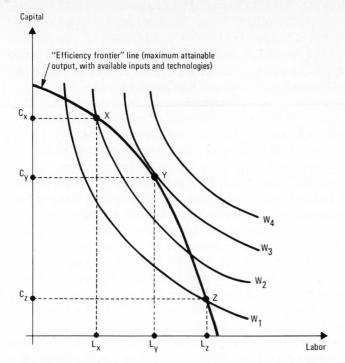

EXHIBIT 11.9

indicates that a maximum output can be achieved by combining capital and labor in many different ways. All possible combinations of these two inputs—all giving the same maximum output—can be represented graphically by a line traditionally referred to as the *efficiency frontier.*

Points X, Y, and Z indicate three of these technologically possible combinations. At each point, different combinations of input quantities are used. For instance, at X, society would use more capital than labor, while the opposite is true at Z. Yet, all three possible combinations are equally efficient in that they produce the same maximum output of products and services.

In discussing the efficiency of resource allocation, we must note that the facts represented in the graph can be approached and interpreted in two different ways. First, at a given level of capital use (say, C_x), output increases as labor is added, up to the level L_x. That is, increasing amounts of labor *cause* an increasing amount of output. Similar results obtain if labor is fixed and the amount of capital is varied. More generally, the maximum output indicated by X is *caused* by using the inputs in the amount (C_x, L_x). Thus, this approach views inputs as *causes* of outputs and may be called the *causality approach.*

There is a second way of looking at the graph. It is frequently impossible—especially in industrialized societies—to produce more output by adding an increasing amount of one input to a fixed amount of another. For instance, a certain machine may require two operators; with only one operator it cannot be run; a third operator would remain idle. Accordingly, to operate n machines of this type, we need 2n operators. In the short run, there are generally *structural* or *proportional* relationships among inputs.

The structural or proportional relationships between the two inputs in the graph can be visualized by a line that begins at the point of origin and reaches some point on the efficiency frontier, for example, point X. This line may be straight: the case of *constant proportionality*. However, as society adds capital equipment, it may adopt newer technologies that change the ratio of men to machines. In this case of *varying proportionality,* the line would be curvilinear. This approach stresses the structural or proportional relationships among inputs rather than causal relationships between inputs and outputs, and may be called the *structural* or *proportionality approach.*

Let us remember these two complementary ways of looking at the efficiency of any economic process: (1) the inputs *cause* the outputs, and (2) there exist optimal *proportions* among inputs for reaching certain levels of output for given inputs' prices. Later commentaries will use these two approaches for a detailed examination of the macro roles of the advertising institution (see Section 3.3 below).

Neither approach, however, answers the question of what society *should* do. This is a matter of *effectiveness.* So far we have simply identified three equally efficient ways for society to reach the maximum level of output attainable with its resources. The choice among the three depends on society's preferences. These are expressed by the so-called welfare function, which is partly represented by the curves labeled W in the graph. The subscripts 1, 2, 3, and 4 indicate that the higher the curve reached by a particular utilization of resources, the more societal preferences are satisfied.

Suppose that, at a particular time, a society's preferences are those indicated by the welfare function W in our graph. The society would then choose the resource combination Y, rather than other equally efficient alternatives, since both alternatives X and Z lie below the level W_3 that is achieved by alternative Y. (Observe also that alternative X is, in turn, preferable to alternative Z since $W_2 > W_1$.)

To summarize, while engineering "facts" may indicate that equally *efficient* alternatives are available to reach certain levels of output, these alternatives may not be equally *effective* in attaining social values. Understanding the advertising institution depends on the ability to compute both efficiency and effectiveness. We need to know how many ways there are to organize efficiently the transmission of economic information via mass media (i.e., we need to compute an efficiency frontier). We must also ascertain society's preference among the various types of efficient institutional organizations.

Both types of knowledge are prerequisites for public policy and social choice. For example, a change in advertising—say a prohibition of national TV ads—may change a society's efficiency or its rate of utilization of different resources. This change may alter the institution's contributions to the economic system (such as sponsorship of TV programs) and eventually affect the level of satisfaction of social preferences. But this chain of effects cannot be traced unless the first change in efficiency can be assessed. And this assessment can be made only on the basis of knowledge of both the internal structure and external relationships of the advertising institution.

Much of the existing literature on the advertising institution amounts only to expressions of the desires of particular individuals or groups. These desires are perfectly legitimate, but they should not be confused with a study of how advertising operates. Even more serious, many writers seem unaware that their preferences imply economic consequences that cannot be evaluated without a systematic inquiry into the efficiency of advertising—an inquiry that has not yet begun.

Research on the question of efficiency is especially necessary since increasing complexity, both technological and social, creates greater reliance on a system of mass communication. Below we consider various methods of gaining the requisite knowledge, beginning with a brief discussion of the problem of gathering data.

2.2 THE LIMITATIONS OF EXISTING DATA

In an age of voluminous data collection and publication by state and federal governments, it may come as a surprise to learn that there are, in fact, no federal statistics directly concerned with advertising. The federal government publishes data on advertising expenditures and other numerical indicators, but these data are literally copied from such private sources as *Printers' Ink* (now *Marketing/Communications*) and *Advertising Age,* who in turn rely on the computations by McCann-Erickson (an advertising agency).

Although these data may be accurate estimates, they are not the most appropriate indicators of advertising at the macro level. As in any other inquiry, we must be careful that our data correspond to the phenomenon under study and that they depict the relevant aspects of the phenomenon. As noted in Chapter 1, the data available on the advertising institution do not shed light on its internal efficiency. Thus, we are compelled to look for synthetic or *macro* data that might indirectly measure the institution's overall behavior.

The difference between micro and macro data can be understood by a comparison with medical practice. When a doctor lacks the resources (time and facilities) to subject a patient to all known laboratory tests, he typically looks at gross indicators, such as temperature. The body's temperature has limitations as an indicator: when it is abnormal, it does not tell what is wrong; alternatively, it may be normal when, in fact, a person is dying of cancer. Generally, however, it signals the presence of some "inefficient" situation.

In advertising there is one analogous macro indicator: total advertising expenditures (AE). Since AE is so often cited when passing judgment on the efficiency and effectiveness of advertising—and since it will be used in the analyses below—its nature and limitations should be understood.

2.2.1 Advertising Expenditures

The main and perhaps only advantage intrinsic to AE is that it exists in a time series reaching back for many years. Further, certain limited types of functional and structural change in the advertising institution can be inferred from available breakdowns of the AE time series. For example, changes in the utilization of different mass media can be observed, as well as the appearance of new types of media. Differences in use by different economic sectors can be noted—e.g., utilization rates by the extractive, industrial, consumer, service, and import/export sectors, or by specific industries within each sector. In general, however, the available breakdowns are insufficient to indicate directly the mechanisms governing such changes and thus to study questions concerning efficiency and effectiveness.

A major limitation of AE is that it collapses on a unidimensional scale (dollar) the many dimensions or components of the advertising institution. Ideally, there should be measures for each of these dimensions.

Another basic limitation of AE is that it reflects only part of the institution—the efforts of senders of messages. All economists know that *costs are not sufficient to measure the efficiency of any economic activity.* We must relate costs to their results, such as the *number of messages sent* per period of time. Telser[1] and others agree that "number of messages sent" is a preferable indicator of the institution's overall work. As mentioned earlier, this indicator can be viewed as a measure of the system's output.

On the basis of our previous discussion, however, still another indicator must be added—*number of messages received.* For instance, an evaluation of the efficiency of an electrical distribution system is based on the difference between the number of kilowatts put into the system and the number actually delivered. In fact, to estimate the efficiency of the advertising institution, a measure of the *number of messages sought* is also necessary. In evaluating an electrical distribution system, the ultimate yardstick is whether the system can meet the demand for electricity at any given time. These indicators—costs (advertising expenditures) and the number of messages sent, delivered, and sought—are minimum requirements for the analysis of the efficiency of any advertising institution.

Looking toward the future, the first step is to measure, at the very least, the number of messages sent. This will probably require some new system of data collection. It will also be necessary to explicate the concept of message in order to obtain meaningful empirical measures (see Chapter 1, Section 3.6). Unfortunately, there is no evidence that private and public agencies have even begun to plan research in this direction.

ADVERTISING AND OTHER CHANNELS OF COMMUNICATION

Still another shortcoming of the advertising-expenditures indicator and the available time-series data (AE) is revealed when we recall that sellers use many means to communicate with buyers. Examples of other channels of information are fairs, exhibits, catalogs, and product and package designs and labels.

An extremely important channel of information is *personal selling* (PS). An idea of the relative utilization of personal selling and advertising at the macro level is indicated by the fact that salaries paid to salesmen in 1970 amounted to $50 billion as against $20

---

[1] L. G. Telser, "Advertising and Cigarettes," *The Journal of Political Economy*, October 1962.

billion for advertising expenditures. It is interesting to note that AE tends to be a higher percentage of PS salaries in developed economies than in less developed ones.

The use of advertising–measured by AE–varies both across industries (see Exhibits 11.3 and 11.4) and across firms within the same industry.[1] It is impossible, however, to derive any conclusion with respect to the role of advertising in the economy without assessing the use of other information channels. Note that, for example, the ratio of advertising to the total of personal selling plus advertising (AE/AE+PS) may lead to better insights into the uses of different channels of communication within the economy over a period of time, especially if such observations are made at different periods in a business cycle.

The relative use of each channel may vary a great deal over long periods of time (say, three or four decades) in one country and, as mentioned, it appears to vary also from country to country, especially in developing countries. If such variations are substantial, then relating AE to macroeconomic indicators (e.g., GNP or consumption expenditures) is legitimate only if these variations are taken into consideration.

Finally, AE does not represent the entire utilization of the advertising institution. For instance, firms' expenditures for hiring labor and white-collar personnel imply some use of mass media, but such expenditures are not identifiable by our present data collection procedures. Furthermore, most public relations expenditures (e.g., press releases, printing and distributing of stockholders' reports) imply some use of the advertising system but may be only partly included in AE. And much of the use of the advertising system by nonprofit institutions, government agencies, and consumer cooperatives is not recorded at all, or is recorded in ways conceptually unrelated to uses of a country's mass communication system (e.g., government printing and mailing, post-office costs).

2.2.2 **Relating Advertising Expenditures to Gross National Product and Other Economic Indicators**
When AE is related to macro indicators, we must again consider the adequacy of the concepts and the data chosen. Do the overall indicators really measure those aspects of the economy that are related to the advertising institution? Mr. Thiele has chosen gross national product and personal consumption expenditures as indicators (see Exhibits 11.1 and 11.6). Let us examine this choice.

Since the 1930s, with the development of the national income accounting system and the macroeconomic theories of Keynes and others, economists have found that *gross national product* (GNP) is a useful indicator for answering questions concerning public policy (e.g., money, taxes, and labor policies) and private management. Intuitively, it would seem useful also to relate AE and GNP in order to develop a quantitative measure of how the advertising institution fits into the economy. There are many *caveats,* however.

---

[1] See periodicals such as *Advertising Age* and *Marketing/Communications,* and R. Buzzell, "The Role of Advertising in the Market Mix," Marketing Science Institute, Cambridge, Mass., October 1971 (this paper is also one of the testimonies presented to the FTC Hearings on Modern Advertising Practices). We shall return to this point in Chapter 12.

The GNP data contain records of economic events that may be related to the advertising institution in various ways. However, some of these events may not be related to advertising at all. First, it is doubtful whether government expenditures (G), a component of GNP, are related to AE. To the extent that G is a varying proportion of GNP, the direct association of AE with GNP may be a meaningless or even deceiving statistic. In addition, many types of personal services, especially public services, may have very weak relationships with advertising. Furthermore, the service sector of the economy is the one that has increased fastest in the sixties. If these observations are correct, statistical computations of relationships between the economy (GNP) and the advertising institution (AE) may be misleading.

Second, GNP summarizes the behavior not only of government but also of the consumer and business sector; however, the relationships of the advertising institution with the consumer sector of GNP may be substantially different from its relationships with the *business sector*. For instance, advertising expenditures representing messages directed to business firms (AE-B) should be related to the purchasing behavior of business firms. The available data on investments by business firms (I) possibly provide an indicator that approximates firms' purchases sufficiently. However, the relationship of AE-B to I, or to other indicators, is not a simple one. For instance, the amount of business expenditures that may be influenced by advertising is constrained by the total amount of *disposable funds* (Yb) that firms have to spend in a given period of time. Even if we were willing to ignore the ability of firms to borrow, and its effect on the value of Yb, we should estimate the relationship of AE-B with the ratio $\frac{I}{Yb}$ rather than directly with I.

Third, GNP reflects the activities of the *export* (Ex) and *import* (Im) *sectors* of the economy. Even in countries such as the United States where foreign trade is a relatively small proportion of GNP, the content of imports and exports may create distortions when the direct relationships between GNP and AE are computed. For instance, exports affect GNP data, but clearly do not call for advertising in the selling country. Imports of raw materials call for much less advertising than imports of consumer goods. Furthermore, for any one country, the content and value of exports and imports may change substantially over time. Whether these factors are of major or minor importance is a question of fact, and therefore cannot be dismissed a priori.

Fourth, recall that the utilization rate of the advertising institution by senders and seekers/receivers of messages may be related to the number of such users (see Chapter 1). Similarly, GNP may also be related to the number of users. We may capture this by considering AE and GNP *per capita*. But even at this primitive level of analysis, there is a danger of choosing the wrong population. For instance, the appropriate population for the consumer part of AE is demographically determined. Yet how shall we define the population of the nonconsumer component of AE? Many social institutions and public agencies should probably be considered along with business firms. Only conceptual developments and empirical analyses will suggest where the lines should be drawn.

Fifth, GNP, AE, and consumption expenditures (CE) are typically measured in *money* (current) *prices,* not in *real prices.* If we report these data in money prices, we are assuming that the rate of inflation in the economy, the advertising institution, and the household sector has been the same.[1] This again is a question of fact. For instance, some professionals feel that inflation in the 1960s was greater in the advertising industry than in other industries. While the cost of living index increased by 45 percent during the 1959-1972 period, salaries paid by publishers increased by 87 percent, and postal rates rose by 47 percent (second class) and by 113 percent (controlled) during the same period.[2]

One factor common to all these conceptual issues must be resolved prior to empirical investigations of how the advertising institution relates to the economy and society. This is the pseudo-homogeneity inherent in each measure discussed. For example, to compare GNP, even in real dollars, across many decades is to compare potatoes and tomatoes. The *content* of GNP has changed drastically in both the industrial and consumer sectors. Until the mid-1950s, data processing equipment consisted exclusively of unit-record equipment (sorters, countersorters, tabulating machines). This equipment differs in kind from computers, and the early generations of computers differ in kind from the later generations. Even such a common appliance as the refrigerator has changed in kind in a number of basic ways ranging from lower consumption of electricity to entirely new design and performance characteristics. Similarly, the advertising institution has changed in kind (different mixes of old and new media, different products and brands being advertised, different themes, and so on).

A new branch of economic theory—hedonic price analysis—is being developed to cope with the inadequacy of comparing GNP (or other indicators) over time simply because it is measured in dollars (real or otherwise). Unfortunately, no practical solution is yet available. We must remember, therefore, that the artifact introduced by our measurement in dollars can be disregarded for certain investigations but not for others.

The pseudo-homogeneity of measures in dollars must also be kept in mind when different indicators are related over time. The results of the computations of these relationships may hide more than they reveal. Further, what they reveal may be deceptive; for instance, statistically significant associations may, in fact, be spurious. For many managerial and public policy issues concerning advertising, the heterogeneity underlying the available time series must be considered explicitly (for an illustration, see Section 3.2 in this chapter).

2.2.3 Relating Advertising Expenditures to the Household Sector

Similar considerations of heterogeneity apply to the investigation of how the advertising institution relates to the *household sector* of the economy—the consumer. Mr. Thiele

---

[1] Telser, *op. cit.*, has argued in favor of considering AE in current prices, but his reason for doing so was his feeling that current price may make AE a better indicator of the number of messages sent through the institution. L. D. Taylor and D. Weiserbs, however, have found that AE in constant dollars show a better statistical relation with CE ("Advertising and the Aggregate Consumption Function," *American Economic Review*, September 1972, p. 650). To deflate advertising expenditures is an arduous task; of the few past attempts, the most promising is in R. Schmalensee, *The Economics of Advertising*, North-Holland Publishing Co., Amsterdam, 1972, Chapter 7, Appendices A and B.

[2] J. B. Koback, "Business Press Turned the Corner in 1972," *Industrial Marketing*, March 1973, p. 52.

suggests personal consumption expenditures (CE) as an indicator of the household sector (see Exhibit 11.6). The same CE and its mirror—savings (S)—have been used in many studies.

In such studies, CE is related to total advertising expenditures (AE). Yet our previous remarks suggest that we should consider only that component of the advertising system that carries messages addressed to consumers—i.e., consumer advertising expenditures (AE-C). More important, AE-C should be related to the total spending *and* saving of households (that is, CE+S).[1] At present, a reasonable estimate of AE-C is not available for periods prior to 1947.

Relating AE-C to CE assumes that all advertising messages attempt to make consumers *spend more.* This assumption, unfortunately, is implicit in the study by Taylor and Weiserbs[2] and others.

But a large portion of advertising messages urge the consumer to spend less and *save more.* Such messages include those by banks (from opening checking accounts to various forms of savings deposits); savings and loan associations; credit unions; insurance companies (both private and group policies); private firms, investment trusts, installment investment companies and stock brokers (to buy stocks and bonds); and by local and federal governments (to buy bonds directly and to pass bond issues). It is thus premature to draw conclusions from current studies relating AE-C with CE.

In principle, advertising expenditures attempting to influence consumer saving decisions (AE-CS) should be related to saving time series (S), and those attempting to influence consumer expenditures (AE-CE) should be related only to consumer expenditures (CE). At present, the suggestion of breaking AE-C into two components (AE-CS and AE-CE) is not feasible. But any a priori judgment that such separate computations are unnecessary cannot be accepted, for it is based neither on empirical nor conceptual evidence. Nor can we resort to the time-honored principle that "things balance."

An alternative indicator of the household sector could be the *disposable income* (Yd) available to the consumer. This is the amount of income that advertisers may influence, not only toward more (less) spending and more (less) saving, but also toward specific types of activities and, ultimately, types of life styles. The possible relationships of Yd with AE-C (not total AE) can be seen as the reflection of the social rather than the strictly economic role of the advertising institutions.

Conceptual and measurement problems abound here, too. We would have to examine, for example, whether the spending and saving behavior of households (and of different types of households) is more closely related to gross income or to income net not only of taxes but also of deductions for retirement plans, group insurance premiums, etc. The composition of disposable and gross income should also be considered.

---

[1] For the moment, we shall not consider the possibilities that AE-C may have direct and indirect effects on business spending and that AE-B may affect consumer spending and saving.

[2] Taylor and Weiserbs, *op. cit.*

Predispositions to spend and save may depend on whether a household's income is mainly from salaries, wages, interest and dividends, or transfer payments.[1]

Finally, it may be more reasonable to relate AE-C *directly* to Yd or to some other indicator (remember that even Taylor and Weiserb's study postulates a direct relationship between AE and CE).[2] The amount of consumer spending or saving that the advertising institution can affect is, after all, limited by how much the household sector can allocate to different alternatives. To know more about this constraint, we should compute relationships between AE-CE (not AE) and the proportion of disposable income that consumers actually spend. That is, for instance, CE/Yd = f(AE-CE).

2.3 SUMMARY

In this section we have limited ourselves to an examination of the internal efficiency of the advertising institution and its possible relationships with the economy and its main components. This was done because it is meaningless to discuss the effectiveness of different institutional designs of advertising without some valid measurements of the efficiency of these alternative designs.

Prior to any empirical work on efficiency, two conditions must be satisfied. First, the concepts to be measured and their possible relationships must be clearly understood. For instance, we discussed whether such concepts as gross national product are, in fact, relevant to a study of the role of the advertising institution in the economy through time. Second, the data used must indeed be appropriate indicators of the concepts chosen.[3] Thus, we discussed whether available advertising expenditures or GNP data are appropriate measures of the concept "advertising institution" and the concept "economy" for the purposes of our inquiry.

Our conclusion is straightforward: future analyses will require better concepts and better measures. Prior to, or at least concurrently with, future analyses, we must systematically develop new concepts and more relevant breakdowns of current data, and collect new kinds of data. In the following sections we shall see that we need more thinking about the possible network of relationships between advertising and the economy and more attempts to translate and analyze possible networks into structural (mathematical) models prior to empirical estimation work. At the same time, we need

---

[1] Transfer payments (unemployment insurance, social security payments, workmen's compensation, Medicare, etc.) have become a new and rapidly increasing component of personal income only in very recent times. In the analyses of long-term time series, it would seem intuitively appropriate to eliminate transfer payments from personal income before making comparisons with consumer advertising expenditures. Concurrently, one should also try to estimate whether there exist specific relations between advertising expenditures and personal income for those households whose personal income includes a large percentage of transfer payments.

[2] For a thorough and advanced analysis of this possible relationship, see Schmalensee, *op. cit.,* Chapter 3.

[3] In our future work we must avoid making the all-too-frequent mistake of having no correspondence between the data structure and the concept structure under examination. For a most lucid exposition of this problem and its consequences, ignored by much of the econometric work in the area of interest to us, see K. Mackenzie, "A Set Theoretic Analysis of Group Interaction," *Psychometrika,* March 1970.

less impulsive use of direct-inference procedures, chosen simply because some time series are available. It is not true that processing available data through some algorithm of statistical inference is "the best we can do." The best we can do is to *formulate a systematic plan* for the development of appropriate concepts and data, and experiment with data analyses (Exhibit 11.10 summarizes the material discussed so far). This plan may appear ambitious, but it is actually only a small step toward understanding both the advertising institution and some aspects of those economies that have become dependent on mass communication.

3 UNDERSTANDING THE ADVERTISING INSTITUTION: SOME MAIN STRATEGIES

The development of appropriate concepts and data is only one prerequisite to understanding the socioeconomic roles of the advertising institution. Once this prerequisite is satisfied, it is still necessary to determine how to go about analyzing the data.

The type of analysis one undertakes obviously depends on the purpose of the study. For our purposes, three strategic questions arise:
1. Shall we observe one or more countries?
2. Shall we observe one or more countries at one point in time (a cross-sectional design) or through time (a longitudinal design)?
3. Shall we approach the data to ascertain relationships of causality or relationships of a structural nature (i.e., relationships of proportions)?

The next section examines the nature and implications of the first two strategic choices; Section 3-2 discusses the type of approach.

3.1 COMPARISONS THROUGH TIME AND/OR ACROSS COUNTRIES

The choices available with respect to time and countries can be represented schematically:

At One Point in Time (Cross-sectional Designs)		Over Time (Longitudinal Designs)	
One Country	*Many Countries*	*One Country*	*Many Countries*
A	B	C	D

There are four choices available, each with advantages and disadvantages. Strategy A is the least informative. It can be used to describe a situation at one point in time (i.e., we can use it to produce a "picture"). Examples include a table showing the breakdown of AE by types of media, or by type of industry, or both. Sometimes data may allow computations of correlations among different descriptors of the advertising institution or between these descriptors and other indicators of the economy. Although such descriptions and computations are useful—e.g., they could suggest the working of the institution—they cannot provide as much information as any of the other three strategies.

EXHIBIT 11.10

THE ADVERTISING INSTITUTION AND THE ECONOMY
SEARCHING FOR APPROPRIATE CONCEPTS, DATA, AND RELATIONSHIPS

A. The Advertising Institution	B. The Economic System	C. Factors to Be Controlled
1. The Advertising Institution Number of messages sent Number of messages received Number of messages sought	*1. The Total Economy* GNP (gross national product) Ex, Im (exports and imports) NNP (net national product)[a] NY (national income)[b]	*1. Real Price Indices* By sectors For AE

2. The Institution's Costs
AE: total advertising expenditures
  – incomplete record of all economic messages sent by all users;
  – records mostly costs of business firms;
	2. The Main Components
	G (government expenditures)
	I (investments)
	Y_b (amount firms can spend)
	} I/Y_b
	Y_d (consumers' disposable income, gross or net)[c]
	CE (total consumption expenditures)
	S (total saving)
	} CE/Y_d
		2. Population
		Demographic
		Business
		Institutions
		Others

AE-B: cost of messages directed to the business sector (industrial, etc.) AE-C: cost of messages directed to consumers (households) AE-CE: cost of messages urging consumers to spend more AE-CS: cost of messages urging consumers to spend less (save) AE-O: all others (esp. by media types)		*3. Other Information Channels Used by the Business Sector* Personal selling (PS as salaries, etc.) Catalogs, fairs, exhibits Designing (product, package, labels) *4. Other Uses–Users of the Advertising Institution* To improve completeness of current AE data To investigate joint costs and benefits

[a]NNP = GNP minus depreciation.

[b]NY = NNP minus indirect taxes and business transfers to consumers.

[c]Net of taxes and/or deductions for retirement systems, group insurance premiums, etc. Also, special attention to transfer payments (social security, unemployment insurance, etc.) in long-term time series.

*The relationships R that are most relevant to an evaluation of advertising at the social macro level are, e.g., (AE-C)R(Y_d) and its components (AE-CE)R(CE), (AE-CE)R(CE/Y_d), (AE-CS)R(S), and (AE-CS)R(S/Y_d).

179

In strategy C, for example, we might take one country and observe a number of indicators (e.g., those in Exhibit 11.10) over a long period of time. We could then calculate a number of possible relationships among the chosen indicators and their changes over time. These measures provide some baseline for inferring whether efficiency is becoming *relatively* better or worse.

These inferences are relative in the sense that there is no a priori measure of what is or should be optimal efficiency. For example, we can compute a priori what are or should be the optimal characteristics of the performance of a new engine. Thus, the behavior of any one engine can always be compared with these optimal characteristics and its performance can be evaluated. But, since advertising and the economy are not mechanical systems, our inferences in following strategy C will remain relative unless we have a control group.

Strategy B allows us to make comparisons across countries. Consider a medical analogy: if only one individual is observed through time, we may note his survival but we cannot know whether our subject could be healthier. It would be impossible to ascertain normal temperature, pulse rate, blood pressure, and basic metabolism. But by comparing a number of individuals—or advertising institutions and economies—similarities and differences can be observed and the conditions associated with such similarities and differences can be identified.

The observation of such conditions is crucial in any scientific effort, because they specify what is normal. To illustrate, the structure of certain metals is such that electricity does not flow through them until their temperature approaches absolute zero. Then the structure of these metals changes, and they become very efficient conductors. Similarly, the human respiratory system changes at very high altitudes in order to process more efficiently the lesser amount of oxygen available. Similar changes in the efficiency of advertising may occur under varying economic conditions.

Strategies B and C are both valuable, but the maximum payoff is achieved with strategy D. Here different systems are observed through time, with a careful recording of the conditions that make them different in structure and function. This procedure is scientific method in a nutshell.

The literature on the socioeconomic effects of the advertising institution has emphasized the C strategy. Basic breakthroughs in statistical analysis of time series have encouraged its use, as has the lack of comparable data describing the economies and advertising institutions of different countries. Unfortunately, this strategy has been used only at the level of an industry; we shall examine its uses in Chapter 12.

AN EXAMPLE OF INTERCOUNTRY COMPARISON
Strategy B has been used rarely, but it has great potential. A recent article by Valli[1] pioneered this approach, with results that illustrate its importance for describing and understanding the advertising institution.

[1] C. G. Valli, "Gli Investimenti Pubblicitari in un'Economia in Fase di Sviluppo," *Studi di Mercato,* Numero 1, 1972.

In the example below (Exhibit 11.11), Valli computes the 1968 per capita advertising expenditures and gross national product for several countries and then the ratio between these two. By setting the ratio "per capita AE/per capita GNP" equal to one for Italy, he can rank several countries.

EXHIBIT 11.11
ORDERING OF COUNTRIES BY THE RATIO OF ADVERTISING EXPENDITURES TO GROSS NATIONAL PRODUCT, PER CAPITA, 1968

Switzerland	3.04
U.S.A.	2.75
Denmark	2.43
Sweden	2.12
Holland	2.05
West Germany	1.89
Great Britain	1.55
Japan	1.43
Belgium	1.07
France	0.94
Italy	1.00

Source: Valli, *op. cit.,* p. 18.

How can we interpret Valli's results? For now, they are just facts—descriptive facts. Anything else is speculation. Descriptions, however, are useful, for they suggest speculations that may, in turn, lead to work explaining why we observe these facts rather than others. And descriptive data alone, even without further work, may correct some of our misconceptions. An American critic of advertising, for example, may be shocked that the United States is apparently not the leading spender. And memories of majestic Swiss mountains, bucolic Dutch windmills, and Swedish social order may make these countries' spending seem surprisingly high. Finally, data like Valli's might suggest methods for changing the facts observed. For instance, an Italian advertising agency might present Exhibit 11.11 to its clients, observing that exports of consumer goods to Northern Europe would probably call for doubling current Italian advertising budgets.

Valli's comparative work also illustrates how to develop insights into the structure of the advertising institution. Exhibit 11.12 shows the allocation of advertising expenditures to various mass media in six countries, thus providing a *tentative* indication of how many messages (ads) flow through which media. Even such a simple descriptive chart as this provides challenging food for thought. For example, countries with high utilization of TV are low in utilizing movie theaters. There is also a strong inverse rank association between TV and print media—so that one is tempted to wonder whether the use of these two media is interdependent, i.e., for a given output of the institution, a lower use of TV requires a higher use of print, and vice versa.

Note also that the countries whose economies have developed most rapidly since

EXHIBIT 11.12

ALLOCATION OF ADVERTISING EXPENDITURES TO DIFFERENT MASS MEDIA

	Germany (1970) %	France (1968) %	Great Britain (1970) %	U.S.A. (1970) %	Japan (1970) %	Italy (1970) %
Total print	81.5	67.7	64.3	57.8	52.4	61.6
periodicals	(31.9)	*	(11.8)	(9.9)	(7.1)	(33.4)
daily	(49.6)	*	(52.5)	(47.9)	(45.3)	(28.2)
Television	10.2	3.4	29.0	27.7	41.7	16.9
Radio	3.3	15.0	0.2	11.0	5.9	8.0
Movie theaters	0.9	2.2	1.4	–	–	5.6
Outdoor, etc.	4.1	11.7	5.1	3.5	–	7.9
Total	100.0	100.0	100.0	100.0	100.0	100.0

*Data not available.

Source: Valli, *op. cit.,* p. 23.

World War II tend to be at the extremes in the utilization of TV and print. Japan scores highest on TV and lowest in print;[1] Germany scores highest in print and next to lowest in TV. But the two countries whose rate of economic change has been relatively more systematic—the United States and Great Britain—are intermediate in their use of both.

Valli's comparisons also provide a yardstick to measure the use of different media within the United States. Outdoor ads are most visible: we are surrounded by them on streets and highways. Yet, as of 1970, United States outdoor advertising was far lower than that of any other country.[2] The United States is also second lowest in its utilization of periodicals (magazines) as an advertising medium.

All in all, through strategy B, comparative descriptions tell us something more about the world we live in; they anchor our feelings by giving them dimensions. Comparative descriptions give us a sort of geographic map; by locating an advertising institution on such a map, they indicate what should be studied to understand the internal workings of the advertising institution and its interactions with the economic system.

Such studies would become even more useful if they were combined with longitudinal studies (i.e., strategy D). If the figures in Exhibit 11.12 were available for the past several decades, what—other than imagination—would limit the amount of understanding we might gain from them?

[1] The low score on print might be related to the high cost of printing Japanese language and the high cost of paper. However, contrary to the notion that the amount of expenditures in a medium is an indicator of the amount of information (ads) in that medium, note that the average Japanese buys two newspapers per day (C. Pizzinelli, "La Stampa in Giappone," *Esso Rivista,* Luglio-Ottobre, 1970, p. 31).

[2] Once again we must be careful in interpreting this fact. For example to establish which country has more outdoor advertising, we should standardize Valli's data—e.g., per capita, per square mile.

The problem discussed so far is essentially one of methodology. Note that this methodological perspective leads to the same conclusions reached in the previous section. To understand the internal efficiency of advertising institutions, their relationships to economic systems, and, eventually, their social roles, we need to formulate and implement a very systematic plan of concept development, new data collection, and experimentation with data analyses.

Choices of time periods and number of countries do not exhaust the problem. One must also decide how to approach the study of the macro roles of advertising (see our third strategic question). Two approaches present themselves.

The researcher may ask whether there exist relationships among advertising and economic indicators that are causal; e.g., do advertising expenditures affect GNP? Or he may ask whether various indicators of the advertising institution and the economy relate in structural (proportional) ways. Here he is interested in discovering relationships of structure or proportionality: e.g., do different types of economic systems require different amounts of mass information?

The first approach may be called the *causality* approach, and the latter the *structural* or *proportionality* approach. Both these approaches were mentioned in introducing the concept of efficiency (see Exhibit 11.9, Section 2.1). The former will be discussed in the following section; the latter, which has received little attention, will be considered later.

3.2   SEARCHING FOR RELATIONSHIPS OF CAUSE AND EFFECT

Positive and negative evaluations of advertising share one key assumption: the belief, implicit or explicit, that the institution *causes* certain events. On the macro level, debate revolves, for example, around whether advertising contributes to economic growth or hinders it, whether it affects or reflects changes in cultural values, and so on. These are basic issues, but the causal nature of the relationship is simply assumed. This assumption has not been systematically studied at the aggregate level. Hence the purpose of this section is to illustrate the conceptual and empirical problems involved in testing the assumption of causality.

Underlying the cause-effect assumption is a view of the entire economy as a gigantic production process. On the one hand, we see the result of this process—the output of products, brands, and services. On the other hand, we see inputs, such as capital, human skills, equipment, and raw materials. Another input required by large and complex economies is a system of mass communication, of which the advertising institution is a part. From this point of view, the literature conceptualizes advertising as an input into the economic process and asserts that it affects the economy's output and, ultimately, society. The view is that, all other things being equal, variations in one input cause variations in the output, i.e., output is a function of input.

How can we apply this reasoning? In the absence of more appropriate measures, let us use the GNP and AE to illustrate the problems involved in the study of whether advertising has a causal role at the macro level. Our reasoning will also apply to more appropriate measures, if and when they become available.

As a first step, let us restate the basic assumption of causality. It says that, all other inputs being equal, GNP is some function of AE:

$$GNP = g(AE), \text{ for all other inputs being equal} \qquad (11.1)$$

Practically all discussions of the effects of advertising depend on whether this hypothesis holds true. It is a prerequisite without which much of the literature makes no sense. More important, the hypothesis is also a prerequisite for any work directed toward resolving the questions of efficiency and effectiveness already discussed. How can we develop a systematic inquiry into this postulated causality? A number of problems present themselves.

The *first problem* is that we must discover whether or not the relationship signified by the function g in the above equation does, in fact, exist.

The *second problem* is the nature of the relationship: is it always positive (or negative, or null), or does it vary with the absolute value of GNP and AE? The latter possibility can be understood intuitively: if a very large economy spends very small amounts on AE, variations in AE may have no effect whatsoever on the economy, for only a reasonably developed institution can produce enough information to affect the economy's processes of production and distribution. Conversely, if an economy is spending very large amounts on AE, even a small increase in AE may imply "too much" information and thus have a negative effect on GNP.

The *third problem* is whether the association of AE with GNP depends on the level of other inputs into the economy. For example, if a country does not have a sufficiently large and well-qualified sales force, a particular level of AE may contribute less to economic growth than it would in the presence of a higher level of sales force input.

These three problems can be explored by observing changes in the relationship between GNP and AE—i.e., the changes in g—both in one country over long periods of time and in several different countries at one point in time. As time series for both GNP and AE become available for more Western countries, this research will become feasible. Given the popularity of theorizing about the effects of advertising, it is mysterious that no one has systematically undertaken such initial inquiries.

The *fourth* problem is more complex, reflecting the possibility that any causal relationship between AE and GNP may be reciprocal. That is, (1) changes in the advertising institution may cause changes in the economy, and also (2) changes in the economy may cause changes in the advertising institution.

Although Equation (11.1) states that AE cause GNP, it is also possible that GNP causes AE. It is reasonable to hypothesize that an economy growing in size and complexity requires a higher level of mass information activities. This hypothesis can be written as follows:

$$AE = h(GNP), \text{ all other things being equal} \qquad (11.2)$$

The same three problems discussed above of course apply equally to the relationship postulated in Equation (11.2). However, when the two equations are combined, a different and more complicated problem arises. If the causality process goes both ways (the g and h functions, respectively), then we are dealing with a problem of interaction over time, that is, the familiar case of the chicken and the egg.

THE CHICKEN-AND-EGG PROBLEM

We shall not discuss here the complex methodological and statistical difficulties involved in dealing with a set of variables interacting over time (e.g., lag effects). But one point must be stressed; if we did estimate the g function in Equation (11.1) without considering (e.g., controlling for) the feedback expressed by the h function, our computations and final estimates would be meaningless—and most likely deceptive —for decision making by private and public managers. The same consideration applies to estimating the h function without controlling for the g function.

With these difficulties in mind, it is possible to explore the currently available time series and observe some suggestive relationships. We are going to ask of our data whether AE tends to lead, follow, or interact simultaneously with GNP.

Remember that AE represents only the cost of sending ads by business firms. Each firm presumably invests efforts in advertising in order to increase, or at least retain, the current level of its sales in the future. If all firms behaved this way, and if they were successful in the aggregate, then we would expect that AE, at any given time, would be associated with future GNP more closely than with past GNP.

If we observed the opposite—a higher association of AE with past GNP—a number of interpretations would be possible. For instance, it may be that, in the aggregate, firms are not even able to retain their current level of sales. Or, again in the aggregate, we may speculate that firms tend to treat advertising as a residual: that is, when sales have gone up in the previous year, they increase advertising while they spend less when sales have gone down.[1]

The available AE and GNP time series for the United States makes it possible to investigate this question. In 1970, S. Banks looked at the year-to-year percentage changes in AE and GNP for the period 1946-1969.[2] Changes in AE and GNP during the same year had a correlation coefficient of 0.6; that is, the strongest tendency was for both time series to rise and fall together. The correlation between changes in GNP for one year, followed by changes in AE the next year, was 0.16. The opposite correlation—i.e., changes in AE preceding changes in GNP—was 0.04.[3]

---

[1] There are other possible interpretations. For example, in January 1973, firms set their advertising budgets on sales expectations for 1973. Yet these expectations may be heavily influenced by their sales experience in 1972. The higher the influence of past experiences on expectations, the more likely that the aggregate AE will turn out to be correlated with past GNP. Although we cannot pursue the topic, we believe that future inquiries will be successful only if we can learn more about organizational decision making and other behavioral processes. For an example of the difficulties in the study of how marketing departments process information regarding their markets, see I. Nonaka, *Organization and Market: Exploratory Study of Centralization vs. Decentralization,* Ph.D. dissertation, Graduate School of Business Administration, University of California, Berkeley, 1972.

[2] S. Banks, "Adapting Marketing Strategy to Changes in Business Conditions: Implications for Promotional Programs," National Industrial Conference Board, 18th Annual Marketing Conference, New York, October 1970, unpublished manuscript.

[3] Banks found a similar pattern for the association between changes in personal consumption expenditures and advertising expenditures. The correlation between simultaneous changes was 0.81; for consumption expenditures leading advertising, 0.24; and for advertising leading consumption expenditures, 0.07.

Let us pursue our question: does AE tend to be associated more with future GNP, current GNP, or past GNP? Exhibit 11.13 shows the results for the United States for the period 1929-1971. The two time series are always highly associated throughout the period. However, AE tends to correlate more highly with past GNP than with future GNP. The advertising expenditures in a given year are correlated with GNP three years later by 0.97, but their correlation with the GNP of three years before is 0.99. All other cases fall in line—exactly between the maximum and the minimum of the observed correlations.

EXHIBIT 11.13

DEGREE OF ASSOCIATION BETWEEN ADVERTISING EXPENDITURES AND GROSS NATIONAL PRODUCT IN THE UNITED STATES, 1929-1971*

Gross National Product	Advertising Expenditures	Correlation
	AE three years before	.972
	AE two years before	.982
GNP of any given year	AE one year before	.987
is correlated with:	AE the same year	.991
	AE the following year	.993
	AE two years hence	.993
	AE three years hence	.994

*Computations by R. Dunkle and T. Kwan, based on federal statistics (see detailed references in Exhibit 11.16).

This regularity is somewhat perplexing. One might expect that in some years AE would be highly associated with future GNP and in other years with past GNP—possibly during periods of expansion and recession, respectively. But the exhibit tells us that, over four decades, the tendency was for advertising expenditures to follow rather than precede, to react to rather than lead. Although very small, the tendency is consistent.

Such persistent regularity may be merely a matter of chance. This should not stop us from wondering whether AE might follow the economy's development. Since the advertising institution is highly decentralized, it might be natural for the growth of the economy to create the need for more distribution of information through mass media. More and more firms would gradually come to recognize this need and try to fulfill it with increasing advertising efforts.

Some additional data also indicate that business firms tend to adjust their advertising decisions to the economy by decreasing (increasing) their ad budgets when sales decrease (increase).[1] Further, in a detailed study Verdon, McConnell, and Roesler observed the relationships of AE to the United States business cycle during the period 1945-1964.[2]

[1] "How to Advertise Out of a Recession," *Printers' Ink,* November 2, 1962, Special Report; and "Advertising in Recession Periods," Buchen Advertising, Inc., New York, 1970 (this report concerns only industrial advertising and sales).

[2] W. A. Verdon, C. R. McConnell, and T. W. Roesler, "Advertising Expenditures as an Economic Stabilizer: 1945-64," *Quarterly Review of Economics and Business,* Summer 1968.

They found that AE predominantly lagged behind the turning points of the business cycle and behind changes in GNP and industrial production.[1] Finally, an impressive series of econometric studies by Schmalensee shows that advertising expenditures tend to follow rather than lead consumption expenditures.[2]

Does Exhibit 11.13 provide additional evidence that the advertising institution tends to follow rather than lead economic change in the United States? It is possible to gain some further insight by following a standard scientific procedure: using existing knowledge to challenge the results presented in our exhibit.

During the period 1929-1971, the United States underwent some major changes. First, it went from the peak of prosperity of the twenties down to the troughs of two depressions in the thirties, and then through a major war in the first half of the forties. We would expect that pessimism would have prevailed during the thirties, forcing advertisers to be extremely cautious in setting their advertising budgets.

> *Proposition A.* To the extent that pessimism prevailed during 1929-1950, we would expect that in this period the correlations we observed would change as follows: (a) AE would lag more and lead less; and (b) AE would be less associated with GNP of the same year.

Second, although the immediate postwar period was characterized by conflicting tendencies, the major characteristic of American society during the fifties and sixties was the increasing discovery of affluence. Optimism prevailed throughout these two decades, and we would expect advertisers to have been much less cautious in setting their advertising budgets. In fact, we would expect them to have been aggressive, i.e., more likely to set ad budgets in expectation of higher future sales.

> *Proposition B.* To the extent that optimism prevailed during the fifties and the sixties, we would expect that in this period the correlations we observed would change as follows: (a) AE would lag less and lead more; and (b) AE would be more associated with current GNP.

It is worth remembering that the bulk of AE reflects ads aimed at the consumer sector. Since there are federal statistics that provide indicators of this sector—namely, disposable personal income (DPI) and personal consumption expenditures (PCE)—we further predict that Propositions A and B above also apply to the associations between AE and DPI and PCE, respectively.

The nature of our reasoning must be emphasized, especially because in recent times the overreliance on statistical methods has resulted in less thinking (especially when initial findings are statistically significant), in confusion of statistics with scientific methods, and, ultimately, in misuse of the power of statistical inference. Our procedure is: if the tentative

---

[1] We shall not discuss whether following rather than leading the economy makes sense from the managerial point of view. The Buchen report cited above presents evidence that business firms that react to decreases in sales by not cutting their advertising budgets during the recession year, or the following year, do much better in sales (and probably in profits) than those that do cut back their expenditures.

[2] Schmalensee, *op. cit.*, Chapter 3, especially Section 3.2.

interpretation of the data contained in Exhibit 11.13 is correct, then it should be even more valid under certain conditions (e.g., during depressions and wars), but less valid under other conditions (e.g., during periods of affluence). That is, the observed correlations are challenged as an artificial average that must be specified.

Exhibits 11.13A, 11.13B, and 11.13C give the results of our explorations into the chicken-and-egg problem. At the aggregate level, these orders of magnitude are *consistently* observed: (1) advertising expenditures are somewhat more likely to follow rather than simultaneously interact with GNP, DPI, and PCE; and, in turn, (2) advertising expenditures are more likely to interact simultaneously than to lead GNP, DPI, and PCE.

Such consistent tendencies were particularly true during the depressions and the World War II years. Even during the expansionary fifties and sixties, there is no evidence that advertising tended in the main to lead the other three indicators. Note that the highest simultaneous association of AE during the depression and war years is with PCE rather than with DPI or GNP—which makes sense for those who are familiar with advertising management problems.

It is important not to conclude rashly that these observed tendencies are established facts, merely because of the magnitudes observed or their statistical significance, but

EXHIBIT 11.13A

**ASSOCIATION BETWEEN ADVERTISING EXPENDITURES
AND GROSS NATIONAL PRODUCT***

Gross National Product	Advertising Expenditures	Correlations for the Time Period		
		1929–1971	1929–1950	1950–1971
	AE three years before	.972	.559	.970
	AE two years before	.982	.785	.979
	AE one year before	.987	.872	.983
GNP of any given year is correlated with:	AE the same year	.991	.916	.990
	AE the following year	.993	.927	.992
	AE two years hence	.993	.940	.989
	AE three years hence	.994	.958	.988

EXHIBIT 11.13B

**ASSOCIATION BETWEEN ADVERTISING EXPENDITURES
AND DISPOSABLE PERSONAL INCOME***

Disposable Personal Income	Advertising Expenditures	Correlations for the Time Period		
		1929–1971	1929–1950	1950–1971
	AE three years before	.971	.572	.973
	AE two years before	.982	.799	.982
	AE one year before	.987	.887	.985
DPI of any given year is correlated with:	AE the same year	.991	.931	.991
	AE the following year	.993	.943	.993
	AE two years hence	.994	.954	.991
	AE three years hence	.994	.968	.988

EXHIBIT 11.13C

ASSOCIATION BETWEEN ADVERTISING EXPENDITURES AND PERSONAL CONSUMPTION EXPENDITURES*

Personal Consumption Expenditures	Advertising Expenditures	Correlations for the Time Period		
		1929–1971	1929–1950	1950–1971
PCE of any given year is correlated with:	AE three years before	.976	.637	.977
	AE two years before	.986	.856	.984
	AE one year before	.991	.937	.987
	AE the same year	.995	.978	.993
	AE the following year	.997	.987	.995
	AE two years hence	.996	.988	.992
	AE three years hence	.996	.990	.990

*Computation by R. Dunkle and T. Kwan, based on federal statistics (see detailed references in Exhibit 11.16).

especially because only one country has been observed. The next scientific step should be to explore whether similar results obtain in other countries as well.

In this brief examination of currently available data, we have purposely avoided the term *causality*, using instead the terms *association* and *correlation*. The high association between AE and GNP cannot be interpreted as *prima facie* evidence of a cause-effect relationship; in fact, in scientific inquiry, any high association is usually suspicious. It is very probable that at least part of the observed association is not causal, but spurious, and so some other explanation should be sought.

These considerations lead to the very heart of the problem we want to solve. How can we establish whether there exist causal relationships between the advertising institution and the economy?

FROM CORRELATIONS TO CAUSATION

Although correlation and other operations of statistical inference are tools that have greatly enriched the scientific method, they cannot themselves identify causality; they can only help the search for causal relationships among events. Correlation, no matter how high, indicates only the possible presence of some direct or indirect causal process. Conversely, lack of correlation between two or more variables does not necessarily mean lack of causality. Furthermore, if measures of statistical association cannot identify the presence of causality, they certainly cannot ascertain its direction, i.e., whether x causes y or vice versa.

How, then, can we examine the high correlation of AE with macroeconomic indicators in a search for causality? In scientific method, the correct posture is an attempt to disprove the observed association. That is, one proposes a program of research and operations that would demonstrate that the observed association is spurious, e.g., the result of an antecedent causal process.[1] If this is, in fact, demonstrated, we know the

[1] In the text, we discuss only one of the several possible operations usually followed in research utilizing nonlaboratory data. The interested reader may pursue the topic by checking advanced econometric literature. At a somewhat easier level, for instance, the following are suggested: H. Zeisel, *Say It With Figures,* Harper, New York, 1957; and P. F. Lazarsfeld, A. K. Pasanella, and M. Rosenberg (eds.), *Continuities in the Language of Social Research,* The Free Press, New York, 1972.

association was indeed spurious. If it is not, we may be one step closer to believing that a causal relationship may in fact exist.

Some advertising literature has already thrown doubt on the assumption that the high association between AE and GNP is entirely causal. One can argue that much of the observed association is simply a reflection of the level of a country's economic development. In fact, if we rank all countries in terms of GNP and AE per capita, we find the United States and other industrialized countries at the top, with several countries that have not yet reached a stage of industrial development at the bottom.[1]

This argument, and similar ones, essentially state that the behavior of AE and GNP is "caused" by antecedent variables. But precisely what antecedent events might affect both GNP and AE? Let us look at a table ranking all countries on GNP and AE per capita.[2] At least part of the ranking reflects variations in the countries' *natural resources,* which are basic to industrialization. The United States and West Germany, for example, are rich in resources, while Greece and Pakistan are relatively poor.

But the correspondence between the countries' ranking by natural resources and by their GNP and AE per capita is still far from perfect. Countries like Brazil are extremely rich in natural resources of all kinds, but they score low in terms of both GNP and AE per capita. Conversely, although relatively poor in natural resources, countries like Switzerland and, recently, Japan score high on GNP and AE per capita.

These observations suggest that perhaps natural resources are only one cause of high GNP and AE. Or perhaps they are a condition contributing to high GNP and AE, rather than an actual cause. The data indicate that lack of natural resources can be overcome by obtaining resources by imports (Japan) or by inserting a country into the international flow of capital (Switzerland).

An *ability to use* resources is a necessary prerequisite of economic development. But it is also a human quality that, in principle, is uniformly distributed over the human race. Why, then, do some countries manifest this ability while others do not?

Two possible answers suggest themselves. First, the kind and level of *education* in a country may be a contributing factor. If the level of literacy is very low, technological and managerial skills cannot be employed. Further, if literacy is high but few people specialize in chemistry, physics, and the applied sciences, then a country lacks the climate in which economic development can flourish.

But education in itself cannot cause a country to use its abilities in a specific way. *A desire to use or acquire natural resources and human skills* toward work, saving, and so on–i.e., toward economic development–is also essential for economic growth; it is the necessary spark.[3]

---

[1] See the revealing computations in J. Simon, *Issues in Economics of Advertising,* University of Illinois Press, Urbana, Ill., 1970, p. 170. The findings reported by Valli are also a hint in this direction; see Exhibit 11.11.

[2] See, for example, Simon, *op. cit.,* p. 170.

[3] Decreases in economic growth may also be related to a gradual extinction of this desire. It is not too difficult to imagine a social group so contented that it shifts its energies from production to consumption: the United States and other "affluent" societies might become examples of this cultural-economic relationship.

Yet this very desire calls for further explanation: what *cultural orientations* may call it into existence? The Protestant ethic has often been suggested as a major factor in determining which countries first harnessed the power of technology for industrialization and economic development. In addition, industrialization requires saving and other sacrifices: it requires current action to achieve future goals. Some cultures, however, are more immersed in the present. Finally, industrialization, as observed in history,[1] requires the presence of specific *political ideologies* and political and legal *institutions*.

Let us pause for a moment and take stock. We started with a description, namely, the high association of AE and GNP. We first wondered whether this implies that the former causes the latter, or vice versa, or whether each affects the other. Then, following scientific procedure, we inquired whether this association is causal by trying to disprove it. Thus, we searched for possible causal mechanisms that would explain why the two measures co-vary.

This search suggested a causal mechanism, represented graphically in Exhibit 11.14. Natural resources may be one cause and/or a contributing condition to the observed GNP-AE association. Natural resources lead to economic growth if a country has the ability to use them. This ability depends on two other variables: education and the desire to use or acquire natural resources. Variations in societies' desire to use or acquire resources may be explained by a number of additional factors: cultural orientations, religious predispositions, political ideologies, and social-legal institutions.

In Exhibit 11.14 we have added to the blueprint of the hypothesized mechanism some possible feedbacks: these give the causal mechanism the dynamic quality necessary to capture the most relevant aspect of life—change. These feedbacks are also tentative hypotheses.[2]

It would not be surprising if this causal mechanism—or some other—were to explain away a large part of the observed association between GNP and AE. The advertising institution, after all, is at most only one of the inputs affecting economic output. Only after we have isolated the effects of other factors can we assess how much of the association between the economy and advertising is causal. And only then can we turn our energies to identifying how much of this observed net causality flows from advertising to the economy and how much from GNP to AE.

The proposed net of cause-effect relationships, as well as others, can be tested at the present time. Methodology and statistics are available, provided they are used

---

[1]S. Kuznets, "Modern Economic Growth: Findings and Reflections," *American Economic Review,* June 1973.

[2]It must be stressed that the proposed mechanism in Exhibit 11.14 is only one of the many that could be postulated at present to ascertain *how much* of the initially observed association between GNP and AE is, in fact, evidence of causality. For instance, suppose we were interested mainly in economic variables and willing to postulate only recursive rather than feedback, fully dynamic interactions over time. We could then postulate a blueprint as follows:

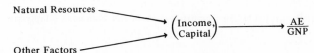

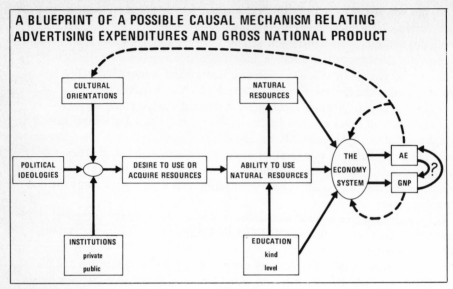

EXHIBIT 11.14

correctly, as are data tapping several of the variables listed in Exhibit 11.14.[1] Although the available data are not the best indicators of the listed variables for the purpose of our inquiry, they do at least provide a basis for systematic inquiries. All that is lacking—and it is a major lack—is the willingness to make the systematic conceptual efforts needed to determine the possible causal roles of the advertising institution in a socioeconomic system. Without these efforts, methodology and statistics will serve no purpose or will be misused, and better data will not be generated. In that case, the advertising institution will remain the topic of cocktail conversations, political discourse, random legislation, and personal preferences, rather than the focus of scientific study.

3.3 SEARCHING FOR RELATIONSHIPS OF PROPORTIONS

Several disciplines, including engineering, find it useful to study the structure of a phenomenon. In this approach, one tries to observe whether there exist optimal *proportions* among the components of a phenomenon (e.g., among the gears in the transmission of a car) or between some components (the sizes of the gears) and the entire phenomenon under study (engine speed, i.e., revolutions per minute). Note that as the level of the phenomenon (engine speed) changes, the optimal proportions among the components (gears' size) may remain constant or may vary, sometimes substantially. That is, sometimes the observed relationships are *constant:* for example, if body

---

[1] Possible sources, for instance, are the United Nations' statistics or the World Data Bank (Marketing Control, Inc.).

temperature increases, so must heartbeat if life is to continue. In other cases, we observe *variable* proportions: for instance, as a child grows, his height gradually becomes a larger and larger percent of the length of his intestine. The questions of what are optimal proportions and whether they are constant or variable are questions of fact, to be determined for each case.

The proportionality approach can provide useful knowledge to decision makers. For example, one first ascertains the value of optimal proportions that correspond to optimal (desired) behavior (performance). With this knowledge, one can correct a suboptimal case before it is too late; e.g., increase the amount of electricity generated by a car engine before the battery is drained completely. Or one can plan, design, and implement new systems whose behavior is "better" since optimal proportions have been built into it.

The proportionality approach has been used relatively little in the study of economic and social phenomena.[1] The well-known exceptions in business are the fields of finance and accounting; for example, the price/earnings and other ratios are used by analysts to judge the well-being and potential of different firms. From engineering to medicine and finance, the study of proportions can indeed provide actionable knowledge.

The study of the structure of a phenomenon must be distinguished clearly from the study of its possible causes. In the proportionality approach, we are interested in observing relationships of proportions (varying or constant), not of causality. In the next two sections, we shall illustrate the potential of this approach to our subject. More specifically, we shall try to measure and interpret the proportion between the size of the advertising institution and the size of the economy in the United States.

3.3.1 On the Proportionality Between the Advertising Institution and the Economy: Some Facts and Possible Interpretations

Let us look at data covering the United States from 1929 to 1971 and search for relationships of proportionality between the advertising institution and the economy. Before doing this, however, we should have a departure point, that is, some working hypotheses to guide our examination. As the dialogue between an initial frame of reference and the data unfolds, new insights, and even some testable hypotheses, will gradually develop. Hopefully, these will guide future research and public policy decisions.

As a point of departure, assume that three statements (or hypotheses) are correct:

A. *The number of senders of messages through the society's mass communication system has increased between the years 1929–1970.* This speculation is based on the following observation. First, the number of nonprofit institutions that advertise for selling, buying, or other reasons (including public relations) has increased. Second, the number of individual consumers who advertise has also increased. In the business sector, while a tendency toward concentration may have decreased the number of legal entities,

---

[1] For some notable exceptions in economics, see, e.g., S. Kuznets, *Modern Economic Growth: Rate Structure, and Spread,* Yale University Press, New Haven, Conn., 1966, and *Economic Growth of Nations: Total Output and Production Structure,* Harvard University Press, Cambridge, Mass., 1971. For an exciting exception in the study of human organizations, see M. Haire, "Biological Models and Empirical Histories of the Growth of Organizations," in M. Haire (ed.), *Modern Organization Theory,* Wiley, New York, 1959.

the number of profit centers with the authority to advertise has increased (from the number of relatively independent companies within conglomerates to the number of divisions and product and brand managers within a company). Although each of these assumptions could be tested, at this junction it is more important to see what may happen if they are correct.

B. *The number of seekers/receivers of advertising messages has also increased over the same forty years.* This statement is true for the demographic component of the United States; the number of consumers and workers looking for information has certainly increased. Applying the reasoning presented above, we assume that the number of seekers/receivers in the business and nonprofit sectors has also increased.

C. *The number of messages per unit of time (say, per year) has also increased.* This hypothesis is the basis of the popular clichés about the good old days. To support this statement, recall that over the last forty years (1) the life cycle of various consumer goods has decreased (see the data in Chapter 4, Section 2); (2) the life cycle of industrial goods has also decreased (due to increasing technological change); and (3) the number of options available in both consumer and industrial goods has increased.[1] These changes are presumably related to (or lead to) an increase in the number of ads.

If the number of all senders, seekers/receivers, and ads has increased, then the *load* on the country's communication system must have increased also. Therefore, the total *cost* of the system must have gone up too. Assuming that the cost of the United States advertising system is measured appropriately by total AE, we know that the system's *absolute cost* has increased (see the first column in Exhibit 11.15).

But what are the changes in the *relative cost* of the advertising institution? That is: if the size of the economy has increased over the last forty years, has the size of its advertising institution increased *proportionately?* More specifically, has the proportion of the advertising system to the economy increased, remained the same, or decreased?

Our tentative hypotheses imply another hypothesis: the cost of the institution should have grown more than proportionately. If GNP and AE are used as measures of the size of the two entities, during the past forty years the proportion of advertising to the economy has never again attained the 1929 level. It first decreased, then increased somewhat, and is now declining again (see the first column in Exhibit 11.16 and its graphical representation in Exhibit 11.16A): the hypothesis seems incorrect.

There are many ways to react when facts do not support a tentative hypothesis. If our initial predispositions toward the hypothesis were negative, we could conclude that the facts are wrong. Conversely, if we believe in our hypothesis, we may argue that we have chosen inappropriate indicators or that the data contain "noise." There is a third possible way to react; we may ask why there is a discrepancy between prediction

[1] Some extremely suggestive computations have been made for six appliance categories advertised in the Sears & Roebuck catalogs for the period 1950–1970, and for a series of nondurable products such as deodorants, toilet soaps, sandwich bags, and margarine, for the period 1960–1970, by W. T. Moran, "Where There Is Choice There Is Value," paper presented to the Annual Scientific Meeting of the Society of Cosmetic Chemists, New York, December 1971, reprinted in *Journal of Advertising Research,* April 1973.

EXHIBIT 11.15

TIME SERIES: ADVERTISING, THE ECONOMY, AND THE HOUSEHOLD SECTOR
(Current Dollars, in Billions)

Year	AE	GNP	NNP	NI	Ig	Ex	Im	PI	DPI	PCE
1929	3	103	95	87	16	7	6	86	83	77
1930	3	90	82	75	10	5	4	77	75	70
1931	2	76	68	60	6	4	3	66	64	61
1932	2	58	51	43	1	3	2	50	49	49
1933	1	56	49	40	1	2	2	47	46	46
1934	2	65	58	50	3	3	2	54	52	51
1935	2	72	65	57	6	3	3	60	59	56
1936	2	83	75	65	9	4	3	69	66	62
1937	2	90	83	74	12	5	4	74	71	67
1938	2	85	77	67	7	4	3	68	66	64
1939	2	91	83	73	9	4	3	73	70	67
1940	2	100	92	81	13	5	4	78	76	71
1941	2	125	116	104	18	6	5	96	93	81
1942	2	158	148	137	10	5	5	123	117	89
1943	2	192	181	170	6	4	7	151	134	99
1944	3	210	199	183	7	5	7	165	146	108
1945	3	212	201	182	11	7	8	171	150	120
1946	3	209	199	182	31	15	7	179	160	143
1947	4	231	219	199	34	20	8	191	170	161
1948	5	258	243	224	46	17	10	210	189	174
1949	5	257	240	218	36	16	10	207	189	177
1950	6	285	266	241	54	14	12	228	207	191
1951	6	328	307	278	59	19	15	256	227	206
1952	7	346	322	291	52	18	16	273	238	217
1953	8	365	339	305	53	17	17	288	253	230
1954	8	365	337	303	52	18	16	290	257	237
1955	9	398	367	331	67	20	18	311	275	254
1956	10	419	385	351	70	24	20	333	293	267
1957	10	441	404	336	68	27	21	351	309	281
1958	10	447	408	368	61	23	21	361	319	291
1959	11	484	442	400	75	24	23	384	337	311
1960	12	504	460	415	75	27	23	401	350	325
1961	12	520	475	427	72	29	23	417	364	335
1962	12	560	510	458	83	30	25	443	385	355
1963	13	591	538	482	87	32	26	466	405	375
1964	14	632	576	518	94	37	29	498	438	401
1965	15	685	625	564	108	39	32	539	473	433
1966	17	750	686	621	121	43	38	587	512	466
1967	17	794	725	654	117	46	41	629	546	492
1968	18	864	790	711	126	51	48	689	591	536
1969	19	930	848	766	139	56	54	751	634	580
1970	20	976	887	799	137	63	59	806	690	617
1971	21	1050	957	856	152	66	65	861	744	665

Sources: AE (advertising expenditures) from *U.S. Statistical Abstract 1971,* Washington: GPO, 1972; GNP (gross national product), NNP (net national product), NI (national income), Ig (gross investments), Ex (exports), Im (imports), PI (personal income), DPI (disposable personal income), and PCE (personal consumption expenditures) from *Economic Report of the President, January 1973,* Washington: GPO, 1973.

EXHIBIT 11.16

ADVERTISING AS A "PROPORTION" OF THE ECONOMY AND OF THE HOUSEHOLD SECTOR (in Current Dollars, in Percentages)

Year	AE/GNP	AE/NNP	AE/NI	AE/Ig	AE/PI	AE/DPI	AE/PCE
1929	3.3	3.6	4.0	21.2	4.0	4.1	4.4
1930	2.9	3.2	3.5	25.3	3.4	3.5	3.7
1931	3.0	3.4	3.8	40.8	3.5	3.6	3.8
1932	2.8	3.2	3.8	162.7	3.2	3.3	3.4
1933	2.3	2.7	3.2	93.0	2.8	2.9	2.8
1934	2.5	2.8	3.3	49.3	3.0	3.1	3.2
1935	2.3	2.6	3.0	26.4	2.8	2.9	3.0
1936	2.3	2.5	2.9	22.4	2.8	2.9	3.1
1937	2.3	2.5	2.8	17.6	2.8	2.9	3.1
1938	2.3	2.5	2.8	29.3	2.8	2.9	3.0
1939	2.2	2.4	2.7	21.3	2.7	2.8	3.0
1940	2.1	2.3	2.6	15.9	2.7	2.8	3.0
1941	1.8	1.9	2.2	12.5	2.3	2.4	2.8
1942	1.4	1.5	1.6	22.0	1.8	1.8	2.4
1943	1.3	1.4	1.5	43.8	1.7	1.9	2.5
1944	1.3	1.4	1.5	38.4	1.7	1.9	2.5
1945	1.4	1.4	1.6	27.1	1.7	1.9	2.4
1946	1.6	1.7	1.9	11.0	1.9	2.1	2.4
1947	1.8	1.9	2.1	12.5	2.2	2.5	2.7
1948	1.9	2.0	2.2	10.6	2.3	2.6	2.8
1949	2.0	2.2	2.4	14.6	2.5	2.8	2.9
1950	2.0	2.1	2.4	10.6	2.5	2.8	3.0
1951	2.0	2.1	2.3	10.9	2.5	2.8	3.1
1952	2.1	2.2	2.5	13.8	2.6	3.0	3.3
1953	2.1	2.3	2.6	14.7	2.7	3.1	3.4
1954	2.2	2.4	2.7	15.8	2.8	3.2	3.5
1955	2.3	2.5	2.8	13.6	3.0	3.3	3.6
1956	2.4	2.6	2.8	14.2	3.0	3.4	3.7
1957	2.3	2.6	2.8	15.2	2.9	3.3	3.7
1958	2.3	2.5	2.8	16.9	2.9	3.2	3.6
1959	2.3	2.5	2.8	15.0	2.9	3.3	3.6
1960	2.4	2.6	2.9	16.0	3.0	3.4	3.7
1961	2.3	2.5	2.8	16.5	2.8	3.3	3.5
1962	2.2	2.4	2.7	14.9	2.8	3.2	3.5
1963	2.2	2.4	2.7	15.1	2.8	3.2	3.5
1964	2.2	2.5	2.7	15.1	2.9	3.2	3.5
1965	2.2	2.4	2.7	14.1	2.8	3.2	3.5
1966	2.2	2.4	2.7	13.7	2.8	3.3	3.6
1967	2.1	2.3	2.6	14.5	2.7	3.1	3.4
1968	2.1	2.3	2.6	14.4	2.6	3.1	3.4
1969	2.1	2.3	2.5	14.0	2.6	3.1	3.4
1970	2.0	2.2	2.5	14.3	2.4	2.9	3.2
1971	1.9	2.1	2.4	13.5	2.4	2.8	3.1

Sources: AE (advertising expenditures) from *U.S. Statistical Abstract 1971,* Washington: GPO, 1972; GNP (gross national product), NNP (net national product), NI (national income), Ig (gross investments), PI (personal income), DPI (disposable personal income), and PCE (personal consumption expenditures) from *Economic Report of the President, January 1973,* Washington: GPO, 1973.

ADVERTISING AS A PROPORTION OF
GNP, Ig, DPI & PCE (in current $)

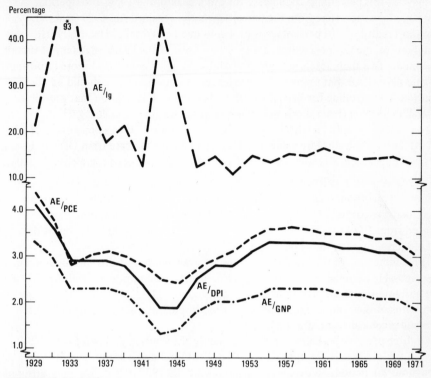

EXHIBIT 11.16A

(hypothesis) and data. The following sections illustrate the latter two kinds of reaction.
Let us begin with a few general remarks about the observed trends and then proceed
with an interpretation of these observations.

ADVERTISING AND THE ECONOMY

It might be argued that GNP is not an indicator appropriate to our inquiry; for
example, the relationship of AE to GNP may be misleading because several components
of the latter are not associated with the former. Such economic indicators as net
national product (NNP) and national product (NI) would presumably contain fewer
components unrelated to the work of the advertising institution. Yet the percentage of
AE in terms of NNP and NI varies over time in exactly the same way as AE as a
percentage of GNP. From 1919 to the mid-forties it declined, then rose again until the
beginning of the sixties, when it slowly fell again. In no case did it ever reach the height
of 1929 (see the appropriate columns in Exhibit 11.16).

The relationship of AE with gross investments (Ig) was relatively unstable, especially during the 1929-1946 period (Exhibit 11.16). Yet after World War II there was the same tendency for this percentage to increase toward a peak in the 1958-1961 period, decreasing thereafter. Here, too, the percentage never regained the 1929 peak. The relative instability of this percentage is probably due to two simple factors. First, investments by the business sectors are inherently one of the less stable components of the economy (see their absolute values in Exhibit 11.15). Second, and more important, only that part of AE that represents messages sent to business firms should be compared, concurrently controlling for the use of other channels of information that prevail in industrial marketing (from shows and exhibits to salesmen and catalogs).

Overall there is only one difference in the time trend of AE as a percentage of GNP, NNP, NI, and Ig: the absolute value of AE as a percentage increase from GNP to Ig. This is so simply because the absolute values of the four indicators are progressively smaller.

ADVERTISING AND THE HOUSEHOLD SECTOR

Much of AE record messages sent to consumers, and our three tentative hypotheses suggest that the cost of advertising relative to the consumer sector should have increased from 1929 to 1971. Much of the popular literature, with its vision of the good old days, suggests the same.

Three indicators of the household sector are available to test this: personal income (PI), disposable personal income (DPI), and personal consumption expenditures (PCE). Their absolute values through time are listed in Exhibit 11.15, while the percentage of AE in terms of these three indicators is reported in the last three columns of Exhibit 11.16 and graphically in Exhibit 11.16A.

All three percentages behave in almost exactly the same way: down from 1929 to the end of World War II; up until about 1958-1961; and down again to 1971. Throughout the period, no percentage again reaches its 1929 height. The only difference is that the absolute value of the percentage in terms of PI is greater than that in terms of DPI and this, in turn, is greater than the percentage of PCE—a fact to be expected since the absolute value of these three indicators decreases in that order.

Overall the relationships of AE with the indicators of the economy are very similar to those with the indicators of the household sector. All the percentages in Exhibit 11.16 show much the same behavior over time.

These findings are based on current dollar measures and do not take into account the demographic changes during the 1929-1971 period. The findings are not altered if we control for demographic variations and for inflation. That is, if we recompute the percentages in Exhibit 11.16, in *per capita* and/or *real dollar* terms, the observed proportions do not change.[1]

INTERPRETING THE OBSERVED RELATIONSHIPS OF PROPORTIONALITY

The observed relationships do not support our prediction: that the weight of the

---

[1] In fact, if we deflate AE by the GNP deflator and PCE by the PCE deflator, the proportion is 4.9 percent in 1929 to 2.9 percent in 1971, a decrease that is greater than that shown in Exhibit 11.16 (4.4 percent to 3.1 percent, respectively).

advertising institution as part of the economy and the household sector should be greater in recent times than in 1929. How can this discrepancy be explained?

We might begin by speculating that, since the institution carries a high load at a lower relative cost, it must be doing its job more efficiently. Yet the oscillations in the observed proportions through time suggest that this explanation—higher efficiency—may be only one of several factors at work. Let us take a closer look at the AE/GNP ratio since 1929, examining each of its three major movements separately.

FROM 1929 TO 1944

It is a popular belief that 1929 was the beginning of the Great Depression. This is incorrect; for most of society, 1929 was the peak of the boom of the late 1920s. Black Friday—and the end of an era—came only in November of that year. In addition, federal income taxes were low. Thus the relatively large size of AE—3.3 percent of GNP—is not especially surprising.

As the depression began to gather momentum, this percentage decreased: however, it gave no indication of the brief recovery and of the second recession of the late 1930s. (Perhaps the AE/DPI and AE/PCE ratios provide some slight indication of these events.) Then, at the end of the period, the United States began to shift its production capacity fo war-related goods, first with its early efforts to send supplies to Great Britain and the USSR and then by entering the war directly. The ensuing centralization of economic decision making and the lid placed upon consumer choice clearly diminished the need for advertising—and the ratio of AE to GNP decreased to a low of 1.3 percent in 1943 and 1944.

FROM 1945 TO 1960

The AE/GNP ratio began to climb gradually but steadily after World War II, reaching an apparent plateau in the second half of the fifties. A maximum of 2.37 percent was reached in 1960. Considering the release of the pent-up wartime demand and the affluence that followed and gradually spread throughout society, this increase in the utilization of the advertising institution is readily comprehensible.

What is surprising is that the ratio did not increase even more. This period saw a rapidly growing population, large increases in discretionary time and real income, the birth of new products and brands, and the shorter life cycle of products. These factors lead us to expect that the load on the institution, and thus its relative cost, should have grown more rapidly than the figures indicate. How was the institution able to cope with a higher load? Was it through increasing efficiency?

At least two factors have been responsible for this apparently higher efficiency. First, the appearance and subsequent growth of television drastically changed the "production function" of society's mass communication system, and thus of the advertising institution. Television's ability to carry more messages at a lower cost per capita per period of time made a basic contribution to the institution's engineering efficiency.

One can also speculate that a change in consumer predispositions may have influenced the AE/GNP ratio. Affluence not only provides more discretionary time and income, but can also bring about some change in basic cultural predispositions. Affluence may increase willingness to try new products, brands, and ideas; abundance may mean less resistance to stimuli urging people to "take it easy," or to realize "you're lucky to live in America," and to other, similar advertising themes of the fifties. In their search for a style of life, consumers learn that trials are within their reach and errors are less costly.

These cultural and economic changes in the household sector require each firm to adjust to society's increased orientation toward consumption. More products and consumers implies the need for more ads, but advertisers may have realized that they did not need to increase the number of messages to the extent that would have been necessary in a society that had continued to be oriented toward work and saving. Thus, what appeared to be an increase in the internal efficiency of the advertising institution may have been due partly to a change in the seekers/receivers of ads.

FROM 1961 TO 1971

After 1960, the proportion of AE to GNP, and to all other indicators, began to decrease, reaching a low of 2.01 percent in 1970 and 1.9 percent in 1971 (versus 3.3 percent in 1929). Since both affluence and fads continued to spread across the United States during the 1960s, this decrease is perplexing.

The decrease of AE incidence on the household sector is also perplexing: the cost of the advertising institution, relative to personal income, disposable income, and even personal consumption expenditures decreased even more rapidly. By 1971, for instance, the AE/PCE had gone from 3.7 to 3.1 percent, substantially lower than in 1929 (4.4 percent).

At first one might speculate that the internal efficiency of the institution had increased still more. But TV could not be responsible, for it had already reached its maximum impact by the beginning of the sixties, while the role of cable television was still marginal. On the other hand, management decisions by message senders, especially business firms, might have improved, for it was at this very time that consumer research came into its own (see Chapter 6, Section 3). It is possible that increased understanding of consumer needs contributed to a more efficient utilization of the advertising institution by an increasing number of firms. Note that, according to Schmalensee's computations, the cost of the "basket" of national ads increased much less than the cost of the entire basket of all goods produced by the economy for the period 1950-67.[1]

Changes in consumer behavior might also explain the declining cost of the advertising institution relative to the economy and the consumer sector. As in the fifties, cultural predispositions toward a consumption life style may have led people to spend more freely and to heed ads more readily. Thus, from the advertiser's viewpoint, equal or better results could be obtained at relatively lower costs. One can also speculate that the nature of much savings may have changed: instead of saving only "for a rainy day," many people might now have saved for the short term in order to buy "luxuries." This would also increase the response to ads.

There are several reasons for suspecting that the increased efficiency of the institution recorded by the AE/GNP ratio was at least partly an artifact of the data. The components

---

[1] Schmalensee, op. cit., p. 254. And, for the period, 1966-1971, media "cost per thousands," has remained practically unchanged despite rising labor and raw material expenses (R. J. Coen, personal communication).

of GNP that grew fastest during the sixties were not related to any substantial utilization of the advertising institution. Examples are: the space program, the Vietnam war, and—most important of all—public services, including social security, Medicare, education, public health, transportation, public housing, farm subsidies, and many others. If the value of these components were deducted from the GNP, the proportion of AE to GNP might not have decreased during the sixties.

Without further research we cannot yet conclude that the weight of the advertising institution has in fact decreased, and thus infer that its structural efficiency has increased. The largest variation has been about two percentage points: 3.3 percent in 1929 and 1.3 percent in 1943 and 1944. The next largest variation is about 1 percent: from 1.3 in 1943 up to 2.37 percent in 1961; then a change of about 0.47 percent—from 2.37 down to 1.9 percent in 1971. The variation for the 1929-1971 period is -1.4 percent. Similar magnitudes apply to the household sector. One may argue that these variations do not reflect basic socioeconomic events at all; they may simply express the large amount of "noise" in most of the data available. This argument obviously applies to all aggregate economic data but, in life, "it all depends." For instance, many take changes in unemployment very seriously, even when they are of an order much smaller than those reported here.

All in all, until further research is brought to bear on the topic, we have a choice between two conclusions. Either we "feel" that the advertising institution is indeed becoming a smaller cost to the economy and the household sector, or we "feel" that, by and large, the "proportion" has remained essentially the same. It is reasonable to conclude, however, that the relative cost of the advertising institution to the economy and consumers has *not* increased during the past forty years.

To stop at either of these two conclusions, however, is to miss the potential the proportionality approach has for mapping out knowledge of relevance to public policy decisions—from planning to implementation to control. Let us illustrate.

3.3.2 On the Nature and Use of the Proportionality Approach

The preceding section has reported trends in the proportions of AE to several indicators of the economy and the household sector. It would be incorrect to assume, however, that these ratios are good measures of structural relationships. An appreciation of the nature of the proportionality approach explains why this is so and illustrates how the approach can provide knowledge useful to private and public decision makers.

A simple illustration of the engineering knowledge that can be gained from the proportionality approach is provided by Kenneth Boulding's famous example of the leaping flea:

> . . . a flea can jump over a scale model of the Capitol, scaled down to the size of the flea. If a flea were as big as a man, however, it could not jump over the Capitol in Washington. Indeed, it could not jump at all. Its legs would break. This is due to the fact that the *strength* of muscles and bones is proportional to their cross section, which is an *area*. The *weight* of an object is proportional to its *volume*. Now, as the size of any object is increased according to scale, its volume increases as the cube of the proportionate increase in length, but its area increases only as the square. Multiply the length, breadth, and height of a flea by 1,000 and you will have increased all its

areas by 1,000,000, and all its volume by 1,000,000,000. You will have increased its weight by a thousand times more than the increase in its strength of bone and muscle. No wonder it would break into pieces![1]

In this case, the behavior (jumping) of the system (the flea) is a function of its strength and weight. Strength is related to the area (a^2) of bones and muscles, while weight is related to volume (w^3). If we increase the size of the flea to improve its performance, its weight will triple but its strength only double. Thus, we should plan accordingly—that is, the bigger flea *can* continue to leap only if its strength and weight remain in an optimal range of proportions.

Let us cautiously consider an analogy. Suppose we want to double the size of an economy. This will require greater use of the mass communication system, and thus we must also increase the size of the advertising institution. But by how much? And how can we conceptualize and measure the size of the economy and the advertising system?

An economy presumably is a space with many dimensions (commodities, human skills, technologies, etc.); let us say that the number of these dimensions is n. The advertising institution is also a space with many dimensions (in Chapter 1 we counted at least six). However, since advertising is only a subset of the economy, the number of its dimensions must be smaller than that of the economy: let us say it is $m < n$.

Given these points of reference, doubling the economy will increase its size by n. But if we simply doubled the mass communication system, we might create an extremely insufficient situation, for its size has increased only by m (which is smaller than n). That is, the *strength* of the communication system may be inadequate to support the larger economy.

Do we know whether this situation applies to the United States or to any other economy? The public policy implications of knowledge necessary to answer this question are crucial. For instance, in planning changes in the economy and its advertising institution, rational decisions are possible only if the values of n and m are known. At present, these numbers are not known. Although macroeconomics suggests a number of dimensions that are relevant in describing an economy, no conceptualization of the structure of the advertising system has yet been systematically attempted. In fact, practically all of us still think of advertising, and study it empirically, as something equivalent to advertisers, the ads, or the dollars spent.

Existing data, furthermore, reduce the multidimensional structure of both the economy and the advertising institution into one dimension (i.e., a line) by using the dollar yardstick. Thus, doubling the size of the economy always means doubling its GNP. But does it mean that we must double AE?

It should be clear by now that the ratios of AE to GNP and other indicators do not yet yield the structural knowledge needed by public policy makers. There is a further reason why this is so. Beyond identifying the number of relevant dimensions, we must also ascertain *how* these dimensions relate to each other. Let us explain.

---

[1] K. E. Boulding, *Economic Analysis,* Harper, New York, 1955, pp. 738-39.

WHAT "PROPORTIONALITY" HAVE WE OBSERVED?

In the Boulding example, note that the area or cross section of a bone is obtained by *multiplying* the length by the width (say, $a \times b$). The size or volume is obtained by *multiplying* length by width by height (say, $a \times b \times c$). The key feature of the flea case is that the *dimensions* of each concept (a and b for strength and c, d, and e for size) relate to each other by a *multiplicative relationship.*

Multiplicative relationships may or may not apply to advertising and economic systems. Research on the structure of the two systems, and on the proportions that must be satisfied for optimal changes in their performance, will have to identify whether linear, multiplicative, or some other complex relationships apply.

The importance of this question may be illustrated with two simple examples. In Exhibit 11.17, we begin with an economy and its advertising institution at time zero. Assume that the dimensions of each system can be measured in dollars; by *aggregating*, a total value for each system is obtained. This aggregation is additive in the linear case and multiplicative in the other. Thus the total dollar values of the economic and advertising systems differ in the two cases because of the difference in the relationships among the components or dimensions. Consequently, the ratio of the advertising institution to the economy is 35 percent in the linear case, 5 percent in the other.

EXHIBIT 11.17

AN EXAMPLE OF LINEAR AND MULTIPLICATIVE GROWTH

	Linear Case (Dimensions)	Multiplicative Case (Dimensions)
Economy	$(a + b + c + d) = X$	$(a \cdot b \cdot c \cdot d) = X'$
Advertising Institution	$(a + b) = Y$	$(a \cdot b) = Y'$
At time zero		
Economy	$\$(3 + 2 + 4 + 5) = \$14$	$\$(3 \cdot 2 \cdot 4 \cdot 5) = \$120$
Advertising Institution	$\$(3 + 2) = \$5$	$\$(3 \cdot 2) = \$6$
Proportion	$\dfrac{AE}{GNP} \cdot 100 = \dfrac{5}{14} = 35\%$	$\dfrac{6}{120} \cdot 100 = 5\%$
At time one (a growth by two)		
Economy	$\$(6 + 4 + 8 + 10) = \$28$	$\$(6 \cdot 4 \cdot 8 \cdot 10) = \$1920$
Advertising Institution	$\$(6 + 4) = \$10$	$\$(6 \cdot 4) = \$24$
Proportion	$\dfrac{10}{28} \cdot 100 = 35\%$	$\dfrac{24}{1920} \cdot 100 = 1.2\%$

Now assume that, by time one, all components of the two systems have doubled. Making the same computations, we obtain:

1. In the linear case, the ratio of the advertising institution to the economy has remained the same: 35 percent, but
2. In the multiplicative case, the ratio has decreased to 1.2 percent.

Note that the value of this ratio would differ if the relationships among the components of an economy and its advertising were other than linear or multiplicative. The ratio could also change if each dimension grew at a different rate, or if new dimensions appeared and old ones disappeared. For instance, if dimensions a and b represented print and radio media in 1929, a new dimension—television—would have appeared by 1971. Further, the values observed in 1929 for print and radio would not need to double during the period as long as television made up for the growth required.

These considerations suggest that even though the relationships within the advertising institution and within the economy may be linear, the ratio between the two systems may not necessarily remain constant.[1] Conversely, even if the relationship is multiplicative, the ratio may not necessarily decrease: here, too, the expected effect may be confounded by changes in the number and intensity of dimensions. Finally, as both systems grow, it is plausible that the relationships between dimensions may themselves change from linear to nonlinear, or vice versa.

Given these caveats, one can only speculate whether the observed AE/GNP proportionality implies a linear or a multiplicative case. However, as our knowledge of the *number* of the economy's and advertising's dimensions increase, we will be able to use the observed proportionality to understand their *relationship*.

It is exciting to think that we may have empirical suggestions that the economy and its advertising systems have grown *as if* the linear or the multiplicative case applies, within the forty years of observations. For evaluative questions and, above all, for planning at the public policy level, it would be useful to know which structural relationship does in fact apply. That is, if we plan for a certain rate of growth in the economy, by how much should we "allow" the advertising institution to grow also?

In conclusion, by studying our subject matter from the viewpoint of the proportionality approach, we can ask many questions that are relevant to policy making. Here is another example. Does doubling the size of the economy require doubling the size of unemployment? Why not? What structural knowledge of the economy makes us believe that 4 percent is the correct proportion in both 1940 and 1970? In fact, we have succeeded so far in keeping unemployment down by reducing the work week to forty hours (less in some cities and industries); increasing the number and lengthening the time of the so-called coffee breaks; increasing the length of paid vacations and sick leave; increasing the amount of compulsory schooling, and so on. The study of the structural design of socioeconomic systems is crucial for gaining the engineering knowledge required

---

[1] Consider a numerical example. Suppose that, at time one in the exhibit, the value of print has increased to 6 and that of radio has remained equal to 2; and suppose that a new medium, television, has appeared and its value is 4. If we replace these figures in the exhibit, we obtain a total value for the economy of 30 and a total value of 12 for the advertising institution, for the linear case. The ratio has now increased to 37.9 percent instead of remaining constant at the level of 35 percent, even though the relationships are still linear.

for the solution of many public policy problems. This is as true of advertising as it is of employment and other socioeconomic phenomena.

4 SUMMARY

Although the advertising institution has been praised and condemned for centuries, both viewpoints are at present based simply on personal preferences. We lack measures of efficiency that would allow us to evaluate the institution rationally. Even though there is much micromanagerial evidence to indicate that buyers and sellers need to acquire and use information by means of mass media, we lack clear concepts and solid data to approach the subject at the macrosocietal level. At this level, an economist has effectively summarized the limitations of current knowledge:

> In fact, it is probably not possible to demonstrate rigorously that too much, too little, or just enough is now spent on advertising. In the present state of welfare economics, there are no rules to help our ideal [public] authority determine its optimal budget. Further, since such an authority would be likely to produce a different information mix than that presently available, proving that the information now conveyed by advertising could be given to consumers at less cost does not answer the question. Finally, as Telser reminds us, in order for any judgement of this sort to have meaning, it must relate to some replacement or supplement to advertising which could actually be implemented, and we know little about such creatures.[1]

In this chapter we have examined the main lines of concern that should guide future research on the macro roles of the institution. Concepts must be operationalized; more and new breakdowns of current data must be provided; altogether new data must be collected; and the emphasis on regression and other inference techniques must be switched toward building substantive models if we are indeed interested in identifying possible causes and effects. Finally, we must also explore the potential of the structural approach, of studying the relationships that may govern changes in the structure of both the advertising institution and the economy in which it works.

Still other avenues of research readily suggest themselves. Macro models describing the United States economy abound, yet no equations specifying the relationships of the advertising institution to the consumption *and* to the investment equations have been included. Similarly, the input/output models recently favored by the United States Department of Commerce could reserve a visible place for the advertising industry, thus giving us some further insights into the ways the economy utilizes its communication system.

The conceptual and empirical knowledge of the engineering efficiency of the institution that can emerge from these efforts will eventually give public policy makers, and citizens, the necessary foundations for making value choices. We shall now turn to an examination of the possible knowledge we might have with regard to more specific roles of the advertising institution.

[1] R. Schmalensee, "Advertising and Economic Welfare," in S. Divita (ed.), *Advertising and the Public Interest,* American Marketing Association, Chicago, Ill., 1974, p. 10.

Chapter 12

On Some Specific Roles of the Advertising Institution

While in the previous chapter we examined the advertising institution at the macro level, in this chapter we turn to more specific roles of advertising, including its relationships with with the press (i.e., society's mass communication system), its function in providing economic information, and its variations across different industries and firms.

In the first section, two publishers discuss how advertising interacts with the entire mass communication system as a whole. Both stress two points: (1) the extent to which the advertising institution pays for the cost of the entire communication system and (2) the extent to which the institution helps to maintain a press free from government control and other pressures and open to diverse viewpoints in politics, religion, and other areas of human concern.

The second section turns to the relatively new and controversial topic known as the economics of information. Contrary to traditional economic theory, new developments start from the premise that information is not free; that humans do not have perfect information. From this perspective, advertising is an industry that produces the information necessary for sellers to find buyers and for buyers to find sellers. Here advertising competes with other channels of information, e.g., word-of-mouth, personal selling, labels, and package and product design. Thus the rate at which different industries and firms utilize mass information varies according to whether or not its relative price is competitive. Finally, we examine a number of empirical attempts to identify and assess the relationships advertising may have with economic concentration, profit rates, and price levels in different industries.

The existing evidence in these research areas is contradictory. In the third section, we shall discuss whether the contradictions may be due to behavioral and organizational differences across and within industries that are ignored by the current Standard Industrial Classification (SIC) system. Some evidence indicates that even firms classified in the same industry differ greatly in their marketing mix, especially in the role that advertising plays vis-à-vis other available informational channels. This suggests the need for data more appropriate to the study of advertising's relationships with industry concentration, profit rates, and price levels.

1 ADVERTISING, COMMUNICATION, AND SOCIETY *(excerpts from N. Cousins, former editor,* Saturday Review, *and editor,* World Review; *and A. Heiskell, chairman of the board, Time, Inc.)*

Advertising, as we have emphasized, is only one use of society's mass communication system, and it thus shares relationships of joint costs and benefits with other uses. For example, when postal rates go up, they affect not only the cost of ads but also the cost of all the information flowing through print media.

Cultures differ in the amount and kind of information that is allowed to flow freely throughout society. In the United States, a free flow has been generally encouraged.[1] For instance, second-class postal rates are seen as a subsidy to readers rather than to magazines and newspapers. Other channels of communication—from private conversations to speakers on soapboxes to TV networks—also can be and have been the subject of government encouragement and regulation. Regulation of any type of information flow faces many problems, which, as T. I. Emerson pointed out, "are not so much technical ones of method and efficiency in communication, . . . as they are questions of political and social control over the effects of communication."[2]

Emerson's point is obvious if we consider the regulation of political communication, such as the equal-time provision to which radio and television are subject. But it also applies to regulation of advertising. For example, social preferences regarding the free flow of information and free access to mass communications will affect the specific

---

[1] Apparently there have been exceptions. In 1917, second-class mail rates were withdrawn by the government from *Appeal to Reason,* with a circulation of more than one million copies, apparently because of the paper's opposition to World War I. This paper subsequently died.

[2] T. I. Emerson, "Communication and Freedom of Expression," *Scientific American,* September 1972, p. 163.

regulation of advertising. And social regulation of one use of the mass communication system will affect all other uses since all are related by joint costs and benefits.

It is not easy to visualize the interdependencies between advertising and other uses of a mass communication system, but the following two testimonies provide a feel for them. First the testimony of Norman Cousins:

> *My purpose here is not so much to comment on the power of advertising as to ponder the implications of the fact that one of the tests of a free society is its attitude toward ideas. For ideas are a prime requirement for the growth and progress of any social organism that has to adapt to changing conditions. Obviously, every society—open or closed—is shaped by ideas. But the sources of ideas, the nature of ideas, the respect for ideas, and the way in which ideas are moved from one point to another, serve to define to what degree a society is open or closed. . . .*

> *So far, these brief statements come under the heading of historical truisms. What is less self-evident, however, is the connection between advertising and ideas in an open society. My contention here is that advertising—more particularly, the creative skills and techniques it affords and puts to use—represents an increasingly vital part of the process by which ideas are circulated and put to work. Advertising has generally been recognized in terms of its ability to move goods. Its ability to move ideas is no less significant in any definition of its function in a modern and dynamic open society.*

> *Some evidence. In 1962, President Kennedy believed it was in the national interest and the human interest to seek a treaty to limit nuclear testing. The President brought private citizens together for the purpose of persuading them to form a citizens' committee that would educate public opinion on the need for a treaty to seek this objective. The situation at the time was that more than two-thirds of the American people, judging by public opinion polls and tabulations of Congressional mail, had been led to believe that unlimited testing was essential to the national security and that there was little substance to the reports of dangers resulting from radioactive fallout. . . .*

> *What was involved here was not just a challenge in mass re-education, but the fact of a stern deadline by which the re-education had to produce a visible result. The President had a timetable: A treaty would be proposed within three months; it had to be ratified within another three months. So long as public opinion was in such a predominantly negative condition, there would be little point in announcing a treaty and even less point in pressing for an early Senate vote. . . .*

> *When the Citizens Committee considered its strategy for mobilizing public opinion, it realized it had to operate on many levels. It had to enlist the open and active support of leaders from all sectors of the national life. It had to get organizations behind it—business, labor, professional, religious. It had to fashion a solid base of scientific opinion. Finally, it had to mount a campaign in the general marketplace of public opinion. Resources were limited.*

> *Given all these requirements and approaches, the Committee decided to put its main thrust into advertising. The approved program called for a series of prominent advertisements—in the nation's leading magazines and newspapers, in television spots, in organization journals. . . . The bottom line [of the ads] called for letters to Congress. And the letters came. They came in large numbers. . . . Within six or*

seven weeks, the clear preponderance of public support against any limitation of nuclear testing had diminished to the point where both sides were just about even.

It was at this juncture that the President publicly proposed a treaty. But he had a long way to go. He needed a working consensus before he could have any confidence in a two-thirds Senate vote. The advertising campaign continued. And the evidence of a growing consensus became apparent. As the Committee anticipated, the opposition forces to the proposed treaty now began to use the same approaches *[stress added], mounting a mass advertising campaign in behalf of their own views. The effect was noticeable but not critical. In the end, the President's position was sustained.*

What happened was the war of ideas became joined on the advertising battlefield [stress added]. The episode is worth recounting . . . . People can be persuaded but the techniques of persuasion are secondary to what is communicated. Given the proper material and the proper sponsorship, and skilled techniques, public opinion can be shaped by skilled advertising but it cannot be manipulated. . . . Whether we are talking about a labor union or a corporation eager to put its case before the public, or a minority group in quest of support, we have to recognize that advertising will be increasingly regarded as the most effective form for the communication of the message. But persuasion is not automatic. . . .

Advertising commands the attention—more than that of any other form, editorial or commentary. But different sides and legions will turn to it—sometimes for opposite and competing purposes. Each will seek victory. There is no sure-fire formula for the use of words with maximum impact to insure such victory. But some things are clearer than others. Those who believe that advertising is a natural device for manipulation or distortion or exploitation are betting on a dubious proposition. Certainly, in any clash of ideas in which advanced advertising techniques are used on both sides, the appeal to good sense, supported by evidence, makes for a strong and often decisive difference.

What are the implications, in terms of national policy, of this major function of advertising as a vital instrument of ideas? First, policy-makers should recognize that advertising must be seen in a larger context than the commercial marketplace alone.

Second, it is the clear duty of government to establish standards for honest labeling, but it is the equally clear duty of government to regard advertising as an integral part of the consensus mechanism of an open society.

Third, just as the advertiser or the editor underestimates the intelligence of the reader at his peril, so government must not underestimate the ability of the average citizen to resist manipulation or exploitation. Nor should government underestimate the extent to which this fact is respected by the advertising profession itself.

Mr. Cousins' testimony underlines a basic feature of the United States mass communication system—its relative openness to diverse ideas. Note that *both* proponents and opponents of nuclear testing were able to use mass media to mount an advertising campaign. A similar openness to diverse political advertisements is visible during any presidential campaign.

But the openness of the media to political ideas extends beyond paid political announcements. During the 1960s, for example, Black Power, participatory democracy, civil disobedience, and other themes of the civil rights and antiwar movements received wide circulation through the mass media. In fact, antiestablishment groups and leaders received substantial coverage from national and local network TV, a medium that depends totally on advertising for revenue.

The next testimony, by Andrew Heiskell, chairman of the board of Time, Inc., publisher of *Time, Sports Illustrated, Fortune, Money,* and until recently, *Life,* discusses the main point of Cousins' presentation in more detail—namely, the relationship between advertising (the flow of economic information) and the flow of all other information in an open mass communication system.

Mr. Heiskell contends that the present advertising institution is basic to the maintenance of a free press and that other organizational designs for the flow of economic information cannot guarantee as free a circulation of all ideas and points of view. Toward the end of his testimony, Mr. Heiskell submits a particularly challenging hypothesis concerning social change. Free access to mass communications may, he argues, be eroded inch by inch. Taken singly, each limitation may appear harmless, even desirable; but their cumulative effects may not be noticed until it is too late. At that point, it may be impossible to recreate a free press.

I have been requested . . . to discuss the relationship of advertising revenues to the maintenance of a free press. I will confine my discussion to newspapers, magazines, and broadcast journalism—both the news and public affairs aspects of radio and television—those portions of the "free press" that are financed largely by advertising revenues. When I discuss the press collectively, I will be referring to each of these elements.

The relationship of advertising to the free press must form an important part of any thorough examination of the advertising industry. . . . In simple economic terms, advertising is the lifeblood of the press. Some $12 billion of revenues are provided to the various segments of the press by advertisers. Almost all of the revenues of commercial broadcast journalism and something like two-thirds of the revenues available to newspapers and magazines come from advertising dollars. I have no doubt that without those revenues the free press, as we know it today, could not continue to exist.

The free press has become such an integral part of our society and political system that we tend to take it for granted. We shouldn't. A few years ago, . . . a major survey of the world's press [was conducted]. That study determined that less than one-half of the world had a free press—that is, a press that was not controlled or substantially influenced by government or special interests. . . . The results of that study indicate that a free and unfettered press may be more fragile and more nearly unique than we like to think.

I think most of us would agree that the free press is necessary to the workings, indeed to the survival, of a democracy. An informed citizenry is possible only with an independent, multi-faceted, and competitive press. . . . The news media . . . make us aware of each other's problems and accomplishments. They are a part of the cement that holds this nation together. We have developed a system, largely financed by advertising, which does those things and which, I believe, does them quite well. I can think of no alternative means of financing that would allow us to do them as well.

The special role of the press has been encouraged as a matter of political and social policy throughout our history. "Congress shall make no law . . . abridging the freedom . . . of the press . . ." is the clear mandate of the First Amendment. But, an effective free press requires much more than the absence of government interference. It requires an affirmative commitment of our people and our government to an open society.

This, too, has become a fundamental tenet of our political system. Thus, our courts have developed a body of case law concerning libel which is carefully designed to maximize freedom of the press. Thus, Congress passed "The Newspaper Preservation Act" to improve the financial viability of the press. Thus, the Post Office has traditionally given special rates to newspapers and magazines. Thus, regulatory agencies, concerned with matters affecting the media, such as the FCC, have attempted to strengthen and encourage the independence of broadcasting and journalism. And, thus, the United States Senate's Subcommittee on Constitutional Rights is these very weeks holding hearings on the problems of the relationship between press and government.

Of course, the press is not without its faults. We are frequently the subject of legitimate and valid criticism. There are, however, two criticisms—both frequently heard, both germane to the subject of this hearing, and both, I contend, quite inaccurate.

The first is the contention that the media have virtually unlimited and, therefore, potentially dangerous power to mold public opinion. Whether or not that criticism has any validity for advertising will be discussed later in this hearing in detail by those far more expert in the field than I. I address myself to this criticism only as it applies to the editorial content of journalism.

Opinions and beliefs are the product of society as a whole. News media play an important, but by no means a monopolistic role. Institutions such as schools, churches, business, and the family are vital and fundamental to the formation of the ideas and beliefs of an educated nation. Because there is such a diversity of means of communications in the country today, there is limited reliance on any one source. I think it is fair to say that the more active a citizen in the community, the more numerous are his sources of information and ideas. Such well-informed individuals are themselves usually an important means of influencing opinion in their communities.

A second criticism frequently heard and equally inaccurate is that advertisers, because they do provide the economic lifeblood of the press, exert considerable influence on the editorial content of the press. This is not so. The free press in America is indeed free. The multiplicity of advertisers, and, therefore, sources of revenue, makes control by any one advertiser or group of advertisers impossible. . . . I can speak best for my own company. We have always had a firm policy of keeping our editorial content entirely separate from advertising considerations and I know of no instance where an advertiser has been able to dictate the editorial content of our magazines. In fact, publishing and broadcasting are the only businesses I know that make a habit of criticizing their own customers. At times, advertisers have become so annoyed with us that they have withdrawn their advertising. Because we have so many different and competing sources of advertising revenues, we have always been able to ignore such withdrawals and most of those advertisers have eventually rejoined us.

Even in areas of great sensitivity for major advertisers, news coverage has been extensive and balanced. Ralph Nader is a household word and every American who knows how to read—as well as some who don't—are familiar with the Surgeon General's Report on smoking, because newspapers, magazines, radio, and television have told the public, in detail and at length, about both. . . .

The economics of the news media are of vital importance to the nation and the government. Because of economic pressures, only 37 U.S. cities have two or more daily newspapers in competition, whereas 10 years ago there were nearly twice as many. So serious did Congress consider that matter that it passed special legislation, "The Newspaper Preservation Act," which permits papers to use joint facilities and combine certain commercial operations without concern for the antitrust laws. We have seen the disappearance of a number of great national magazines—most recently Look *magazine.* Look *suspended publication this month in large part because its publisher saw no hope of economic survival in the face of the enormous increase in postal rates now being proposed. At the time of its demise,* Look *had six and a half million subscribers, but this demand was not enough to overcome its economic problems. [*Life, *another well-known and highly circulated magazine, also stopped publication about a year after this presentation.]*

In 1970, advertising revenue will provide some $12 billion toward direct support of the free press—about 1% of our G.N.P. Almost 100% of commercial television and radio broadcast revenues, of course, are derived from advertising. Some two-thirds of newspaper and magazine revenues are also generated by advertising. . . . The conclusion is inescapable that without these revenues the free press as it has evolved in America could not exist.

Advertising, of course, is more than a source of revenue for the press. . . . We in journalism have found that, in general, the public wants advertising. The old PM *in New York, for instance, was originally published without advertising and financed entirely by circulation revenues, but soon found that its readers insisted on advertisements as a service. How else were they to learn about new movies, shows, and concerts, or the price of food at supermarkets, or clothing sales in the big downtown stores? . . . Last year slightly more than half of the $12 billion total spent on advertising in the press went into local advertisements—classified, retail and the like. . . .*

Advertising, then, is a part of the service provided by the press and desired by the American consumer. . . . Is advertising the only way to support the free press as we know it? I must confess that I can think of none better. Consider the alternatives: There is the possibility of government subsidy. The danger inherent in such a situation, the possibility of control of content, is clear. In the American context, at least, the government has been kept out of the press and denied any power, economic or otherwise, that might lead to control.

Another possibility is that special interest groups who wish to reach and influence the public—such as political parties—might finance major organs of the free press. Such a situation—which exists in quite a few countries—seems little more desirable to me than the possibility of government subsidy. The press in this country has been a "fourth estate" and, if it is to continue to function as it traditionally has, it must continue apart from direct participation in the political process.

Another method of financing that has received considerable attention is greater payment by the consumer. In the first place, increasing reader costs for magazines and newspapers is probably not economically feasible. Time, Inc. studies show that higher subscription rates generally reduce circulation and, therefore, circulation revenues, by roughly the amount of the gain of the higher rates. In the second place, such a substitution would involve a very substantial amount of money for the individual reader. Without advertising, the annual cost of Time *magazine would go from $15 to $45; the cost of a newspaper such as the* New York Times *would rise [from] 15¢ to 40¢ daily.*

Those figures are misleading because they assume no change in circulation; but, as must be clear, all our experience indicates that circulation falls as prices rise. Since a sizeable portion of our costs are fixed and others are kept low by economies made possible through volume buying, prices for the subscribers who remained would rise, causing more subscribers to cancel, causing further rises, and so on. A Time *magazine that goes to, say, 200,000 buyers would be a very different magazine and would play a very different role in informing the public, sparking discussion and inquiry, and in helping bind us together than the* Time *of today which is purchased by some 4.2 million people in the United States. Such a situation would limit access to news and information to the affluent. . . .*

The broadcast industry faces similar problems. A nightly half-hour network news show costs in the neighborhood of $10 million a year. Even if the mechanical problems of billing and collecting from the public could be overcome, the cost of maintaining network news facilities would be enormous. All possible means of financing, then, would in some way diminish the present system.

We like to think of the free press in the abstract, but it does not exist in the abstract. It exists in the very real economic world with which all businessmen must deal daily. There are expenses and income and, to stay in business, the press must make a reasonable profit. Like many other industries, the great demand for capital has forced many publishing companies that were long privately held to "go public." That means that, over the long run, the press must achieve a profit margin more or less comparable with other investment opportunities.

The courts have recognized the special role of advertising as the economic lifeblood of the free press. Taxes which have singled out advertising revenues have been struck down largely on First Amendment grounds.

It is my firm belief that the greatest danger faced by the free press stems not from any deliberate or planned action by individuals or agencies in the government, but rather from a climate of indifference to what may appear minimal damage to First Amendment principles combined with expediency exercised in the desire to achieve what is often a good end. First Amendment freedoms always involve a process of balancing. In recent times, despite court decisions, there has been an alarming tendency on the part of some government officials and agencies to weight the scales against freedom of the press.

The desirability of convicting a criminal takes precedence over the protection from subpoena of a reporter's notes or a television producer's out-takes; the need for secrecy of state papers takes precedence over the press' duty to inform the public; the political gain to be made by attacking reporting takes precedence over the chilling effect of criticism by government officials; the need for state and local revenues to be gained from special taxes on advertising takes precedence over the dangers of hitting directly at the revenues of the press; the need to increase postal revenues takes precedence over the damage that a sudden large increase has on expenses, profitability and even the existence of a portion of the media.

Individual actions by individual agencies cannot be considered independently. They have a cumulative effect. That fact should be, but often is not, weighed in the decision-making process. I am a publisher and not a lawyer or constitutional scholar. Nonetheless, it is my view that, possibly as a matter of constitutional law, and certainly as a matter of public policy, First Amendment guarantees should extend to business and industry. I believe that any product which may be legally sold or traded in this country should have the right to publicly advertise itself. Indeed, if it does not have such an inherent right, it might as well not exist. I also believe that the various sections of the press should be able to decide for themselves the content of their pages—both editorial and commercial content.

Obviously, these First Amendment rights are subject to the same reasonable limitations that apply to any other exercise of freedom of speech and freedom of the press. I do not for a moment advocate the right of businessmen or advertisers to make false or misleading statements. This commission must and should carry out its congressional mandate to regulate such advertising.

The free press in the U.S. does have its faults and we must continue to try to correct them. On balance, however, we have developed a press of high quality, free from control by government or special interest, and easily accessible to the public. In our highly complex, industrialized, and sometimes fragmented society, our many-faceted press both fills the needs of groups and individuals and provides one major force that holds a large and varied country together.

Competitive and diverse, the press provides an outlet for all shades of opinion and forms the marketplace of ideas necessary to the functioning of the democracy. That such a system is so rare indicates that we should take special steps to safeguard it. Advertising is an integral part of the system we have developed and any actions which affect advertising will affect the system itself.

Our form of government depends on carefully developed checks and balances of which the press is a key element. As the power of government grows, and it does every day, it is important that the balance be kept by strengthening, not weakening, the free press.

2 ADVERTISING, INFORMATION, AND COMPETITION *(excerpts from H. Demsetz, professor of economics, University of California at Los Angeles)*

The next testimony, by Professor H. Demsetz, provides a more quantitative approach to the socioeconomic roles of advertising. Two features of this testimony are of special importance.

First, Professor Demsetz summarizes a new trend in economic theory: information is no longer viewed as a free good, but as a good that, like others, has its own costs, and for which there is a supply and a demand.[1] Second, he illustrates the applications of

---

[1] There has been an increasing interest on information in economics during the past three decades. The work presented by Professor Demsetz represents one of the several research interests that have emerged; for a review of all other developments, see J. Hirshlaifer, "Where Are We in the Theory of Information?" *American Economic Review,* May 1973.

this new perspective to the study of the advertising institution. This perspective allows economists to raise new questions concerning the genesis and functioning of the advertising institution in an economy, and to undertake new empirical studies. Professor Demsetz reviews these studies in the context of previous theoretical and empirical work, especially earlier work on the relationships of advertising to industry concentration, profit rates, and price levels.

In 1776, a vintage year for great works, Adam Smith began his treatise on the Wealth of Nations with the sentence

> *The greatest improvements in the productive powers of labour, and the greater part of the skill, dexterity, and the judgment with which it is any where directed, or applied, seem to have been the effects of the division of labour.*

The quotation contains the key to understanding the main social function of advertising. Specialization cannot succeed without communication. In order to move closer to the life style to which we aspire, it is necessary to work and produce in a manner that is increasingly specialized, and this cannot be accomplished without increasing the resources we devote to communication.

The productivity increase brought about through specialization has allowed us to enrich our lives with product and travel variety, fewer work hours, and more time for leisure activities. Without the effective use of resources for communication, these forward strides would have been much more difficult. One of the important ways to use communication resources effectively is by advertising.

That advertising is primarily a method of communicating efficiently is revealed by the systematic variation in its use. Where customers are few, advertising expenditures tend to be small, and when products are new and less well known, these expenditures tend to be greater. For communicating with mass markets, the messages conveyed are appropriately nontechnical, whereas for buyers who are specialists, the messages are more like invitations to inquire further.

These variations in advertising efforts are not due to happenstance; there is a consistency across national boundaries[1] and through time that provides convincing evidence that the patterns we observe are due to the comparative advantage offered by advertising in solving certain communication problems. These problems are encountered more frequently when and where economies have become highly specialized in social organization. Since economic organization here has reached a higher degree of specialization, this helps to explain why advertising expenditure in the United States is a somewhat larger percentage of Gross National Product than it is in other industrialized nations.[2] As our economy continues to take advantage of specialization, we can expect to observe a slight upward trend in the fraction of our resources used in advertising. . . .

[1] On this, see the studies by the U.S. Federal Trade Commission, *Distribution Methods and Costs,* Part V, *Advertising as a Factor in Distribution* (1944); and N. Kaldor and R. Silverman, *A Statistical Analysis of Advertising Expenditure and of the Revenue of the Press,* Cambridge University Press, England, 1948.

[2] Advertising outlays are slightly over two percent in the United States and slightly under two percent in the United Kingdom and Canada.

An economy built upon the productivity of specialized industries requires more than information about the availabilities and prices of products. Encouragement must be given to make product improvements and to avoid carelessness and deception.

The activities of labeling, branding, and advertising are important in establishing producer responsibility. Thus, suppose persons would like their cereal to contain more vitamins and minerals, and that they are prepared to pay the cost of adding these dietary supplements. . . . If each manufacturer is allowed to identify his product by branding and by advertising the vitamin-mineral content, . . . each will have an incentive . . . to promote an improved cereal. By the same token, producers of highly advertised brands, precisely because they are more easily identified and remembered, stand to lose a great deal if their products are found to be faulty. Thus, branding and advertising greatly facilitate responsible decision making in an economy of specialists. Even the Soviet Union has found it desirable to reintroduce branding and advertising in its attempt to discipline managers and workers.

Most popular discussions of advertising give only lip service to its importance as communication. However popular are concerns about monopoly, fraud, and persuasion, and whatever element of truth these concerns may reflect, they can have relevance only to a very small fraction of advertising. The bulk of advertising activity is readily explainable as a response to the highly specialized economic activity which characterizes our society.

The cost of communicating would be significantly higher . . . and the main effects of a public policy seeking to reduce the use of resources in advertising would be undesirable. Exchange opportunities would be limited and specialized production hampered, with a resulting reduction in living standards; and resources would be diverted into less efficient selling methods. Even if some of the popular concerns about advertising do reflect real problems, these may be but a small price to pay for the considerable advantages offered to us by this method of communicating.

Studies of advertising undertaken by economists throw light on some of these popular concerns. Professor Lester G. Telser has studied the problem of advertising and monopoly.[1] His work seeks to discover whether there is a relationship between advertising intensity and the share of industry output enjoyed by the four largest firms in an industry. The degree to which output is ooncentrated in the hands of the four largest producers is a frequently adopted proxy for monopoly power.

Professor Telser has been unable to establish a significant correlation between concentration ratios and advertising expenditures *per dollar of sales. There have been other studies of this problem. . . . Taken in total, the evidence argues strongly against any significant relationship between advertising intensity and industrial concentration. It is surprising to me that we should expect such a relationship. Indeed, advertising must be one of the main tools for upsetting established purchasing patterns, allowing new rivals, such as Toyota and Volkswagen, to compete more easily.*

All firms have access to advertising, just as they have access to raw materials and labor. There is no more reason to expect the use of advertising to be a source of monopoly than the use of labor. The use of advertising, just as the use of labor, can

---

[1] See, especially, L. G. Telser, "Advertising and Competition," *Journal of Political Economy,* December 1964.

be imitated by rivals. It may be the case that some firms have a particular knack for managing advertising, and others for managing labor, but such differences reflect competitive advantages and not monopoly.

There also have been some studies of scale economies in advertising, although it is not quite clear just what the policy implications of any conclusions about scale economies would be. If the per unit cost of advertising should fall as more messages are purchased, or more customers are contacted, or more dollars of sales are made, it does not follow that it would be wise policy to restrict advertising, for that would merely force buyers to bear less efficient communication methods.

Be that as it may, no broad assertion of scale economies in advertising can be supported by existing empirical work. Such is the conclusion reached by Professor Simon in his survey of advertising cost studies,[1] and studies by Dr. Blank[2] and Professor Peterman[3] offer convincing evidence that television advertising rates do not generally favor large advertisers. The supposition that there exist scale economies or favored treatment in advertising seems to be incorrect, and so the argument that advertising scale economies lead to monopoly, an argument that is built upon illogical leaps of Olympian dimensions, is rendered irrelevant.

Professors Comanor and Wilson[4] have studied the relationship between profit rates and advertising in forty-one industries. Their results suggest that a significant relationship exists between profit rates, measured from accounting data, and advertising intensity, measured by advertising expenditure per dollar of sales.

This finding is difficult to interpret. A similar relationship exists between research expenditures and profit rates, but hardly anyone would argue that research activity leads to monopoly power. Successful product development may simultaneously cause profit rates and advertising intensity to go up. Product failures are not long advertised. Air transportation continues to be advertised because it is successful, while railroads spend little to attract passengers because such traffic has proved unprofitable. Because of this we would expect to observe a correlation between profitability and advertising that has little to do with monopoly.

Moreover, it is not clear just why advertising expenditures per dollar of sales constitutes an appropriate measure of any supposed barrier to competition. A product which sells for a low price can exhibit a very high advertising intensity when such a measure is used, even though the total amount spent on advertising is small. There are many such commodities, and with respect to them it would hardly seem that the advertising expenditures of firms pose a serious obstacle to those who wish to compete. I quickly note that the same criticism can be made of Telser's use of advertising expenditure per dollar of sales in his study of industry concentration. Comanor and Wilson did include an alternative measure of advertising activity in their

[1] J. L. Simon, "Are There Economies of Scale in Advertising?" *Journal of Advertising Research,* June 1965.

[2] D. M. Blank, "Television Advertising: The Great Discount Illusion, or Tonypandy Revisited," *The Journal of Business,* January 1968.

[3] J. L. Peterman, "The Clorox Case and the Television Rate Structures," *The Journal of Law & Economics,* October 1968.

[4] W. S. Comanor and T. A. Wilson, "Advertising Market Structure and Performance," *The Review of Economics and Statistics,* November 1967.

study—advertising expenditures per firm. But this measure of advertising activity proved to have little relationship to profit rates.

The implicit value judgments contained in many studies of advertising, including that by Comanor and Wilson, should be noted. The premise is that advertising is unproductive. Hence, if advertising causes profit rates to be high, this represents a socially undesirable increase in the rewards to industries that use advertising. But advertising is a form of communication—it is a service, or a product, that serves useful social ends—and just as other products can be produced wisely and with good taste, so can advertising. A given physical product advertised poorly is not the same product if it is advertised well; poor advertising makes it more costly or painful to communicate and raises suspicions about the tastes of the manufacturer with respect to other properties of the product. We are quite prepared to say that the producers of well-designed products should be rewarded with higher profits; by the same token, well-designed advertising campaigns are deserving of higher profits.

In my final reference to empirical work, I would call attention to the forthcoming research of Professor Lee Benham.[1] *Benham compares the prices paid for eye examinations and eyeglasses in states that prohibit the advertising of these services and products with prices in states that allow advertising.*

This study directly confronts the notion that advertising adds to the cost of a product and therefore to its price. A significant difference in prices was found to exist after taking account of income and demographic variations among state populations. The prices for eye examinations and eyeglasses averaged $4.43 less in states allowing advertising. His work indicates that the use of advertising to convey information allows these services to be sold through larger commercial outlets at lower prices. Such outlets depend on being able to communicate with large numbers of prospective buyers, which advertising allows them to do at low cost. Where advertising is permitted, these firms can be successful in lowering product prices.

The underlying association between advertising and low prices observed by Benham should not surprise us any more than the relationship between the assembly line and low-priced model "T" Fords. Both techniques are geared to succeed only if mass markets can be tapped successfully, and this can be accomplished only if the real price faced by the buyer is lowered. The notion that cost and price can be kept lower by eliminating advertising ignores the impact of advertising on the size of the market to be served.

But in one respect, studies such as Benham's will tend to underestimate the benefits of communicating through advertising. In the absence of advertising, we might very well observe lower nominal prices, as popular notions would lead us to expect. But the real price must include the cost of acquiring information about the product and its producer. The consumer will bear a larger portion of this cost in the absence of advertising, and the information-gathering cost that he does bear may very well exceed that which would have been passed on to him through the product price if it had been advertised. The nominal price observed in a regime without advertising will be an underestimate of the true cost of the product to the buyer. With advertising, a significant portion of the communicating cost is contained in the product's price, but

[1]L. Benham, "The Effect of Advertising on Prices," *Journal of Law & Economics,* forthcoming.

without advertising the cost of communicating may be hidden in the expenditures by consumers to acquire information about the product.

It is possible, even probable, that there do exist families of products in which advertised products sell for more than unadvertised. Advertised brands and the firms that produce them may be more reliable, and the expenditure made directly by the consumer to become acquainted with unadvertised brands may offset the advantage offered by lower prices.

More important than such price comparisons is the question of what advertising does to the entire structure of prices. An examination of the price structure with and without advertising would be of great interest. The Benham study is able to shed a little light on this problem because some states have been silly enough to forbid the advertising of eyeglasses and examinations.

Such controlled conditions are difficult to find in economics; consequently, data bearing on this problem are not abundant. Theoretical work on the economics of information by Professor George J. Stigler[1] does suggest that if advertising is a low-cost method of communicating, then general restrictions on its use can be expected to result in a distribution of prices exhibiting a larger range and higher mean. Lower-cost methods of acquiring information reduce the cost of search to buyers, thereby encouraging them to search more for better combinations of price and other commodity characteristics.

The empirical work that I have been discussing does not lend support to the myth that oligopolists rely on advertising to keep out competitors and that the expenditures incurred to do so are passed on to the customers in the form of higher prices. No significant connection between advertising and oligopolistic structures has been uncovered, and industries that do advertise more intensely seem to be characterized by less stable market shares. What little work has been done on comparing prices for the same type of products suggest that the entire structure of real prices faced by buyers may be increased by arbitrary limitations on the use of resources for advertising.

Much criticism of advertising seems to be founded on two notions—that commodities possess intrinsic value and that persuasion through advertising is undesirable if not unethical. Neither of these notions can be justified. A glass of water at Niagara is hardly worth a glass of water in the Gobi Desert, and neither is an economist or lawyer. . . . There is nothing intrinsic about the value of the commodities and services that are offered to us. Their worth depends on how we perceive them and on the quantities available to us. . . .

Underlying the idea that commodities have intrinsic value is the belief that we are motivated by basic, stable, and simple wants. If man ever was so motivated, that primordial time, thank heaven, has long since passed. Only its ghost lingers to haunt discussions about advertising. We court new experiences while we strive for stability, we seek variety and new faces but hold on to old ways and friends, we desire to interact with others but carefully maintain the privacy of our homes. . . . Our wants are fascinatingly complex and sophisticated, not simple and basic. Professor Frank H. Knight writes: "What men want is not so much to get things . . . as . . . to have

---

[1]G. J. Stigler, "The Economics of Information," *Journal of Political Economy,* June 1961.

interesting experiences. . . . Most conscious desire is ultimately a wish to play a role, to be some kind of a person in some kind of a human world."[1]

New directions in these wants are difficult to decipher, and catering to them is not only a matter of the physical properties of commodities, which have little direct connection to social roles and states of mind. . . . We may like or dislike the complexity and dynamism of our wants, but if we are to form an intelligent policy toward advertising it is necessary to recognize them for what they are.

Virtually all of the specific forms in which our wants are expressed are learned. The complex process of want formation undoubtedly is affected by advertisers. Politicians, professors, and churchmen also play a part in this learning process. In a sentence, we are persuaded to most of the wants we hold.

Persuasion is an important element in all communication. At the least, an attempt to communicate suggests that the other party would be better off taking note of the proffered information rather than turning to some other task or other information. . . . Information cannot be communicated voluntarily without persuasion, which is the only practical alternative to coercion.

Communication requires the attention of the listener. All teachers know how difficult that is to obtain—even when they have something to say. Listing the dry statistics of the American economy is a sure way to cut class enrollment. . . . I suspect that dry statistics on products would have the same effect. . . . However, it is a delusion to believe that persuasion would be missing from such advertising. The seller clearly would be implying that these physical characteristics are more important to the buyer than the infinite number of others that might be presented.

In this business of persuasion it is not at all clear that Madison Avenue has a special advantage. Advertisers enjoy neither the protection of Congressional immunity nor the privilege of academic freedom. More important, advertising is necessarily exposed to millions of people. Such exposure surely reduces the risk of serious misrepresentation. This cannot be said for personal selling techniques, whether practiced in an office on Pennsylvania Avenue, a classroom in Cambridge, or on the doorstep of a home.

But I think that the risk of serious misrepresentation in this nation is greatly exaggerated. We still have a society that tolerates healthy competition between those who wish to persuade us, and therein lies our most effective defense. We are exposed to a very large collection of persuaders, especially in the marketplace. . . . And the government is given free press coverage to present its case. . . . An expansive competition between those who would persuade us is what protects us from the the excesses more characteristic of closed societies. If we have no confidence in ourselves when we are offered a great variety of options and suggestions, then how can we be confident of our decisions if we wear the blinders of censorship? . . . Since most men's wants and beliefs are learned, meaningful freedom must involve the right to choose between the offering of those who wish us to learn one life style rather than another, purchase this commodity instead of that, accept one suggestion rather than another. The free society keeps open the avenues of persuasion, and it encourages us to walk along these avenues. What threatens the free society most is the blocking of avenues of persuasion.

---

[1] F. H. Knight, *Risk, Uncertainty, and Profit*, Houghton Mifflin Company, New York, 1921.

2.1 CHANGES IN PERSPECTIVES AND IN FACTS

For several decades economists presented conceptual perspectives and even empirical evidence suggesting that advertising has, or may have, negative effects on the economy. The new perspective and empirical studies presented by Professor Demsetz not only challenge earlier thinking and facts, but also raise new questions relevant to public policy decisions.[1]

The debate among economists concerning the old and new is presently very spirited, and differences and contradictions abound. It throws new light on the problems faced by advertisers, advertising agencies, and mass media, as well as on the problems of regulating the advertising decisions of these firms. The nature and implications of this new literature thus deserves further consideration.

2.1.1 Information as an Economic Good

In conceptualizing and measuring the possible effects of advertising, traditional economics has relied on an image of the world in which both firms and consumers have *free and perfect information.* According to the new literature, this image is incorrect and tends to predetermine the results of traditional analyses of advertising.

To begin with, traditional theory assumes that consumer preferences, technology, resources, and products are *given* and *known* by all concerned. There is a crucial relationship between the terms *given* and *known.* If givens were to remain constant, one might think that consumers, firms, and public agencies might eventually learn all of them. A consumer, for example, might gradually come to know both his own preferences and all the properties of all the products available on the market.

Psychological research, however, shows that humans do not have the ability to acquire, store, and use this much information. For instance, in such a relatively simple situation as a chess game, Herbert Simon and others have found strong evidence that even chess masters do not compute all possible moves and countermoves. On the contrary, their processing of information rarely goes beyond the third move.

Even if humans could acquire, store, and use large quantities of information, they would face a very severe handicap living in a world where the givens change. Societies evolving through industrialization to affluence are just such a world; technology, resources, products, cultural values, institutions, and life styles all change with increasing rapidity. The more frequently such givens change, the more difficult it is for humans to know what they are.

Yet some information is necessary for any mental activity, especially decision making. Herbert Simon once noted that a decision is a conclusion derived from premises. This leads to the second assumption of traditional theory that is challenged by the new perspective.

Traditional thought portrays a world in which information is free and in which humans have perfect information. From the time of Ricardo to the present, the stock

---

[1] Note that the literature cited in the testimony dates from the end of the 1950s. For readers interested in the foundations of this new literature, see Stigler, *op. cit.*

exchange has often been cited as a place in which free and perfect information exists. But, in reality, on-the-floor information is *neither* perfect *nor* free. From the business viewpoint, traders do not buy and sell stocks; they trade information. More precisely, they exchange either different information and/or different evaluations of the same information about a certain stock; they trade forecasts.

Traditional economics has not viewed—empirically or even theoretically—information as an economic good. Thus past economic research was inherently unable to handle the advertising institution conceptually and empirically. The general conclusions of traditional economics do flow from its premises: in a world in which information is perfect and free, advertising is bound to look like evidence of human irrationality and a waste of resources.

A noted economist has observed that information

> . . . occupies a slum dwelling in the town of economics. Mostly it is ignored; the best technology is assumed to be known; the relationship of commodities to consumer preferences is a datum. And one of the information-producing industries, advertising, is treated with a hostility that economists normally reserve for tariffs and monopolies.[1]

In the future, meaningful studies of advertising and its effects will need to recognize explicitly that information itself is a basic part of the economy. Several economists, especially those who have studied marketing and consumer behavior, have long viewed information as an economic good, i.e., a scarce good. Both consumers and firms buy and sell information, and this acquisition, storage, and use of information implies costs and benefits. In a classic article, Holton explained that one of the key elements in a consumer's approach to any good is the perception of the costs and gains connected with search. For example, if the cost of searching for information about a brand's attributes is greater than the benefits to be gained from the additional knowledge, then a consumer will not bother to learn about that brand's attributes. Using this insight, Holton could parsimoniously explain why marketers had long observed, since the early twenties, that consumers treat goods as either convenience, shopping, or specialty goods.[2]

Similarly, marketing economists have had little difficulty in explaining why some consumers develop brand loyalty. If their first experience with a brand is satisfactory, consumers "know" what to expect from it the next time. Consequently, no new search for information, with its inherent cost, is necessary. Thus, since at least the 1940s, marketing literature has recommended that firms develop a brand name as a service to consumers.

All economic actors need and search for information. If advertising is viewed as an information-producing industry, then it is possible to ask descriptive and explanatory questions that are relevant at the macro level. For example, what is the cost of search

[1] Stigler, *op. cit.*

[2] R. H. Holton, "The Distinctions Between Convenience Goods, Shopping Goods, and Specialty Goods," *Journal of Marketing,* July 1958. For further consideration, especially on the relationship between the so-called rationality and the cost/benefits from search for information in consumer behavior, see Nicosia, *Consumer Decision Processes, Marketing and Advertising Implications,* Prentice-Hall, Englewood Cliffs, N.J., 1966, Ch. 2, Sect. 3.2 and Sect. 4.

by buyers for sellers and by sellers for buyers in different economies? As an information-producing institution, does advertising substitute inexpensive information for expensive search costs? What is the optimal allocation of an economy's resources to personal selling and advertising? Why does this allocation vary from country to country, from industry to industry, and from firm to firm?

Part 1 stressed that, at the micro level, each firm is compelled to recognize and deal with the economics of information. The emerging economic literature cited by Professor Demsetz indicates that some economists have also begun to deal with information at the macro level.[1]

2.1.2 Some Specific Economic Effects: Issues and Recent Findings

Even without considering the new questions raised by the literature described by Professor Demsetz, it is fair to say that "there is a good deal of uncertainty among economists about the economic effects of advertising. Therefore, there is more scope for personal values to influence policy decisions."[2] To illustrate, some theoretical and empirical work has tried to demonstrate that advertising has the power to affect choice of brands and product classes. But this view "runs counter in spirit to another hypothesis of many economists concerning advertising. This is the notion that a great deal of advertising in most industries is both ineffective and wasteful."[3]

Be that as it may, there is some structure in the work inspired by the traditional economic view of the world. Let us sketch the key questions that have been investigated, though without pretense of doing justice to the complexity underlying these research efforts and the possible uncertainty of their results.

One key question has been whether there are *increasing returns to scale* in advertising. That is, if a firm were to increase its advertising expenditures, would it obtain proportionately larger and larger returns? If this were true, then it could also be true that large firms would tend to become larger; smaller firms would tend to withdraw; and fewer and fewer firms would survive in an industry. Thus, increasing returns might work as a barrier to entry by new firms and lead to concentration and an increase in potential monopoly power. Many researchers have studied this question empirically in different industries. With one exception, there is no evidence that advertising leads to more

---

[1] Other branches of economics have also turned their efforts to the study of information; see, for example, the writings by Jacob Marchack and Roy Radner. As for the role of information within marketing, still at the macro level, see the very new approach and interesting results concerning traditional economics in H. Baligh and L. Richards, *Vertical Market Structures,* Allyn & Bacon, Boston, Mass., 1967. See, also, L. P. Bucklin, *Competition and Evolution in the Distributive Trades,* Prentice-Hall, Englewood Cliffs, N. J., 1972, *infra,* and his earlier work, *A Theory of Distribution Channel Structure,* Institute of Business and Economic Research, University of California, Berkeley, 1966, Ch. 5.

[2] H. G. Grabowsky, "Advertising and Resource Allocation—Discussion," in S. Divita (ed.), *Advertising and the Public Interest,* American Marketing Association, Chicago, Ill., 1974.

[3] *Ibid.* That is, the view here is that most advertising, especially in oligopolistic industries, is defensive in character, with the result that one firm's expenditures cancel out the expenditures of its rivals.

concentration because of increasing returns to scale; in fact, the general finding is that decreasing rather than increasing returns to scale prevail.[1]

The next question is whether advertising expenditures have a *carryover effect.* That is, do current advertising expenditures affect current or future revenues? If response to advertising continues over long periods of time, then advertising efforts are an investment, not an expenditure—that is, they are an addition to capital. The consequence of this possibility would resemble the case of increasing returns to scale: large firms could spend more on advertising and thus add to the size of their capital; new firms would find it harder to enter the market, and compete; and, as in the cases of technology and equipment, advertising would be a barrier to entry and lead to concentration and the danger of monopoly.

Past studies have found evidence of carryover effects.[2] Note that these are investigations at the industry level and thus the findings cannot apply to each firm in an industry. Very recently, applications of advanced estimation techniques have raised some doubts about the size of the carryover effects determined previously. For instance, Clarke and McCann have reanalyzed the data of a well-known study and found that the estimated duration of the effect decreased from nineteen months to three months.[3]

Other studies have focused "directly" on whether advertising is a *barrier to entry.* One group of studies has essentially asked whether industries with higher advertising expenditures are also the ones with *high concentration* (i.e., industries in which a few firms hold a large share of the market). Another group of studies has been concerned with an even more direct relationship: do firms with high advertising expenditures also record *higher profits?* A third group has studied a variety of effects that may or may not be related to those just listed, e.g., does advertising contribute to *higher prices* or to "too much" product and brand differentiation? In general, answers to these questions have tended to be controversial or inconclusive. And they have been heavily criticized on many grounds, ranging from the appropriateness of the research assumptions to the data and inference techniques used.[4]

---

[1] For a concise summary and some new evidence, see W. A. Luksetich, "Some Economic Issues and Policy Implications of Studies on the Competitive Effects of Advertising Expenditures," *Journal of Advertising,* 1973 (no month given). For a thorough discussion, see R. Schmalensee, *The Economics of Advertising,* North-Holland Publishing Co., Amsterdam, 1972, Ch. 7.

[2] M. Nerlove and F. Waugh, "Advertising Without Supply Control," *Journal of Farm Economics,* November, 1961; Telser, *op cit.*; K. Palda, *The Measurement of Cumulative Advertising Effects,* Prentice-Hall, Englewood Cliffs, N.J., 1964; and H. Bloch, *Advertising, Competition, and Market Performance,* University of Chicago Press, Chicago, Ill., 1971.

[3] The previous study is the pioneering work by Palda, *op. cit.* The new analysis is reported in D. G. Clarke and J. M. McCann, "Measuring the Cumulative Effects of Advertising: A Reappraisal," Paper No. 410, West Lafayette, Ind.: Institute for Research in the Behavioral, Economic, and Management Sciences, Purdue University, May 1973. These authors note that many econometric studies in the marketing literature are still using the same inference procedures used by Palda.

[4] The debate often inverts the basic assumptions of current thinking. For example, Schmalensee has examined analytically the assumption "advertising causes barriers to entry" and has found that it does not hold true under a number of possible and plausible conditions (R. Schmalensee, "Brand Loyalty and Barriers to Entry," *Southern Economic Journal,* April 1974).

Most of the questions asked in the past pay little attention to the consumer, i.e., *to his demand for information.* The perspective presented by Professor Demsetz, of course, strongly stresses the fact that consumers do search for information and advertising may be an inexpensive way for them to obtain it.[1] Some empirical work from the consumer viewpoint has, however, now begun to appear. For instance, Farley found that the amount of search will depend on expected gain relative to information acquisition costs. Nelson has found support for the idea that consumers are likely to seek more advice with regard to "experience" goods (where the qualities of a good can be assessed only through purchase and use, e.g., a washing machine) than with "search" goods (where the qualities can be reasonably assessed prior to purchase, e.g., a dress).[2]

All in all, there is no doubt that consumers use advertising as one channel to gain information concerning choice of brands, products, services, and stores. But, in a comprehensive study, Bucklin[3] warns us that consumers use other channels as well, and, more importantly, that many social psychological variables lead to different modes and levels of search, and consequently to differences in consumers' use of available channels. Public policy must examine and evaluate the roles of advertising in the context of the richness and complexity of consumer search for information.[4] As we shall see in Chapter 13, however, policy makers are totally unaware of the knowledge that Bucklin and others have been accumulating. The consequence of this is unavoidable: even though there seems to be a genuine interest in developing methods to improve consumer search activities, regulatory efforts tend to be focused on marginal and often irrelevant issues.

The debate between the old and the new is very lively at present. Its most important contribution is at the conceptual level, for the new perspective suggests how previous questions and findings can be recast in a different framework. Consider the following case: within the framework of traditional economics, evidence of carryover effects leads one to think of potential monopoly and its inherent dangers, thus suggesting the need for one kind of regulatory decision. But if information is viewed as an economic good, attention is focused on different considerations. One of these is that advertising should be treated like investment in equipment and R&D. Two widely quoted studies have found a positive association between advertising and profit rate; however, they treated

---

[1] At the present stage of development, the new perspective assumes that information is a homogeneous commodity. That is, for example, it is assumed that the information sent by advertisers is that demanded by consumers or that the meaning of an ad is equal to all consumers.

[2] See R. Ferber, "Consumer Economics from Neo-Classical Times to the Present," Paper No. 100, March 1973, College of Commerce and Business Administration, University of Illinois, Urbana, Ill. See, also, P. Nelson, "Information and Consumer Behavior," *The Journal of Political Economy,* March-April,1970.

[3] L. P. Bucklin, "Consumer Search, Role Enactment, and Market Efficiency," *Journal of Business,* October 1969.

[4] When this is done, issues and possible solutions are clearer; see, e.g., R. H. Holton, "Consumer Behavior, Market Imperfections, and Public Policy," in J. W. Markham and G. F. Papanek (eds.), *Industrial Organization and Economic Development,* Houghton Mifflin, Boston, 1970.

advertising as an expenditure, not as capital investment.[1] Let us illustrate how this distinction may alter the findings.

In their study, Comanor and Wilson[2] state that "Industries with high advertising outlays earn, on average, at a profit rate which exceeds that of other industries by nearly four percentage points. . . ." One can show, however, that if the authors had treated advertising outlays as a capital investment, their results could have been different. In a recent paper, Professor Brozen explains why:

> . . . [Comanor and Wilson's conclusion] is reached by using grossly understated net worth for the firms in such industries [those firms with high advertising outlays]. Since firms do not capitalize their investment in advertising for balance sheet purposes, the omission of this asset leads to an understatement of net worth which is large for firms with high advertising sales ratios. As a consequence, the rate of return is overstated. For example, a firm spending 10% of sales on advertising, earning 8% on sales, and whose stated equity equals 50% of sales, will be earning a 16% accounting rate of return. If the firm's advertising has a five year life and its sales and advertising have been level during the past five years, then current outlays on advertising will be equal to depreciation of past advertising. Its current income will be unaffected by capitalizing current outlays and straight line depreciating past outlays. Its equity, however, will be increased 60% by the depreciated value of capitalized past advertising. It will become equal to 80% of sales and an 8% margin on sales will show a 10% return on corrected equity instead of the 16% return on stated equity.
>
> Comanor and Wilson have discovered only the fact that the upward bias in accounting rates of return for "industries with high advertising outlays" is four percentage points greater than the upward bias "of other industries." They have not substantiated the presumption that advertising is a barrier to entry.[3]

The second study showing a positive statistical relationship between high advertising and high profit rate (i.e., return on capital) is the *Economic Report on the Influence of Market Structure on the Profit Performance of Food Manufacturing Companies*, 1969, by the Federal Trade Commission. Here too, however, advertising was treated as a current expenditure rather than as an investment. Furthermore, Brozen points out that the commission's study did not use the actual advertising outlays of the firms it selected; instead it inputed to these firms the *average* level of advertising for the firms in an industry, ignoring the large variety among these firms!

This FTC study has been repeated, by treating advertising as an investment and using the firms' actual expenditures. The results do not confirm those of the FTC study; they

---

[1] The advertising data used by these studies were obtained from the Internal Revenue Service. But the IRS does not allow firms to capitalize advertising outlays. Thus, accounting data report advertising as expenditures (i.e., in the profit and loss statement) rather than adding them to net worth (i.e., in the balance sheet).

[2] Comanor and Wilson, *op. cit.*, p. 437.

[3] Y. Brozen, "An Ivory Tower View of Advertising," University of Chicago, Chicago, Ill., June 1972, p. 4, unpublished manuscript.

indicate that advertising is a means of entry into a market rather than a barrier. In this sense, advertising resembles any other investment in equipment, technology, and R&D.[1] A dynamic model has also been proposed supporting the idea that advertising is a cost of entry that can be explained in exactly the same way as the accumulation of any other form of capital stock.[2] The model describes the time path followed by advertising expenditures during the introduction of a new product and during its subsequent life cycle. Brozen evaluates this model as follows:

> It is easy to point to evidence supporting Professor Gould's view. We all know that advertising outlays are very frequently much larger relative to sales in the first year or two after introduction of a product than in subsequent years. Frequently, they are so large relative to sales early in the life of a product that no sane man could possibly argue that they are current expense. A drug manufacturer does not spend 80 to 150% of the first year's sales of a drug promoting and advertising the drug in the expectation that the expenditure will be currently profitable. . . . That first year outlay must be looked upon as an investment upon which a return will be realized in future years—not in the year the outlay is made. . . . The National Commission on Food Marketing found that the advertising to sales ratio for new products in the cereal industry average 47% in the first year declining to 22% in the second year. It also found that typical new cereal did not reach a break even point until after it had been on the market at least two years. Again, it is obvious that the first and second year expenditures on advertising are investments—not a current expense—which supports Professor Gould's view of outlays on advertising being a capital accumulation process.[3]

Esentially, policy makers need to know facts: what effects does advertising have and what are the magnitudes of these effects? But the debate just sketched teaches us a fundamental lesson. Questions of fact are not answered by establishing that numerical results are statistically significant, but by establishing whether research (1) has begun with an appropriate conceptualization of the phenomenon under study, (2) has used the appropriate data, and (3) has followed an appropriate scientific methodology. Here, as in Chapter 11, we find that questions of fact lead to questions of method.

2.1.3. Questions of Method

The term *effect* implies that one thing causes another. But we have already noted that statistical associations are neither an indication of the direction of causality nor evidence of causality, and that truly creative work is necessary to interpret statistical associations in a causal sense (Chapter 11, Section 3.2). Few, if any, of the studies reported in the literature satisfy the elementary scientific canons needed to establish causality. For example, if advertising expenditures are positively associated with profit, our work has

---

[1] Bloch, *op. cit.*

[2] J. Gould, "Diffusion Processes and Optimal Advertising Policy," in E. S. Phelps, *et al.* (eds.), *Microeconomic Foundations of Employment and Inflation Theory,* Norton, New York, 1970.

[3] Brozen, *op. cit.,* p. 6.

only begun. We must then try to disprove the observed association. Concurrently, we would have to respect another necessary scientific canon: causality can be inferred only if an experimental group is compared with a control group. The control-experimental design is admittedly difficult to obtain in the social sciences, especially at the macro or industry level. However, statistical procedures other than regression should be explored to approximate the ideal of a laboratory control-experimental design.

Future work must also be directed by more open-minded conceptualizations. For instance, the causal link is not only from advertising to profit, but also from profit to advertising. Both are real possibilities. A firm, like any organism, exists only as an expression of the dynamic tensions within it and between it and its environment, which includes its competitors, potential customers, and suppliers. Any action will evoke a number of direct and indirect reactions. And the situation is even more complex because past research has been concerned not with one firm but with an industry, i.e., a *population*. One does not need to be a student of demography or genetics to realize that what happens to an individual firm is only partly the result of what it does; what other firms do also plays a role.

Yet none of these considerations seems to have explicitly guided the literature on the roles of advertising at the industry level. For instance, the widespread use of a limited number of statistical techniques reveals that researchers try to ascertain whether advertising has an effect on profit, and then assume that nothing further will happen—like the fables of old in which the king married the princess and lived happily ever after. But social history does not end so simply. Moreover, by aggregating firms, one ignores dynamic interactions among them. Naive conceptualizations of the world lead to misuses of statistical inference and to establishing incorrect facts.

Finally, as stressed in the previous chapter, research is quantitative only if the *concepts* of interest are clearly specified and the numbers used are indeed measures of those concepts. So far, these conditions have generally been violated in the study of advertising effects at the industry level.

Without going into detail, we note that such concepts as market structure, concentration, and power are too blurred and vague for explication in the context of empirical measurement.[1] There are even more basic problems. Buzzell[2] has noted that traditional economic analysis tends to include advertising expenditures as an element defining *both* the concept of structure (is an industry's structure like that of competition or of monopoly?) and of conduct (is an industry behaving as if it were structurally competitive

[1] See the critique of the so-called concentration measures in C. Marfels, "Some Recent Developments in the Measurement of Business Concentration," Paper No. 7001, Department of Economics, Dalhousie University, Halifax, Canada, n.d.; K. Mackenzie and F. M. Nicosia, "Marketing Systems: Toward Formal Descriptions and Structural Properties," in R. L. King (ed.), *Marketing and the New Science of Planning,* American Marketing Association, Chicago, Ill., 1968; and J. M. Vernon, *Market Structure and Industrial Performance,* Allyn and Bacon, Boston, 1972. See, also, the literature in, e.g., *The Journal of the American Statistical Association* and the *Review of Economic Statistics.*

[2] R. Buzzell, "Marketing and Economic Performance: Meaning and Measurement," Marketing Science Institute, Cambridge, Mass., August 1972, pp. 7–8.

or monopolistic?). To the extent that this occurs, the two concepts are not logically distinct, *and* their empirical measures will necessarily be statistically associated.[1]

This remark leads to a major shortcoming of past studies: most of the data used are federal statistics that are not measures of the concepts under study. Even the Bureau of the Census stresses that the data it collects were not developed as measures of such economic concepts as concentration, oligopoly, profit, etc. That is:

> ... [the classification system was] developed over a period of years to serve the general purpose of the census and other governmental statistics. Although the basic data are extremely useful and widely used for a variety of purposes in marketing analysis, the classifications were not designed to establish categories necessarily denoting coherent or relevant markets in the true competitive sense, or to provide a basis for measuring market power.[2]

The general problems that follow from the lack of fit between data and concepts have been discussed by Bock.[3] In a nutshell, government data such as that provided in censuses, National Income Accounting, and the Internal Revenue Service ultimately depend on the criteria used to define an establishment and an industry in the Standard Industrial Classification (SIC) system. These criteria concern the chemical and physical properties of inputs and of technologies; thus the numerical descriptions of the economy and of industries that can be derived from the SIC system are not descriptions of decision-making activities and/or decision centers. At the micromanagerial level, a firm examining alternative policies always complements SIC data by (1) further elaborations, (2) additional company-based or newly collected data, and (3) a great deal of judgment. These laborious operations attempt to overcome the lack of fit between government data and those concepts that actually deal with the dynamics of decision making.

Since the concepts of profit, concentration, market power, brand loyalty, and consumer demand are measures of the dynamics of decision making, it is plausible that a similar lack of fit applies to the study of advertising effects. For the future, we must hope that researchers will not use government data simply because they exist, but will instead show the imagination necessary to match data with concepts.

2.1.4 Public Policy and Ambiguity of Concepts and Data
Although the questions discussed in these commentaries are few, they are enough to convey the picture of the present state-of-the-art. Studies of advertising effects at the industry level are characterized by both a proliferation of blurred concepts and

---

[1] Another crucial problem concerning the explication and measurement of these concepts is whether data such as advertising expenditures, firm sizes, etc. are market-related or firm-related. Apropos of this, see, e.g., the empirical explorations in J. M. Vernon and M. B. McElroy, "A Note on Estimation in Market Structure-Performance Studies," Marketing Science Institute, Cambridge, Mass., July 1972.

[2] Bureau of the Census, "Concentration Ratios in Manufacturing Industry, 1963," report prepared for the Subcommittee on Antitrust and Monopoly of the Committee on the Judiciary, United States Senate, Government Printing Office, Washington, D.C., 1966, Part I.

[3] B. Bock, *Concentration, Oligopoly, and Profit: Concepts vs. Data*, The Conference Board, New York, 1972.

inappropriate data. But it is the conceptual ambiguity that hinders policy making most deeply. An example may clarify why conceptual ambiguity is so critical.

Consider the well-known questions: Is brand proliferation necessary? Does brand loyalty imply monopolistic power? Is the existence of brand names a good or a bad thing? Since firms use advertising to develop and maintain a brand name, the questions necessarily apply to advertising also. But the answers are predetermined by how one views the appearance of brand names in modern economies. At least *two* very different perspectives are possible, with very different implications for public policy.

From a managerial viewpoint, the development and maintenance of a brand name is an expensive effort. Why, then, does each firm try to differentiate its can of tomato paste from that of competitors? If information is viewed as an economic good, the answer is relatively simple: whatever real or imagined attributes a brand may have, such attributes represent information that may be meaningful to at least some consumers. This information may be price, taste, color, texture, the shape of the can, or simply the assurance that the consumer will find exactly the same attributes in the same intensity on repurchase. Some people may argue that it is irrational to choose a brand because of its can rather than because of its price or taste. But the firm's point of view is: "I found that some consumers prefer a particular combination of attributes and I will differentiate my tomato paste can accordingly."

Each firm tries to associate a particular combination of attributes with a brand name, hoping that some consumers will become loyal to it. This loyalty will benefit these consumers in that they no longer must pay search costs, and it will also benefit the firm, because its planning will be easier and its costs and revenues more predictable. In conclusion, if we view information as an economic good, the development of brands has advantages for both consumers and firms.[1]

We would arrive at a different conclusion if we adopted the point of view of traditional economics. In perfect competition, every can of tomato paste would be "equal" in all respects; thus, no consumer would prefer one firm's can to another's. But if a firm is "allowed" to differentiate its cans along some attributes, then the extent of consumer loyalty observed in the market can be seen as the degree of "monopoly" gained by the firm. That is, if a firm increased the brand's price, consumers would tend to pay the increase. In other words, the degree of loyalty a consumer has to a brand is a measure of the degree of a firm's monopolistic power over that consumer. Thus, from the traditional perspective, brand loyalty has disadvantages.

What can legislators, regulators, and courts do when confronted not only with ambiguity but, as in this case, with opposite conclusions? The answer was suggested by Grabowsky's statement mentioned earlier: it is in these numerous situations that "there is more scope for personal values to influence policy decisions." Historically, when personal values are brought into the picture, the technical questions concerning the possible economic effects of advertising at the industry level fade into the background.

---

[1] It can be argued that consumers are not actually better off since advertising has the power to make them prefer this or that attribute. We shall return to this in Chapter 13.

At the present time, there is a clear differentiation among two opposite value perspectives about man and society. These value perspectives essentially debate whether consumers have a choice in the market and, more importantly, whether they have the "right" information to make a choice.

As we saw in Part 1, managers consistently answer "yes," from the introduction of new products and brands on through their entire life cycle. And behavioralists who have observed consumers conclude that there is no evidence that firms can dictate consumer choice.[1] But others, with a different image of man and society, answer "no." The extent to which consumers are seen as passive and ignorant is so high that a writer, C. Kaysen,[2] has even suggested that "experts" should decide whether a new car model should be introduced.

It is doubtful that these two viewpoints can be reconciled and it is certainly impossible to predict which of the two will prevail. It is, however, plausible to argue that legislators, courts, and—more subtly but more basically—regulators may affect the results. By their daily decisions, they will contribute to the dominance of one or the other. They cannot escape this historical responsibility. Nor can they reach their decisions on the basis of "perfect information," for none of us knows what people are or what they want.

3   THE ROLES OF ADVERTISING IN DIFFERENT INDUSTRIES *(excerpts from A. A. Achenbaum, senior vice president and director of advertising services, J. Walter Thompson Co.)*

In earlier chapters we saw that advertising expenditures varied considerably from firm to firm as well as from product to product and from industry to industry (see Part 1 and Chapter 11, Exhibits 11.2, 11.3, and 11.4). We also learned that, at the firm level, management can communicate with its potential customers through many channels such as visual means, product and package design, salesmen and mass media advertising. Variations in the optimal *mix* of these channels among firms, and even for brands within a firm, are dictated by many factors, some internal and some external to the firm.

These variations must be taken into consideration in assessing advertising roles within the entire economy (see Chapter 11, Section 2.2.1) and within each industry. In the next testimony, Mr. Achenbaum considers four different types of transactions. In each case, both buyer and seller need to acquire information, but the structure of each transaction varies and so does the importance of giving or receiving information through advertising.

> *. . . it should be abundantly clear that market communications between buyers and sellers are a critical element in consummating transactions. While the buyer can be*

---

[1] G. Katona, B. Strumpel, and E. Zahn, *Aspirations and Affluence*, McGraw-Hill, New York, 1971. See, also, Chapters 13 and 14 below.

[2] Cited by H. P. Root, "Should Product Differentiation Be Restricted?" *Journal of Marketing*, July 1972, p. 7.

exposed to advertising in the course of making a transaction, advertising is only a part of the process. . . .

How important advertising is in the role that communication plays in a transaction or sale—and we are only concerned in these hearings with the sellers' communication . . . and the response of buyers to it—will largely vary with the type of good or service being sold and the channels of distribution used for getting it to the consumer. This perhaps can best be seen schematically as a continuum from a rudimentary sale, which is quite typical in the sale of a house, to some of the more complex transactions, which are most typified by self-service/self-selection products sold in the supermarket.

The Rudimentary Transaction—A House Sale

Let's start with a house just built by an artisan builder as the object of sale, where no middleman is involved. The maker in this case is also the seller. The prospect or ultimate user (or owner, if you wish) is the buyer. The agreement is such that money flows from buyer to seller and the product flows from seller to buyer. All communication is personal, direct, and two way. All elements of the agreement are discussed and negotiated personally.

We have here a situation where almost no advertising is used. If manipulation, deception, or compulsion is used, no one would ever know it. In fact, the advertising often used is of a "classified" nature and is given as an example by many critics of good advertising because it is informative.

[Imagine] a typical classified page from [a newspaper]. What's so informative about it? It has all the earmarks of what is criticized in national advertising except that it is small and done by individuals. But how many cases do we each know of where the seller, who was not the head of his corporation doing national advertising, forgot to mention the wet basement to the buyer?

The Automobile Sale

The real difference between a rudimentary sale and a more complex one is the injection of middlemen or selling agents to the maker into the picture. This means that from the time a product is made until it is bought by the ultimate consumer, more than one set of buyers and sellers is involved.

Let's take as our first example of a complex sale the sale of an automobile. An insurance sale by an exclusive broker is similar. So is a gasoline sale. Here the maker—the automobile manufacturer—works through an exclusive dealer who deals directly with the user or ultimate buyer. The manufacturer has no direct relationship with the final consumer sale itself—except through warranties that it expressly grants.

In the early days of the automobile industry, . . . the manufacturer did little, if any, indirect communication with the consumers. This was a role left to the middlemen. But it became readily apparent—even though the middlemen were exclusive agents of the manufacturer—that communication with the consumer could not be left to them alone. There were things the individual dealer could not do. And so national manufacturers' advertising became an important element in automotive market communications.

While advertising plays a role in the sale of an automobile, it is a limited role. To a large extent, its purpose is to create the proper competitive context for consumers to make a decision and to induce traffic to the dealers' showrooms.

Because the automobile dealers are often direct extensions of the manufacturer, personal selling still remains the crucial means of market communication.

Since the terms of the sale vary considerably from place to place and dealer to dealer, manufacturer-sponsored advertising of automobiles cannot cover certain information in their national advertising—in fact, they are quite restricted from mentioning the complete terms of sale. Negotiation of terms is such a key part of the automobile market that personal selling normally takes precedence over all forms of market communication.

The Appliance Sale

The sale of household appliances [involves] a more elaborate distributive structure including wholesalers and retailers. This is still somewhat typical of home furnishings and clothing (Exhibit 12.1). Here the "distance" between the maker and user is great. Moreover, the retailers are usually not exclusive agents of the maker. Merchandise and dollar flow go through two institutions in getting to the ultimate consumer. Likewise, personal communications.

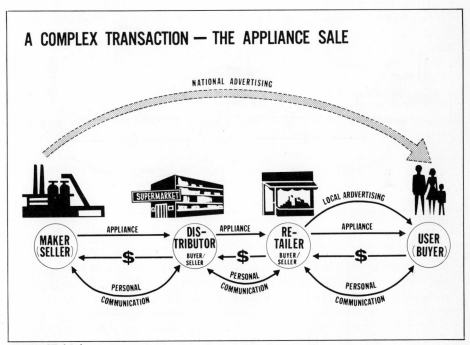

EXHIBIT 12.1

Under these circumstances, if the maker wishes to have some effect upon his demand, he must communicate with the marketplace indirectly. In relation to cost, advertising plays a relatively important role in market communications. Yet, personal selling at the retail level will be found. But more than in the case of the automobile sale, the maker must undertake the major share of market communication with the ultimate consumer since the interests of the retailer are not always served by moving a particular maker's merchandise.

The Packaged Good

And finally, let's look at the packaged good . . . soap . . . typical of most process foods, toiletries, and cosmetics. This is a key group because a great deal of national advertising takes place in this category (Exhibit 12.2).

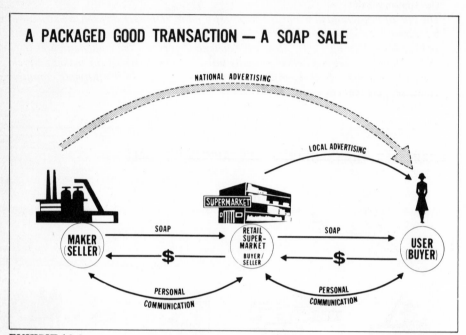

EXHIBIT 12.2

But there is another reason—women make most of the purchases in this category. Unfortunately, it is men who are often most critical of the ways of the marketplace, particularly the role that advertising plays. But for the most part, they are quite ignorant of how it really operates, particularly with respect to women. . . . Yet, in acting as the purchasing agent for the household, women are in fact knowledgeable. Our experience in surveying them is that they are articulate in telling you what they think, in knowing what they want, and in being skeptical of what is offered for sale. There is nothing passive about most women buyers. You need only observe them in a department store or supermarket to know this.

In these industries, the wholesaling function has been absorbed by the manufacturers and the retailers. The typical middleman is the large retail chain supermarket. Self-service/self-selection is the rule, where the personal communication between even the retailer and the consumer is nil. Thus the entire communication job for any one brand is the burden of the manufacturer.

This is not to say that the retailers do not rely on advertising. They do. But it usually is to advertise specific prices or sales in an effort to induce store traffic. However, as some of the retail chains have developed important brands of their own — in coffee, for example — they have done national advertising, which is much the same as that done by national makers.

Communication Feedback — Market Research

For many years, makers only communicated to the marketplace impersonally through advertising. There was almost no direct *feedback from the consumers. Essentially they relied on their own sales data and, later, on retail sales data obtained from independent auditors, like Nielsen, to ascertain how they were doing with consumers. But they soon learned that these were inadequate methods of feedback. They had to learn more from the consumer than just how many sales they were making.*

Forty years ago the maker willingly accepted the middleman's information about the market. But, in recent times, the maker learned that the middleman did not know accurately what the user thought and often didn't care, and [he] had more than one maker to worry about and didn't see any reason to give one maker more information than any other.

The maker then decided he would get the information himself — much the way he at one time decided to do the advertising himself. And so, modern market research was developed. The growth of market research in the last twenty years has been phenomenal . . . market research actually closed the communication circle — making it much more like the personal communications in the rudimentary sale — a two-way proposition. What makes this development important is that it shows that the intent *of the maker is constructive, not manipulative; it shows his desire to ascertain what the user has in mind so that he can more readily satisfy her. . . .*

Summary

As I said before, the amount and type of market communications depends on the type type of product and the distributive structure. Let's now summarize how much of each is involved in each of the examples I gave (Exhibit 12.3).

EXHIBIT 12.3
ROLE OF PERSONAL AND IMPERSONAL COMMUNICATION IN CONSUMER TRANSACTIONS

	House Sale	Automobile Sale	Appliance Sale	Soap Sale
Role of Middleman	None	Exclusive retailers only	Distributor and nonexclusive retailers	Chain retailers only
Personal Selling to Consumer	All important	Very important by retailer	Not too important by retailer	None at retail
Need for National Advertising	None	Important, but not relative to cost	Somewhat important relative to cost	Very important
Need for Research Feedback	None	Important relative to cost	Somewhat important relative to cost	Very important

It is obvious that the more direct the transaction is between maker and user, the less likely impersonal market communication—either advertising or market research— will be used. Since none of the communication is recorded, it is difficult to know what takes place in the negotiation, which is likely to be most active.

On the other end of the continuum is the packaged good sale where there is virtually no personal selling at the point of purchase. Advertising and market research are used a great deal by the maker in communicating with the marketplace. In fact, without this advertising and market research, the maker would in effect have no direct influence on the sale of his merchandise. Wanting to have such an influence, however, does not suggest a desire to manipulate.

The Competitive Milieu

As I have shown, impersonal market communication—particularly for certain forms of merchandise and services—is a key part of the marketing process at the level of the individual transaction. What I have left out, of course, is the competitive milieu in which these individual transactions take place.

Competition, needless to say, is a crucial element in the picture. Quite simply, to the degree that there is more than one maker—and usually there are many to choose from, although again it depends on the industry and the distributive structure— the user is in a position to get more than one story about the product he wishes to buy. In fact, the competition of impersonal communication is a very key element in the two-sided marketing mix.

Much has been said that the only real marketing competition pertains to price. This is an interesting idea, but without communication about the merits of what is offered and all of the terms of the offer, and without this communication by all the competitors being widely disseminated, we really cannot have price competition. In fact, unless we have the competition of communication, we are going to restrict trade, not free it. Thus, the competition of communication is what truly precludes the possibility of manipulation.

3.1   IF ADVERTISING'S ROLES VARY ACROSS INDUSTRIES AND FIRMS, THEN WHAT IS AN "INDUSTRY"?

In the four theoretical cases discussed by Mr. Achenbaum we have seen that structural differences call for a different *communication mix*, i.e., differences in the relative use of the many available channels. The empirical evidence presented below suggests that the communication mix varies not only across industries but also across firms.

EVIDENCE ON THE VARIETY OF ADVERTISING ROLES ACROSS INDUSTRIES
A revealing and challenging picture of the possible roles of advertising has been prepared by Dr. Charles Ramond.[1] He has ranked the 125 largest advertisers among the *Fortune* 500 largest United States firms in terms of (1) level of advertising expenditures as a percentage of sales and (2) level of profits as a percentage of sales (Exhibit 12.4)

The results are striking. First, any combination of advertising, sales, and profit values seems possible. For soaps, for example, advertising is a high percentage of sales,

---

[1] Professor at New York University and president of Marketing Control, Inc.

EXHIBIT 12.4

INDUSTRIES GROUPED BY THEIR AVERAGE ADVERTISING EXPENDITURES AND PROFIT MARGINS, 125 LARGEST ADVERTISERS, 1968

Advertising as a Percentage of Sales	Profit as a Percentage of Sales		
	Low (under 6%)	*Medium (6%–8%)*	*High (over 8%)*
Low (under 3%)	Tires (4)* Automotive (4) Appliances (3)	Metals (4) Airlines (6)	Oil (6) Chemicals (4)
Medium (3%–10%)	Food (20) Beer (4)	Liquor (3)	Tobacco (6) Paper (2)
High (over 10%)	Soaps (4)	Soft drinks (3)	Gum and candy (3) Toiletries and cosmetics (10) Pharmaceuticals (4)

*Number in parentheses indicates number of firms in this industry which were among the 25 largest advertisers in 1968 and also were listed in the *Fortune* 500. Companies with high advertising/earnings ratios that year are shown in Exhibit 12.5.

Source: C. Ramond, "Measurement of Sales Effectiveness," in R. Barton (ed.), *Handbook of Advertising Management*, McGraw-Hill, New York, Ch. 22, pp. 22–26.

but profit is a low percentage of sales; oil and chemical firms have low advertising but high profits relative to sales; and other firms exemplify intermediate cases. At present, it would be premature to suggest the factors that account for these substantial variations. Yet their very existence warns us that any statistical association between advertising and profit would hide the heterogeneity of the underlying situation. At the very least, part of any statistical association would necessarily be spurious.

A similar caveat applies even to firms usually thought to be substantially similar in their consumer orientation. Consider the bottom row of the exhibit. All firms in this row—soap, soft drinks, gum and candy, toiletries and cosmetics, and pharmaceuticals— spend large absolute amounts of money on advertising (they are among the 125 largest advertisers). They also spend the highest percentage in terms of sales (over 10 percent). On the basis of these two factors, one might reasonably conclude that the three groups are similar, differing in degree, but not in kind.

Such conclusions overlook key differences. The group of soap firms has a profit rate of less than 6 percent of sales; the soft drinks group realizes a profit of between 6 and 8 percent (like the firms in the metal industry!); while the third group (gum, etc.) achieves a profit of over 8 percent. In the behavioral sciences, such data suggest differences in kind rather than degree—that each group may be a type.[1] And if this is

---

[1] For a variety of reasons, much economic analysis has not dealt with the problem of "differences in kind." A basic introductory article here is A. H. Barton, "The Concept of Property-Space in Social Research," in P. F. Lazarsfeld and M. Rosenberg (eds.), *The Language of Social Research,* Free Press, Glencoe, Ill., 1955. For a more recent discussion of index construction (cases of differences in degree) and typology construction (case of differences in kind), see the entire Section I in P. F. Lazarsfeld, A. K. Pasanella, and M. Rosenberg (eds.), *Continuities in the Language of Social Research*, Free Press, New York, 1972.

so, the effects of advertising should be studied for each group separately; to aggregate them leads to misuse of statistical inference.

To date, these differences have been ignored. In fact, researchers have assumed that the industries under study are homogeneous; that is, they have assumed that the relationships between profit and variables such as advertising and market share do not vary across industries. This assumption has also been made by the often-quoted study made by the Federal Trade Commission of food manufacturing companies (see Section 2.1.1). Bass[1] has begun testing whether such homogeneity holds using the FTC data (97 firms in 13 industries). His early results indicate the presence of strong heterogeneity not only among several industries but also among firms in the "same" industry.

EVIDENCE ON THE VARIETY OF ADVERTISING ROLES ACROSS FIRMS

If the relationship between advertising and profit or some other variable is studied by subjecting the firms in an industry to the same statistical procedure, one assumes that these firms are, for the purpose at hand, comparable. But few studies check this assumption. Present research in this area resembles consumer research before investigators realized that a population of consumers may not be homogeneous, that there may exist consumer types, and that each type must be analyzed separately.

Ramond's study suggests that there are indeed strong structural differences among firms in the same industry. Consider the findings in Exhibit 12.5. Recall that in Exhibit 12.4 all four pharmaceutical firms were in the same high advertising-high profit percentage cell. But when we consider the ratio of advertising to earnings, the four firms are scattered. Similarly, Procter and Gamble, the largest advertiser in the United States, has an advertising/earnings ratio of only 1.0 to 1.49, whereas Colgate-Palmolive and Lever Brothers, its smaller competitors, who spend considerably less on advertising, have ratios of over 3.0. One may be tempted to infer that the quality of advertising is responsible for these differences. Yet many other structural factors differentiate these three firms: from the structure of their marketing mix (e.g., the sales force and relationships with dealers) to the structure of their production and distribution costs to their financial features. These three companies are not sampled from a homogeneous population (e.g., from an urn containing a population of balls that are perfectly equal in all respects except one, say, color). Instead they are structurally different. Their use of advertising and its effects on earnings, prices, and the like can be properly studied only if these structural differences are explicitly considered.

If we neglect to ascertain differences in kind, so-called quantitative studies of advertising's effects may give numbers that are just as meaningful as the total weight of a box containing both tomatoes and potatoes. Armed with this figure, we could determine shipping charges, only to discover later that the box arrived at its destination with the tomatoes squashed and the potatoes rotted—a result presumably not desired by consumers, business, or public policy makers.

---

[1] F. M. Bass, "Market Structure and Profitability—Analysis of the Appropriateness of Pooling Cross-Sectional Industry Data," Purdue University, Paper No. 424, Lafayette, Ind., October 1973.

EXHIBIT 12.5

ADVERTISING/EARNINGS RATIOS OF MAJOR UNITED STATES ADVERTISERS, 1968

Ratio	Number of Companies	Drugs and Toiletries	Food and Soft Drinks	Beer and Liquors	Soaps, Autos, Airlines, Tobacco, Etc.
Over 3.0	4	Miles Laboratories			Colgate-Palmolive Lever Brothers Rapid American
2.00–3.00	3	Sterling Drug	Pillsbury		Mattel Inc.
1.50–1.99	6	Bristol-Myers Chesebrough-Pond's Richardson & Merrill	General Foods Standard Brands Armour		
1.00–1.49	12	Warner-Lambert	National Biscuit Norton Simon Quaker Oats General Mills Wm. Wrigley Kellogg	Jos. Schlitz	American Motors P & G Liggett & Myers Loews Theaters
0.75–0.99	11	Revlon	Beatrice Foods Campbell Soup Borden Carnation H. J. Heinz Pepsico	Seagrams Heublein	TWA Gillette
0.50–0.749	13	Johnson & Johnson Pfizer Smith, Kline & French American Home Products	Coca-Cola Ralston-Purina	Anheuser-Busch Pabst	W. R. Grace Purex Phillip-Morris United Airlines American Airlines
Totals		11	18	5	15

Source: C. Ramond, "Measurement of Sales Effectiveness," in R. Barton (ed.), *Handbook of Advertising Management*, McGraw-Hill, New York, Ch. 22, pp. 22–26.

Because of the multitude of factors bearing upon industries and firms, Buzzell has noted that "the only general statement that can be safely made about the role of advertising [in different firms and industries] is that 'it depends.'"[1] He then illustrates, at length, enormous variations in the level of advertising expenditures, its objectives, and its results, even among firms in the same industry. Three of Buzzell's illustrations of variations in advertising expenditures are presented in Exhibits 12.6a, b, and c.

Note that government statistics—i.e., those generated by the SIC system—consider each of the pairs of firms in the Exhibits to belong to the same industry. Most economic studies do the same, in that their data base is indeed generated by the SIC classification. But the striking variations in the use of advertising among such firms again suggest that, *behaviorally,* the firms may be very different.

---

[1] R. Buzzell, "The Role of Advertising in the Marketing Mix," Marketing Science Institute, Cambridge, Mass., October 1971.

EXHIBIT 12.6a

THE COSMETIC "INDUSTRY": AVON VS. REVLON

	Avon	Revlon
Distribution	In-home (40% commission)	Stores (35–40% margin)
Advertising	1.5% of sales	7.0% of sales

EXHIBIT 12.6b

THE VACUUM CLEANER "INDUSTRY": ELECTROLUX VS. HOOVER

	Electrolux	Hoover
Distribution	In-home (30–35% commission)	Stores (20–25% margin)
Advertising	Little or none	$1.5 million (Est. 1970)

EXHIBIT 12.6c

THE HOME-LAUNDRY PRODUCT "INDUSTRY": PUREX VS. MAJOR LAUNDRY-PRODUCT FIRMS

	Purex	Major Competitors
Advertising	Relatively small	Major means of competition
Trade Promotions	Heavy emphasis	Relatively minor

Source: R. Buzzell, "The Role of Advertising in the Marketing Mix," Marketing Science Institute, Cambridge, Mass., October 1971, Appendix.

ARE THE SIC INDUSTRIES RELEVANT TO THE STUDY OF ADVERTISING EFFECTS? The SIC criteria for classification of firms concern the form and/or chemical and physical properties of products. It obviously follows that cosmetics, vacuum cleaners, and home-laundry products are different in kind, and that firms producing these products are different in kind. Thus, the concept of *industry* (a population of homogeneous and comparable firms) is peculiarly anchored to the *product* class produced by firms.

But both the evidence in the preceding exhibits and professional knowledge indicate that firms in the same SIC industry may not be homogeneous, but may differ in kind with respect to their internal structure (e.g., production, distribution, and finance) and their decision processes. And these are the differences that count in understanding and evaluating the roles advertising may have in the economy.

The implications of this evidence are far-reaching. If the organizational decision process of a firm in one SIC industry is similar to that of a firm in another SIC industry, the findings discussed in the previous section may be misleading in two ways. First, comparisons of advertising effects across SIC industries are meaningless, for different industries may include firms that are similar in their decision-making structure. Second, if firms in the same SIC industry differ in kind, they cannot be aggregated into one industry. As mentioned previously, if we add the weight of potatoes and tomatoes, we produce a number (total weight) that is meaningless and even misleading in most problems dealing with their handling and use. Different types must be studied separately.

Future empirical studies of advertising effects at the industry level will have to consider very carefully the fact that the SIC data base classifies firms using criteria that may be irrelevant for the study of advertising management decisions and their effects on the economy. At the very least, future studies must take into account that advertising is only a part of each firm's search for an optimal communication mix, and this mix, in turn, is only a part of each firm's marketing mix. Undoubtedly, it will be difficult to identify similarities or differences among firms—i.e., types—on criteria that are relevant to the study of advertising effects. But this work is necessary, for successful studies must begin with models of reality.[1]

4   SUMMARY

In this chapter we examined several specific roles that the advertising institution might play in society and in the economy. In the opinion of Mr. Cousins, advertising cannot be evaluated solely in economic terms. He argued that advertising provides the means for free access of ideas—economic and noneconomic—into society's mass communication system. At the same time, he asserted, advertising enables mass media to be independent of government and special interest groups.

Only this independence, according to Mr. Heiskell, assures free access to the mass communication system. Mr. Heiskell presented data showing that advertising pays for practically all the costs of broadcast media (radio and TV) and about two-thirds of those of print media (newspapers and magazines). That is, advertising not only pays its own way but also largely supports the flow of all other types of information—political, religious, social, and cultural.

Mr. Heiskell also asserted that the advertising institution could not control the mass communication system. He testified that, in his experience as a publisher of several mass circulation magazines, advertisers had not sought to control his editorial and general press decisions—even when editorials and reporting were critical of firms' behavior. In fact, he appeared more concerned about government interference than about interference from advertisers.[2]

---

[1] F. M. Nicosia and B. Rosenberg, "Substantive Modelling in Consumer Attitude Research: Some Practical Uses," in R. I. Haley (ed.), *Attitude Research in Transition*, American Marketing Association, Chicago, Ill., November 1971.

[2] One may obviously challenge the witnesses' assertions that, in their experience, advertisers have no control over the functioning of society's mass communication system. It could be argued, for example, that both witnesses are ignorant. Or, perhaps, they are both, together with their employees, unaware that they are being manipulated by the same occult powers advertisers use to manipulate consumers. Alternatively, we could argue on the basis of empirical data, an approach that would certainly be more convincing than any other.

The testimonies by Cousins and Heiskell illustrate clearly the problems posed by joint costs and benefits in a mass communication system. If we wish to abolish the current advertising institution, the funds needed to obtain a certain quantity and quality of information flow will have to come from somewhere else. In this age of ecological thinking, it should be clear that there is no such thing as a free ride. Thus any change in the present advertising institution must begin with an examination of how the cost of maintaining any mass communication system can or should be allocated.

Beyond allocation of costs, of course, each proposed alternative must also consider qualitative value premises. For instance, does society wish to keep its mass communication system free from intervention by government and possible panels of professionals? If so, how? But, as stressed in Chapter 11, these questions of values cannot be discussed rationally without detailed knowledge of costs and benefits—i.e., of efficiency. Unfortunately, existing proposals for change have been conspicuously silent on the costs of such changes, on how they should be allocated to the members of society, and, above all, on opportunity costs.

With the testimony of Professor Demsetz, attention shifted to the possibility that advertising might create barriers to entry, contribute to monopoly power, and raise profit rates. Traditional economic theory has argued that society is better off when perfect competition exists, and that deviations such as monopolistic competition, oligopoly, and monopoly are to be avoided. To the extent that advertising contributes to such deviations, it can be assessed negatively.

However, Professor Demsetz pointed out that this chain of reasoning assumes that information is free and that all members of society have or can gain perfect information. He reviewed several studies that departed from traditional economics. These studies begin with a model of the economy in which buyers and sellers need information and must pay for it. They fail to support the conclusions of research based on the traditional image of man and society. At present, we must stress a most important conclusion: the differences in current findings on advertising effects are not *contradictions* so much as expressions of the fact that different researchers adopt different views of human affairs as points of departure.

In discussing Professor Demsetz' report, we also noted serious methodological shortcomings in much of the popular literature. One of these was brought to the fore by the theoretical situations illustrated by Mr. Achenbaum: different combinations of structural factors tend to create differences in kind even across firms classified in the same SIC industry. The empirical evidence provided by Ramond and Buzzell strongly supports Mr. Achenbaum's illustrations. The observed variations suggest that the organizational decision processes of firms differ in kind; that the role of advertising changes in different marketing and communication mixes.

But the SIC classification of firms is not based on differences in marketing and communication mixes nor on other decision-making characteristics. Unfortunately, many economic analyses of advertising effects have taken these SIC data as their point of departure, thus assuming that the population of firms in each SIC industry is homogeneous and that firms in different SIC industries are heterogeneous (see Bass' study).

It is inappropriate, however, to ask "what is the mean contribution of advertising to profit" in a population of firms that differ in kind with respect to their advertising strategies. As an analogy, suppose we wanted to inquire into the role of the battery in the behavior of a sample of automobiles. If our sample included cars operating on both combustion engines and electric batteries, we would obtain a peculiarly meaningless answer, even though we used the most sophisticated tools of statistical inference in our analysis.

All in all, while we have too few concepts and data to study the overall role of the advertising institution in the entire society, we also have too many blurred concepts— e.g., power—that are difficult to measure, and certainly too much inappropriate data when we begin to study some specific economic roles. Future research, especially that attempting to help public policy, must begin to refine the vague concepts used so far and become aware that there must be correspondence between concepts and their measures, i.e., data.

Chapter 13

Advertising and the Manipulation of Consumers

In our search for the roles that the advertising institution may play in a socioeconomic system, we have thus far emphasized economic roles. We now turn to an area that is essentially social: the possible effects of advertising on consumers. We shall focus on the question of manipulation: can advertising make people do things against their own wills and interests? This is a legitimate and pressing question, and one that encompasses most, if not all, the social roles of advertising.

The question is difficult to answer directly, for the term manipulation is used in many different ways. It may refer to the intent of the advertiser, who wishes the consumer to alter his behavior, or to a quality of the message itself: lies, deceit, and distortion are viewed as manipulation and counterposed to objective information. Manipulation may also refer to the various psychological processes that operate upon external stimuli. Further, the meaning attributed to any of these types of manipulation may range from the original sense, "to handle or mediate," to the modern, pejorative connotation.

Any definition we choose poses serious questions. For example, the distinction between manipulation and persuasion may remain fundamentally subjective. If John convinces Sarah to act in her own interest, he *persuades* her. But if John convinces her to act against her own interests, he *manipulates* her. The distinction, in principle, is clear. But what if we disagree on the desirability of some particular behavior—e.g., investing in United States savings bonds? In this case, there will remain an irreconcilable conflict, rooted in different values, about whether an ad for United States savings bonds is persuasive or manipulative.

Although we cannot neatly resolve all the ambiguous cases, we shall see that certain types of advertising manipulation can be detected; that their adverse consequences are clear; and that government regulatory action is both feasible and desirable in preventing them.

To pinpoint these undesirable types of advertising, we must review some basic knowledge in social psychology and communication research. First, we want to know what happens when a human receives a message. In Sections 1 and 2, we find that even a captive subject—a person exposed to a message in a laboratory experiment—himself manipulates (handles) the stimulus he receives. The results of these manipulations—the subject's perception of the information (i.e., his *information processes*)—tend to be different, because subjects differ from one another.

In Sections 3 and 4, we turn our attention to a close examination of what is meant by *information*. Many have argued that certain types of information may manipulate consumers. What are the qualities that make information manipulative? We shall search for operational definitions of manipulative information—definitions that can be used objectively by legislators, regulators, and courts. The reason for this emphasis should be clear: public agencies must be helped (1) to identify such types of information and (2) to prevent such information from flowing through the advertising institution.

1   SOME FACTS AND PRINCIPLES FROM COMMUNICATION RESEARCH
(excerpts from Dr. H. E. Krugman, manager of public opinion research, General Electric Company)

The following testimony reviews, in nontechnical terms, some features of the psychological processes through which the consumer perceives advertising messages. To begin with, manipulation obviously cannot occur unless individuals are exposed to the manipulative stimulus. Further, manipulation requires that, once a stimulus has been physically perceived, the information it contains is assimilated in its entirety—content *and* meaning—with no loss and/or distortion. Third, the meaning of this information must be remembered. Finally, at the moment of purchase, the message's information and meaning must actively and predominantly affect the subject's decision.

Thus, even omitting the philosophical question of the true interests of human beings, verification of the presence of manipulation requires that we establish: (1) that a message is *registered* by the subject, (2) that the content and meaning of the message is *accurately* perceived, (3) that the message is remembered, and (4) that the message is a major influence on the subject's behavior. Dr. Krugman presents examples and evidence bearing on all four of these topics.

> To begin, I'd like to mention a pioneer psychologist, Dr. Daniel Starch, who in 1923 devised a method for measuring readership and recognition of print advertising. In February of 1932 he established the Starch Continuing Readership Research Program which each year covers more than 1,000 issues of consumer and farm magazines, business publications, and newspapers. More than 240,000 personal interviews are made each year in carrying on this program.
>
> To provide a relatively current answer to the question of how many people notice an ad and read an ad, I took the most common single type of ad—the one-page, four-color ad—and totalled the Starch scores for all such ads in all major magazines for all of 1970, i.e., 47 magazines in all and 20,374 individual ads. I found that, on the average, 44% of readers of a publication claim to notice a particular ad, 35% read just enough to identify the brand, but only 9% of readers of a publication read most of a particular ad. In other words, almost half of all ads are noticed, a third to the point of brand identification, but less than a tenth are of enough interest to be read by the typical reader (see Exhibit 13.1).

EXHIBIT 13.1
ALL ADVERTISEMENTS/TOTAL

Number of Magazines	One-Page, Four-Color Ads			
	Number of Ads	Percent Noted	Percent Associated	Percent Read Most
47*	20,374	44.3	35.0	8.7

Noted is the percent of readers of the ad-containing issue who remembered that they had seen the advertisement in the issue

Associated is the percent of readers of the ad-containing issue who saw some part of the advertisement which clearly indicated the brand name.

Read Most is the percent of readers of the ad-contianing issue who read half or more of the words in the advertisement.

*In some magazines, separate scores were available for males and for females. Thus, for the 47 magazines, a total of 59 sets of data were used in averaging of percentages.

> There are many variations to these overall answers, depending upon the size, content, and position of the ad, or depending on the receptivity of the reader, i.e., the sex, age, and income of the reader, and especially whether or not he or she is currently in the market for the product being advertised. The point is that a minority of available advertising is fully perceived at any one time.
>
> The situation in television is similar. Dr. George Gallup, another psychologist and a pioneer in media research as well as in public opinion research, instituted what he called a Total Prime Time Survey in which, for example, a cross-section of

Philadelphia was phoned the day after an evening of television, the viewers of all prime-time programs identified, and then asked to recall the commercials on the shows. On the average, only 12% of those who had seen the show the previous evening could recall the commercials on the show.

It has been demonstrated in many different ways that people can screen or filter huge amounts of advertising. For example, [in a] large national sample, . . . respondents were equipped with counters and asked to register every advertisement they saw. Each respondent enlisted for half a day. The modal group of counted exposures was only 11-20, suggesting that the perceptual screens of the respondents were very effective, indeed.[1]

I mention these data on the limited attention to advertising not to suggest that advertising lacks effectiveness or force, but to suggest the enormous competition among ads for the reader's attention. The reader is, so to speak, shopping for information, is aware of much advertising, but fully consumes or perceives only that minority which is of current interest. . . . To get answers to such questions as "How persuasive is advertising?", "Has it no effects on an uninterested audience?", or "Can it make people buy things they don't want?", one probably should begin by asking first "What is the difference between the really effective ads and the majority that don't get through to the public?", i.e., what is the nature of advertising effectiveness? When we can see how the successful ads accomplish their effects, we may judge better how far such effects can go. If I may, then, I'd like to suggest how successful ads work.

There seem to be three ingredients of successful advertising: information, reasoning, and emphasis. The mix of these three ingredients will, of course, vary greatly in particular cases.

Information is the simplest ingredient. It is news. If what you have to say is that gold has been discovered in California, the advertising skills themselves are not critical to the success of the ad. The agency that first reported the ADA's endorsement of Crest toothpaste had a relatively easy job in producing an initially successful ad. The nature of the information almost guaranteed a successful ad. This is not a common phenomenon, but many manufacturers of new products do hope that the availability of their brainchild will be accorded a similar reception.

The second ingredient of successful advertising, reasoning, is one that provokes thought on the part of the viewer, that stimulates interest, evaluation, judgment, and decision-making inside the viewer's head. This type of response is most common when the viewer happens to be in the market for the product or service in question, and when his response to an ad is a type of shopping behavior. The involvement with the advertising is a prelude to, a substitute for, a supplement to, contacts with salesmen and with stores. It facilitates pre-planning. . . .

The virtue of successful ads based on a reasoned response is that the ad is explicitly trying to be as persuasive as it can, and the viewer's attention is clearly on that persuasive attempt, i.e., the viewer has every opportunity to bring his judgment to bear on the sales attempt. An ad that survives this scrutiny is likely to elicit from the consumer a clear explanation of what it was in the ad that convinced him. . . .

[1] R. A. Bauer and S. A. Greyser, *Advertising in America: The Consumer View,* Division of Research, Graduate School of Business, Harvard University, Boston, Mass., 1968.

Now I come to the third ingredient of successful advertising, emphasis, and here is where the topic becomes more complex. For it is here that we are more likely to meet the relatively less expensive products, . . . products with less clear differences among the brands represented. This means that the consumer is relatively less interested in the advertising and more likely to screen it out. This situation sets up conditions such that the advertiser is more likely to emphasize only a single theme, which he repeats more frequently in order to gain attention and make his message familiar to the public. This is the most difficult, the most skillful (when it works), the most TV-oriented type of advertising. It is the type that receives the most criticism from citizens concerned with taste, but which also contributes the most entertaining and best-known commercials of all.

Moreover, the amount of advertising and media effort in comparison with the size of the output seems disproportionate in the eyes of many. They assume waste or, at the other extreme, some hidden but more powerful effect—something which might seem to justify all the repetitions of rather simple themes.

The fact is, however, that inexpensive and what may seem to some like minor products also have to be bought. For many fortunate people, such products do not merit enough concern to require involved types of comparison shopping, but are instead bought quickly and put, almost all at once, into a shopping cart. The advertiser then cannot hold a long discourse with the shopper at the time his ad is seen, but can only hope that a little effect will still be left later on at the time of purchase. In short, advertising by emphasis aims for small delayed effects, just enough effect to tip the scales in favor of brand A over B. . . .

The exaggerated power that some attribute to repetitive advertising by emphasis is based on an assumption that something is or must be happening at the time of exposure to the advertising. It is not generally recognized that the advertising is designed to have some effect still alive and working after perceptual screening *and* forgetting *have taken their toll. And since it is a later or delayed effect that is involved, the toll taken by forgetting is especially dramatic. Advertising students, as well as advertising managers, have long been awed by the demonstrated curves of remembering and forgetting. One in widespread use in today's textbooks is by Herbert Zielske, based on his 1959 article entitled, "The Remembering and Forgetting of Advertising." His chart demonstrates that much advertising will be quickly forgotten if not continuously exposed (see Exhibit 13.2).*

The chart summarizes a comparison between an ad exposed to one group thirteen times in thirteen successive weeks vs. the same ad exposed to a group every fourth week thirteen times during the year. A sample of each group was surveyed once a week for ad recall every week during the year. For those who saw the ad every week, ad recall climbs up to over 60% during the thirteen-week exposure, but then, without further re-enforcement, declines to almost zero by the end of the year. For those who saw the ad every fourth week, ad recall declines sharply during the weeks between exposures, but when re-enforced every fourth week attains a new and slightly higher peak. In the first group, the overall forgetting, and in the second group, the repeated forgetting, illustrate the nature of the need for repetition of the advertising stimulus.

The purpose of advertising that succeeds by emphasis, then, is to make some small point stick or survive—at least through the "cooling off" period between advertising exposure and a visit to the local supermarket.

WEEKLY PERCENTAGE OF HOUSEWIVES WHO COULD REMEMBER THE ADVERTISING

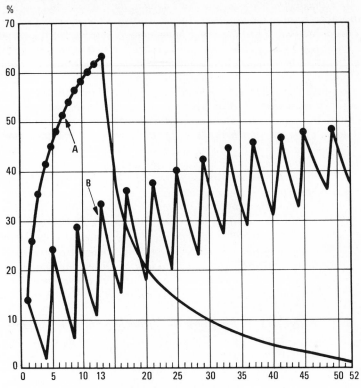

A = Exposed to advertising thirteen weeks in a row.

B = Exposed to advertising every fourth week thirteen times.

Source: Zielske, H. A., "The Remembering and Forgetting of Advertising," *Journal of Marketing,* January 1959, p. 240.

EXHIBIT 13.2

Now what about persuasibility? . . . how far can I go in persuading those who don't want my product to begin with, and/or are not satisfied with it after purchase? With the first two approaches, information and reasoning, the repugnant expedient, as in any form of selling or persuasion, political or commercial, is simply deception. The audience . . . has little immediate defense against deception. The intended deceptions are usually the most potent but also the most quickly exposed, e.g. in the contrast between what is said about a product in an ad and what one learns about it in the store. It is perhaps the unintended "deceptions," which all salesmen have to guard against, that are of most concern here. . . .

Apart from intended deceptions, the consumer is well equipped to shop and debate and evaluate the importance to him of reasoned types of advertising for expensive, important, or involving types of products. Advertising by emphasis, however, is a different story. Here the consumer is not on guard at the time he is exposed to advertising because the products are similar, inexpensive, and less involving. However, because the products are inexpensive, he or she can, over a period of weeks or months, try all the major brands before settling down with one as the more or less regular brand. Because low-cost products represent primarily a high-turnover, repeat-type of business, the impact of deceptive advertising would be quickly and frequently countered by product experience.

Overall, I am suggesting that the weight of advertising and the attempt to gain familiarity, which is characteristic of the emphasis approach, can be used once or twice in the individual case to sell what turns out to be an unwanted product—when the audience doesn't care very much about it. On the other hand, looking at the open and visible salesmanship of the reasoned approach, it takes something else to sell an unwanted product to a shopper who does care and has his guard up.

Coming back now to the general topic of attention and persuasibility, I would summarize the condition of advertising as follows: At any one time, advertising is competing mightily for the attention of large numbers of not-too-interested viewers, while at the same time, smaller numbers of serious shoppers are seeking out information from all sources, including advertising. The less-interested viewers are primarily made more aware of the product by advertising, while the serious shoppers are primarily made more thoughtful about the product by advertising. Both processes are effective as sales tools, awareness contributing to convenience and choice within the marketplace, and thoughtfulness contributing to the rationality of the shopping process.

On the whole, consumers shop for information from advertising in the same way they shop for products in stores. Some items take very little attention, and some take a great deal. Deceptive information, just like faulty products, can be screened out by pre-testing.

2 HOW PEOPLE MANIPULATE ADVERTISEMENTS

Communication, personal or through mass media, is an active two-way process. Throughout Part 1 we saw how each firm is compelled by market realities to recognize this basic factor in the engineering of human interaction. Firms have learned from their daily experience and from the behavioral sciences that *humans manipulate information for their own purposes.*

Yet at the macro socioeconomic level, critics of advertising and public policy makers are often unfamiliar with the psychological processes through which any human being perceives any stimulus about any topic, be it economic, political, or religious. If we are to regulate mass communication processes in the interest of society, it is absolutely mandatory that existing knowledge be disseminated, understood, *and* applied. Note that we are concerned with technical knowledge—*how* people perceive, not what they *should* perceive.

The presentation by Dr. Krugman has sketched, in nontechnical language, some of the basic psychological processes that should be familiar to all those concerned with manipulative advertising. He has stressed that humans screen or filter whatever information reaches them, from whatever source and medium. Some of this screening is due to shopping for information, either consciously or unconsciously. Information that is relevant to some need or interest is more likely to be noticed, while information that is not relevant is either discarded or, at most, stored in some memory reservoir. This is the classical case of *motivated perception.*

Parallel to motivated perception, Dr. Krugman has discussed *motivated forgetting and remembering.* Laboratory and survey research confirm again and again that humans are most likely to remember information that they use frequently, that is important to them, and that makes sense to them. Conversely, humans tend to forget information that is rarely used, that is unimportant, or that makes no sense.

There is another well-known type of psychological manipulation of perceived stimuli. When a subject is faced with information that is dissonant or incongruent with respect to his previous knowledge, beliefs, and values, he may not understand it and thus, in effect, may not "see" it; he may distort it to make it fit with what he "knows"; or he may store only those parts of the message that are consonant or congruent.

In particular, Dr. Krugman has stressed that how each individual interprets information contained in a stimulus depends on his kind and degree of interest and involvement. Similarly, interest and involvement will determine what information will be remembered and for how long. Finally, even when a message is remembered, its effects on behavior will vary according to: (1) the number and kind of *events that intervene* between its receipt and the moment of choice, and (2) the number and kind of *events surrounding* the subject at the moment of choice. The latter include both *immediate* situational events, such as the store surroundings, and *anticipated* events, such as the subject's perception of his future use of the product under consideration.

Dr. Krugman's testimony only skims the knowledge available to public policy makers and to students of the advertising institution. Most of the basic findings are reprinted in a careful selection by Kassarjian and Robertson.[1] Applications to consumer behavior, with clear implications for administrative action, can be found in the literature.[2]

2.1 DOES THERE EXIST OBJECTIVE INFORMATION? PHYSICAL VERSUS PSYCHOLOGICAL PERCEPTION

Basic literature has established that if the information in a stimulus—an ad, a label, or a package—makes sense, the *specific sense* depends on the people who perceive the stimulus. And different people tend to perceive the same stimulus differently. This is true even of so-called objective stimuli, such as the size of coins: an experiment showed that poor

[1] H. H. Kassarjian and T. S. Robertson (eds.), *Perspectives in Consumer Behavior,* Scott, Foresman & Company, Glenview, Ill., 1973; see, also the earlier 1968 edition.

[2] For instance, see Chapter 6 in F. M. Nicosia, *Consumer Decision Processes: Marketing and Advertising Implications,* Prentice-Hall, Englewood Cliffs, N.J., 1966; also J. A. Howard and J. Sheth, *The Theory of Buyer Behavior,* Wiley, New York, 1969; and J. F. Engel, D. T. Kollat, and R. D. Blackwell, *Consumer Behavior,* Holt, Rinehart and Winston, New York, 1973.

children tended to see coins as larger in size than did rich children. Another experiment showed that some subjects perceived the length of one bar as longer than another, simply because they heard others say it was—even though the bar was "objectively" shorter.

If even objective simuli may be perceived in varying ways, consider the interpretations that may be placed on more ambiguous stimuli. Our symbol for poison—a skull and crossbones—supposedly warns "everyone" that the contents of the package are dangerous. Yet research has shown that, to some children, this symbol of danger may actually represent mystery, curiosity, and interest. Thus this warning symbol may only serve to lead the child into discovering, and even possibly trying, the product so labeled.

Examination of the process of perception reveals why diverse interpretations of the same stimulus exist. Let us first fix some basic ideas. When a subject is physically exposed to a stimulus, he will already have a certain amount of information stored in his memory. After he has *physically* perceived the stimulus, *he will select some subset of the stored information and match it against the information in the stimulus.* Through this matching he decodes at least some of the information in the stimulus, thus perceiving it *psychologically.* The *meaning* of the stimulus depends in part on the specific subset of information a subject uses to decode the objective information in the stimulus; the meaning is thus bound to be subjective.

Common sense reveals the nature and extent of this subjectivity. Although the color "red" can be objectively defined in terms of physical qualities, the psychological perceptions of red vary greatly. Even in prerevolutionary China, red was the color of happiness and played an important role in wedding ceremonies. Yet in our culture, a bride-to-be might well react negatively to a suggestion that she be married in a red dress. However, her reaction to red might not always be negative: although a red wedding dress might connote sin, red roses from her fiancee might be happily accepted as a sign of warmth and passion. In both these cases, *different subsets of information are used to decode* the same objective stimulus: red. The information used by the subject may vary according to the culture (Chinese versus American), the situation (roses versus a wedding dress), and the subject herself (some American brides might be attracted by the novelty of a red wedding dress).

Let us describe more explicitly the psychological mechanism of perception. Assume that the engineering department of a firm must develop blueprints for a new airplane wing. Different groups of draftsmen are assigned to different parts of the design. In the sequence of work, Group A develops one part of the blueprint and passes it to Group B; Group B develops another part, puts it together with the part designed by Group A, and passes the combined plans to a third group. The part of the blueprint to be developed by Group A is shown in Exhibit 13.3. Let us ask ourselves: is the angle α greater than, equal to, or less than ninety degrees?

Note that all readers perceive α physically, through their eyes. With the exception of such modification as glasses that correct physical differences (myopia, astigmatism, etc.), all human eyes follow exactly the same physical processes in transforming the component parts of α into a pattern of neural signals that are then sent to the brain. Also, the language of these neural impulses is the same for all humans. The information

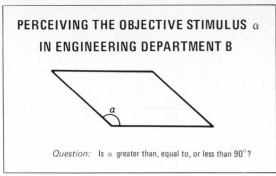

PERCEIVING THE OBJECTIVE STIMULUS α

IN ENGINEERING DEPARTMENT B

Question: Is α greater than, equal to, or less than 90°?

EXHIBIT 13.3

carried by these neural impulses will be interpreted (decoded) by the information most readers acquired in high school geometry.

Although this description of the chain of decoding and reincoding "whatever α is" has been greatly simplified, it serves to establish one point. If all readers have gone through exactly this same chain, then they must all agree on the specific meaning of the α. That is, all readers will agree that α is greater than ninety degrees.

If a reader disagrees with this interpretation of the meaning of α, several explanations are possible. Perhaps some of his physical processes differ from those of the normal eye and its normal connection with the brain. Perhaps his recollection of high school Euclidean geometry is somewhat incorrect. Or, the reader may simply refuse to cooperate with the author's point. This is a typical phenomenon in communication: the receiver's psychological perception of the source of a message affects the meaning imputed to the message. In this case, the uncooperative reader has discovered the well-documented phenomenon of *source effect,* which is another class of variables that also frequently make "subjectivity" so prevalent, and "objectivity" so meaningless.

Having established that α is greater than ninety degrees, we now move to the draftsmen working in Group B. After preparing their part of the blueprint, these draftsmen will fit it together with the one from Group A.

The part of the blueprint designed by Group B is a cube—without its top—and is portrayed in Exhibit 13.4. In this exhibit, we also show the part received from Group A and how it is fitted with the blueprint prepared by Group B. Suppose we were the draftsmen in Group B and were asked one specific meaning of A's blueprint—namely, whether α is greater than, equal to, or less than ninety degrees.

Once again, all of us would go through exactly the same decoding and reincoding processes physically performed by the eye and its neural connections with the brain. Yet all of us will agree that now α is equal to ninety degrees.

Why has the meaning of the "same" α changed? The answer could not be simpler. In the first instance, the reader was looking at the Euclidean space of a page, i.e., a two-dimensional plane. *Using this information* (that is, matching a two-dimensional plane against α), the reader sees α as being more than ninety degrees. But in the second

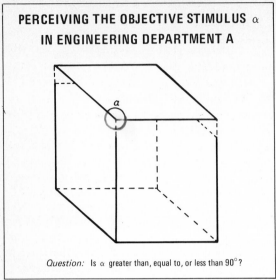

PERCEIVING THE OBJECTIVE STIMULUS α

IN ENGINEERING DEPARTMENT A

α

Question: Is α greater than, equal to, or less than 90°?

EXHIBIT 13.4

instance, the reader uses the information acquired by looking at the cube. Matched against this information (the cube), the meaning of α becomes equal of ninety degrees. *The meaning of the stimulus depends on the information a subject uses in decoding the physical information contained in the neural impulses conveyed to the brain.* When the information of a *plane* (a two-dimensional plane) is used, the meaning of a stimulus is bound to differ from the case in which the information used is that of a *cube* (a tridimensional plane).[1]

In this example, we have tried to establish two key principles. First, we have shown that even the most passive and captive receiver of a message actively manipulates the information contained in the received stimulus. Second, in this active manipulation, a person is bound to be subjective in that he uses some of his own information to make some sense out of a stimulus' information. In real life, *different people will tend to use different information in giving meaning to an ad,* and thus no ad can have one, and only one, objective meaning.

Firms learned long ago that it is extremely dangerous to assume that "most" people will perceive a given stimulus in one specific way: every ad has multiple meanings. As we saw in Part 1, in developing and pretesting any ad, the key question is: "How many people have indeed perceived the ad in the manner we intended?" The same principle

---

[1] It must be stressed that the example in the text is very simplified. The interested reader may pursue the topic of physical and psychological perception further by reading, for instance, U. Neisser, *Cognitive Psychology,* Appleton-Century-Crofts, New York, 1969. I must add that the example is not original; unfortunately, I do not remember the elementary textbook—in psychology or social psychology—to which I should give the proper credit.

must be recognized by all those who are concerned with the functioning of the entire advertising institution.

This basic knowledge is at odds with what many of us want to believe. Western man has searched for some objective order since the time of the Greek philosophers. Most of us would like to know that something "out there" exists. But even before social psychology had confirmed that what is "out there" is partly a function of what is "in" a person, Goethe had already noted that "we see only what we know."

Obviously, there are boundaries that limit the number of meanings each of us can give to a stimulus. In the extreme, if a man does not psychologically perceive the presence of a glass door, he will physically perceive it rather strongly when he tries to walk through it. Contrary to our deep-seated hopes, however, these boundaries operate only in extreme situations. The areas of ambiguity and subjectivity are enormous; they probably include more than 90 percent of all the ads we perceive in all mass media.

In sum, any message, no matter how clear its physical properties may be, is always manipulated by processes of interpretation, and the resulting interpretations—i.e., meanings—will tend to differ from individual to individual and, for the same individual, across products, situations, and time. Consequently, *no* message contains objective, clear, unambiguous information.

This conclusion, well-grounded in psychological research, poses a major challenge to public policy makers. On the one hand, it makes the task of regulating advertising extremely complex, for it undercuts the assumption that one can investigate only the objective meaning of ads. Further, it indicates that regulators must recognize that consumers are diverse; i.e., that different consumers may perceive the same ad in different ways. On the other hand, application of this knowledge can make regulation more realistic and more efficient. As we shall see, recognition of the existence of different meanings for the same ad will also allow regulators to distinguish between choice of efficiency versus choice of values.

Before pursuing the possibilities, however, we must turn to another aspect of manipulation. Admitting the subjectivity of perception, what information *can* we define as manipulative?

3   DEFINING INFORMATION, PERSUASION, DECEIT, AND OUTRIGHT LIE
(excerpts from T. Dillon, president, Batten, Barton, Durstine and Osborn, Inc., and from A. A. Achenbaum, senior vice president and director of marketing services, J. Walter Thompson Co.)

To manipulate is a transitive verb; it implies a subject (the sender of a message, in our case), an action performed by the subject (i.e., creating a message), and the object of the subject's action (i.e., the seeker/receiver of the sender's message). In previous sections we have focused on the object; here we turn to action—creating the *content* of an ad.

We have already seen how it is necessary for a firm to define the content of an ad in terms of seeker/receiver needs. At the macro socioeconomic level, we have essentially the same emphasis—public regulators and students of the advertising institution are clearly concerned with the content of the information that flows through society's communication system in terms of the public interest.

One question raised is whether specific information is objective, persuasive, deceitful, or, to put it more operationally, false. A second question is which of these types of information is manipulative. Some consider only false and deceitful information as manipulative; others include persuasion in this category. In his testimony, Mr. Dillon argues that equating persuasive information with deceitful information is incorrect.

> . . . The creating of advertising is essentially a technique of creating a persuasive message. There are many people in the world who equate persuasion with deception. Plato, for example, deplored persuasion in the marketplace and described it as a method of making the worse seem the better. He conceived of a society in which the forces of persuasion would be eliminated. By creating an elite body of philosopher kings who had been trained in complete objectivity, he hoped to direct every detail of a citizen's life in the citizen's own best interest.
>
> In this, he differed with Aristotle who pointed out that virtually all communication has some persuasive effect. His proposal was that the truth is best established by setting up institutions whereby persuasive arguments are encouraged on every side of issues affecting the public.
>
> At the present time, the world is still divided on this issue. The totalitarian states do not permit persuasion to exist except in support of the elite group which purports to act objectively in the best interest of the citizen.
>
> Democracies, on the other hand, have adopted the Aristotelian concept. We require in our courts that both sides of an argument be heard, and we train lawyers in the techniques of persuasion to that end. Our legislative structure is such that we require the members to repeatedly exert persuasive skills on the public to be elected to office, and then to exert their persuasive skills on each other to arrive at legislation.
>
> Our society encourages the development of persuasive skills in editorial writers, salesmen, lawyers, politicians, and, indeed, teaches its techniques in our public educational system. . . . We are committed to a theory of government that assumes he [the American citizen] can listen to the political persuasion on various sides of the most complex social and economic issues and arrive at a common-sense decision in the voting booth. On the other hand, if one has contempt for the judgment of the American people, one is likely to assume that those who engage in persuasion are necessarily engaged in deception. One then sees politicians as charlatans, lawyers as perjurers, salesmen as bunko artists, and advertising men as sly deceivers.
>
> Advertising is boldly and openly persuasive of a point of view which is clearly identified with the advertiser—one of a few forms of persuasion in which the interest and the source of persuasion are always clearly labeled [emphasis added]. . . .

Mr. Dillon implies that there is a difference between persuasive and deceitful (false) information. We shall see that this difference can be made operational for public policy and regulatory purposes (see Section 4 below). Let us now turn to the distinction between objective and nonobjective (persuasive) information. Does manipulation imply the use of nonobjective information? In the next excerpt, Mr. Achenbaum begins with a summary of the ways in which advertising information is commonly considered manipulative; he then argues that it is hopeless to try to make a distinction between objective and nonobjective information.

Without referring to the specific literature of criticism, there are presumably seven more commonly mentioned methods [of manipulation]:

- *First, by using* emotional *appeals, by not talking rationally to consumers, by using appeals directed at fear, sexual desire, status, etc.*
- *Second, by being* incomplete, *by not giving consumers all the information they need for making a decision.*
- *Third, by being* irrelevant, *by not giving people the salient information they need to make a choice, particularly about the quality and price of the product.*
- *Fourth, by being* noncomparative, *by not giving people information about competitive products, by forcing the consumers to make their own calculations in making their judgments.*
- *Fifth, by the* overwhelming weight *of the advertising, by just doing so much advertising that consumers are seduced into doing things they normally wouldn't do.*
- *Sixth, by being* subjective, *by not informing consumers about the objective criteria for measuring product quality, such as ingredients, but rather by talking about its benefits and uses.*
- *And last, by* deception *or* misrepresentation, *by not telling the truth, by using phony demonstrations, testimonials, presenters, and comparisons.*

MEANING OF MANIPULATION

But are all these methods truly manipulative, do they make people do things involuntarily, . . . ? I think we can rule out of our discussion any physical meaning to manipulation. . . . At least no one to date has suggested that [advertising] has that power.

In the nonphysical sense, then, the word manipulate is an interesting one, for as we shall see, the case for or against advertising can fall on its meaning. . . . words . . . such as influence, inform, persuade, and convince are not pejorative, do not imply physical force. Yet, even they appear to have a hierarchy of meanings. If we were to place all of the words on a continuum, it would seem that they would fall in the following order from bad to good:

MANIPULATE   INFLUENCE   PERSUADE   CONVINCE   INFORM

There is no responsible person in the advertising industry who will argue in favor of involuntary choice or compulsion. If advertising does either, it is contrary both to a free market and a free society. I also don't believe you will find anyone in the industry who will condone or defend deception or misrepresentation. These are patently illegal. . . . No one will question the right of the FTC to investigate and to prevent any and all of them.

If manipulation is limited to mean these situations and only these situations—I need go no further. Unfortunately, there are some who feel that influencing, persuading, or convincing people are not legitimate means of getting people to act under the Federal Trade Commission Act, that only informing people is the legitimate purpose of advertising. Thus, we are to a large degree dealing with a semantic problem.

Compulsion, *which connotes physical duress, we can all agree is manipulative. Involuntary choice would almost seem to be in the same category. The consumer would have to be a rather passive participant in the sale for this to occur and, as I shall show later, that is not the case [see Chapter 14, Section 1]. I think we can agree, too, that there is a distinction between* deception *and persuasion. Deception is a form of misrepresentation. It is fraudulent, untruth is involved. . . . If an advertiser is in fact guilty of deception, he should be stopped and penalized. But what constitutes deception is not always clear-cut. And to say that emotion, subjectivity, incompleteness are deceptive is not necessarily so.*

But the manipulative case against advertising is not made only in terms of deception. It is made on the basis of persuading, *influencing, or convincing people. The less kind believe this is a form of deception or market seduction and therefore manipulation. We cannot accept this definition as competitively fair or socially acceptable.*

Professor Taplin, in his book, Advertising, *makes the reason for this quite clear.*

At the lower limit it may be impossible to have any kind of social relationship without an implicit minimal element of persuasion. . . . It may not be the most satisfactory of devices whereby human beings affect each other's behavior. But it is equally certain [that it is] not the least satisfactory. There may be something in it from which the fastidious intellect shies away. But at least it is among the more human of the means of social influence.

Politically speaking, it would be necessary to state the case for persuasive procedures more positively. They are characteristic of and essential to democracy. Far from its being necessary to excuse them, it is of paramount importance that they should be preserved and strengthened. The more "natural" tendency in political institutions appears to be in the direction of authoritarianism and compulsion, so that is is necessary to be on guard against encroachments on the area of personal freedom. The price of liberty is external vigilance. This argument can certainly be extended into the economic sphere.[1]

THE ROLE OF INFORMATION

It has been suggested that advertising's only legitimate role should be to inform buyers—that is, describe the product and the terms of sale. Some have said that unless the description is complete, it is inadequate. Accordingly, some have even gone so far as to suggest that if the medium doesn't economically or feasibly permit a complex description, it shouldn't be used.

I dwell on this point about information because informing people is not considered manipulation. It is when you go beyond informing consumers that you are presumably—by definition—manipulating or at least getting close to manipulation—influencing, persuading, or convincing them to act. But let's look at the meaning of information or description more closely. I think I can most graphically describe the problem by describing an experience I had some years ago at Arden House at a McCann-Erickson-sponsored meeting on general semantics and information flow.

At that meeting, a group of 20 executives were told to sit in a circle. The group

[1] W. Taplin, *Advertising: A New Approach,* Little, Brown, Boston, Mass., 1963, pp. 64–65.

leader asked us to describe an apple, and passed one to the first person he came to. The obvious answer of the first person was to say that it was red. The next—following the color lead—said it was also yellow; another said it had green in it; the next said it was mostly red. . . .

There then followed a whole series of descriptions on its shape (some saying it couldn't be measured) until someone remarked that we were only talking about the outside. How about cutting it in half and describing the inside? Once more someone mentioned its color and said it was white; the next person said it had pits which were brown or black. This was followed by statements that it had a peel, it felt moist, it was cold, it contained water, it was pulpy. And then suddenly someone realized that the apple's color changed. In the half hour we handled that poor apple it turned somewhat brown and a bit grey on the inside. The dynamics of this began to play a role in the description. Now we noticed it was softer than before, it lost its stem, etc. It was well over an hour, after hundreds and hundreds of descriptions—this was truly a creative group, none of whom ever wrote a piece of copy to my knowledge— and not one thought of tasting the apple, or trying to describe its taste, or how it could be used or eaten.

But once that subject was brought up, another plethora of descriptions came forth until the question of nutrition was raised. And off we went on another track. The exercise, I must tell you, continued for two hours. In that time, over four thousand words or phrases were used to describe the apple, and I am sure we did not exhaust the list.

My point (and the point of that exercise in perception) is quite simple. Any tangible item has almost an infinite number of descriptions and to communicate them—to inform the buyer of all of them—is virtually impossible. Ah, but we are not that silly the critics say; what we want is for the advertising to communicate only the relevant items to the people.

But what are those relevant items? Was its size, shape, color, dimension, feel— the so-called objective sensory items. Or was it the nutrient value? Or was it its taste? And if it's the latter, how do you describe such a subjective quality? And whose description do we use—the farmers, the shippers, or the retailers?

Obviously, what is relevant will depend on the purchaser. To the mother concerned with the health of her family, it may be nutrition. To a man interested in dessert, it may be taste. To the storekeeper, its ability to stay firm. To another housewife, its perishability over time, its ease in cooking. But as you can see, it all depends on who wants it. . . . No one is being deceived. Nor is anyone being irrational.

There is another issue. The number of apples available for sale is often beyond the reach of the buyer to inspect or evaluate. How could one weigh the value of each individual description in order to come to a perfect judgment? But what's more critical is how could an advertiser possibly compare his product with all others available for sale? He would face the same impossible task that the prospective user would.

For the fact is, to say that informing is what is necessary is to beg the issue. And to say that communicating salient information is likewise begging the issue. And to say that you must give a comparative description begs the issue still further.

Is it not for the seller or the maker to decide what he thinks he is selling to decide?

And for the buyer to evaluate it—as she most certainly does? If she doesn't like what is said, doesn't believe it, or doesn't care, she will ignore that seller's communication and seek another.

THE NATURE OF PERSUASION

While communicating information is obviously one role of advertising, there is another—persuading the buyer to come to terms. That is what negotiation in the transaction is all about, whether the buyer accepts the offer with or without further discussion. . . .

Two major issues of persuasion are involved insofar as the national advertiser is concerned: Should persuasion be permitted as an element in advertising products or brands? and If it is permitted, are there any limits to the form of that persuasion?

Should Persuasion Be Permitted?

Upon reflection, it is almost a ludicrous argument to suggest that persuasion in advertising can be eliminated. To begin with, persuasion is a key aspect of the negotiating process. It is certainly not questioned in the personal selling situation. Why should it be questioned in advertising?

In any transaction, the ultimate buyer has the option to accept, reject, or discuss the terms of the offer. If the buyer is not content, he may very well have to do some persuading to get the terms changed. Nor is the seller precluded from telling the buyer what he thinks about his wares and terms, or to make the buyer feel that what he is offering is of a certain value. Nor has anyone suggested that the personal salesman not show pictures of the product in use, be pleasant, dress in a certain way, or do all sorts of things which could enhance the chance of sale as long as he doesn't misrepresent the product. . . . Why, then, because we change the form of communication to print or to the airwaves, must we suddenly change the criterion of communication to the description of product and the terms of the sale only?

But there are more fundamental reasons why persuasion must continue to be a part of the market communication process. First of all is that descriptive information and persuasion are inseparable. One just cannot convey descriptive information of any relevance without it also being persuasive *[emphasis added]. . . . [Further,] once* we decide to limit what we say to salience, we are already being persuasive *[emphasis added]. . . .*

The more we study the meaning of information, the more we realize that it doesn't mean objective description only. Description is sterile unless put into context. To the degree that advertising is educational (it must be that if it is to reduce consumer ignorance), *description must be related to use, to performance, or to product benefits.*

People buy goods and services to satisfy needs and wants. A need or want has relevance only with respect to the benefit a product can perform—to the way the need or want is satisfied. But once you indicate how the descriptive quality will satisfy a need or want through some benefit, you are in fact being persuasive. . . .

There are two other reaons why we should not permit the elimination of persuasion from advertising. One is that it is a part of the democratic process. It is the way reasoned judgments are made in a free society. I have already pointed out that it is by far a better means than any other for getting human action. But there is also an economic reason. If advertising were neutral—not persuasive—it would have to be ineffectual. Under such circumstances, it would truly be wasteful. Now there is a paradox. . . .

Should There Be Limits To the Form of Persuasion?

If persuasion in advertising is either desirable or unavoidable, should we place limits on its form? Perhaps this can best be decided by reviewing how persuasion is thought of in advertising.

Persuasion in advertising has essentially five basic purposes: to convince a person to use a product he never before used; to convince a consumer to use a product more frequently—either sooner or in greater quantity; to convince a consumer to use a particular brand of a product he currently uses; to convince a user to buy a particular form or size of the brand; and to convince a prospective user to take some action which could lead to the use of a brand, e.g., to go to a particular store to see the brand on display.

The first two of these purposes deals with generic demand. In the former instance, this occurs only with new products. But nowadays there are few truly new consumer products. It therefore has little relevance to today's advertising. In the second instance, it is usually the matter of getting people to buy more, which is quite difficult because usage patterns are rather stable in the short run. In both cases, we are dealing with human values or priorities. Advertising no doubt has some influence on them, but probably far less than is usually supposed. Certainly, movies, television, the news media, churches, schools, and the home all play a big role. To single out national advertisers as the culprit is somewhat unbecoming. But perhaps more important is the question as to whether the government has a right to regulate these values. . . . Up to now we know that such regulation of values on a widespread basis has no Congressional sanction.

Moreover, it is a rare national advertiser who spends his money trying to use advertising generically. The overwhelming dominance of national advertising is competitive in nature—dealing with the three latter competitive purposes mentioned above. Only to the degree that the totality of a product category's brand advertising sells products does it have generic influence. And no one has yet to show how much this generic influence has affected the economy's product-mix in the short run. In trying to be competitive, advertising attempts to affect people's attitudes—to get them to like a brand more than they did previously—often by having people change an attitude on some attribute of the product.

These attributes need not be of a physical character. They can be sensory, evaluative (where people must make a deliberate judgment) or emotional (something people intuitively feel). They all count. They are all real. The emotional ones are no less real and desirable to consumers than the sensory or the evaluative. To preclude the use of them is to reduce the area of human satisfaction, and there is nothing in our legislation that broadly permits that.

Nor can we say that the presentation of a persuasive argument must be objective or verbal. Certainly pictures and music have informational overtones. But even the tonality or environmental context of the advertising should not be precluded from the presentation. Who wishes to be persuaded by unpleasant individuals? Must we accept ugly surroundings in negotiation? We would certainly not condone a surly, sloppy salesgirl in an unkempt store. Why must advertising be otherwise?

To sum up, there is nothing manipulative in the selection of the information to be conveyed or its withholding. Nor is there anything manipulative when comparisons are not made or when subjective views are conveyed. Information communicated is or is not persuasive, influential, or convincing only [with respect to the point of view] of the receiver. If it is conveyed honestly and without duress or compulsion, manipulation is not involved.

We therefore cannot accept the idea that only by informing consumers about a product and the terms of the offer is one legitimately communicating; that reasoned, voluntary choices cannot be made on grounds other than so-called objective information; or that such choices are in fact irrational. Nor can we accept the view that the arguments for persuasion cannot be subjective; that they must always present complete information; that the information must be salient to some official board; that it must compare one brand with another; or that advertising per se by its weight is seductive in and by itself. Not only have we seen no evidence that these practices are themselves unfair or deceptive, but we do not perceive them as being manipulative.

Action is not based on information alone, but on a point of view or attitude about that information. Information is meaningful only when it is put into context. It cannot be divorced from persuasion. We don't vote for a President because we know everything about him. Nor do we expect the candidate to provide complete information or comparative information or only objective information. Nor can we divorce what he says about himself from how he says it, where he says it, and the context in which he says it. We vote for the man whom we are persuaded is going to do the best job of governing, based on everything we perceive about him, although even that isn't always the criterion used. And the same is true about courtship, religion, and education. It is also true of buying behavior.

4   THE REGULATION OF THE CONTENT OF ADS: SEARCHING FOR OBJECTIVE CRITERIA

To study whether advertisements do manipulate consumers, we first turned our attention to the question of whether any message sent by any medium could manipulate people. In the first two sections, we saw that human beings are themselves engaged in physical and perceptual manipulation of any stimulus. Psychological perception, we observed, is the interpretation of a stimulus' information and is subjective.

Two main results followed from this. First, it is practically futile to search for information that is objective. To contain human meaning, information must be subjective. Also, the more humans differ from one another, the more likely it is that the meanings of a stimulus will differ in number and kind. Second, there are limits to the number of possible meanings that can be obtained from any particular stimulus. The upper limit to this number is physical—to perceive a poisonous drink as an elixir of long life could be unfortunate.

Within physical limits, the number of possible meanings a stimulus may have is still astronomical. However, functionally, social groups devise ways to decrease the enormous ambiguity with which they would otherwise be confronted; if they did not, it would be literally impossible for members of a social group to interact meaningfully. These devices run the entire spectrum of a textbook in sociology: cultural values, norms, rewards, and sanctions are the most obvious. Taboos, stereotypes, beliefs, role-playing, and finally institutions and laws also serve the purpose of allowing people to relate to each other through one or another form of communication.

Within each social group such devices confer relative objectivity to many stimuli, i.e., they reduce the number of meanings that particular stimuli may have. Yet, even within these boundaries, millions of large and small differences allow each individual to develop his own private meanings. For all practical purposes, we can say that, in the great majority of cases, any one ad will have meanings that will differ from one individual to another.

Equipped with this basic knowledge, we turned in Section 3 to the consideration of the term manipulation. We saw that the term is intimately related to the content of a message, namely, to the qualities of the message's information. The review by Mr. Achenbaum suggests that information is usually defined in one of the following four ways: *objective, persuasive, deceitful, or false.* Presumably these four attributes could be used to define information operationally, i.e., in a measurable way. Unfortunately, they fail to do so.

To begin with, the attributes are not mutually exclusive (i.e., they are not independent coordinates). Overlaps between two or more attributes make it impossible to identify every bit of information as falling into one and only one category. Thus, we cannot operationally distinguish, for example, between objective and persuasive information in each case. Nor can these four attributes be used to construct quantitative measures that might eventually provide objective regulatory criteria.

There is a further problem. Some of the literature looks at the four attributes as describing gradations of acceptable-unacceptable information. But there is serious disagreement on where one should draw the line between acceptable and unacceptable. For example, advertising professionals argue that only deceitful and false information should be proscribed, whereas many of their critics would prohibit persuasion too. Such disagreements cannot be resolved until we agree on measurable definitions of information.

There is an urgent need to define information operationally—at least to the extent necessary to guide regulatory agencies in identifying which type of information is, in fact, contained in an ad. We cannot continue with the present situation. Lacking an operational definition, regulation of the content of ads has been necessarily unsystematic, piecemeal, and essentially unsatisfactory to all those concerned.

In the following pages we shall argue that we can move toward some beginning answer. In Section 4.1, we shall discuss the term *false information.* Here it will be relatively easy to show that we do have simple and acceptable ways to go about determining objectively whether an ad contains false information.

We shall then turn to objective, persuasive, and deceitful information. Our major difficulty will be one of perspective. On a micromanagerial level, a successful firm recognizes that the meaning of products as well as of ads is highly subjective. Consequently, management searches for a subgroup of consumers to whom its product (and the ads about it) are meaningful. But on a macrosocietal level, we have not yet learned how to cope with such heterogeneity of meanings. If we recognize that what is good or relevant to some is bad or irrelevant to others, how can we determine what is in the public interest?

The concept of public interest is one that can be interpreted only if we have some common denominator that takes into account consumer heterogeneity. Legislators, regulators, and courts daily attempt to find such denominators. The total array is bewildering,[1] but we can identify two major approaches that have been used.

The first approach, to be discussed in Section 4.2, suggests that the content of ads should be limited to objective information. Objective here means information about the physical, chemical, engineering, and similar technical attributes of the product being advertised. The second approach, to be discussed in Section 4.3, argues that all human needs can be defined on a *natural*, and thus objective, basis. Two different classifications of natural needs are frequently proposed: (1) rational-irrational needs, and (2) functional-emotional needs. Advocates of both classifications hope that their classification can be used empirically, and thus that advertising can be limited to information related to rational, or functional, needs.

We shall review these criteria and argue that they have not worked and cannot work, because they disregard basic knowledge about perceptual processes. We shall particularly stress, by examples, that when we try to define operationally what is meant by *physical* characteristics, or by *natural* needs, we are bound to be subjective. That is, the person who defines physical or natural is subjectively defining the public interest.

Beyond issues of false information, we do not have objective criteria. Definitions of objective, persuasive, and deceitful information are necessarily subjective. Understanding these facts is the basis for the unavoidable conflict between the firm-consumer pair and the public interest discussed in Chapters 9 and 16. Further, the realization that public policy decisions concerning the content of information are subjective choices of value—choices that cannot be avoided by references to objectivity—will clarify much of the prevailing confusion between facts and values and thus offer some basis for the formulation and implementation of objective regulation.

4.1 DEFINING FALSE INFORMATION OPERATIONALLY

Although there are no facts in the absolute, there are large classes of information that can be transformed into fact relative to some yardstick whose nature is known and generally accepted. For instance, to reduce the uncertainty in any human interaction, most societies have developed concepts of weight, length, volume, voltage, amperage, and the like. Such concepts—and the related measurement procedures and instruments—are useful to all; they provide common denominators that transcend the heterogeneity of human perception.

---

[1] See, for example, the excellent, concise picture of the "buts," "ifs," "perhapses," and "maybes" that underly this daily work in D. A. Aaker, "Deceptive Advertising," Working Paper No. 86, Institute of Business and Economic Research, University of California, Berkeley, November 1972.

Such concepts and standards make it possible to define false information operationally. If we can approach the information in a message and ask if it contains facts *relative* to some agreed-upon measurement concept, we can then test whether or not this information is false. Thus the public interest is served by the development of standard measurement procedures and instruments and by their applications to the information content of ads.

Given the present medical knowledge, for example, we can test the accuracy of a statement that a bottle of "Mom's Miraculous Mender" will cure gout, kidney stones, and peptic ulcers, as well as increase sexual potency. Similarly, suppose that a certain brand of bread advertises that it is enriched to contain more vitamin K than other brands. This statement is either true or false: we can test it simply because we have agreed on the measurement of a vitamin's quantity. Of course, some of us may wonder how much more vitamin K is required in order to justify the term "enriched to contain more"— 7.155 percent more or 9.321 percent more? Public agencies are hard-pressed for time and may not find it practical to pursue such refinements.

In addition to the scientific yardsticks of measurement, we also have legal criteria that allow us to evaluate whether or not the information in an ad is acceptable. Even though in this case we cannot determine that information is true or false in the sense above, we have the same situation of relative objectivity. Any society has legal norms or yardsticks; while there may be disagreement on the desirability of these norms, their existence provides objective criteria for determining the acceptability of an ad. For example, an enterprising young man would not be allowed to advertise hard drugs as part of his attempt to satisfy the desire of some consumers.

We must realize, however, that legal norms change, as do scientific standards. The frontier of knowledge is moving: received truths change, and new concepts are explored. For example, medicines and food additives that appeared to be safe, and were *so certified* by public agencies, have been discovered to have serious side effects. In other cases, we are discovering that we do not yet have sufficient knowledge to determine what is true and false. For instance, differences in the structure of chemically equivalent vitamins were at one time thought unimportant from a clinical viewpoint, but this is now being questioned. The nutritional sciences community appears outraged at the assertions made by Adelle Davis, yet finds it difficult to prove that her claims are false.

Similarly, we are told that ads for all sorts of pills *do* encourage use of hard drugs, and that smoking marijuana *does not*. Even though these two assertions may not conflict, the point is that we cannot yet scientifically agree whether either one is true.

Despite these shortcomings, there are cases in which society can establish—by the use of legal and/or scientific yardsticks—whether the information in an ad is permissible. It is unfortunate that this ability is not used more often and more thoroughly. To emphasize this point—namely, that government should deal promptly with information that can be assessed as true or false—let us consider a case in which several human deaths have already disproved advertising claims that a wide range of products and brands were noninflammable and self-extinguishing.

About ten years ago, a relatively small number of chemical companies introduced cellular (foamed) plastics (polyurethane and all forms of polystyrene) for use in roof and wall insulation, furniture, cushions and bedding, panels and siding, cabinets, chairs, tables, pipes and lighting, plumbing fixtures, and even airplane interiors. Intermediate processors and thousands of applicators rapidly accepted and used these raw inputs: it has been estimated that more than one billion pounds of these plastics were marketed in 1972 alone. Firms promoted the final products very aggressively in both industrial and consumer media. Advertisements for these plastics, as recently as the summer of 1972, claimed they were "nonburning and self-extinguishable."[1]

Yet, in 1969, a fire broke out in the basement of a private home in Kohoka, Missouri, causing the deaths of two children and total destruction of the house. A Missouri court established that the inherent flammability of such plastics, which were applied to the walls of the basement, was a contributing factor in the deaths and in the destruction of the house.[2] Apparently the high flammability—measured in terms of speed and intensity, degree of heat, and density of toxic fumes—of the plastics also caused the death of 145 teenagers in a dance hall in France in November 1970. In August 1970, a fire involving foam plastic seats completely gutted a just-completed (but not yet open to the public) wing of the BOAC Terminal at Kennedy International Airport. At breakneck speed, the fire consumed 600 seats along a 330-foot length.[3]

These cases raise two questions. The first is obvious: why did the industry continue to advertise such products as nonburning as late as 1972? At least three years earlier their flammability potential had been proven by actual events, and two years earlier the "industry's own surveys had revealed the inadequacy of the American Society for Testing Materials and Underwriters Laboratory tests on which these self-extinguishing claims were based."[4] All available evidence suggests that the ads were known to be false. Thus their continued use would indicate intent to manipulate consumers against their interest—to lead them to buy products that would increase the probability of injury and death.

The second question is less obvious but more serious. Why did government agencies not act immediately with respect to the production, marketing, and advertising of such consumer products? The Department of Commerce and the Department of Health, Education and Welfare are the public agencies directly responsible by law for intervening and ruling in these matters. Also responsible are the National Commission on Fire Prevention and Control, the relatively new (since 1968) National Product Safety

---

[1] Mary Gardiner Jones, "Social Responsibility: The Regulator's View," in S. P. Sethi (ed.), *The Unstable Ground: Corporate Social Policy in a Dynamic Society,* Melville Publishing Co., Los Angeles, Calif., 1974.

[2] *Childress* v. *Cook Paint & Varnish Co.,* Case No. 11,077, Cir. Ct., Schuyler County, Mo., October 6, 1971.

[3] From J. C. Abbott, "Fires Involving Upholstery Materials," *Fire Journal,* published by the National Fire Protection Association, July 1971. Mr. Abbott is the Fire Protection Manager at BOAC.

[4] Jones, *op. cit.* Incidentally, this is also an illustration of how reliance on technical standards cannot make the identification of false advertising an easily applicable basis for objective criteria, especially since, in high-technology societies, new and untested products are continuously appearing on the market.

Commission, the National Bureau of Standards, and, of course, the Federal Trade Commission. None of these public agencies had taken any action, until the FTC filed a complaint in May 1973.

The inability of public agencies to meet simple criteria of public accountability and social responsibility is both deplorable and alarming. Equally alarming is the practical impossibility for consumers to hold these agencies responsible. Note, furthermore, that the Federal Trade Commission itself has no direct jurisdiction in the above cases: the advertising claims are legally correct for they passed the present ASTM and UL tests. In order to file a complaint in May 1973, the FTC had to build a complex case asserting that the firms involved knew that the test standards were inadequate.

All in all, the public is confronted here with a number of paradoxes. For example, instead of investigating and regulating the production of these plastics, the community of public regulators seemed satisfied with merely investigating their advertising. There are many other cases that reveal similarly strange priorities; for instance, at the same time as the plastics were being produced, marketed, and advertised, the FTC was spending public funds to determine whether or not athletes could be considered acceptable experts on the benefits of breakfast cereals.

Be that as it may, society has the operational ability to identify false information. It would be reasonable for public agencies to concentrate most vigorously on policing the truthfulness of the information that flows through the advertising institution. By giving the highest priority to seeking out false information, such agencies might at least forestall the most serious cases of advertising manipulation. If time and budgets allowed, public agencies could then afford to study whether it is possible *and/or* relevant to distinguish between persuasive and objective information.

4.2 CAN PHYSICAL, CHEMICAL, AND OTHER PRODUCT ATTRIBUTES BE EVALUATED OBJECTIVELY?

We have seen that it is often possible to determine by measurement whether the information in an ad is true—that is, whether the advertised product has or does not have a certain quality, in a certain quantity, and producing a certain effect. Many critics of advertising, however, insist that ads should contain information that is objective as well as true.

But what *is* objective information? One popular answer is that information about the physical, chemical, and/or engineering qualities of a product is objective. Let us discuss these objective qualities in terms of the meanings they may have in the mind of the seeker/receiver of ads.

With the characteristic urge of Western man to find solutions to human problems in science, the argument is made that any technical feature has one and only one meaning; that this meaning is perfectly clear to anyone; and that it is the same for everyone. Therefore, to advertise technical attributes is to send objective information. It is also assumed that this objective information is neither persuasive nor deceptive. That is, its effect on the consumer is presumably not manipulative.

On the basis of the behavioral research presented earlier, consumer researchers find it difficult to accept this. The three examples that follow illustrate the conceptual and empirical problems involved in using the objectivity criterion to regulate the content of ads.

The first example concerns *price*. It is widely believed that price is an objective quality of a product, and thus many argue that all ads should provide price information. Yet empirical research tells us that price does not have the same meaning to all consumers.

In our daily work with the consumer, we find that price, like any other bit of information, is subjectively perceived by each person. A person who cares for his car may refuse to consider a "low-premium, economy" car insurance; some respondents frankly admit that they want their auto to be in "good hands" or protected by a company as "solid as a rock." Any text on consumer behavior is filled with examples of the ways in which price is intimately connected with social-psychological needs and, ultimately, with the subjective meaning of the product under consideration.

Implicit references to economic theory are often used to argue that price is objective. This is in conflict with the traditional economic theory of demand (from Marshall to Slutsky and Hicks, to the refinement in, e.g., Debreu) and also with the extensions proposed by Lancaster and others. According to economic theory, price is a measure of value and thus reflects the subjective preferences of each consumer! If one argues that price is objective, he is not using any economic theory known at present; in fact, he is probably expressing a particular aspect of his own utility function.

If price has no objective meaning, can physical, technical, or engineering characteristics provide a basis for objective regulation of ads? For example, is objective information provided by data on the torque curve—or, more precisely, the *shape of the torque curve*—of a car's engine? If he knew several other attributes of the engine *and* the intended uses of that engine, an engineer might see in it *one* indicator of reliability. But the same curve may be perceived as an indicator of safety by a skillful driver; as the means of showing off when the stop light turns green by a young "hot-rodder;" or mean absolutely nothing to another consumer.

In this example, the same piece of technical information means different things to different people. Furthermore, since any object has a very large number of technical features, a regulatory agency must decide which features are important. This is a subjective task, since the relevancy of the features depends upon the individual consumer. Therefore, an agency must investigate how many consumers are interested in which technical features.

The regulatory goal would be the development of a minimum list of technical features relevant to a large number of consumers. Here the agency would find what we already know: (1) most consumers do not think and act in terms of technical features; (2) most do not know or understand even the most basic technical features; and (3) most do not use the large amount of technical information already available on the market—often in simple language—in such media as *Consumer Reports* (which is available in most public libraries). Consequently, rather than requiring that ads contain specified technical information, a regulatory agency may conclude that its truly functional task is to ensure that only accurate information is presented.

Let us consider a third and final example in order to stress, once and for all, that technical attributes cannot help us distinguish between objective and nonobjective information and thus cannot identify persuasive or misleading information.

Suppose that a car manufacturer wants to reinforce the widely held image that his *cars are robust, rugged, strong, and durable.* In a carefully developed five-year plan, the firm decides to communicate this idea by using several themes: undercoating and several coats of paint will permit the car to survive many winters of snow and ice; there are five main engine bearings (for use in media catering to sophisticated car buyers); a large percentage of this firm's older cars are still on the road today; and the body shell of the car is very strong.

As we noted in Part 1, the next task is to encode each of these themes into specific messages. To express the last theme, the firm's advertising department and its agency agree to use a picture of seven cars piled on top of the firm's model. The copy will say, "See how strong my car is!"

Now let us analyze this ad from the viewpoint of both the advertiser and the public. To begin with, let us ask: what factual, objective information does it contain? If we were .to answer that question on some "absolute" basis, we could only say that the ad says that the car is strong—at least strong enough to support the weight of several other cars. The truth of this statement could be easily tested.

In the past, neither advertising critics nor regulatory agencies have been satisfied to ask such questions from an absolute point of view. They would argue, in fact, that the ad says much more than this; that people are led (manipulated) to all sorts of interpretations because the ad does not state the car's strength in some objective—unique meaning—fashion.

Let us see how the consumer might actually interpret this ad. Following established survey procedures, let us suppose we showed the ad to a sample of consumers and asked them—in the most open-ended way—to tell us something about the ad. An analysis of their responses would permit us to identify several classes of meaning. These meanings are displayed in the first row of Exhibit 13.5. One of these is strength. Continuing our open-ended interview, we ask the respondents who mentioned strength what it was in the ad that suggested this quality. The second row of the exhibit shows the frequency of different answers.

From the advertiser's viewpoint, these results are unusually good. To begin with, the ad seems to communicate the intended meaning to 73 percent of the respondents (such a high score is usually registered only in classroom examples). Moreover, the specifics leading to this perception do not signal any potentially dangerous quirk of perception; no elements in the ad appear to detract from perceiving that the car is strong. Whether it is the body shell, or the suspensions, or the tires that is the element in the ad that leads respondents to perceive the total car as strong does not, in principle, distort the intended purpose of the ad; each quality is, in fact, a specific objective correlative of the abstract concept of strength.

Now let us take the point of view mentioned at the beginning: that only technical properties inform rather than mislead. Continuing our interviews from this perspective, we ask those respondents who mentioned "body shell" to specify what they meant by a strong body shell—strong with respect to what?

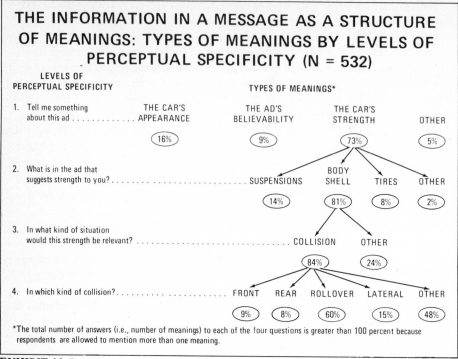

THE INFORMATION IN A MESSAGE AS A STRUCTURE OF MEANINGS: TYPES OF MEANINGS BY LEVELS OF PERCEPTUAL SPECIFICITY (N = 532)

LEVELS OF
PERCEPTUAL SPECIFICITY   TYPES OF MEANINGS*

1. Tell me something   THE CAR'S   THE AD'S   THE CAR'S
   about this ad . . . . APPEARANCE   BELIEVABILITY   STRENGTH   OTHER

        16%   9%   73%   5%

2. What is in the ad that   BODY
   suggests strength to you? . . . . SUSPENSIONS   SHELL   TIRES   OTHER

                          14%   81%   8%   2%

3. In what kind of situation
   would this strength be relevant? . . . . COLLISION   OTHER

                              84%   24%

4. In which kind of collision? . . . . FRONT   REAR   ROLLOVER   LATERAL   OTHER

                                  9%   8%   60%   15%   48%

*The total number of answers (i.e., number of meanings) to each of the four questions is greater than 100 percent because respondents are allowed to mention more than one meaning.

EXHIBIT 13.5

In the third row of the exhibit we see that a high percentage of respondents mention "collision." Our interviewer continues his probing by asking: what kind of collision? The answers are tabulated in the fourth row of the exhibit. We must note that even though our interviewer probed only one of the original four classes of meanings (the car's strength), he has already generated eleven subclasses of meanings. Even if he had stopped at this micro specific level of perception (which is, nevertheless, molar), he would already have ascertained that the meaning of the ad is a rather complex structure of information. And, furthermore, this complexity is generated by the fact that different respondents have different hierarchies of meanings.

Consider the 60 percent of respondents who feel that body shell is an indicator of strength in a rollover type of collision. Here a public agency could argue that the forces in a rollover collision would affect a car's roof in a manner substantially different from the forces operating when several cars are stacked atop another's roof. In this technical sense, then, the ad *is* misleading.

An agency might also believe that the existence of multiple meanings, especially those that could be considered misleading, is due to the lack of technical information in the ad. Suppose it prescribed that the ad copy should clearly state: "The strength of the body shell of this car is X number of psi (pounds per square inch)." Unfortunately, had this copy been used, we would not have changed the perceptual possibilities of the ad's content for anyone.

To an engineer, the bit of information "X psi" is meaningless unless put into context. And, if the number X were put in the context of a rollover collision, then an engineer would need much more information about the car's body shell *and* about the various types of rollover situations in order to pass any quantitative judgment. Moreover, since all this relevant information would take several pages of print, no ad could use it. At best, an ad might indicate where a reader could find more detailed information. If we were to generalize to all properties that could make some sense to chemists, physicists, engineers, etc., we would face a rather impractical situation. And technological change and improvement would necessitate continuous monitoring and revisions.

And what about the consumer? The new X psi copy would certainly not change his perceptual processes. This and the earlier picture both contain, in principle, the same information: the car is strong enough to support (1) several other cars, or (2) X psi. And if we were to show the ad with the technical copy to a sample of consumers, we would produce results equivalent to those already discussed. That is, we would again observe a cascade of meanings, varying by type of respondent and level of perceptual specificity.

As for the advertiser, we find that he has been fairly successful in putting across the intended meaning of the ad—the car is strong and rugged (see the first two rows of meanings in the exhibit). Recall that the notion of *intended meaning* has often been suggested as a criterion for regulation. Even if this notion could be implemented practically (a difficult task, since even in criminal cases the notion of intention is unsettled), our example demonstrates an all-too-frequent dilemma: the firm has conveyed its intended meaning; yet a number of other meanings—some potentially misleading—still obtain in reality.

One could argue that each advertiser should ensure that his ads do not have additional misleading meanings. This suggestion is not only impractical, but also misses the crux of the process of psychological perception. Looking at Exhibit 13.5 again, we see that the information content of any message is a variable that usually takes on (1) values in breadth and depth across a population (see each row in the exhibit), and (2) values for each individual in the population (see each branch of each tree in the exhibit). The information content of an ad is not a single-value variable, but a complex, partially ordered set. As the exhibit illustrates,[1] for any information—objective or otherwise—we shall always observe a cascade of meanings, varying by type of respondent and level of specificity.

It is virtually impossible for any advertiser to create an ad that has one and only one meaning or class of meanings. This is why firms try to test whether the intended meaning is perceived by a sufficiently large number of consumers. This fact has nevertheless been overlooked by legislators and especially by regulators. Neither reference to objective information nor to the intended meaning provides the basis for workable laws and rules.

---

[1] Somewhat misleadingly, because of our desire to present a simple graphic illustration of the structure of information in a stimulus.

The only goal that can be attained is to assure that consumers are given accurate information. That is, regulatory efforts will be most profitable to society if they are directed to a vigorous pursuit of false information.

The fact that there is no truly objective information does not mean that regulation should be limited to false information. On the contrary, it is perfectly within the tradition of Western societies to establish that, independent of any subjective meaning perceived by firms and/or consumers, certain facts, however true, cannot be contained in an ad. Lawmakers and regulators can intervene in the communication between a firm and a group of consumers and rule out any number of topics.

The case of hard drugs is a clear example—whatever the private meanings of drugs may be, no open commercial communication about them is allowed. Or suppose we are examining an ad that describes how a particular brand of gasoline will decrease the emission of those visible particles that contribute to the formation of soot. From a managerial point of view, it is legitimate to communicate this fact to those consumers who are personally annoyed by soot; it is also legitimate for such consumers to search for gasoline that reduces soot.

There will be some consumers, however, who may infer that the same brand of gasoline will also decrease the invisible parts of air pollution. On the surface, this misunderstanding might seem a logical basis for ruling that the ad is unacceptable. But the ethical and legal basis for the ruling would be neither the presence of such misunderstanding nor the number of people who share it. The legal strength of the ruling would be rooted in the fact that laws have established the need to fight a certain kind of pollution, and that possible misunderstandings of this need must be avoided. In other words, the existence of a misunderstanding is not a sufficient basis for intervention in the dialogue about soot between a firm and a group of consumers, for there will always be some "misunderstandings" of any ad; but a misunderstanding can trigger regulation if it is relevant with respect to some clearly established public need.

When legislators clearly state public needs, then regulatory agencies may legitimately check the contents of ads. Concurrently, when social choices are clearly made by legislators, advertising management can also assess the boundaries impinging on its choices.

4.3 CAN THE SO-CALLED NATURAL HUMAN NEEDS MAKE INFORMATION OBJECTIVE?

Behavioral research indicates that the perception of information is a function of what each subject sees. Much of what is seen, in turn, is determined by the subjects' needs. Several proposals to regulate advertising implicitly accept this principle. They then argue: if we can determine the existence of "natural" needs—i.e., needs shared by all humans— we can limit advertising to information relevant to such needs. In other words, cultural homogeneity with respect to such needs would reduce multiplicity of meaning and enable us to assess whether the ad's information is acceptable to society.

The implementation of this reasoning depends on our ability to define operationally the concept of natural need. Let us examine two proposed classifications of natural needs and the extent to which they may provide a workable basis for regulation of the contents of ads.

THE RATIONAL VERSUS IRRATIONAL NEEDS CLASSIFICATION

From the perspective of this classification of natural needs, ads could legally appeal only to rational needs. Consider the following definition of rational need. If two goods are identical except in price, the consumer ought to choose the least expensive one. Since it is practically impossible to find any two products that are exactly alike except in price, supporters of this view argue that differences among products (say, among the colors of cars) are only perceptual, forced upon the consumer by various marketing gimmicks. Thus, the consumer is manipulated to spend more for satisfaction of "unnatural" needs.

To apply the "rational-irrational" classification, we must be able to slide a long list of human needs into one category or the other. It is curious that here, too, writers invoke economic theory to justify their assignment of certain needs to one class or the other. Demand theory in economics, however, only says that *given* (1) a certain set of preferences, (2) some goods available on the market at certain prices, (3) some means to buy such goods, and (4) the desire to spend such means to satisfy as much as possible the given preferences, *then* the consumer is rational if and only if he does act (purchase) according to all the givens above.

By assuming any person's preferences as given, demand theory—in its neoclassical form, its refinements, and its newly proposed extensions—is amoral. It does not tell us which human need is rational. Those who invoke economic theory to define rational needs are either revealing their own preferences or saying that others *should* have these preferences. They are thus either making a moral judgment on others or revealing ignorance of economic theory.

Throughout the coldest regions of North America and Europe, a large number of women recently wore miniskirts for several winters. This would be irrational if we were to assume that clothing is worn solely as a protection against cold weather. But the motivations of a young girl who wants the immediate attention of the opposite sex are different from those of a cohort who equates clothes with comfort. From the viewpoint of economic theory, the behavior of each is equally rational.

The futility of attempting to define what is rational is best embodied in a newly emerging case concerning low-calorie or "empty-calorie" food products.[1] Many concerned citizens view the production, marketing, and, above all, advertising of these products as one of the most blatant examples of manipulation of gullible and/or irrational consumers. Producers usually respond that they are merely responding to consumer preferences. And the usual counteranswer is that advertising causes these consumers to behave irrationally. Rationality is here defined as eating a sufficient and balanced number of calories per day—no more, no less.

Recently, however, this specific basis of rationality has become questionable. It would appear that consumers who buy low-calorie food may be rational, after all, in exactly the sense meant by those who criticize such foods in terms of the need to be healthy. Recent research at the nutritional division of the FAO (the International Food

---

[1] Empty calories are those whose composition is not highly nutritious with respect to some of the known human requirements.

and Agriculture Organization) has documented that the average citizen of some Western societies tends to be overfed, both quantitatively and qualitatively—i.e., his intake of proteins (animal and vegetable), carbohydrates, lipids, minerals, and vitamins is, on the average, far above the requirements of his daily activities. At the same time, in these societies, there is an increase in obesity, diabetes, and diseases of the cardiovascular system, all of which tend to be associated with overeating.[1]

FAO was originally founded to help improve the amount and content of food intake, but in affluent societies it may be faced with the emergence of a completely reversed situation—overeating—one that the growing popularity of low-calorie foods may help to resolve. Whereas the *manifest* function of these foods seems to be that of providing frills—that is, catering to irrational psychological needs—their *latent* function may be one of enabling people to reestablish physiologically healthier diets.

Since health is defined as a rational need by those who criticize the foods in question, we are faced with a case of irrational behavior. To make this behavior rational, the critics should actually lobby for legislation favoring the production, marketing, *and* advertising of low-calorie food.

In conclusion, there is no theoretical concept nor empirical evidence that suggests how a regulatory commission could develop an objective classification of human needs as rational and irrational. Furthermore, it is not clear that such a classification would enable regulators to determine whether ads contain purely objective information and are thus permissible.

THE FUNCTIONAL VERSUS EMOTIONAL NEEDS CLASSIFICATION

The reference to the nutritional content of food leads us to another proposed classification of natural human needs: *functional* versus *emotional.* If we had an a priori way to classify human needs into these two classes, and if we knew that functional needs are good and emotional needs are bad, then clear-cut laws, regulations, and enforcement would follow.

Neither of these two conditions can be fulfilled. To illustrate, consider the possible needs that may be satisfied by drinking liquors at a cocktail party. One person may drink cocktails to quench thirst—a physiological need. Another may view it as a means to meet people, perhaps his boss—an aspirational need. And some unhappy soul may want to escape from a bad experience.

How can a regulatory agency decide which of these needs is not functional and therefore unlawful with reference to liquor ads? Note that even the need to use liquor to allay thirst is questionable, since water is probably physiologically and economically a more appropriate way to quench thirst. To go even further, we note that even drinking water may satisfy a variety of emotional needs, beyond quenching thirst, as William Saroyan spelled out when he described his return to the San Joaquin Valley, his valley, his Sierras, his people, his home.

During the question and answer period following the ANA/4As presentation to the FTC, some commissioners probed deeply into the question of whether the content

---

[1] J. Périssé, "L'Homo Economicus Sta Ritornando Ai Menu dell'Etá della Pietra?" *Notiziario*, Food and Agriculture Organization, Roma, Italy, Luglio 1972.

and/or forms of certain ads concerned the "functional" or "other, nonfunctional, emotional, psychological" uses of the advertised product. It would appear that the commissioners were trying to determine whether such a distinction could provide the basis for determining the lawful content of ads, e.g., only those ads that catered to functional needs would be lawful.

If such distinctions were to become a basis for regulation, several consequences can be foreseen. First, it will be impossible to arrive at an empirical definition of functionality. For the sake of concreteness, let us think of or liquor case. Since different consumers use liquor to satisfy different needs, it follows that (1) each behaves functionally with respect to his own particular need, and (2) the ad that caters to such a need is also functional *for the consumer who experiences that need.* There will be different perceived functions; in fact, for some religious groups we shall also observe cases of perceived disfunctionality.

Second, how are the regulators to choose, once they observe that there are many types of functionality? They might decide on the basis of personal preferences. For instance, they might rule that only ads referring to thirst are lawful. Or they might ask advertisers to pay for research measuring how many people drink liquor to satisfy particular needs. Then, in a new version of Solomonic justness, they might announce the most popular needs, and thus make the related ads lawful.

In this latter case, legislators would be behaving in a manner very similar to that *already* practiced today by advertisers; but, instead of TV ratings, legislators will use consumer-needs ratings! More important, advertising management would still confront uncertainty, since (1) consumer needs and ratings change, and (2) the introduction of new kinds of alcoholic drinks and their ads might be related to some new types of needs. Finally, the least popular consumer needs would be precluded from the consideration of those firms economically able to cater to them. Short of declaring all alcoholic drinks unlawful, the rating procedure would only assure that discrimination against minority needs would not depend on the preferences of regulators but on those of the majority of consumers!

Finally, let us consider the impact of such regulation on the firm. Imagine that an advertiser wants to introduce a new tropical drink—say, piña colada—to the U.S. market. Consumer research and common sense suggest that a growing number of Americans travel, or would like to travel, to tropical countries. Research confirms that awareness and perception of the new drink will be enhanced if the drink is presented in the context of visiting or living in tropical countries. From copy to visual themes, it is decided that all ads will stress tropical settings. But, like a member of a medieval guild, management now has to research whether this theme is permissible. If the legal staff finds no previous ruling on the need to visit tropical countries, could the firm assume that the need for such visits is part of a more general class of needs—for instance, daydreaming or escape? Back to the files, to see whether this class of needs is officially recognized as being functional. In such a situation, lawyers might be better off, but not the firm, whose costs would increase, or the consumer, whose taxes would pay for such regulatory efforts.

FUNCTIONAL NEEDS AND "EXPERT" TESTIMONIALS

The functional-emotional distinction has already affected present regulation. Recall that in Chapter 7 a witness made a passing reference to a sudden new FTC rule on testimonials. The ruling essentially states that only an expert can vouch for the goodness of a product. This ruling would further private or public interests if we had some criteria for identifying experts. The ruling seems to rely on the functional relationship of a person to a product's attributes; but it is not clear what such relationships might be. For instance, who is an expert about coffee? The grower? A chemist? The tasters used in some South American wholesale markets? The housewife next door? Ratings by consumers? (We already have these ratings, for such services as MRCA and SAMI periodically report the market shares of different brands of coffee.)

On the light side, we cannot avoid thinking of how many wine-drinkers and jam-eaters might be horrified to learn that labels such as ". . . by appointment to Her Majesty" have now obviously become unlawful.

More seriously, however, the FTC seems to be disregarding the fact that different consumers have their own notions of who is an expert. Instead of consulting the literature on opinion leadership and mass communication research, the commission seems to have relied on ambiguous and subjectively interpreted concepts such as objectivity and expertise. Because of this, the commission is exposing itself to the question: what expertise do regulators have in deciding who is an expert? Why, for instance, should a wine expert be a chemist? And what kind of chemist?

But the commission also seems to disregard a most important factor in human behavior: motivation, a factor that is basic to the functioning of each individual and, ultimately, of society. It further disregards the fact that, in communication, it is necessary to give concrete form to abstract concepts. Even the poet needs "objective correlatives" to communicate feelings.

Let us use an example to illustrate the importance of motivation. Most children periodically exhibit peculiar eating behavior. They may refuse to eat altogether, or they may limit their food to breadsticks or ice cream or apples. Directly or "deceitfully," most parents have, at one time or another, had to urge their children to eat a reasonable quantity and quality of food. "Why?", the child asks. "Because it's good for you," is the first impulse answer. The next obvious question is another "Why?" Here, one parent responds, "Because I tell you so"; another, "It will make you grow tall"; a third "It will make you pretty."

Most parents have also tried the ploy: "Because it will make you strong." Physical strength is perceptually meaningful to children and culturally cherished in our society. To be strong is not only permissible, it is desirable.

The copy on milk cartons uses the word "fortified" rather than "added." Food advertisers do not need consumer research to tell them that Americans want to feel healthy and strong and want their children to be healthy and strong also. They further know that many Americans like a generous breakfast and train their children to eat accordingly. Manufacturers of breakfast foods must be able to relate their own food— a specific object—to some need. Needs are usually experienced in a generic form—

strength, health, beauty. Thus, the communication problem is one of finding a specific entity, a concrete referent, that interprets and gives life to a generic need. The communicator needs an objective correlative, in the same way as a falling leaf captures the large domain of feelings associated with an approaching autumn.

Food manufacturers and their advertising agencies may have not been as inventive as great poets, but they have catered to the generic desire of most children and their parents to be healthy and strong by choosing an athlete as an objective correlative of that need. Milk producers may choose a United States president as a referent, fruit juice canners may refer to sunny beaches, together with many other more or less successful attempts to suggest that each of these foods can be a component of a "good" meal.

If we decide that athletes are not really experts on cereals, we still have not decided who *is* an expert—especially in terms meaningful to the different potential users of cereal. But above all, we completely misunderstand the processes by which children are induced to eat. While attempting to define the public interest, we have forgotten that a few hours earlier we may have told our children that if they swallow a few more spoonfuls, they will grow as strong as Vida Blue, Daryl Lamonica, or Mohammed Ali—the reference depending on our sports preference or on whom we, and the child, might have seen on television the day before.

Essentially, the commission has disregarded the fact that we all manipulate others by using their aspirations to channel their behavior into what we hope are socially acceptable directions. Aspirations, and their concrete manifestations in some referent figure or reference group, are extremely critical to the functioning of any society. When black leaders ask Abdul-Jabbar, Mohammed Ali, and other famous black athletes to play with the children in ghetto schools, they do not intend that all black children will become athletes. On the contrary, they want these children to become successful in all walks of life through emulating human qualities that are most easily understood by children as well as adults.

The ruling on testimonials is rationalized under an idealistic—or perhaps politically motivated—belief that there is some *objective* notion of objectivity. But it is based, in fact, on the personal opinion that it is bad to motivate children by making use of their desire to identify with referent figures relevant to them. If athletes are not experts on breakfast cereals, neither are they experts on school matters. To be rational, then, the FTC should forbid using black athletes and entertainers in ads that attempt to motivate black children to become integrated into the full spectrum of economic and social activities. Nor should they allow athletes to appear in antidrug commercials.

For advertising managers and for all consumers, the minimum type of rationality that is needed is internal consistency. In the above, and in many other examples, internal consistency could be easily achieved by recognizing that motivation is what makes people tick. At present, it might be argued that the FTC is inconsistent when it uses the "expert" criterion in the case of breakfast cereal manufacturers but not in the case of farmers' cooperatives (operating in fruit juice and milk product industries) and black organizations.

FULL DISCLOSURE AND PERFECT KNOWLEDGE

The tendency of lawmakers and regulators to justify moral decisions by reference to objectivity and other vague or unworkable notions affects advertising management and consumers in yet another way. Recall that any society needs to ensure that its members have access to optimal amounts and quality of information. In the case of quality, consumers should be guaranteed that advertising claims are true. Although much effort is needed to achieve this goal, there is now a trend to shift already scarce resources *away* from enforcement of truthfulness and *toward* guaranteeing consumers an increasing amount of information.

The trend seems to be toward requiring that each ad say "everything." Like the testimonial rule, this trend disregards what we know of consumer information processes and complicates advertising management decisions. Nor is it clear how it can help the public to make better decisions.

First, since some complain that there is already too much advertising and that the consumer is already suffering from an information overload, it could be argued that requiring additional information would simply increase the burden on the consumer. Second, it is not true that all consumers want perfect knowledge. If they did, the excellent *Consumer Reports* would have an enormous circulation and, above all, would be used! Third, since the use of one product may fulfill different needs, different consumers are interested in different kinds of information. Fourth, by demanding an increase in the information load carried by the mass communication system, we create obvious economic inefficiences whose consequences cannot be guessed. Fifth, insistence on a total-information type of ad implies that we are asking a central agency to tell consumers that they must know everything about each possible brand before buying one, i.e., we are ultimately faced once again with a subjective moral posture.

To conclude, in this section we have searched for criteria that might inspire objective, rational regulation of the informational content of advertisements. Manipulative information, which leads people to do things they would not do otherwise, is not acceptable. We thus searched for objective criteria that would permit us to measure whether or not an ad contained manipulative information.

If manipulative information means false information, we already have objective criteria for recognizing falsity and thus eliminating it. Manipulative information can also be that which is deceitful. If deception implies the use of false information, the same criteria apply here also. Deception may also imply not mentioning some information relevant to a consumer. Examples abound here. For instance, if a cold remedy makes some people drowsy, they should certainly be cautioned to this effect.

These cases can be treated with fairness to all—the consumer, the firm, and the public. By requiring that certain information be spelled out on the product's package and in added brochures, rather than in national ads, the regulation of the Federal Drug Administration is a good example of understanding human behavior (i.e., providing the right kind of information at the right stage of decision making). Another good example of regulation of cases concerning the omission of information is the rules evolved by the Securities and Exchange Commission. In principle, similar rules could be developed for all ads concerning safety and financial information.

If by deceit one refers to persuasion, we are suddenly in a whole new ballgame. As we noted, some individuals feel that all persuasion is bad. Since this posture is admittedly subjective, it is not amenable to an examination from the point of view of the technical knowledge we have borrowed from the behavioral sciences and consumer research. Others, however, believe that there is a technical distinction between objective and persuasive information; from their viewpoint, objective information is permissible, but persuasion is objectionable and should not be allowed to flow through the advertising institution.

It is here that public regulation encounters its major problems, for there is no objective way to distinguish between persuasive and objective information. The distinction itself is subjective, since it will vary from person to person. It is thus impossible to develop regulations on this basis, unless we are willing to assume that the subjective distinction perceived by one group of "experts" will also be perceived by all concerned parties.

Nor is it possible to identify the type of information that is objective. This, too, begs the issue, since all humans perceive information subjectively. Thus, the shape of the torque curve of an engine, the chemical properties of a lipstick, and even the physical properties of a color may mean different things to different people, and even different things to the same person, depending on a multitude of factors. Finally, proposed classifications of human needs as rational-irrational or functional-emotional do not offer criteria to identify objective information; these classifications, too, are completely subjective and, in practice, unworkable.

As observers of human behavior, we cannot escape the consequences of what we know about consumers and their decision processes. At one end of the spectrum, we know how to identify false information. At the other end, we know that any stimulus will have meanings whose number and content vary according to the type of person and the level of perceptual specificity at which we operationally define meaning. The vast majority of ads fall into this class of multidimensional meanings.

Most societies have mechanisms, democratic or otherwise, to intervene in communication processes and to define which messages are unlawful. These interventions are not based on objective criteria but on values and subjective choices. Thus, for instance, wine can be advertised but marijuana cannot.

Legislators and regulators cannot escape their legal and historical responsibility; with the exception of seeking out false information, their decision as to what is permissible information is a value choice. To search for objective criteria in the vast majority of ads is naive; it takes funds and staff away from the task of eliminating false information, and it will not satisfy any interested party. Ultimately, it may undermine the respect for the law that is so necessary to keep a society together.

5 SUMMARY

In this chapter we have turned our attention to a specific role the advertising institution may have—that of manipulating consumers. We have addressed ourselves to the question of whether any mass stimulus *can* manipulate humans as a prerequisite to answering the question of whether the institution *does,* in fact, manipulate consumers.

The analysis unfolded in two steps. First, we asked the behavioral scientists to tell us how people perceive stimuli—any stimuli carried by any medium. Second, we asked ourselves whether we can operationally define manipulation.

The answer to the first question was rather simple. Humans manipulate (i.e., operate upon) the information contained in any stimulus: even the most passive or captive receiver is actively engaged in manipulating that which he perceives physically. Psychological perception is a process whereby a subject uses some of the information he has within himself to decode whatever information he has perceived with one or more of his five senses. Thus, decoding is an eminently subjective operation.

Since different people tend to use different information to give meaning to the content of a stimulus, and since the same subject may use different information to decode the same stimulus at different times and in different situations, the meaning of any stimulus is multidimensional. The number of meanings a stimulus may assume in a society depends on the number of people it reaches and the level of perceptual specificity at which we want to measure meaning.

Societies develop mechanisms by which the number of possible meanings an entity may have is reduced to a manageable size—e.g., norms, standards, taboos, stereotypes, prejudices. Yet even within these boundaries, any stimulus still has a large number of possible interpretations. This variety is probably the basic factor allowing for the richness of human personal experiences and for the level of flexibility, or "slack," a society needs to adapt to environmental changes. The more a society cuts down on this variety, the more questionable would be its survival and the more certainly it would tend to become a mechanical, closed-end system rather than a social, open-ended one.

The answer to the question of what manipulation is, and how to eliminate it from advertising, depends essentially on the answer we have just received from the behavioral sciences. We can objectively determine false information and thus avoid its use for manipulative purposes.

But we cannot operationally define the other proposed kinds of information— deceitful, misleading, persuasive, and objective. We have examined the major criteria proposed as bases for identifying these kinds of information and have consistently found them to be unworkable and/or subjective. Beyond outright lies, the decision of what information is permissible is a subjective value choice. Here we must note that elected officials tend to reflect the subjective views of their constituents, and, when they fail to do so, they may be replaced. However, regulators are appointed, and therefore their ability to respond to consumers tends to be functionally weaker. Moreover, the pertinent literature also suggests that regulatory agencies tend to respond to the climate of the political milieu in which they operate; this phenomenon is bound to increase as the number of regulatory agencies proliferates at all levels of government.

The relative insulation of regulators from the pressures of the public is, in part, a price we must pay to assure their independence. Recent arguments suggest that one way to make regulators more responsive to the public interests is to encourage them to find out what the consumer wants. This is certainly a step in the right direction. But even here there are many caveats and difficulties we must be ready to face. Among these, we shall mention only two.

First, there is no average or typical consumer, and the heterogeneity among consumers becomes increasingly greater as society reaches higher levels of affluence. It will not be easy to find rules that are fair to consumers with different and often opposing interests and perspectives. It should probably be emphasized, however, that most consumers undoubtedly care about health, safety, and truthful advertising. If this is a reasonable assumption, then it would also be reasonable to expect public agencies to concentrate their future resources, as scarce as they are, on such priorities. If and when the common needs of health, safety, and truthfulness are met, then public agencies are morally justified in turning their efforts toward learning what consumers think and feel about other types of information, if there exist types other than false/not-false.

Second, as public agencies turn to consumers to learn about their heterogeneous ways of perceiving information, they will necessarily have to rely on the theories and research methods developed in the behavioral sciences.[1] Like firms, these public agencies may also be tempted to overbuy what the behavioral sciences can offer. We must hope that this will not happen, for a mistake at the public level is much most costly to society than a mistake at the managerial level. Behavioral sciences and the emerging discipline of consumer behavior can help regulators only if they are used with great caution and a real understanding of their limitations.

---

[1] Apropos of the recent FTC program concerning visits by consumer researchers, see W. L. Wilkie and D. M. Gardner, "The Role of Marketing Research in Public Policy Decision Making," *Journal of Marketing,* January 1974.

Chapter 14

Does Advertising Manipulate Consumers?

OUTLINE

In the preceding chapter we explored the concept of manipulation of human behavior. We now turn to a set of testimonies that discusses whether advertising does in fact manipulate behavior.

The first testimony presents a large amount of data bearing on our question (Section 1). In the second testimony, we move from data to *words* and, in an almost humanistic manner, examine whether words manipulate consumers (Section 2). Then we turn our attention to two critical areas: the possible effects of ads on children and the possible relationship between ads and the use of illegal drugs (Section 3).

It would be naive to assume that these testimonies are the last word on whether information flowing through the advertising institution manipulates consumers. But the data and thoughts presented in them provide a starting point for rational discussion and future research.

1 ARE CONSUMERS MANIPULATED? *(excerpts from A. A. Achenbaum, senior vice president and director of marketing services, J. Walter Thompson Co.)*

In Part 1 we saw how firms have learned that it is impossible to make people do things against their wishes, desires, and needs. We also learned that a firm can be successful only if it can identify certain needs (physical and/or social-psychological); interpret those needs through a set of product attributes; and relate these attributes to the identified needs via its marketing mix—including appropriate ads.

In Chapter 13 we learned that it is difficult to relate product attributes and ads to the specific needs of a group of consumers. The major difficulty is that any stimulus (e.g., the attributes of a product or the themes in an ad) is always actively manipulated by consumers themselves. These manipulations—diverse, subjective, and numerous—cannot be controlled by the stimulus sender.

We might deduce from these findings that ads cannot manipulate consumers. We might also reach the same conclusion by recalling that despite the great attention firms devote to planning the introduction of new products, many of these products fail—even the well-advertised ones introduced by large and "oligopolistic" firms (see Chapter 4). But by and large, these were experiences of single firms. It is desirable to have a more comprehensive picture.

In part of his testimony, Mr. Achenbaum presents data on nineteen dfferent national brands—some with a large market share, others with a small one—from seven packaged goods categories; analgesics, cigarettes, coffee, denture cleanser, hair spray, mouthwash, and peanut butter. National brands in these product categories are among the most heavily advertised in the United States. It is in these cases that we would most expect to find evidence of stimulus-response conditioning, or a sheeplike attitude, or any other sign that consumers are manipulated by mass communication.

Since Mr. Achenbaum presents a great deal of data, and since it is easy to be swamped by a mass of statistics, it will be useful to sketch here the general line of his discourse. He first presents the *aggregate ratings* given to all brands by a sample of consumers in three different waves.[1] These ratings tend to tap the overall opinion or, to use a more colloquial term, attitude a subject may have about an entity such as a brand.

At this aggregate level, we find that brand ratings are fairly stable. But, as we noted, just as firms tend to be heterogeneous (Chapter 12, Section 3.1), so, too, are consumers. To look at *aggregates* of consumers or firms, either at one point in time or through time, assumes homogeneity among consumers or firms. This often leads to misleading results, which the use of sophisticated statistical methods cannot overcome.

Since he has panel data, Mr. Achenbaum can challenge the observed stability in the aggregate data. He first investigates how many subjects change their brand ratings or opinions. As we would expect from the knowledge we have acquired from the behavioral sciences, he finds a very high rate of instability. That is, many consumers change their

---

[1] The term *wave* is used in panel or longitudinal analysis. In this type of survey design, the *same* subjects are interviewed at successive points in time (each called a wave). The popularity of this design increased during the sixties within the business community, and by the late sixties, some government agencies had also begun to use it. Not much has filtered down into the academic literature—for an introductory overview of panel designs and analyses, and their role in marketing and advertising, see, e.g., F. M. Nicosia, "Panel Designs and Analyses in Marketing," in P. D. Bennett (ed.), *Economic Growth, Competition, and World Markets,* American Marketing Association, Chicago, Ill., September 1965. For a more technical discussion of panel biases, see F. M. Nicosia, "On the Implementation of Panel Designs and Analyses," Consumer Research Program, Survey Research Center, University of California, Berkeley, December 1972, mimeo.

ratings from the first to the second wave, from the second to the third, and from the first to the third. These changes are both upward (subjects give a better rating that they did the previous time) and downward.

He repeats this analysis for the *buying* of the nineteen brands. Here too, a high degree of aggregate stability hides an enormous amount of brand switching over time, indicating that these consumers change their minds *and* their buying behavior over time. This finding is very common in daily professional work; it essentially confirms the difficulty of solving the communication equation that we discussed throughout Part 1.

These findings might be somewhat surprising to those who believe in the manipulative power of advertising. If ads had the power to make people do things, we should see consumers "hooked" into a stable pattern of opinions and buying behavior. So far, however, we have observed a very high degree of switching in both opinions and buying.

It would be premature, though, to conclude that consumers think and act independently. Thus, Mr. Achenbaum continues by exploring the possible relationships between *changes in opinion and changes in buying habits.* Here he does find a strong relationship. Consumers who rate a brand highly are more likely to buy that brand (and vice versa), not only at one point in time but also over a period of time. Further, those consumers whose opinion of a brand has improved are more likely to buy it than those whose opinion has deteriorated. This internal consistency applies to both users and nonusers of the nineteen brands under examination.

Since changes in opinion are related to changes in buying, Mr. Achenbaum is now ready to ask the general question: *What are the possible factors that cause changes in opinion, or in buying, or in both?*

One obvious possibility is *advertising.* If the information that flows through the advertising institution is capable of mesmerizing consumers, we would expect that, in these heavily advertised product classes, advertising would be strongly associated with opinion changes. Mr. Achenbaum does find a relationship, but it will be disappointingly weak to those who believe in the magic power of mass communication. Common sense, of course, can help allay this disappointment. In addition to ads a myriad of *other factors,* impinge on consumers' decision processes—from other marketing variables (e.g., price, packaging, shelf position, and type of store) up to and including economic and social events.

One obvious factor affecting opinion and buying is the *personal experience* a consumer has had with a brand. Note that if consumers are mesmerized by mass communication, their opinion of brands will not be affected by their experience—they will keep on buying the same brand or brands regardless. Once again, however, Mr. Achenbaum's data confirm what common sense would suggest: changes in buying are related to changes in brand ratings. Advertising does not seem to have much "holding" power;[1] a consumer's

---

[1] Recently, several professionals have recognized this fact of life and are arguing that much more effort should be made to find out how advertising can help in at least retaining one's own customers. See, e.g., W. T. Moran, "Holding and Switching Strategies," in M. K. Starr (ed.), *Production Management Systems and Synthesis,* Prentice-Hall, Englewood Cliffs, N.J., 1972, and "The Law of Conservation of Advertising Energy," in C. W. King, and D. J. Tigert (eds.), *Attitude Research Reaches New Heights,* American Marketing Association, Chicago, Ill., Marketing Research Techniques, Bibliography Series Number 14, n.d.

personal experience with a brand seems to be a much greater determinant of the next purchase.

In addition to these indications of consumer initiative and independence in opinion and action, Mr. Achenbaum shows that *consumers are very active in trying different brands.* Finally, he concludes by noting that his findings tend to hold true for those who are either rich or poor and those with different levels of education.

> *If consumers were truly being manipulated by advertising, we would expect them to act against their better interest when exposed to advertising: (a) we would expect that their attitudes toward the various brands would be extremely stable; (b) we would likewise expect that they would loyally refrain from moving from one brand to another and that they would not move on the basis of changed attitudes; (c) we would also expect that the attitudes held or changed were not deliberate, but random; and (d) we would expect that certain demographic groups – the lower-income, less-educated people – would behave differently.*
>
> *The empirical evidence suggests otherwise. Obviously, I only have time to show you the tip of the iceberg of the data available. . . . Most of the material I am going to present was obtained in a nationwide study among 2000 females who head up their households. The study, conducted by Grey Advertising, was done in three waves over a six-month period. The study covered 19 different brands – some large and some small – in 7 packaged good categories, where advertising plays a major role in the marketing. Included were analgesics, cigarettes, coffee, denture cleanser, hair spray, mouthwash, and peanut butter. Only national brands were measured, some I might add that are accused of advertising manipulation. I shall also use some copy-testing data developed by Grey and some material obtained from Ogilvy and Mather, another major advertising agency.*

CHANGES IN ATTITUDES

To begin with, attitudes would seem to be on the surface very stable. As you can see, almost the same number of people rated the 19 brands about the same in each of the three periods measured (Exhibit 14.1). Although I am showing you summary data, these data were obtained for each brand. Let me assure you that anything I tell you about the summary applies for each individual brand as well.

But what these data hide is the intrinsic dynamism in attitudes which actually exists in the marketplace. Since the same people were measured in all three waves, we were able to ascertain how each individual changes her attitudes during the three points in time (Exhibit 14.2). And what we found was that 53% of the consumers actually altered their opinions at least once toward a brand between Wave I and Wave II (a three-month period) and another 48% changed them again at least once between Wave II and Wave III. In fact, the extent of attitude change, brand by brand, between two waves ranged from 41% for a small hair spray brand to 61% for a medium-sized denture cleanser brand (Exhibit 14.3).

While it was true that so-called loyal users (those who continued to use the brand through all three waves of the study) changed their attitudes less frequently than consumers who moved from one brand to another, there was always more change in attitude than no change, no matter what the usage pattern (Exhibit 14.4).

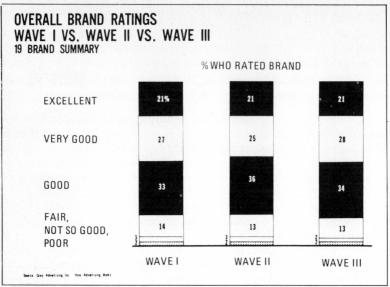

EXHIBIT 14.1

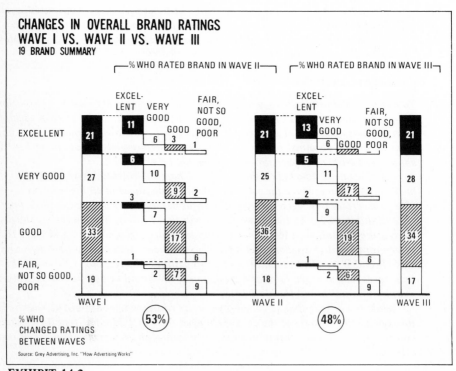

EXHIBIT 14.2

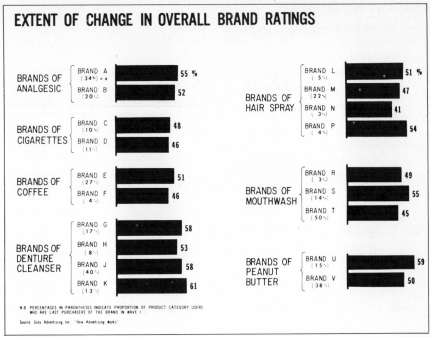

EXHIBIT 14.3

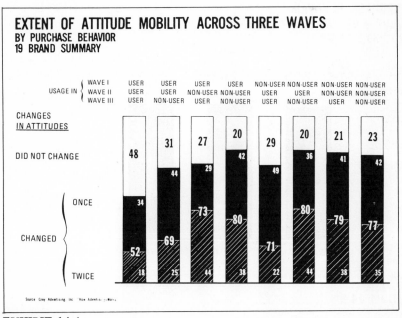

EXHIBIT 14.4

PURCHASE BEHAVIOR

The data in this study also revealed that purchase behavior, like attitudes, appears stable on the surface. . . . there is apparent stability in brand shares among the brands measured (Exhibit 14.5).

But, again, underlying this surface stability is a very substantial amount of change (Exhibit 14.6). . . . 13% of the consumers switched brands between Wave I and Wave II, while another 12% switched between Wave II and Wave III. Obviously, there is not as much switching as with attitudes, but we should not expect much more since purchase behavior occurs much less frequently than those forces that affect attitudes. Bear in mind that people, even for the repeat-purchase items we measured, are not back into the market that often during a six-month period.

In total, then, 73% of the consumers changed their ratings of the brands between the three waves and 21% changed the brands they used during this period (Exhibit 14.7).

THE RELATIONSHIP OF ATTITUDES TO BEHAVIOR

Noting the changes I just described, one would certainly expect a relationship between the two. And so there is.. . . a very clear-cut correlation between brand attitudes and usage (Exhibit 14.8). But I guess one should expect a user to like his brand. Yet, even in a dynamic sense, we see this correlation (Exhibits 14.9 and 14.10). . . . when users change their attitude downward between two waves, the probability of using the same brand drops substantially. On the other hand, among nonusers, if attitude toward a brand is enhanced, consumers are more likely to become users of that brand.

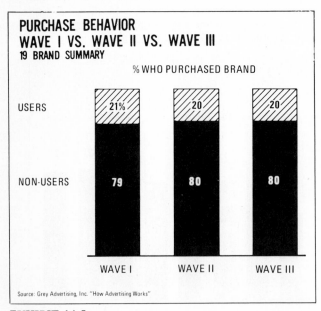

EXHIBIT 14.5

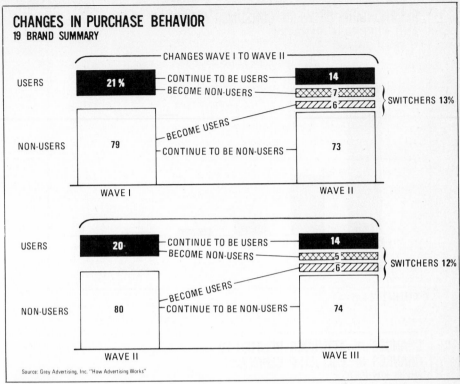

EXHIBIT 14.6

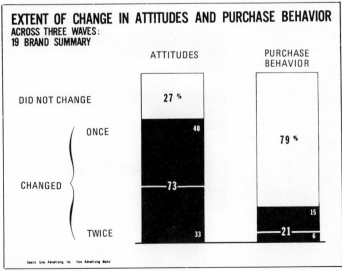

EXHIBIT 14.7

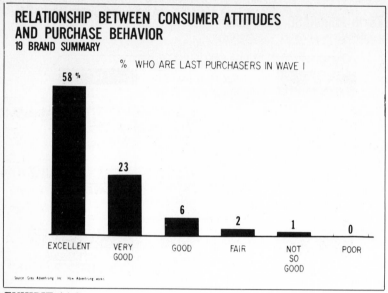

EXHIBIT 14.8

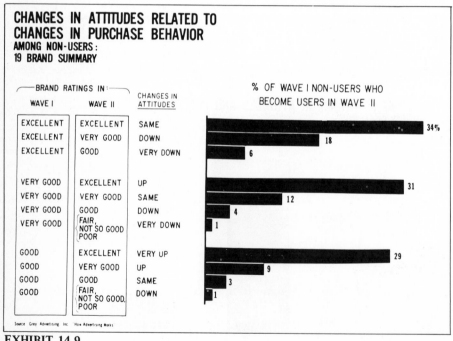

EXHIBIT 14.9

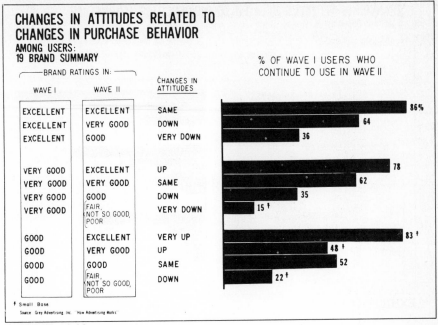

EXHIBIT 14.10

In the most predictive situation, we found that if people changed their attitudes downward between the first two waves, they are less likely to remain users in the subsequent wave. And this is true for both nonusers and users alike (Exhibits 14.11, 14.12, and 14.13). However, users tend to retain their loyalty to a brand more than nonusers when their attitude shifts downward. Yet we were able to infer from some other data in this study, which I am not showing you, that if the less positive attitude persists, the user will eventually switch away from the brand.

What all these data suggest so far is that people do not think or act like automatons. They are, in fact, quite prone to change their opinions and usage, to do so frequently, and to do so in relation to their changed feelings.

But the data revealed another crucial point—that while there is a correlation between attitude and behavior, it is not a one-to-one relationship. All attitude changes do not get translated into behavior changes. Other forces are obviously at work.

THE EFFECT OF ADVERTISING ON ATTITUDES

In an effort to see if advertising affected attitudes, Grey tried to measure whether different levels of exposure to advertising affected attitude levels. And so it did, although the correlation is not terribly robust (Exhibits 14.14 and 14.15).

Much about the method of measurement could explain this, but it is not that important since they got at this relationship in another way—one that is perhaps

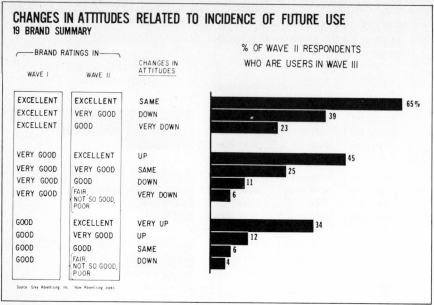

EXHIBIT 14.11

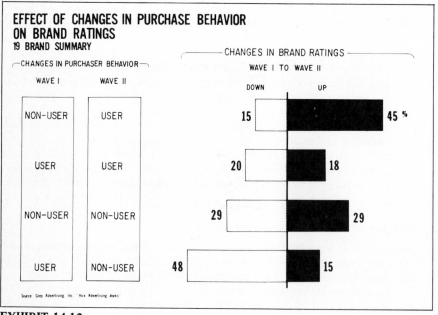

EXHIBIT 14.12

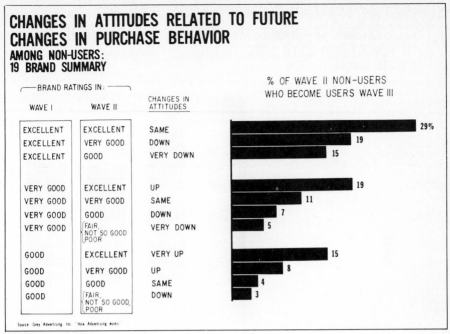

EXHIBIT 14.13

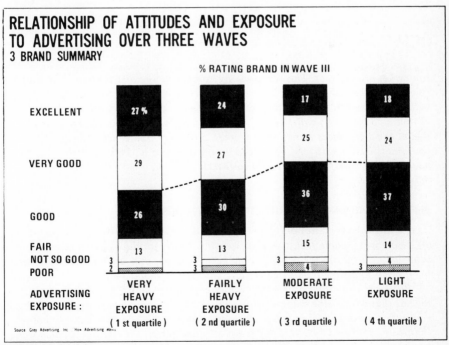

EXHIBIT 14.14

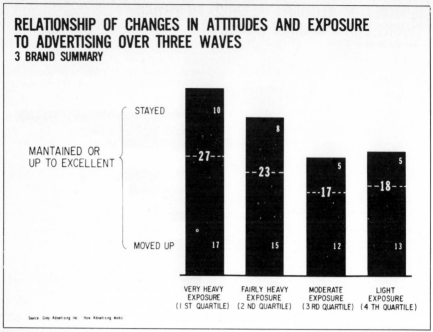

EXHIBIT 14.15

somewhat more direct. This was done by comparing the distribution of attitude changes induced by exposure to an individual commercial in 189 separate copy tests with the distribution one would expect if the changes were purely the result of chance. . . . there was a difference—exposure to advertising did change attitudes. Again, the differences were not very great. Moreover, there were cases where consumers were negatively influenced by the advertising. This is hardly a case of people feeling what they were told to feel. In fact, they were downright independent. . . .

EFFECT OF PRODUCT EXPERIENCE ON ATTITUDES

As one might expect, not only does the way a person feels affect usage, but usage will affect the way people feel, too. Experience with the product plays a role in consumer behavior. As you can see, when people become users, they are more likely to like the brand than to dislike it and vice versa (Exhibits 14.16 and 14.17).

But there is another aspect of product experience which would inferentially suggest that advertising manipulation cannot be a factor in consumer behavior. The amount of product trial in many of the packaged goods categories is very high (Exhibits 14.18 and 14.19). For example, in analgesics, the top four brands were tried at least once by over 75% of the population. Since the repeat-purchase rates on

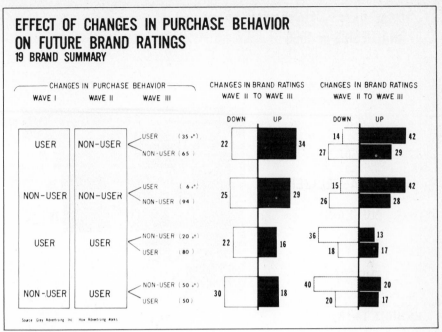

EXHIBIT 14.16

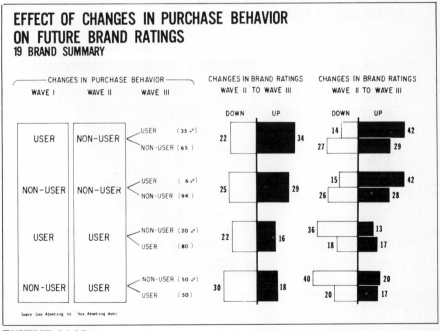

EXHIBIT 14.17

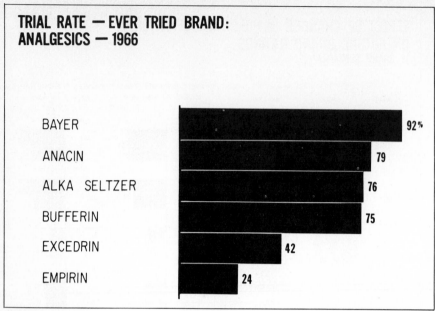

EXHIBIT 14.18

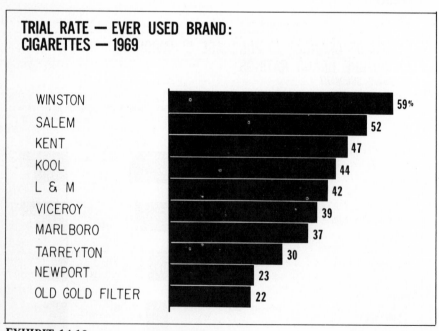

EXHIBIT 14.19

many of these highly advertised brands are also quite high, we must believe that consumers, irrespective of the advertising, are choosing brands based on positive production experience. If advertising were truly manipulative, this would not be the case. . . .

HOW DELIBERATE ARE THESE ATTITUDES

Now one could argue that these measurements of attitude are a function of the questioning technique, that they really aren't measuring how people feel. On the contrary, built into this study was an experiment to find out just how deliberate attitude measurements are. The data quite clearly show that people know exactly how they are rating the brands.

To begin, six different measuring sticks of attitude were used. The correlation between these measuring sticks was extremely high—in most cases over .75. Moreover, when the two most widely used attitude measures were correlated between waves, a similarly high correlation was found to exist. For this to happen by chance would require people to remember how they scored two different scales three months before, a highly unlikely possibility.

DIFFERENCES BETWEEN DEMOGRAPHIC GROUPS

. . . One might question whether these relationships hold true among all groups in the population. After all, the poor and less educated may very well react differently, may be more prone to act as they are told. While I cannot show you all of the data by different demographic groups, let me at least show you the data on the relationship between attitudes and behavior by income and education (Exhibits 14.20, 14.21, 14.22, and 14.23) [for both users and non-users].

I use these data because they are the most relevant and are typical. As you can see, there is no significant relationship between above- and below-average-income householders or among the well-educated and less-well-educated consumers.

THE ROLE OF INFORMATION ON ATTITUDES AND BEHAVIOR

As we discussed earlier, there are some who believe that all advertising must do to effectively do its job in the marketplace is to convey information. Yet we have considerable evidence to show that the communication of information alone will not change attitudes or behavior.

A standard measure of the amount of information communicated in advertising is "related recall." Using a typical case, Grey correlated the related recall scores with attitude shift scores from 15 individual copy tests on one brand. . . . there was no correlation between the two measures.

In a study done by Ogilvy and Mather, they found (and I am only showing one typical piece of evidence from that study) that usage did not change on the basis of the information recalled. As you can see, it didn't seem to matter whether more or less information was recalled, usage remained basically the same. Thus, contrary to what our critics say, consumers do not react—either in the way they feel or in the way they act—on information alone. . . .

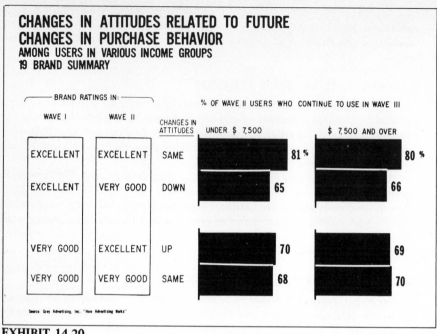

EXHIBIT 14.20

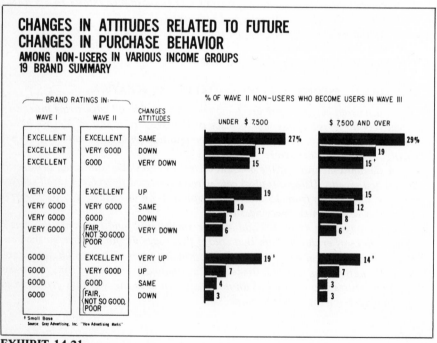

EXHIBIT 14.21

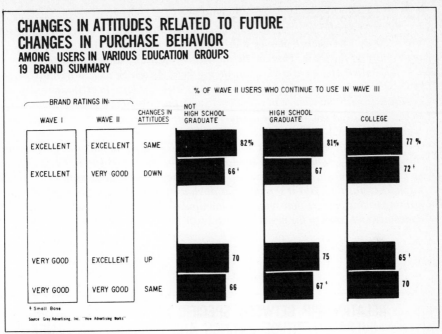

EXHIBIT 14.22

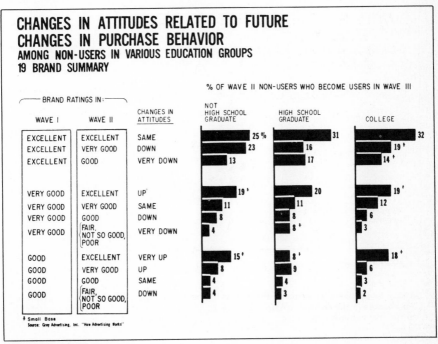

EXHIBIT 14.23

HOW DOES THE ADVERTISING PROCESS WORK?

. . . Based on empirical data, it would appear that the process works something like this . . . a positive change in overall attitudes, we know, will positively affect the probability of purchase. This can be shown schematically using actual data.

Some attributes have more clout than others. As can be seen in Exhibit 14.24, the more salient the attribute, i.e., the more correlated a change in attitudes on an attribute is with the change in overall attitude, the larger the effect on future brand share. As you can see, in the next chart (Exhibit 14.25), Attribute Y has less salience than Attribute X.[1]

Thus, we can empirically see why the advertiser wants to know what is salient to the consumer. . . . unless he can support the claim on that salient factor, and unless he can communicate it in a persuasive manner, he will have done nothing to enhance his market position. But it should be as obvious to you as it is to us that there is nothing in this process that smacks of manipulation. Advertisers either consider the consumer and cater to his needs and wants, or they are doomed to market failure.

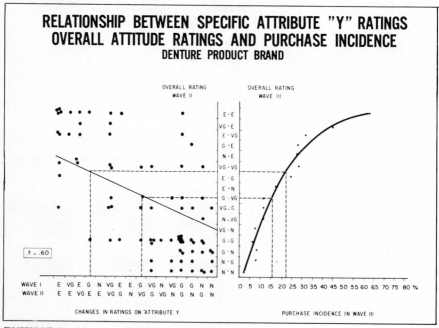

EXHIBIT 14.24

---

[1] Thus, the purchase incidence in Wave III is higher for changes in the ratings of Attribute X than for changes in the ratings of Attribute Y (e.g., 18% and 27% versus 16% and 22%, respectively, in the two exhibits). Ed. note.

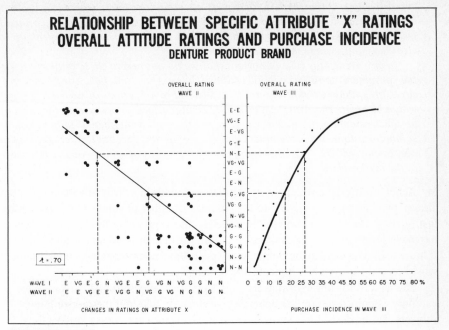

RELATIONSHIP BETWEEN SPECIFIC ATTRIBUTE "X" RATINGS OVERALL ATTITUDE RATINGS AND PURCHASE INCIDENCE
DENTURE PRODUCT BRAND

EXHIBIT 14.25

CONCLUSIONS

. . . I do not deny that there is some genuine deception in advertising. But this deception, when seen in the perspective of the billions of transactions that take place each year, is a relatively minor part of all consumer activity. Moreover, we could have an honest difference of opinion as to what is in fact deceptive. . . .

. . . empirical evidence makes it quite plain that advertising is not manipulative. Consumer's attitudes are extremely variable, as is their behavior. They do not slavishly stick to any one brand. While advertising affects their attitudes, it hardly mesmerizes them. Moreover, product experience plays an important part in influencing future behavior. . . . Certainly, information alone does not appear to have an effect on either consumer attitudes or behavior. . . .

. . . if we force advertisers to move away from advertising as a means of communication with the marketplace, or if we force them to stick to some impossible standard for conveying information alone, we shall be opening a pandora's box. The consequence will mean more personal selling, which is hardly a way to bring truth and objectivity to the marketing situation.

There is an irony to this criticism of advertising. In those areas where manipulation, or for that matter, persuasion, can operate unabated—in religion, education, courtship, and politics—we seem to be calling for more liberalism, more permissiveness. Only where influence affects the pocketbook, where it is often not terribly critical to a person's overall welfare or happiness, is there so much fuss. It seems strange that those who are so concerned with American values speak up so vigorously only where money is concerned.

In any event, it is very important that we do not permit these critics to destroy the consumers' confidence in advertising. Unless Americans have confidence in advertising, they will not rely upon it. The cost ramifications of such a situation would be great. The American economy cannot afford to operate on the basis of personal communication. Nor can it afford to rely on ineffectual impersonal communications. While we must eliminate unfair and deceptive practices, we must not, in our zeal, destroy advertising as a viable means of selling goods and competing in the marketplace. . . .

Mr. Achenbaum's data, which concern nineteen brands in heavily advertised product classes, provide only a glimpse into the complex question of whether the advertising institution conditions consumers. Nonetheless, this is probably the first time that business has made public such a wealth of information.[1] Although it would certainly be desirable if more such data were made public, we expect that a comprehensive collection of data would tend to confirm Mr. Achenbaum's conclusions.

The reasons for this expectation come from the viewpoints and facts we have carefully examined so far. The advertising institution does not mesmerize human subjects. To the best of our knowledge, both laboratory and survey studies show that ads or any other stimulus have effects on seekers/receivers, but these effects vary considerably for different types of people and goods. Furthermore, they vary from negative to zero to positive (from the viewpoint of the sender). Note that, if all factors other than ads are controlled, the positive effects of ads are obtained only when the sender has been able to (1) understand the needs of some group of seekers/receivers, and (2) relate to such needs by developing messages (from choice of themes to their encoding, to the choice of media and the appropriate timing) that are relevant to the subjective needs of a specific group of seekers/receivers.

From basic to applied communication research, we have yet to find concepts or data that give support to the notion of audience conditioning. On the contrary, we do have cases of countries where the entire mass communication system has been used for decades for the purpose of conditioning thoughts, feelings, and actions about political ideologies or drinking habits—apparently with disappointing results.

These results, after all, are to be expected. The information flowing through mass media is only a very small part of the total stimuli that impinge on each member of a society. More importantly, humans are a very rich, lively, and independent form of life; historically they have shown a very great ability to overcome environmental forces far stronger than ads can ever exercise.

---

[1] The data in Mr. Achenbaum's presentation not reported in this book are in his written testimony submitted to the FTC and, presumably, should be available to the interested reader.

2 THE USE OF WORDS: A HUMANISTIC POINT OF VIEW *(excerpts from A. J. Seaman, president, SSC&B, and chairman, operations committee of SSC&B–Lintas International)*

In the preceding section, the emphasis was on numbers; in this section, it is on words. Here, too, we are searching for evidence on whether the advertising institution manipulates consumers. The testimony asks: do words manipulate consumers and, more generally, humans?

One could search for an answer by choosing among several methods of inquiry, e.g., the scientific method, the statistical method, or the historical method. For eons, words have been intimately related to the nature of humans and their interactions; even the above methods of inquiry depend on words. Words probably provide the most distinctive feature of human nature: a humanistic approach to the role of words in communication can give us insights that we might not otherwise obtain.

A. J. Seaman's approach to the question can be described as humanistic in the above sense. We should not expect to see empirical evidence or "proofs." Instead, we must shift gears and try to depict feelings, to sense Mr. Seaman's image of mankind.

> . . . *Lately, the fashion has been to downgrade language, except for what we used to call barnyard words, in favor of visual communications, body language, and the like. I think we should remind ourselves that even the old Chinese idea that "One picture is worth a thousand words" achieved its full impact only when the idea was expressed in* words.
>
> *To know the power of words, we need only to listen to our memories:*
>
> *"Man shall not live by bread alone . . .";*
>
> *"There are more things in heaven and earth, Horatio, than are dreamt of in your philosophy";*
>
> *"We hold these truths to be self-evident: that all men are created equal . . .";*
>
> *". . . government of the people, by the people, and for the people shall not perish from the earth";*
>
> *"The only thing we have to fear is fear itself";*
>
> *"I have nothing to offer but blood, sweat, toil and tears."*
>
> *The power of words! In every age and in every tongue, words have sounded louder than guns. It is no accident that every generation has endorsed again that "the pen is mightier than the sword." If advertising is to remain a vital force for the development of our economic system, it must have access to the vigorous use of words.*
>
> *Words do not work alone. They work in harness with concepts and pictures, with music and sound effects; yes, even with a kind of contrapuntal relationship to silence. They do many things—some of which cause the critics of advertising to view with alarm. Words motivate. Words make pictures. They goad people to action. They persuade and convince. They cause laughter and tears.*
>
> *Words do other things as well—not so much in advertising as in other places—law, politics; labor unions, reform groups; and modern international diplomacy. Yet, also in novels, the movies, and the theater. Words arouse and feed prejudice. They stir ancient hatreds and fan new ones into burning heat. They confuse and mislead. They*

conceal when they pretend to reveal. Indeed, words are so powerful that through the ages, including the brilliant periods of classical Greece and of the Renaissance, they got confused with the things they only represented. People still make that mistake, today. . . .

Advertising people frankly view words as the indispensable tools of their trade. We want the freedom to use them to create images, to set moods, to motivate, to persuade and to sell. We love words; we respect them; and we know we must use them with judgment and restraint.

Is our judgment never faulty? Are we never carried away by enthusiasm? The questions almost answer themselves. Of course we're not free of fault. If this were not so, the lexicon of government speechmakers, academicians, and consumer crusaders would be poorer. They would miss such wonderful weapons as "weasel words," "puffer," "uncompleted comparatives." Their tirades against bad grammar would be limited to everyday speech, to examination papers of college students, to politicians, and the like.

Yes, there are weasel words in advertising—but not nearly so many as there used to be and not so many as critics pretend. Yes, there is puffery, but I gather that few regulators are really concerned about this. Yes, there are uncompleted comparatives, but I think that good advertising people are as strongly against these as our critics. Why? Very simple. Because an uncompleted comparative doesn't have the force of a completed one. That simple fact doesn't apply, however, when the completion of a comparative involves a lot of legal trivia, painfully added to be sure that there is not a single person in the United States for whom the statement is not 100% true.

Yes, there is bad grammar. There are several reasons for this. One is that people speak with what scholars say is bad grammar. Shakespeare did, too. I don't condone bad grammar. I am, to the best of my ability, a purist. But I recognize that language is a living, evolving thing. Using "like" instead of "as" is an abomination, but I fear that such complex distinctions will disappear in the heat of our verbal melting pot. Advertising must talk to people, naturally and effectively. Sometimes—sometimes— bad grammar really does it better. Another reason for bad grammar, I fear, is that some practitioners of our craft don't know the difference between good and bad. What's more, they don't care. They would rather trust their own ears than trust the good graybeards who wrote the grammar books. Perhaps that's where idiomatic speech came from in the first place.

I haven't mentioned taste. I am sure I can't define good taste any more successfully than our highest courts can. Indeed, when one goes to the theater or the movies, he must wonder if there are any bounds at all. Compared to that, advertising language has almost the moral purity of a Gregorian chant.

The vast majority of advertising people I know—agency and advertiser alike—are against bad taste in advertising. Most would not permit it to run even if they thought it would do them some good. But good taste is a changing thing. I find, when I talk to the eighteen-year olds, the college students, and the young marrieds that I am an arch-conservative, practically a man of the cloth. Maybe some of advertising's critics are, too. If you ask advertising leaders where we stand, it's solidly in the corner of good taste. Contrary to what many "experts" say, I believe that there is a consensus in any society at any given time with clear ideas of what good taste—or, at least, bad taste—really is. But in judging advertising, let us be sure we represent good taste and not an unworldly piety.

I have given you these observations about language not as a scholar of language but as a student of advertising. However long we study or however hard we try, we shall find language a difficult and sometimes unpredictable tool. In fact, a common understanding of the difficulties of language is a bridge we must build between advertising and those who regulate it and criticize it. I can see why people outside the advertising business think we have an unlimited supply of scientific tools and techniques—so magical we can manipulate almost anything. The fact of the matter is we are successful in selling good products and unsuccessful in selling poor ones. In the end, consumer satisfaction—or lack of it—is more powerful than all our tools and ingenuity put together. . . .

The use of language is not a science; it is an art. It rises to the status of high art only in the hands of a few, and then not all the time. Mostly it is earthbound, struggling to be heard, trying not to be misunderstood, hoping to communicate a thought.

Whether you are a lawyer, a journalist, a priest, a poet, or an advertising man, words are like mercury on a table top: they glitter, they move, they look solid but they slither and slide and slip through your fingers with the greatest of ease.

For one reason, words don't always mean what they mean. One authority claims that twenty of our simplest verbs enter into 155 different combinations, leading to over 600 distinct meanings or uses. A great strength of the English language is the number of words. I am told that there are 600,000 words in the English language. An average American has an active vocabulary of 10,000 words and a passive vocabulary of slightly over 30,000 words. A child entering school has a vocabulary of three to four thousand words.

With so many words rattling around in 200,000,000 heads, it is not strange that the same words can have different meanings to different people. The simple word "wind" may mean a zephyr in Arizona, a fresh breeze off the Maine coast in summer, or an icy gale in the Dakotas in winter. It means condition to the athlete, sounds to the musician, a rest for a horse to a horseman, and a lot of hogwash to the man who doesn't agree with you. Words are not easy.

Advertising is not the only field for which the meaning of words is an ever-present problem and challenge. Take the law, for example. Trained and skillful men write contracts designed to be clear to other trained and skillful men. They are not bound by economic limits. Whereas advertising may have to make itself clear and meaningful in a 30-second TV commercial or a 200-line newspaper advertisement, lawyers can take as much space and time as they want. A contract can use 500 pages, if need be. Talk about information! Talk about precision! Yet what happens?

The law courts are jammed. The calendar is backed up for months and even years. Why? People can't agree on the meaning of the words. One side says they mean one thing; the other side says they mean something very different. Sometimes, in the end, erudite judges vote 5 to 4 in favor of one side or the other. Even they can't agree.

How realistic, then, are critics and regulators when they say advertising language must never be subject to two different interpretations? Advertising simply could not exist under such requirements—nor could the law, the government, or even the church.

Now I come to the last and perhaps the most challenging problem words present to those who write advertising, those who hear and read it and those who regulate it.

This aspect is what one semanticist, S. I. Hayakawa, refers to as sponsored poetry. *T. S. Eliot, by this system, wrote unsponsored poetry; copywriters write sponsored poetry. If you think that's farfetched, so do I, but even Aldous Huxley wrote, "The advertisement is one of the most interesting and difficult of modern literary forms." In any case, after quoting a Wordsworth poem, [Hayakawa] writes: "A poet, however, cannot let a yellow primrose remain merely a yellow primrose; his function is to invest it with meanings. In the poet's eye the primrose comes to symbolize many things: the joy of early spring . . . the benevolence of God, the transitoriness of life, or other things. Similarly, whatever the object for sale is, the copywriter, like the poet, must invest it with significance so that it becomes symbolic of something beyond itself. . . . the task of the copywriter is* the poeticizing of consumer goods."

You may think that poeticizing is what we don't *need in advertising. Well, that brings to mind the story of Noah Webster of dictionary fame. He was kissing the parlor maid one day when Mrs. Webster suddenly opened the door. "Why, Noah,"* she said, *"I'm surprised!" Webster looked up and said, "No, my dear, I am surprised. You're* astounded!" *Poeticizing is a good thing; life would be dull and barren without it. It is different from lying and deceitful distortion. . . . Sometimes critics of advertising, like Mrs. Webster, are not precise enough in seeing the difference.*

Whether we call it "poeticizing" or . . . rhetoric or colorful language, the function is similar. We are trying to relate the product and its attributes in a meaningful way to the needs, wishes, and desires of the consumer. It must be clear to any observer that people buy products and services for more than physical performance . . . psychic satisfaction is just as important as mechanical satisfaction—often more so.

To rob advertising of its ability to communicate in terms of psychic and emotional satisfaction would be to deprive the consumer of valid understanding and experience. It would severely detract from the life style which hundreds of millions of Americans enjoy—and which people all over the world truly envy. It would not be too unlike asking the sportscaster, the lawyer, the preacher, or the politician to do his work without rhetoric and without metaphor. They would all die of verbal anemia and we would lose one of our favorite indoor sports.

Awareness that we have problems does not make us complacent. Far from being complacent about our craft, we are active in trying to improve it. We are active and we are worried. We are worried about a lot of trends which we think can result in making advertising less effective without making the world any better.

Before I set some particulars before you, let me state the base for my concerns and my conclusions. I have a very clear philosophy about advertising. I have spent my life in it, and I have never been more willing to waste my life than you are to waste yours. I believe that advertising has value and advertising has a mission. Of course, it has the job of making companies more successful and more profitable. It also has the mission of making the lot of all mankind richer—richer in comfort and health, richer in its capacity to create and enjoy. I rest my case simply on three points.

1 *The people of this country and the whole world would rather have prosperity than penury. You don't have to make surveys or consult oracles. It's as plain as the nose on your face—whether you're talking about India or Indiana, whether you're concerned with countries like the United States and Western Germany or the evolving nations of Africa. People have a very clear way of counting worldly goods as high priority items. What the social philosophers want for them is quite a way down the priority list of everyday people.*

2 *Prosperity is the product of business. Business, by creating what the public wants
   and delivering it at prices more and more people can afford, builds prosperity and
   a stronger economy. Let me be candid. I believe business is right to create new
   wants as well as to satisfy existing wants. There was no widespread, crystallized
   demand for the toothbrush, the electric refrigerator, frozen foods, or the
   transport plane. But we have all benefited.*
3 *Advertising['s] . . . job is not just to inform. Its function is to sell. Sell products.
   Sell ideas. Sell styles of living—which are often better than the ones people create
   for themselves, as a trip to some backward nation will quickly show. . . .*

*Now let us examine language and the concerns we have about shackling it in terms
of advertising's basic function—selling. Selling is competitive. Selling is enthusiastic.
Selling is persuasive. Selling must be resultful. What does that mean in our relatively
advanced consumer economy? It means there are lots of fine products. It means
selling yours against the other fellow's calls for ingenuity, enthusiasm, skill, and
tenacity. One may ask what benefit there is for the consumer in all this. A very big
one! The desire to sell more—and that means in part having a more persuasive
advertising story—spurs the manufacturer on to build a better product.*

*In this upward spiral of improving products, breakthroughs are few and far
between. . . . Products improve little by little. Competition soon catches the pioneer.
The margins are small. Our job is to make those small margins of superiority
meaningful to the consumer—and thus make the race for better products even swifter.
To do this, we need the language of enthusiasm. We need the luxury of harmless
puffery. We need the right to make those margins meaningful because they are the
small steps on the stairway that lead to better products, greater satisfaction, and more
prosperity.*

*There is no fight between advertising and the regulatory and legislative bodies
about information—or, to put it another way—about facts in advertising. Facts are
often the building blocks of a sale. We want to use them. But there are two major
reasons why restraint should be used in the drive for more and more facts or
"information" in advertising. First, consumers don't consider every purchase so
important as to make them want to study an encyclopedia. If you make us overload
the ads with facts, you'll bore the consumer to death, and decimate the number of
people who hear and read. . . . Second, we are dealing with very small advertising
units. For example, about 80% of network television commercials are only 30
seconds long. . . . We tell our clients: make your main promise, make it convincing,
ask for the order, and stop there. That's all you can do effectively. I say the same
to you.*

*So, we are asking you to understand the mission of advertising; i.e., to sell. We ask
you to accept that selling means motivating and persuading. . . . We ask you to give
advertising language the freedom, the naturalness, the elbow room to do this in what
has been called the "grammar of gossip"—the day-to-day language of people, without
vulgarities but, also, without the cold hand of the grammarian.*

*Realize that words are like chameleons, ever-changing, subject to many meanings
and shades of meaning. Recognize that "poeticizing" is different from deceiving, that
poeticizing helps to brighten the marketplace and give color to a world which is too
often drab.*

*I have one more worry and, therefore, I would ask one more bit of sympathy
from you. In an attempt to make sure that consumers have every protection possible*

from making a mistake or—it sometimes seems—from being totally satisfied without possessing as much knowledge as some crusader thinks they should have, there is a growing requirement for more legal notices in advertising. Although this example may seem exaggerated, perhaps you will enjoy it with me and recognize my point at the same time. In his book, The Art of Plain Talk, *Rudolf Flesch says the following: ". . . there are things John Citizen has to read whether he wants to or not. One of these must items is his income tax instructions; and they are—or were—written like this:*

> *(3)* Substantial Underestimate of Estimated Tax. *In the case of individuals other than farmers, if 80 percent of the tax (determined without regard to the credits for tax withheld on taxfree covenant bonds and for Income and Victory Tax withheld on wages) exceeds the estimated tax (increased by such credits), and in the case of farmers, if 66-2/3 percent of the tax (determined without regard to such credits) exceeds the estimated tax (increased by such credits), there shall be added to the tax an amount equal to such excess, or equal to 6 percent of the amount by which the tax so determined exceeds the estimated tax so increased, whichever is the lesser.*

. . . As your guide, I can tell you that it contains 107 words, 21 prepositions, 11 past participles, and 8 places where you have to do some arithmetic. And just to save you a sleepless night, here is the gist of it: if you guess your tax too low, you'll have to pay a fine but they can't fine you more than 6 per cent of your error."

Advertising is being asked to carry more and more legalese announcements, which are really unnecessary in today's consumer market and which complicate the message, reduce the effectiveness of the advertising without helping the consumer. . . .

I have addressed myself here to the use of language in creating advertising to sell goods and services on a national or regional basis. I know, as you do, that this is not the whole universe of advertising. In fact, figures published by your Commission show that the most frequent consumer complaints come from local *advertisers and business rather than national advertisers or larger regional companies. The 4A study of consumer attitudes indicated the same thing.*

Please do not make the rules required to stop the excesses on the periphery so broad and general that they smother enterprise and excellence at the core. If what I have said sounds as if I do not appreciate the difficulty or the necessity of your task, that is not so. If it sounds as if I am concerned about some of the things you have done and apprehensive about some of the things you might do, then I have used our language with reasonable effectiveness.

There are several scientific approaches to the study of words and languages (e.g., semantics and psycholinguistics) that we could have chosen to investigate whether the use of words in ads does manipulate consumers. Or we could have pursued the basic theme of psychological perception—first, by noting that the diversity of meanings discussed in Chapter 13 applies to any symbol, and then by reviewing the basic and applied literature specifically concerned with words (and sentences and paragraphs).

Mr. Seaman has taken another approach and has arrived, probably more effectively, at the same conclusion, namely, that it is not realistic to expect that advertising messages —or any other kind of message—can use words that are subject to *only one interpretation.*

Mr. Seaman reaches another conclusion that is familiar to behavioral scientists: words are one of the main vehicles by which humans interact. When this interaction concerns economic matters, we speak of buying and selling. Presumably, when words are used in buying-selling interactions, they have neither more nor less manipulative power than when they are used for interactions concerning education, religion, and politics. Furthermore, a large body of research suggests that the power of words sent through mass media is usually much lower than the power of words in face-to-face situations.[1] Thus, if advertising is subjected to more stringent regulation than other means of communication, we may be creating an unjustified and counterproductive double standard.

3 ADVERTISING, CHILDREN, AND DRUGS *(excerpts from Dr. S. Banks, vice president and manager of media and program research, Leo Burnett Co.; and from B. A. Cummings, chairman of the executive board, Compton Advertising)*

Since the beginning of this book, we have stressed that societies with advanced technology must rely heavily on mass communication. Although the information contained in ads is only a small part of the total information flowing through the mass communication system, advertising expenditures pay for much of the cost of the other information. Thus the advertising institution is directly responsible for the content of information in ads and indirectly responsible for the content of many specific programs, especially TV programs, that single advertisers may choose to support. (We pointed out in Chapter 12 that this does not include the content of editorials and general news programs.)

We now turn our attention to the possible effects of the advertising institution on particular segments of society—children, the aged, and the poor. The first testimony, by Dr. S. Banks, covers extensively many aspects of advertising directed to children. Dr. Banks provides data on viewing time, summarizes applicable research on child development, indicates how this research is used in developing products and ads directed at children, and sketches public attitudes toward such ads. Finally, he argues that child-oriented ads are a valuable component of the process of consumer socialization, preparing the child for eventual participation in the adult world.

INTRODUCTORY COMMENTS

. . . In today's marketing and advertising world, segmentation is the norm—campaigns are developed with specific groups of people in mind, defined in terms of geography,

---

[1] See the still classic findings concerning choice in the areas of breakfast food, fashion, and movies in E. Katz and P. F. Lazarsfeld, *Personal Influence,* Free Press, Glencoe, Ill., 1955. Not only do the roles of different channels of information in consumer decision processes vary a great deal, but the relative effect of these channels is highest for word-of-mouth among peers, much lower for salespeople, and lowest for mass media ads. This pattern of roles and relative effect has been found to apply to choices of new farming methods and new farming machinery by farmers, to doctors' choices of new prescription drugs, to the choice of air conditioners, the selection of auto insurance, and so on. For a brief summary of these basic and applied findings, see the appropriate readings in H. H. Kassarjian and T. S. Robertson (eds.), *Perspectives in Consumer Behavior,* Scott, Foresman & Co., Glenview, Ill., 1968; and J. A. Howard and L. E. Ostlund (eds.), *Buyer Behavior: Theoretical and Empirical Foundations,* A. A. Knopf, New York, 1973.

demographics, product usage, psychographics, or life style. Under this concept, all audiences are "special. . . . Nevertheless, we recognize that, for sincere emotional reasons, children are the most special of audiences and [we] intend to devote the bulk of our discussion to them. . . .

VOLUME OF ADVERTISING TO CHILDREN

In discussing advertising to children we shall concentrate on television because it seems to be of greatest concern and because the data are most easily available.

First, let me show you the data on set usage. . . . The average United States household uses its sets 42.2 hours a week on an annual average basis—more in the Fall and Winter, less in the Spring and Summer. Households with children, particularly those with children under the age of 6, use their sets 9 to 10 hours weekly more than average (Exhibit 14.26). . . .

Nielsen made a study of children's viewing of television in 1970 . . . (Exhibit 14.27). These data show that prime time, Monday–Sunday, 7:30–11:00 P.M., is the time when children's viewing is heaviest—this is the period of adult programming. Regularly scheduled network children's programming is shown with but few exceptions in the Saturday/Sunday, 8:00 A.M.-1:00 P.M. time period. This period receives 14% and 12% of the total viewing of children aged 2–5 and 6–11, respectively. In total clock time, this type of programming is watched 3.2 and 2.6 hours, again respectively.

We do not have any data that identifies the amount of time spent viewing Captain Kangaroo, a network program televised in the 8–10 A.M. period or to children's programs put on by individual stations, so let us arbitrarily double the time spent viewing weekend daytime programming. Hence, we are speaking of 5 to 6 hours a week of programming addressed to children and bearing child-oriented advertising.

Now a word about expenditures. According to Broadcast Advertisers Reports, an industry source of advertising expenditures, the 1970 advertising expenditures in TV network, weekend, daytime programming and Captain Kangaroo was $81 million. Again let us double that for local children's advertising—for a total of $162 million. This is 5.8% of all television advertising revenues in 1970 and 2-1/2 percent of all United States national media expenditures.

SUMMARY OF RESEARCH ON CHILD DEVELOPMENT

As part of our investigation, we have examined the available research literature from the fields of children's cognitive and attitudinal development as well as . . . the relatively small body of work dealing with television advertising's effect on children. . . .

A copy of that research summary is made available for your records. . . . This presentation will draw upon my interpretation of the significance of that material for the discussion at hand, although it must be stated that no brief statement can do justice to a vast and growing literature, containing disagreements among even the most well-qualified of experts.

One of the most significant findings of this investigation of infancy and childhood is the contrasting amount of attention paid to different areas. Two areas have received a great deal of attention—understanding the child's preparation for and performance

EXHIBIT 14.26

ESTIMATES OF AVERAGE HOURS OF TV USAGE PER WEEK
(7-Day 24-Hour Total)

NAD Report Periods	Households			Households By Household Size			Persons					
	Total	With Child −18	With Child −6	1-2	3-4	5+	Total	Men	Women	Teens	Child 2-5	Child 6-11
Oct. '70	42.48	50.53	54.62	34.22	45.19	55.05	23.52	21.81	28.15	17.65	23.36	20.77
Nov. '70	45.69	54.26	58.59	36.52	49.05	59.05	25.44	23.81	30.05	19.77	25.72	22.31
Dec. '70	45.48	53.53	57.93	36.80	47.68	59.66	25.62	23.98	29.20	20.17	27.03	24.17
Feb. '71	48.14	57.35	61.67	37.71	52.55	62.33	27.24	24.24	32.59	21.50	26.93	25.71
May '71	38.66	44.98	48.31	31.68	40.96	49.21	20.83	19.17	25.62	15.83	19.88	16.83
July '71	36.44	42.95	42.18	28.86	38.49	48.68	20.33	16.77	24.25	19.47	16.55	21.39
Straight average	42.82	50.60	53.88	34.30	45.65	55.66	23.83	21.63	28.31	19.07	23.25	21.86
Weighted average	42.25	49.90	52.93	33.82	45.08	54.93	23.49	21.15	28.03	18.94	22.62	21.66

Source: NTI

Weighted Average – Oct(8) Nov(4) Dec(6) Feb(10) May(10) July(10) = Total 48 Weeks.

EXHIBIT 14.27

CHILDREN'S VIEWING BY DAY PART, FALL, BY AGE
(All Times—Eastern Time Zone)

			Hours Viewed Per Week			
			2-5		6-11	
			#	%	#	%
Mon.-Sun.	7:30	– 11:00 P.M.	6.1	27	9.1	42
	11:00 P.M.	– 1:00 A.M.	*	1	0.6	3
Mon.-Fri.	7:00	– 10:00 A.M.	2.7	12	0.9	4
	10:00 A.M.	– 5:00 P.M.	5.0	22	2.4	11
	5:00	– 7:30 P.M.	3.4	15	3.5	16
Sat.-Sun.	8:00 A.M.	– 1:00 P.M.	3.2	14	2.6	12
	1:00	– 5:00 P.M.	0.9	4	1.3	6
	5:00	– 7:30 P.M.	1.1	5	1.3	6
			22.6	100%	21.7	100%

Source: Nielsen
    Set usage 1970/71 Season—% breakdown by day part Oct. 69.

Copyright 1971—A. C. Nielsen Company. This Confidential Report is Nielsen's property and is for the exclusive and confidential use of the Client to whom it is lent pursuant to contract. All persons are subject to liability for unauthorized use, reproduction, publication or divulgence of the contents or any portion thereof. The Nielsen estimates in this Confidential Report have been compiled by the Service referred to herein and are subject to the definitions and reminders contained in the Reports of Said Service.

in school; and the development of the attitudes and values he receives from or expresses in various social groupings, particularly families and peer groups. By contrast, very little basic research has dealt with the origins and dynamics of attitudes and behavior in the work-a-day world—his life as a worker or as a consumer.

With that caveat, let us turn now to the field of child development and attempt to draw out those items of greatest importance for this discussion. First and foremost, it is clear that a child's parents are the most significant influence in his life. This is not merely a question of discipline but the entire interaction process among the various members of the household, including the parents' responses to the child's own activities. A recent college text states:

> *Parents are the single most important determiner of the normal child's attitudes toward the world around him. Next in importance come the siblings in the family and the child's age-group companions during his formative years, then close relatives, school teachers, and religious leaders, and finally heroes and heroines the child reads about, hears about, or watches on television. For any given child, one may be able to find exceptions to this rank ordering, but in general it is a fairly accurate rating of influence. When parents are asked to draw up such a list, they often put such minor sources as television at the top of the list. In past generations, parents blamed their offspring's behavior on radio, comic books, pulp magazines, and, at the turn of the century, dime novels. These days, the "tube" bears the brunt of the projected blame. . . . What children make of television, and how it affects them, is determined to a large extent by what their parents teach them to make of it.* [1]

[1] *Developmental Psychology Today*, CRM Books, Del Mar, Calif., 1971, pp. 296–297.

A few paragraphs from Dr. Ner Littner, Director of the Extension Division and of the Child Therapy Training Program, Chicago Institute for Psychoanalysis, also bear on the question of parental influence on their children (see Appendix). He states on the basis of over 20 years of diagnostic and therapeutic work with both normal and disturbed children:

> *It has been demonstrated repeatedly that the nature of a child's mothering and fathering experiences in the first five years or so of his life is absolutely crucial to his mental and emotional development. For the child the adequacy of his care by his parents in these first five years is far more important than all of his television viewing. . . .*
>
> *When seen in this greater context, we must recognize that, if there are any harmful effects at all on children from watching TV advertising, their traumatic impact is like that of being stepped on by a fly as opposed to being trampled on by an elephant when contrasted with the effects of possible harmful handling by their parents. . . .*
>
> *It must be recognized that not all parents buy items advertised on TV just because they are pressured by their children. Parents do have a choice. When a parent fails to make a choice that is based on his judgment of what is right for the child, then the issue is not the impact of the TV advertising on the child. Rather, the issue must be laid squarely where it belongs: Why are the parents being ineffective in this crucial area? . . .*
>
> *Finally, we might give some thought to the fact that the impact of TV advertising on children pales by comparison with the force, the strength, the pressures, the bribes, the threats or the intimidations used by the average parent in his attempts to get his child to eat something that the parent considers important.*

. . . There continues to be fundamental support for parental warmth and permissiveness, but a question is now being raised as to the optimal level of such parental attitudes and behavior. Extreme parental hostility has been demonstrated to have undesirable consequences (when the child perceives it as such) but some authorities, such as Urie Bronfenbrenner and Diana Baumrind, are beginning to ask whether some spirited give-and-take within the household or even an occasional exchange of openly hostile interaction between parent and child may actually facilitate the child's ability to cope with the realities of independent living within our society and to express aggression in self-serving and pro-social causes and accept the occasional unpleasant consequences of such actions. There is support for the position that authoritative control by parents can achieve responsible conformity by the child with group standards without loss of individual autonomy or self-assertiveness.

One of the chief complaints made about advertising to children is that it puts parents into the awkward position of having to say "no" to their children. We're not advocating training parents to deny their children's requests but are pointing out that some experts in the field say that they need not fear that task either.

It's hard to put the child's own development second to parental influence since the most recent research has indicated amazing cognitive interest and development among even the youngest of infants. There are two errors one can fall into in dealing with children's cognitive abilities. . . . One can either believe that children are infinitely malleable and subject to manipulation by a simple stimulus-response mechanism; or he might treat them as adults, small in stature but possessed of mature decision-making powers. Obviously, the truth lies in avoiding both of these extremes, in good part, by recognizing that children exhibit an age-graded pattern of development.

The last decade has seen a very substantial expansion of both theoretical developments and empirical research into children's intellectual processes. Nevertheless, there is not one but two major theories or concepts of the learning process. One is associated with Jean Piaget and suggests structural stages of intellectual capabilities or powers . . . however, Piaget emphasizes the child's working on his environment as the force moving him from one stage to the next rather than biological development. The other approach draws from learning theory but is much more sophisticated than the classical conditioning concepts associated with Pavlov or Watson because they were unable to explain such developments within the child as symbolic representation, categorization, and problem-solving. The newer learning theory approach considers both external inputs and the child's own internal situation —his developmental status, past experience, and motivational state. . . .

Let us summarize the literature as emphasizing that the impetus to learn is within the child [who] strives to learn within the limits of his physiological capabilities and the emotional climate and cultural pattern of the family and social groups of which he is a part. The old stimulus-response model is inadequate to deal with long-run developmental processes since the perceptual powers of the child help determine or select the stimuli he responds to.

Although there is substantial difference on why things happen as they do, there is fairly general agreement on the facts of child development. It is clear that the period prior to school entrance is one in which children are being prepared (by a combination of internal and external forces) for formal schooling, for a switch from concrete operations on things to abstract or symbolic thought processes. It is suggested that the almost universal practice of sending children to school at ages 5 to 7 indicates that society is responding to the massive changes in perception, cognition, and behavior that occur at this time rather than vice versa. Below the age of four, children's perceptual, cognitive, and vocabulary skills are still incomplete and quite simplified in organization, hence lacking in discrimination and inconsistent in classification schemes. However, after that, the richness of the child's intellectual apparatus increases dramatically both quantitatively and qualitatively. The early school years show a continuation of growth of perceptual and cognitive skills. . . .

Parallel to the development of the child's cognitive and intellectual capacity is the development of his value system. Again we see a similar age-graded pattern of development since the level or content of moral conformity a person develops, his appreciation of the proper sex role, and the rudiments of both the emotional structure of aggressive motivation and repertoire of aggressive behavior are likely to be formed during the child's first four or five years.

Peer groups start to be influential in children's lives somewhere between 2 and 3 years of age, usually. However, such influence seems to peak during the early school years although the specific age at which this peak appears apparently varies, depending upon class, race, or other cultural factors.

ILLUSTRATION OF THE USE OF RESEARCH IN DEVELOPING CHILDREN'S PRODUCTS

. . . As part of the preparation for this presentation, a number of manufacturers and agencies were asked about their use of consumer research. . . . The director of marketing research for a major toy manufacturer started her answer by stating:

First, as I believe you are well aware, our Marketing Research Department does most of its consumer research prior to the time when the product is turned over to the advertising agency, that is during the product's development. We know, as I am sure you do, that no type or amount of advertising will successfully sell a product to the consumer unless the product itself is "right." All of our consumer research studies have as their ultimate objective, coming up with the "right" product. The "right" product must have an inherent appeal, must be optimally engineered for mechanical precision and safety, [and] user dexterity; and it must be durable, that is, able to stand up to prolonged play by its user.

. . . Many firms bring mothers into their consumer research effort, either in addition to children or in their place, especially small companies who don't have a formal research staff. An interesting case of mother-testing was:

. . . a girls' hair care device for girls 8–11. We were concerned about possible mother's hostility to "rushing" the maturation of her child, about her estimate of the toy's appeal, and about her interaction with her daughter via the vehicle of hair care and fashion. We were delighted to find very positive attitudes, incidentally. Had the mothers objected, the product would have been dropped. As it was, changes were made in the directions and package copy to reinforce the positives the mothers saw.

Several of my respondents—all from large companies—work with outside consultants from the fields of child psychology and education at leading universities. For example, a major toy company writes that one complete line was 2-1/2 years in development under the constant supervision of the head of a pre-school project at a major graduate school of education. . . .

ILLUSTRATION OF THE USE OF CONSUMER RESEARCH IN DEVELOPING AND EVALUATING ADVERTISING ADDRESSED TO CHILDREN

General Background Studies

A major advertising agency has had a child psychologist in its Research Department for many years to aid its creative and research people in developing and evaluating advertising addressed to children. Here are some highlights from a document circulated in the agency, prepared on the basis of comments in the literature on children's behavior and development plus more than one hundred lengthy interviews with children she or co-workers conducted:

Traditionally, in advertising, we consider children in the age range from 5 to 6 through 12 as one body. Yet, as we all know, little kids are quite different from big kids, therefore there is a need to approach them differently in our commercials. I'd like to talk to you about how the child in the early years of school, from age 5 to 8, looks at the world, and then compare this with the view of the child in later grades, age 9 to 12.

The Child from 5 to 8

Bigger is Better. *At this stage of development, the child is diminutive in relation to his environment—he sits in a chair and his feet dangle, the ceiling of a room seems awfully high from his vantage point. . . . The child quickly learns to associate large size with power and superiority. Thus the child from five to eight years is keenly interested in things which might physically enhance his self-concept in relation to his environment: he wants to grow taller, and to acquire big things, to go fast, and to be strong.*

Best Age—A Little Bit Older. *What is the best age anybody could be? For the five- through eight-year old this age seems to be just a little bit older than they are right now. Children said they wanted to be old enough to be bigger, or as one girl put it, "to be twelve, because twelve is a high number."*

Limited Life Space. *Another characteristic of the child under nine years seems to be that he lives in a rather limited life space, and is most comfortable with things that are familiar to him. . . .*

Mother and Father: The Models and Criterion. *Within the limited life space of the child under nine, the mother and father provide the models he seeks to emulate. Young girls wanted to be mothers or nurses. Actually the nurse is a paid, professional mother.*

Things in Abundance. *Having an abundance of things he really likes also seems to give the child a feeling of power. Walt Disney Productions has a new movie called "One Hundred and One Dalmatians." Part of the charm of this movie is that at the end a child gets to keep all those 101 Dalmatians. . . .*

Heroes. *A popular fantasy for children under nine is that of being an authority figure, a mom, or a dad, a policeman or such. Dolls and other toys serve as excellent vehicles for these fantasies as they are small-scale models of things in the real world. Pets, too, give the child a chance to try out adult powers. . . .*

There are two other types of heroes appreciated by the five- to eight-year-old child. These are contradictory hero types, representing contradictory sides of the child's nature at this stage. . . . The first, the "authority upsetter," is portrayed by a comparatively small figure. His job is to upset the calm, or deflate the ego, of a larger figure. . . . The Tom and Jerry cartoons exemplify this approach—Jerry always out-maneuvers Tom. The "conformist" hero type, on the other hand, is the one who always manages to retain the image of the model child. Corey of the "Julia" program generally is the recipient of Julia's praise—his behavior constantly reminding us that he is a "good boy."

The Child from 9 to 12

Now let's climb up the ladder of child development a few rungs and speak about the child from nine through twelve years.

Acculturation. *By this age the child has digested many of the cultural values of our society and hence we see in him goals which are more similar to our own, though obviously narrower in scope. . . .*

A New Arena—The Peer Group. *By nine the child is physically capable of participating seriously in competitive sports. He is no longer content with playing with toys and pets. Instead he now wants to demonstrate his newly acquired prowess through peer group activity and to achieve recognition among his peers in his goal. Good deeds seem to have value too. Thus, one child was proud of saving a bird's life and another of helping a chipmunk out of a bear trap.*

Expanding Life Space. *Boys frequently chose locales to visit mentally that offered sporting opportunities: Minnesota, the Swiss Alps, Hawaii. The trips for girls, on the other hand, emphasized people and sights. . . .*

Goals Become Individual. *Another difference was evident in their plans for the future. While the younger child most often thought about the future in terms of what his parents are like, for the nine- to twelve-year-old, goals and future are individual things.*

The Best Age—Adolescence and Young Adulthood. *The best age anybody could be for the nine- to twelve-year-old, generally was either the years of adolescence, or those of young adulthood, from thirteen through twenty-one years. Both boys and girls now strongly associate the best age with achievement of independence. . . .*

Heroes Become Sex-Differentiated. *Each sex begins to seek a hero from among his own sex. Girls prefer TV shows in which a female has the leading role or is at least the object of some man's desire. Boys seek out more aggressive "masculine" heroes. . . .*

What Makes Children Laugh?

Slapstick is a type of humor that has appeal for all ages. An element of slapstick action that is used quite a bit is falling: for instance, somebody always seems to be falling down in children's animated cartoons. . . . This seems to illustrate the close relationship between humor and anxiety. Afraid of falling themselves, children laugh when it happens to others.

The Absurd and Impossible. *The absurd joining together of events is another way to provoke laughter among children of all ages. For example, a car that can talk or a lion that cries. . . . A word of caution, however, for using such devices with the kid market. While children certainly seem to enjoy the fantastical devices, they may not always comprehend the point being made. For example, a child may want to buy Imperial margarine because he might get a* crown, *rather than because it tastes good enough for a king.*

Verbal Humor Should Be Tied to Action. *Another means of provoking humor is the word pun or the phrase with double meanings. . . . Further visualizing the verbal pun with action makes the pun far more effective. . . .*

Findings from Research on Commercials

Professor Wells' article on communicating with children, both as research subjects and as the audience to commercials, essentially corroborates many of these comments.[1]
. . . First of all, children have a different view of "reality" than do adults, whether one is dealing with the actual physical world or the world of fantasy. Wells states that children are willing to grant a program producer or advertiser the poetic license required by almost any fantastic situation but demand conformity to the rules of that situation. . . .

Wells suggests that it is more accurate to refer to a child's acceptance of a commercial as "not scorned" or "not rejected" rather than "believed." He states that most children do not actually believe that monsters exist or that a candy bar will make a child strong enough to conquer an adult; however, disbelief is suspended if the commercial meets the child's test of reality. But if the monster turns out to be "blobs and globs and all kinds of dumb stuff like that" or if the child-hero stops to deliver a message from the sponsor in the middle of a fight with a gang of crooks, the commercial has violated the rules of the game and the verdict is merciless.

Since children do not handle abstractions well and are not adept at verbal associations, effective communications to them require showing them the product in graphic motion, particularly doing something that demonstrates the product's qualities or ability to satisfy his wants. . . .

Case Histories

Let me close this section of my presentation with two case histories. The advertising agency for a cereal company states:

We conduct research among children to develop advertising and products based on determining children's needs and desires. We do not attempt to alter them through advertising but, rather, we alter advertising to be compatible with the existing child attitudes. . . . our standard procedures . . . are: (1) determine what aspect of the product children perceive as most important; (2) determine what type of advertising children enjoy, i.e., cartoons or straight facts, or live with other children, etc.; (3) develop advertising that deals with the aspect of the product the children have told us is most important to them, avoiding any type of communication they have told us would turn them off; (4) when we test among children . . . we try to find out which of our ideas they like best or if there is an idea we have not considered that they like better. . . .

[1]W. D. Wells, "Communicating with Children," *Journal of Advertising Research*, June 1965.

The advertising agency for a toy manufacturer writes:

(1) If a toy or game prototype is considered acceptable for inclusion in the line on the basis of testing with children of the appropriate ages, and further, as a TV advertised item, two story-boards . . . are developed. These are filmed in color with soundtrack, and tested against controls among the target group using essentially our normal sampling and interviewing procedures as above. (2) If one of the commercials qualifies per our norms, it goes into production following those changes and/or additions suggested by the storyboard tested. If neither qualify we start from scratch. (3) The filmed commercial is then tested at the interlock stage, against controls (in interlock form) and among the appropriate target group. Similar methodology applies. If it qualifies, changes suggested by the test are made and the commercial finished. Over the past six years, we have conducted between 150 and 200 tests; . . .

PUBLIC ATTITUDES TOWARD TV ADVERTISING TO CHILDREN

On the basis of public opinion surveys, the American public is predominantly in favor of the principle of advertising to children, although they criticize particular commercials. Between December 1959 and November 1968, Roper Research Associates conducted six studies of public attitudes toward television and other media for the Televison Information Office. In January 1971, the Roper Organization conducted a seventh such study (Burns Roper, former president of Roper Research Associates, is now president of The Roper Organization, Inc.; otherwise there is no connection between the two firms).

These studies have found, over the years, that most Americans take commercials well in stride and only 1 out of 10 disagree with the statement that having commercials on TV is a fair means of supporting it (see Appendix). The proportion of respondents selecting favorable statements toward commercials has risen slowly but steadily since 1963 when this subject was introduced in the questionnaire, from 55% to 62%. A steady 10% have said that they dislike practically all commercials. A question designed to elicit attitudes toward the U.S. system of supporting television by commercial sponsorship, showed a 5 to 1 ratio of acceptance of this concept in 1963 but leaped to 8 to 1 in 1964 and this ratio has held constant (see Appendix).

Because some concern had been expressed about commercials in children's television programs, the January 1971 survey added two questions about the possible elimination of such commercials. The question and the results are as follows:

Now, I'd like to ask you about commercials on children's television programs—and I mean all kinds of children's programs. Some people think there shold be no commercials in any kind of children's programs because they feel children can be too easily influenced. Other people, while perhaps objecting to certain commercials, by and large see no harm in them and think children learn from some of them. How do you feel—that there should be no commercials on any children's program or that it is all right to have them if they don't take unfair advantage of children?

| | | People Who Have Children | | |
| | Total Sample % | Under 6 years old only % | 6–16 years old only % | Both under and over 6 years old % |
On Children's Programs:				
Should be no commercials	18	20	18	21
All right to have them	74	78	79	78
Don't know or no answer	8	2	3	1

To test the strength of negative feelings, respondents who answered "no commercials" were asked a further question:

If eliminating all commercials on children's TV programs meant considerably reducing the number of children's programs, which would you favor...?

	%
Eliminating the commercials and considerably reducing the number of children's programs, or	7
Keeping the commercials to keep the children's programs	9
Don't know or no answer	2
Total "should be no commercials on children's programs"	18

Obviously, one key but unanswered question has to do with people's opinions as to commercials taking unfair advantage of children. We can merely infer people's opinions from their answers to the first question but not definitively so. Nevertheless, it is worth pointing out that the vote on having commercials in children's programs, given the stated qualifier, was 4 to 1 in favor of the principle and that that ratio obtained among the parents of young children to the same degree as among those without children. When those who felt there should be no commercials were asked, if push came to shove and they had to make a Hobson's choice between programs with commercials versus considerably fewer programs, fully half voted to allow the use of commercials to keep the programs. However, the same small minority against commercials showed up again—7% of the sample were willing to reduce the number of children's programs by eliminating commercials.

Putting the two sets of responses together, the Roper survey indicates five out of every six Americans are in general support of the current principle of supporting children's programs by advertising—and this figure holds for parents of young children as well. This figure is conservative since it assumes that those responding "don't know" or giving "no answer" were really opposed to the proposition.

JUSTIFICATION FOR ADVERTISING TO CHILDREN

We feel it is useful to discuss some basic research on children's response to advertising as the springboard for the presentation of a social justification for the practice of advertising child-oriented products directly to children.

As was said previously, it is an amazing contrast to turn from the fields of educational psychology, child-rearing behavior, and child development through the literature on mass media to studies of television advertising and children. One is immediately struck with the paucity of the literature in the last field; perhaps this is due to the nature of the advertising industry, research is regarded as having competitive value and is therefore kept confidential. However, we believe there is a real lack of research from which we all suffer.

Of the relatively few published research studies dealing with children's responses to advertising, Professor Ward's is of greatest interest to us. Incidentally, an example of the current research climate is the fact that, of the 23 current research projects approved by the Surgeon General's Scientific Advisory Committee on Television and

Social Behavior, only one, that of Professor Scott Ward, dealt with commercials, while twelve dealt with aggression or violence. We know he will discuss his work with you but we want to point out that his interest was on the process by which children develop their attitudes, skills, and norms relative to consumption behavior—the process of consumer socialization. One of his findings was that even teenagers did not necessarily go out and buy after being exposed to advertising; instead they talked to their parents about the advertising, the nature and qualities of the goods offered for sale and about the buying and consumption process in general.

The discussion which follows on the value of the consumer socialization is based primarily upon suggestions by social psychologists and conjecture rather than upon hard data derived from studies in these areas, which, incidentally, are lacking. However, they are quite compatible with discussions that one finds in the literature on child-rearing practices.

We suggest that the social justification for advertising to children arises from the process of consumer socialization—experience as a purchaser—both in its own right and as a training ground for other types of decision-making. A significant test of maturity is the ability to make reasonably good choices and decisions in a wide variety of circumstances. We believe that the discussions children have with their parents about product purchases as a result of exposure to advertising, as well as experience with actual purchases, contributes to maturation, Involved in this long and painful process (but no more so than other maturation processes) is the learning of the proper criteria to use in evaluating products, the value of money spent now for several small items versus the purchase of a larger item later, the determination of the standards appropriate to a particular age, class and way of life, and finally, the development of character.

The ultimate result of this experience in making decisions and appreciating their consequences, within a framework created by his parents as appropriate for him, is that the child builds a sense of responsibility for his own actions, stronger and more resilient than if he is asked to be or is made responsible about choices others make for him. In addition to the creation of self-confidence, the child learns to know what he himself wants. Knowledge of one's self arises from experience in making decisions and knowing their ultimate results.

One might express concern about a child's ability to participate meaningfully in the process. However, during the period of a child's greatest susceptibility to persuasion—say, under the age of 5, he makes few purchases on his own. Instead, his parents are the actual purchasers. As he grows older, his growing maturity earns him an allowance to spend with much more freedom—typically, the allowance increases with maturity; this maturity, as we have seen, in a wide variety of research studies, including Ward's, gives him the basis of making more selective choices and drawing inferences from the consequences of those choices. . . .

RESEARCH PROPOSAL

To us, the most significant insight that has come to us in the course of preparation for this presentation is the realization of a great vacuum in our knowledge. In the scientific sense, we know almost nothing about the processes by which children develop their skills of purchasing and consuming. . . .

We wish to call attention to the lack of basic research on the processes by which children learn about the meaning of money and its various uses; the practices of budgeting and planned purchases versus impulse buying; the criteria for choosing one product or brand over another, etc.—in short, the various roles or activities that individuals perform as consumers.

These data will be of great significance both in their own right and as inputs for policy decision-making. For example, we believe it is difficult to plan for educational programs to improve people's buying practices without knowing what those practices are, their origins, and their dynamics.

In addition, we are interested in longitudinal studies in which children are followed up through adolescence into adulthood to determine whether there are long-run subtle effects from exposure to advertising which can be distinguished from the effects of other aspects of their entire cultural milieu. Therefore we are presenting a list of some basic questions which are illustrative of the issues we feel demand investigation before any action program can be responsibly undertaken (Exhibit 14.28).

EXHIBIT 14.28

PROPOSAL FOR BASIC RESEARCH ON THE PROCESSES BY WHICH CHILDREN ACQUIRE KNOWLEDGE AND ATTITUDES TOWARD CONSUMER ROLE

Some basic questions:

1 What is the relationship between general patterns of child-rearing practices and attitudes and practices of consumer socialization of children? What roles do parents' own budgeting and financial practices play as a direct or mediating variable on children's attitudes and practices? How do these practices vary by class, urban-suburban-rural, race, etc.? Practices of the poor are of particular interest.

2 How do children learn about purposes of advertising? What exactly do parents say? At what age does this start? What is role of siblings, peers, teachers in this process?

3 How do parents handle children's request for advertised products? In what ways is this procedure related to those used for other types of requests? How is this affected by parents' demographic and psychological characteristics?

4 From what sources do children acquire their knowledge and attitudes toward money and its uses? What are current practices in giving children spending money—allowances, individual requests, etc.—and demanding accountability? How do these vary by children's ages and characteristics of households?

5 What is the relationship between children's attitudes toward and use of money and other personal characteristics: aggression, conformity, IQ, moral character? How do these relationships vary by child's age and demographic status?

For our part, we pledge effort to get this program of research started.

THE AGED AND THE POOR

In today's American population, there are more aged and poor than there are children; nor, in the scale of human values, are their needs less important. However, these groups are much more diffused and heterogeneous than are children. Almost, by definition, these groups represent much less purchasing potential than their numbers indicate. . . . because of the difficulty of pinpointing these groups through the processes of media selection and the relatively low return if one does, the advertising community has sought to find means, other than advertising, of helping these segments of our population.

Perhaps the chief instrument used for this purpose is the Advertising Council. We are making their Annual Report a part of this presentation. Some of their 1970 campaigns of particular significance to the aged and the poor were: Drug Abuse Information, Continue Your Education, Rehabilitation of the Handicapped, Technical Education and Training, Minority Business Enterprise, National Alliance of Businessmen, and United Community Campaigns.

In addition, individual companies are attempting to cope with the problems of the aged and the poor through the development of special products or educational efforts. For example, a major cereal company has charged a senior marketing executive with responsibility for nutritional projects designed for special categories of the population such as low-income ethnic groups; the equivalent of at least one full-time staff nutritionist will be involved in contributing to nutritional programs beyond the normal scope of business; they also set up a budget for special programs designed to reach out to low-income people with nutritional education messages.

Dr. Banks has referred to several appendices and other documents submitted to the FTC as part of his testimony, but we shall not reproduce this material here for the sake of brevity. Also for the sake of brevity, we shall not reproduce the items submitted as part of the testimony by B. A. Cummings on the possible relationships between the advertising institution and the use of drugs. From Mr. Cummings' testimony we learn the following:

. . . Let me take just one area: drug abuse and the drug culture. The question has been raised about whether advertising of over-the-counter drugs encourages or even induces widespread use of hard drugs by the young. This is a most serious question. Unfortunately, so far as we know, there is no conclusive answer.

We are deeply concerned as a business, and I am equally concerned as an individual, about the drug problem. You may not know that my company, Compton Advertising, was the anchor agency for the Advertising Council anti-drug abuse advertising campaign for the Department of Defense, the Department of Health, Education and Welfare, and the Department of Justice. In addition to the months devoted to preparation of advertising materials for the campaign, my colleagues and I spent countless weeks going over all available evidence, research, and experience of the best practitioners and institutions in the field, as well as agonizing interviews with addicts.

This experience has reinforced my opinion that little is known about the real causes of drug addiction. To substantiate this opinion, I would like to insert five items into the record:

1 The full list of the National Commission on Marijuana and Drug Abuse, chaired by by Raymond P. Shafer, former Governor of Pennsylvania, a commission authorized to spend $4,000,000, and remarkable for the scope and eminence and diversity of its members.

2 *A letter dated October 6, 1970, from Michael J. Halberstam, M.D., with his views on the lack of causal relationship between drug advertising and drug abuse.*

3 *A letter dated September 4, 1970, from Maurice H. Seevers, M.D. and Ph.D., Chairman of the Department of Pharmacology at the University of Michigan, with his views on the lack of causal relationship between advertising of over-the-counter drugs and drug abuse.*

4 *A reprint of an article from* Family Health Magazine, *issue of May 1971, an interview by Judith Ramsey with Henry Brill, M.D., with his views about the lack of a causal relationship between advertising of medications and drug abuse.*

5 *With the permission of the Proprietary Association, for which it was prepared, a report of the social scientists' studies on this subject, prepared by the research firm of Oxtoby-Smith.*

For some of the questions raised during our presentation, there simply may be no available answer. I would add that this is a fact, and that opinion is no substitute. We have, however, tried to answer with fact and research your questions about children and whether consumers are subject to exploitation or manipulation. We have described the safeguards we set up, and the process and measurement of advertising. . . .

4 SUMMARY

After having studied in Chapter 13 whether or not the advertising institution *can* manipulate consumers, we turned in this chapter to the question of whether it in fact *does.* Mr. Achenbaum presented data concerning nineteen brands in very heavily advertised product classes. He found evidence that confirmed the points made in Part 1 and in the beginning chapters of this part: consumers show a great deal of independent initiative in their purchasing behavior and respond to many factors, especially their personal experience with the purchased brands.

Mr. Seaman examined the power of words, not only in ads but in all human relationships. From his humanistic perspective, he reached the same conclusion that would have been provided by voluminous scientific evidence: any interaction among humans has an effect on each of them; words are one of the means by which humans interact; and thus words do have an effect.

As is true of any other stimulus, words have different meanings to different people. In advertising, as in other cases, the sender must realize, and adapt to, this subjectivity of meaning. The senders of ads use words for the explicit purpose of gaining the attention of the seeker/receiver and, hopefully, of persuading him to try this or that brand. There is no reason to think that words may have more or less persuasive power—in a manipulative sense—in advertising than in any other context.

On the contrary, words may well have more power when used by parents, siblings, peers, teachers, and ministers to shape the cognitive and emotional growth of children. This theme underlies the testimony of Dr. Banks. Primary groups are the main sources of influence and socialization: whatever a child makes out of an ad, a TV program, a newspaper headling, a radio announcement, or the picture of a woman on a magazine cover is largely determined by what his society has taught him about life.

Of course, it is also true that the entire mass communication system of a society—including the advertising institution—has a socialization role for adults as well as for children.[1] And by their reactions, as measured by the media to which they expose themselves, children and adults will affect society's mass communication system, a typical chicken-egg situation, such as we have already seen in our previous discussion of the possible relationships between the advertising institution and the economy (see Chapter 11, Section 3.2).

In practice, we know very little about these macro relationships. And what we do know through theoretical and empirical research simply confirms common sense. For instance, an increasing body of literature shows that TV violence tends to have some undesirable effects on some children under certain conditions. The review of past evidence and the addition of new evidence contained in the five-volume report to the U.S. Surgeon General points in the same direction.[2]

But the practical question concerning violence or pornography in television or in any other medium is not whether these effects exist, but whether we can distinguish between what is part of human life and human nature and what is simply cheap cliché. That is to say, all the information flowing through a society's mass communication system will always reflect, as well as affect, the moral fiber of a social group. A recent article captures this dilemma most effectively:

> *Violence in the media is merely . . . [an] expression of the passions that . . . suffuse wide areas of our collective life. It is fatuous to argue that these forces would abate if the media were to ban all showings of Macbeth and confine newscasts to the happy side of life, as some have already done. Yet we cannot dismiss the importance of TV violence merely because other, much more powerful forces are also at large to stimulate aggressive fantasies and to arouse emotions that lead to aggresive acts.*
>
> *Violence can never be eliminated from TV [or other media], because violence is part of life and part of art. As long as . . . news reporting stays free, the violence and brutality of our real world should and will be reflected in it. And as long as TV gives time to plays and films of artistic integrity, it will show violence as a dramatic aspect of human affairs.*
>
> *As every TV professional knows, the real issue is not the use of violence that honestly reflects the passions and conflicts of our troubled world age. The issue is the deliberate use of cliché violence, violence contrived to formula, violence as a commodity that can be packaged for sale.*[3]

---

[1] Advertising's contributions to children's socialization is the focus of inquiry of a recent series of studies; see, e.g., S. Ward and D. Wackman, "Family and Media Influences on Adolescent Consumer Learning," *American Behavioral Scientist,* January/February 1971.

[2] Surgeon General's Scientific Advisory Committee on Television and Social Behavior, *Television and Growing Up: The Impact of Televised Violence,* Report to the Surgeon General, U.S. Public Health Service, Government Printing Office, Washington, D.C., 1972. For recent findings based on extensive field experiments, see I. Milgram and R. Lance Shotland, *Television and Antisocial Behavior,* Academic Press, New York, 1973.

[3] L. Bogart, "Warning: The Surgeon General Has Determined That TV Violence Is Moderately Dangerous to Your Child's Mental Health," *Public Opinion Quarterly,* Winter 1972–73, p. 519.

All in all, the testimonies in this chapter call to our attention that the behavior of the advertising institution, and especially the information flowing through it, is merely a reflection of the much larger forces of society and its institutions.

There will be no successful regulation of society's mass communication system, and of the advertising institution, unless the enormous influence of parents, peers, teachers, churches, and other groups on the behavior of children and adults is taken into consideration.

Let us consider an example to locate one focus of responsibility. Those who are over forty may remember that at one time parents *compelled* their children to go to bed after dinner. There were exceptions, of course; for example, if a child were failing in school, he might have been compelled to stay up and study. But now many parents *allow* children to stay up after dinner to look at television. The order of magnitude of this responsibility was shown in Exhibit 14.27. The amount of time that children between the ages of two and five are allowed to spend in front of a TV set after 5:00 P.M. equals 47 percent of their total TV viewing time; for children between six and eleven, it amounts to 67 percent.[1]

Attempts to regulate only ads—or other media content—are equivalent to attempts to straighten out a tree by working on its leaves rather than on its trunk. By the same token, however, a tree cannot be strong and beautiful if we do not prune away dead leaves and sick branches. Regulation here can be very useful to all concerned. In the next chapter we examine present trends in regulation and self-regulation.

---

[1] It is puzzling to observe that many academicians and other groups quote only daytime viewing by children; see, e.g., M. E. Goldberg and G. J. Gorn, "An Experimental Approach to the Effects of Television Advertising on Children," in S. Divita (ed.), *Advertising and the Public Interest*, American Marketing Association, Chicago, Ill., 1974.

Chapter 15

Public Regulation and Self-Regulation

OUTLINE

1 **Reflections on Regulation by the Federal Trade Commission** (excerpts from L. Loevinger, attorney, Hogan & Hartson, and former member of the Federal Communications Commission)

2 **Self-Regulation: New Developments** (excerpts from H. H. Bell, president, American Advertising Federation)

3 **Summary**

Since the golden age of Greece, Western man has attempted to find a balance between the rights and responsibilities of the individual and the rights and responsibilities of the group in which he lives. In principle, this balance can be easily defined in terms of individualistic values. Each member of society is free to live the life he wants. The freedom of any one member cannot, however, limit the freedom of any other. Thus, each person's freedom can exist only if the freedom of others is recognized. Personal freedom, in practice, is defined by the limits set by the respect of others' right to freedom.

Historically, however, it has proved difficult to implement this principle. In Western societies, most laws and many institutions have developed in an attempt to reconcile the interests of the individual with those of the community. But conflicts of interest are not limited to those between one individual and the entire community; groups also may be in conflict. In the case of the advertising institution, for example, we noted in Chapter 1 that the media have historically been caught between the pressures of changing technology and changing life styles. And, in Chapter 3, we saw that the birth of advertising agencies resulted from stresses caused by the social and economic changes in the United States during the past century.

In this context, the task of legislators, public agencies, and courts is highly complex. We have ample evidence of how each firm searches for a group of consumers with whom it can establish rapport, and how each consumer actively searches for a firm whose brand has the attributes he prefers. We also saw that the advertising institution emerged as an attempt to find an economically rational solution to the problem posed by the need for an almost infinite number of contacts among agents sending and/or seeking information.

But how can we assure that these searches are conducted within lawful boundaries? That no false information flows through the institutions? That no individual or group is unduly favored or handicapped? And that the public interest is not only protected but, in fact, better served?

There are essentially two institutional paths through which we can work toward fair answers to the above questions. One is public regulation—laws, rules, and court decisions; the other is self-regulation by participants in the advertising institution itself. The testimonies that follow deal with these two approaches.

1   REFLECTIONS ON REGULATION BY THE FEDERAL TRADE COMMISSION
(excerpts from L. Loevinger, attorney, Hogan & Hartson, and former member of the Federal Communications Commission)

The testimony of L. Loevinger is addressed to the question of how laws, rules, and court decisions can reconcile the ever-present conflict between the interests of the individual and those of society. Mr. Loevinger stresses the role of the FTC in the regulation of the advertising institution.

After reviewing the statutory power and constitutional mandate of the commission, he points out that in recent times the FTC has tended to assume an activist role. Such a role, he asserts, changes the nature of regulation. He argues that, rather than working to attain a balance between the rights of the individual and those of the state, the commissions's present activities tend to favor the state over the individual. He then discusses the problems that emerge when a public agency (whose five commissioners are appointed rather than elected) takes on an activist role in promoting social change.

. . . In the following statement I have sought to distill what I have been able to learn from . . . experience, augmented by some research on the present subject, into a coherent view of the proper relationship of contemporary government, specifically the FTC, to the oversight of advertising.

WHAT IS ADVERTISING?

. . . . In its most basic meaning, to advertise is to give notice, to inform, to notify, or to make known. The term comes from the same root as "advert" which means to turn the mind or attention to. Thus advertising is any form of public announcement which is intended to attract public notice. . . . This ancient and well-established meaning of the term is illustrated by the Shakespearean aphorism, "We are advertised by our loving friends."[1]

The FTC is not, however, concerned with the broadest meaning of the term, although it must be aware of it, but rather with advertising in its commercial usage. In this sense advertising means a paid public announcement and is commonly a form of selling. . . . We are all familiar with the great variety of functions that advertising

[1] William Shakespeare, *King Henry VI,* Act V, Scene 3, line 18.

performs in the modern media. However, these are not new. In The Tatler *for September 14, 1710, the editor said:*

> Advertisements are of great use to the vulgar. First of all, as they are instruments of ambition. A man that is by no means big enough for the Gazette may easily creep into the advertisements. . . . A second use which this sort of writings have been turned to of late years, has been the management of Controversy. . . . The third and last of these writings is to inform the World where they may be furnished with almost everything that is necessary for Life. If a Man has Pains in His head, Choloc in his Bowels, or spots in his Cloathes, he may here meet with proper Cures and Remedies. If a Man would recover a Wife or a Horse that is stolen or strayed; if he wants new Sermons, Electuaries, Asses' milk, or anything else, either for his Body or his Mind, this is the place to look for them in.[1]

Similarly, criticisms of advertising are centuries old. In 1758 Dr. Samuel Johnson said:

> Advertisements are now so numerous that they are very negligently perused, and is therefore become necessary to gain attention by magnificence of promises and by eloquence sometimes sublime and sometimes pathetick. Promise, large promise, is the soul of an advertisement. . . . The trade of advertising is now so near to perfection that it is not easy to propose any improvement.[2]

In the Eighteenth and Nineteenth Centuries advertisers were not very responsive to criticism. However, in the Twentieth Century there has been a voluntary assumption of responsibility by advertisers and a response to criticism and elevation of standards. In 1911, Printer's Ink, *a leading advertising journal, sponsored a model statute which made dishonest advertising a misdemeanor, put the responsibility for untruthful, deceptive, or misleading statements on the advertiser and held the advertiser responsible for statements of fact but not of opinion. . . . In 1912, the Associated Advertising Clubs of the World adopted the motto, "Truth in advertising" and established a National Vigilance Committee in the United States. . . . This committee has since developed into the National Better Business Bureau and has also organized a large number of local bureaus with the same goal.*

It is notable that these efforts were undertaken long before the Federal Trade Commission Act was passed. The result of these efforts, and of the growing sense of social responsibility among advertisers, has been a steady increase in standards throughout the Twentieth Century. . . . In 1937 the National Association of Broadcasters promulgated an advertising code for radio, and in 1952 for television; and both codes have been actively enforced since then.

In the spring and summer of 1971 a National Advertising Review Board was established through joint efforts of the Association of National Advertisers, the American Association of Advertising Agencies, the American Advertising Federation, and the Council of Better Business Bureaus [see next testimony].

---

[1]*Encyclopedia Britannica*, title "Advertising."

[2]*The Idler*, January 20, 1758.

WHAT IS THE BASIS OF CURRENT CONTROVERSY ABOUT ADVERTISING?

The question that confronts us now is: What are the issues that have engendered the present FTC concern about advertising? The Commission has announced that this proceeding is merely an inquiry designed to inform the Commission, but the announcement of the proceeding inevitably suggests certain assumptions.[1] *There appear to be four major assumptions which underlie this proceeding. These are: (a) that advertising may unfairly exploit human emotions, (b) that new techniques of advertising may facilitate deception, (c) that advertising may have some special effect on children, and (d) that the FTC should be concerned with more than the truthfulness and accuracy of advertising and should somehow seek to monitor its emotional and psychological effects.*

In addition to these assumptions, there is at least a hint of an emerging notion that the FTC should do more than prevent untruthful, misleading, or deceptive advertising and should, on the one hand, require a complete, dispassionate statement of all information relevant to evaluate a product or service and, on the other hand, prohibit any appeal to emotions or suggestion of an irrelevant statement in purchasing any commodity or entering into a transaction. Recent speeches by Commissioner Jones[2] *and Mr. Thain*[3] *espouse substantially this concept.*

The question arises why these ideas are being espoused at the present time. . . . The fact that the gross abuses of the past have been largely eradicated may provide the opportunity for examining more subtle problems. However, there seem to be more basic causes.

One of the fundamental and overriding phenomena of our time is the continuously increasing population and its concentration into metropolitan masses by the continuing trend to urbanization. On top of this there has been an immense increase . . . in business . . . following the inhibiting influence of the depression of the 1930s and the war of the 1940s [review Chapter 11].

Another important element is the rise of broadcasting in the last quarter century. Radio and television have become mass media in a sense which we have not previously had . . . and have brought commercial advertising to the entire population, including segments which, because of poverty or illiteracy, were never reached by the printed press. . . .

There also appear to be other factors that contribute to the present questioning attitude toward advertising. One element is a distaste of many for the intrusiveness of television advertising. Print advertising, whether in a newspaper, magazine, or notice on a church door can be readily disregarded by the uninterested. However, television seeks to enlist the attention and interest of the viewer. It engages him with entertainment and news. Advertising is a diversion and interruption and it is unavoidably intrusive. . . .

---

[1] 36 Fed. Reg. 16698, August 25, 1971.

[2] Commissioner Mary Gardiner Jones, speech on Consumerism to the 18th Annual Marketing Conference of the National Industrial Conference Board, October 14, 1970.

[3] Speech by Gerald J. Thain, Assistant Director for Food and Drug Advertising of the Bureau of Consumer Protection, May 12, 1971.

A second and even more powerful motivation seems to be an objection to the products that are advertised. Advertising, like the media, is attacked as a surrogate for hated but inaccessible targets. Those who object to cigarettes, automobile fumes, sedatives or pain-killing drugs, various types of cosmetics and hygienic products, and other similar products find that public demand will not permit a direct attack on the objects of their disfavor so they attack the ads that sell these products. . . .

Third, there is an obvious zeal to reform the entire social order implicit in the attack on advertising. Many partisans of this view feel that we should not permit the waste of social and economic resources that they see in the production, advertising, and use of automobiles, drugs, and frivolities such as cosmetics, deodorants, and perfumes, and that it is the proper function of government to prevent such alleged waste. In this view, government has the paternalistic job of guiding individual conduct into socially useful and approved paths and to "rational" and sensible decisions.

WHAT IS THE PROPER ROLE OF GOVERNMENT IN REGULATING ADVERTISING?

The question presented by this analysis and by the present FTC inquiry undoubtedly is: What is the proper role of government with respect to advertising? The Commission presumably is seeking to formulate its own ideas as to the appropriate role for government to play as a guide to its own future efforts and activities. It is altogether proper for it to do this.

The first point responsive to this question should scarcely need articulation, much less emphasis, yet it does seem to require statement in view of the attitudes of some critics. Clearly, the proper role of government is not to suppress, to destroy, or to cripple advertising. It is clear that advertising is an integral part of the distributive process. . . . Advertising is one of the least expensive and least coercive techniques of distributing goods. If advertising were eliminated, or substantially curtailed, other competitive methods would surely be substituted. These are most likely to be various forms of personal selling which would certainly be more expensive, less efficient, and more coercive to the consumer.

Complaint is sometimes heard that advertising is excessive, wasteful, over-competitive, and untruthful. In specific isolated cases probably each of these charges has been true. It is the case that there are many abuses occurring in any institution as large, widespread, dynamic, and changeable as business. Many complaints have been, and will continue to be, made about business, and specific instances are likely to be found that warrant each specific complaint. However, this does not mean that business as a whole is subject to these, or any, indictment. . . .

The complaints that are directed to advertising are really complaints against the institution of private business. Advertising, as a part of business, shares the strength and weakness, the virtues and vices of business. Business and advertising are far from perfect, being human institutions, but it seems fair to say that they are no more imperfect than other comparable human institutions, including government itself.

In addition to the function of advertising as an integral part of the distributive aspect of business, it also performs the vital role of providing and supporting American journalism and the apparatus of mass and specialized media. . . . A recent communication from the American Association for the Advancement of Science, one of the largest and most important scientific organizations in the world, states that some 60% of its revenue has been derived from advertising in its prestigious publication Science.

Furthermore, the multiplicity of advertisers gives publishers and broadcasters independence not only from government but also from any single advertiser. Thus any action that significantly curtailed the volume of advertising would have an inescapable and disastrous effect upon our news sources in this country, the entire system of journalism, broadcasting, newspapers, magazines, and all other mass and specialized media.

There is no significant dispute that it is a proper function of the FTC to forbid and prevent false, misleading, and deceptive representations in advertising. A review of cases demonstrates that the FTC has ample powers to do this.[1] *. . . There can be no doubt that FTC cases are attentively watched and widely discussed and that the overwhelming preponderance of business firms voluntarily comply with all established precedents that are applicable to their respective activities.*

Furthermore, voluntary elevation of the standards of advertising has been taking place over a long period of time and there has been self-regulation and self-discipline within the field of advertising prior to the establishment of the FTC. Of course, there are always, and always will be, some abuses and violations of standards of legality or propriety by the few who are ignorant or incorrigible. There are, and always will be, borderline cases where views differ as to the application of precedents and principles. These will not be eliminated but proliferated as the volume of precedents and principles increases.

It is important to note that the fundamental approach in this field has been to forbid or prevent abuses but not to prescribe required standards of conduct or disclosures. This is consistent with and an outgrowth of the American economic and social system. In most fields, and certainly throughout most of the economy, the law forbids certain types of action which are thought to be improper but does not prescribe the norm.

There are manifold reasons for this approach. It is the most practical because it puts the least burden upon government and requires the least governmental investigation and governmental enforcement apparatus. It is compatible with American ideals because it allows the greatest degree of freedom to the individual and the individual firm. The choices open to the individual are as wide as the range of conduct that is not prohibited. However, when government undertakes to prescribe a required standard, then the individual must act according to the government-promulgated standard and has a much more limited range of choice. . . .

Established legal principles indicate that the FTC role should be primarily prohibitory rather than prescriptive. It has been argued that the prohibition against false advertising also requires affirmative disclosure of all relevant facts. The statute provides that in determining materiality the Commission shall take into account "the extent to which the advertisement fails to reveal facts material in the light of such representations or material with respect to consequences which may result from the use of the commodity to which the advertisement relates under the conditions prescribed in such advertisement or under such conditions as are customary or usual."[2]

[1] See I. M. Millstein, "The Federal Trade Commission and False Advertising," 64 *Columbia Law Review,* 439 (1964); FTC v. Colgate-Palmolive Co., 380 U.S. 374 (1965).

[2] 15 USC Sec. 55.

On occasion, the Commission, some of its members, and even some judges have felt that the Commission should go beyond compelling the disclosure of facts that involved material consequences resulting from use of the advertised product, and should compel advertising to provide the purchaser with information that might be useful to him in reaching a decision whether to purchase. This view has been authoritatively rejected by the Court of Appeals for the District of Columbia in an opinion by Judge Prettyman which says:

> We think that neither the purpose nor the terms of the act are so broad as the encouragement of the informative function. Both purpose and terms are to prevent falsity and fraud, a negative restriction. When the Commission goes beyond that purpose and enters upon the affirmative task of encouraging advertising which it deems properly informative, it exceeds its authority. . . . We think that the negative function of preventing falsity and the affirmative function of requiring, or encouraging, additional interesting, and perhaps useful, information which is not essential to prevent falsity, are two totally different functions. We think that Congress gave the Commission the full of the former but did not give it the latter. . . .
>
> . . . it seems to us that the limit of the Commission's power is to require that a product be truthfully represented, and that it has no power to require additional negative statements except as the act itself indicates, i.e., where the affirmative representations require further explanation or where the consequences of using the product require further warning.[1]

A basic legal issue is whether advertising comes within the scope of the First Amendment in any respect. In the Chrestensen case in 1942 the Supreme Court remarked that the First Amendment did not apply to "purely commercial advertising."[2] Some years later, in a concurring opinion, Justice Douglas said that this ruling had been casual, almost offhand, and commented, "It has not survived reflection."[3] The court has made it evident that Justice Douglas was correct in saying that advertising as such was not outside the First Amendment protections. Thus, in the leading case of New York Times v. Sullivan,[4] the court applied and extended the protection of the First Amendment to a statement which appeared only as a paid advertisement in a newspaper. Two years later the Court held that First Amendment protection was not limited by the fact that the expression in issue was made "for trade purposes."[5]

On the other hand, the Court has pointed out that the right to communicate information of public interest is not unconditional or unlimited in commercial settings as illustrated by federal securities regulations, mail fraud statutes, and common law actions for deceit and misrepresentation. . . .[6]

Where commercial advertising, even advertising directed solely to promoting the sale of a product, is not false, it does come within the protection of the First Amendment, regardless of the fact that it may be objectionable on grounds of taste or other aspects that do not violate the law. Thus, it has been held that: "If the

[1] Alberty v. F.T.C., 182 F2d 36, 86 US App. D.C. 238 (1950), cert. den. 340 US 818.

[2] Valentine v. Chrestensen, 316 US 52 (1942).

[3] Cammarano v. U.S., 358 US 498, 514 (1959).

[4] 376 US 254 (1964).

[5] Time, Inc. v. Hill, 385 US 374, 396–397 (1966).

[6] Curtis Publishing Co. v. Butts, 388 US 130, 150 (1967), reh. den. 389 US 889.

advertisement is not false, defendants have a constitutional right to utilize it even though its content and blatancy may annoy both the Commission and the general public. The issue is falsity. . . ."[1]

Ultimately the difficulty is that the government, and any government agency, simply lacks knowledge of the infinite number of relevant facts and variables, lacks the ability to predict or foresee all possible future circumstances, and thus lacks the ability to prescribe standards appropriate to the infinite variety of business situations.

There is a good deal of verbal deference paid to "administrative expertise" but I indicate no disrespect to the FTC when I assert, on the basis of considerable experience, that this is largely a legal fiction. There is no member of the FTC who is qualified as an expert in business, in advertising, or in the behavioral sciences. What the FTC does have is a full-time job which enables and requires it to concentrate on certain limited aspects of economic activity. By virtue of this concentration, it may acquire a greater fund of information over a period of time than is known to the average person or to the ordinary non-expert in these fields. However, it is crucial to note that the situations which come to the attention of the FTC in the normal course of its operations are not representative of either business or advertising in general.

The FTC does not see a random selection of cases or business practices. What does come to the attention of the FTC is a body of complaints and of actual or alleged abuses or violations of law. Thus, the experience of the FTC in business and in advertising is confined to the dark end of the spectrum where the extremes and the economic evils are concentrated. It is both unfair and unreasonable to generalize on the basis of this experience or to regard this experience as constituting expertise in the field.

Surely we all realize that Presidential appointment does not endow those so favored with either omniscience or infallibility. Recent incidents illustrate this. A few months ago the public was being told that it should avoid using detergents containing phosphates. Now the public is being told that detergents containing phosphates are less harmful than the alternatives. Without passing any judgment on the controversy whatever, it is obvious that the government which has issued both statements is not infallible. Similarly, for many years government agencies have been forbidding food manufacturers to advertise saturated fat and cholesterol content. Serious consideration is now being given to requiring such disclosures. Such examples . . . simply illustrate that the knowledge and foresight of government agencies is as limited as that of other human institutions and that it is, therefore, unwise to erect the current views of any government bureaucracy into rigid and universal standards beyond the necessity of protecting the public against known dangers.

There are, in fact, discernible dangers in the prescription of required standards of advertising by the government. Although such a course might satisfy the demands of some advertising critics, it would be inconsistent with the antitrust objectives of the FTC. The increasing scope, complexity, and rigor of government regulation *generally* is not only a burden to business but a substantial barrier to the entry of new business *[emphasis added].* It is becoming more and more difficult for advertisers to be sure that they comply with all government demands and taboos, and they are becoming

---

[1] F.T.C. v. Sterling Drug, Inc., 215 F. Supp. 327, 332 (S.D.N.Y. 1963), affirmed 317 F2d 669 (C.A. 2d 1963); accord, L. G. Balfour Co. v. FTC, 442 F2d (CA 7th 1971).

increasingly dependent upon lawyers, both to enable them to operate and to avoid the continuing threat and burden to litigation. While established business may be able to bear this burden, it is an additional and substantial expense which serves as a significant barrier to the entry of new enterprises.

An insistence upon adherence to some government standards of selling or advertising is, in the long run, inescapably monopolistic for still another reason. Consider the hypothetical case where the government specifies all of the items that can and must be set forth in every advertisement. These include the measurable qualities considered important by the regulatory agency and the prices for specific standard sizes, quantities, or models. Hypothetically, the price-quality ratio might also be required. It would then appear (whether or not it was the fact) that one or a few brands or makes was the best value and the most desirable purchase. Any attempt to present considerations other than the price-quality ratio would be forbidden as unfair and therefore illegal. If purchasers were rational in the sense this regulatory scheme postulates, they would all prefer and purchase the officially certified "best buy." Such a process would clearly promote monopolistic dominance in every field subject to such regulation.

Regulations prescribing required standards inevitably would impose a much greater burden of policing than rules which merely prohibit untruthfulness. With a larger burden of policing there would be a larger government bureaucratic apparatus and the entire system would thus be more burdensome and oppressive than the present system.

Furthermore, there is no evidence that any requirement for specifying the disclosures that should be made in advertising, even if such a set of rules could be promulgated, would be helpful to consumers. Demands for more detailed and comprehensive disclosures both in news and in advertising are old and clamorous. Nearly half a century ago Walter Lippmann commented on a similar demand with respect to news by saying: "We misunderstand the limited nature of news, the illimitable complexity of society; we overestimate our own endurance, public spirit, and all around competence. We suppose an appetite for uninteresting truths which is not discovered by any honest analysis of our own tastes."[1] What Lippmann said regarding news in 1922 is applicable with even greater force to advertising in 1971 and 1972.

.... The notion that it might be possible to convert advertising into a kind of prospectus for products can be dispelled by examining either an actual prospectus for securities, of the kind accepted by the SEC, or a catalogue containing specifications for common consumer items, such as a high fidelity apparatus. These are not merely uninteresting but largely unintelligible to the man in the street.

While the FTC should certainly require that advertisements state only the truth, it should not attempt to require or impose any standard of either good judgment or good taste. Standards of truth and accuracy are things which can be reduced to objective tests that permit impartial determination. However, there are no such objective standards of judgment or taste. What is important to one consumer may be unimportant or irrelevant to another. What is attractive to one person may be repellent to another. . . .

[1] Walter Lippmann, *Public Opinion*, Chap. XXIV (1922).

The Supreme Court has said in a number of cases [that] the purchaser has a right to make his own selection although his choice "may be dictated by caprice or by fashion or perhaps by ignorance."[1] *But to insist that advertising shall be directed entirely to matters deemed rational and relevant by the FTC [emphasis added] is to deny the consumer the right to learn about other aspects and elements and, therefore, to deny his right to select on the basis of taste, caprice, or any basis other than that approved by the FTC. An insistence upon confining advertising to elements deemed rational and relevant by the FTC is an attempt to impose upon the consuming public the Commission's own version of rationality and is a denial of the right of the public to be "irrational" or capricious in its choice if it so desires.*

Regulation of necessity looks to tangible and definable aspects and quantities. Thus, regulation tends to regard price as the paramount factor in selling and buying. But a buyer's values are by no means encompassed by a price or even by a ratio between price and various measurable qualities. Immeasurable but important qualities of this kind include such things as appearance, style, color and aroma, scarcity and exclusivity, prestige, and a host of other intangibles. . . . The values which the public seeks and finds in many, if not most, of its purchases may be wholly unrelated to price, or may be related to price only within some narrow range. There is no formula and no method for determining this. Probably each individual has his own schedule of values for each commodity, and price is no more than one element in a number of elements which go into the individual judgment of value.

When advertisers have sought to excuse misrepresentations on the ground that the facts misrepresented were not material or relevant to a rational choice, the FTC has responded that this was no excuse because people make purchases on an unpredictable and irrational basis and have a right to do so. Thus, the scope of FTC jurisdiction has been expanded on the premise of the consumer's right to be irrational [emphasis added]. The FTC cannot now reasonably repudiate that premise and undertake to specify what shall be officially permitted in advertising. . . . In any event, it is presumptuous to assert that consumers are irrational simply because their basis of choice differs from that which an agency or an official might favor.

In fact, there is every indication that consumers are not only rational by their own standards but relatively astute. People may buy relatively cheap, nondurable items, such as beer or soap, on the basis of an advertising appeal and . . . shift from brand to brand readily. . . . On the other hand, things that are more expensive and longer lasting are much more likely to be closely inspected. . . . Practically no one buys a house on the basis of an advertisement.

It seems to be a general tendency of government agencies to overestimate their own wisdom and their own ability to formulate rules for the guidance of others and to underestimate the ability of individual citizens to discriminate among the many appeals to them and to select those which do best meet their individual needs and values.

In the face of the contemporary public dialogue about government and business it needs to be said that the FTC is not authorized and should not attempt to reform the economic or the social structure of this country. The members and the staff of

[1] F.T.C. v. Colgate-Palmolive Co., 380 US 374, 387–388 (1965).

the FTC are entitled to whatever views they may individually hold as to the desirability of economic and social reform, and to express those views in the individual capacity. However, the legal mandate of the FTC was and is to prevent false and deceptive advertising and not to change the economic system or to attempt to impose the economic and social philosophy of its members upon society. If there is to be a basic change, whether reform or not, in the social and economic structure of this country, it must constitutionally be made by a different agency of government, presumably the legislative branch, and by different legal procedures than are available to the FTC. . . .

The role of the FTC and its statutory purposes are neither small nor confining. The prevention of untruthful advertising and unfair competition in as highly developed an economy as that of the United States is a task which challenges the full resources of any agency. Furthermore, the power of the FTC has been generously construed by the courts to give it a wide area of latitude and discretion. But the Commission need not and should not push all of its powers to their ultimate limit. . . .

Indeed, the government in a country such as this simply won't work unless business and the public generally comply voluntarily with the laws most of the time, and unless government exercises self-restraint in the exertion of its powers over business and the public most of the time. Any other course would lead to the situation in which business and the public were in constant conflict with the government and in which law enforcement depended upon the exertion of power in every case. No matter what the democratic theory of our government might be, such a situation would soon create a police state. . . .

Just as the FTC demands and needs a wide area of latitude and discretion in order to execute its legal mandate and achieve its statutory objectives, so does business also need a wide area of freedom and a large amount of elbow room and breathing space in order to survive and provide its proper functions. Legal counsel may be a permanent and inescapable necessity for business in the United States, but government bureaucrats and private lawyers cannot take over the control of American business with any hope of operating it successfully or to the satisfaction of the public.

It is instructive to observe that government itself cannot operate on the basis that some are urging for business. The kind of disclosure being advocated for advertising is most assuredly not followed by the government itself when it advertises, as in the case of savings bonds or recruiting ads. The well-known phrase "credibility gap" does not refer to the skepticism with which the public views advertising but to the skepticism with which the public views statements by government officials. Examples could be multiplied and brought closer to the present field of inquiry, but it is unnecessary in order to make the point. There is no contention that either government or business should be permitted to make false representations. But it is most emphatically asserted that business should be subjected to no more rigid or rigorous standards than government itself is willing to observe.

. . . . The power of government today, if not unlimited, is great. It is indeed larger than would appear from the statutory grant of authority or the law books. In the case of the FTC the mere issuance of a complaint with its attendant press release and publicity is much more than an accusation. For most of the public it stands as an official conviction. Even now the assertion is being made that an advertisement which has been attacked by the FTC should not be permitted to be heard on broadcasting.

Despite the limitations of budget and manpower, the government can litigate endlessly. It matters little to the FTC that the final determination of a case may take . 1 or 2 or 3 or more years and go through the full trial and appellate process. But such an ordeal of litigation can literally be ruinous to a business. The burden of responding to FTC inquiries, not to mention of defending against FTC charges, can easily exceed the financial ability of any but a very large business. The FTC can as easily prosecute a small business as a large one. By government standards, the FTC prospers as it brings more cases and becomes more aggressive, but the business subject to extensive FTC investigation or defending litigation against FTC charges is heavily burdened and may be crippled or destroyed.

All this does not, of course, mean that the FTC should hesitate to apply its statutory standards whenever it believes that false or deceptive advertising is being practiced. It does mean that the FTC should exercise restraint in jumping to conclusions, should authorize formal proceedings only when its staff has substantial evidence of a violation, and should treat borderline cases as matters appropriate for discussion on the basis of different judgments rather than as crimes showing malicious intent to defraud. Above all, it means that the FTC should not undertake the promulgation of new and more restrictive standards in this field. . . .

The present inquiry involves not merely a commercial convenience or business profits but the richness and diversity of our economic culture, the right of the individual consumer to make his own choices and the survival of free and independent mass media in America. What is at stake ultimately is even more than the survival of advertising or of business; it is the whole character of our society. The members and the staff of the FTC must always remember that liberty is the reciprocal of regulation. As the area of government control is extended, the area of private freedom is diminished. It is true that liberty cannot exist without government and laws. It is also true that where the government and the laws seek to control all conduct, there is no liberty.

There must be a wise balance between law and liberty. The fundamental postulate in American society is that the most important value is liberty and that laws exist to preserve and protect the liberty of the citizen. As liberty and regulation have a reciprocal relation, those government officials who exercise a wise self-restraint in using power only to the degree necessary, and not as far as authority can be pushed, best serve American ideals and democracy.

2 SELF-REGULATION: NEW DEVELOPMENTS

(excerpts from H. H. Bell, president, American Advertising Federation)

For decades, members of the advertising institution have developed private and semi-private forms of self-regulation. One of these, unique to the United States, is the well-known Better Business Bureau (BBB). The potential benefit from self-regulation is high. In practice, the major weakness of self-regulation has generally been the inability of private groups to discourage malpractice by their own members and, above all, by nonmember firms.

Although the testimony of H. H. Bell was not part of those organized by the ANA/4As group, it is important to report its content—namely, a description of a new private initiative to regulate the content of advertisements. While this new program does not have the power of enforcement, it appears to be by far the strongest attempt at self-regulation to date.

The American Advertising Federation (AAF) is an organization whose roots extend back to 1905. Its membership embraces all segments of advertising at the national and local levels, including more than 180 advertising clubs throughout the country; 450 company members comprising advertisers, agencies, and all media, and some 30 advertising and media associations. . . .

The Federation engages in a variety of activities affecting all advertising, including government and public affairs, advertising education, and advertising standards. In recent years we have appeared before this Commission on many issues, including the introduction of the AAF model deceptive practices act for adoption by states in dealing with misleading practices locally. We have recognized the need for a strong and effective Federal Trade Commission and on numerous occasions have supported increased funding and authority, including legislation to grant the Commission injunctive relief powers under certain conditions. . . .

Because of the extensive nature of subsequent presentations on the role and functions of advertising, the Federation wishes to confine its comments essentially to two aspects of advertising that relate to its performance in today's marketplace. First, we want to emphasize the role of advertising as a competitive tool of small businesses and retailers in this country. Second, we want to express our views on advertising's responsibility to the public and set forth for the record industry's plans to strengthen the commitment to high standards.

ADVERTISING AND SMALL BUSINESS

All too often advertising is equated with big business. However, a substantial portion of advertising is local on behalf of small business. For example, most of the 40,000 persons associated with advertising through the 180 advertising clubs in the AAF fall into this category. Generally speaking, the advertising clubs represent the practice of advertising on Main Street, U.S.A., as distinct from Madison Avenue and Michigan Avenue, although these centers are fully represented. . . .

Main Street, U.S.A., is where competition in this country is joined. The retailers of this nation in all categories—food, shoes, jewelry, cars, restaurants—all need and rely on advertising to compete daily in the local marketplace. The new retail establishment can only gain a foothold in the market through the use of advertising and the established store cannot compete without it.

The reliance of local business on advertising is illustrated by examining the billing figures of several major media that deal in both local and national advertising— newspapers, radio, and television. For two of the three categories, local billings far outstrip national usage. Of approximately $5.7 billion spent in newspaper advertising in 1970, $4.7 billion came from local advertisers, of which $3.2 billion was retail display and $1.5 billion was classified advertising. A little more than $1 billion was in national business. Of approximately $1.2 billion spent in radio in 1970, approximately $840 million was spent by local advertisers, with the balance of $398 million coming from national and regional business. In television—a major medium for national advertising—of $3.6 billion spent in 1970, $706 million was spent by local advertisers. The volume of local advertising in local media every Thursday and

Friday testifies to the strong reliance of the consumer on such advertising as a basis for weekend buying decisions.

ADVERTISING RESPONSIBILITY

. . . the Federation undertook a study of advertising self-regulation some fifteen months ago which culminated in the announcement on September 28 of significant new machinery to deal with the truth and accuracy of national consumer advertising.

Specific public proposals dealing with the mechanism of such a self-regulatory program first were presented in September 1970. . . . Throughout the evolving stages of the plan informal consultations with the Commission and its staff were most helpful in developing a sound and effective program, and avoiding possible legal problems. We are deeply grateful for the assistance and the encouragement received.

The new program of self-regulation in advertising as finally adopted involves a two-tier system. The first element is the new National Advertising Division (NAD) of the Council of Better Business Bureaus (CBBB). . . . The second tier is the newly created, independent National Advertising Review Board (NARB) . . . [with] a full-time executive director, William H. Ewen, . . . In addition to the chairman, the NARB consists of 50 members—30 representing advertisers, 10 representing advertising agencies, and 10 representing public or nonindustry fields. . . .

In the development of this program there were two essential elements that were uppermost in importance in establishing a system that would be effective, respected, and credible. The first was the desirability of public representation in the structure itself so that the consumer would have a role in its functioning. The second essential element was that there be adequate enforcement machinery, consistent with existing laws.

The plan which evolved through many stages contained both features. During its development in consultation with government and industry leaders, the effort was joined by the American Association of Advertising Agencies, the Association of National Advertisers, and the Council of Better Business Bureaus.

These organizations and the AAF became the steering committee which now comprises the National Advertising Review Council, a separate corporate body which has been formed to implement the project. While the president and chairman of each sponsoring organization serves on the Board of Directors of the corporation, their responsibilities relate to the housekeeping matters of the corporation. They are precluded from involvement in the decision-making process of the National Advertising Review Board.

The machinery and functions of the National Advertising Division (NAD) of the CBBB and the National Advertising Review Board (NARB) may be summarized as follows.

The NAD will receive, evaluate, and act on complaints with regard to truth and accuracy in national consumer advertising. The complaints may come from any source—public, industry, or even government. In addition to handling complaints, the NAD staff will engage in monitoring to cover possible abuses on its own initiative. It also will render advisory opinions in advance to advertisers and/or agencies on planned advertising as a means of offering early guidance to help avoid problems.

In the handling of complaints, the staff will seek to evaluate the merits of the issues raised. In most cases this will mean checking the representations made in the advertising with the available information on the performance of the product under accepted standards of truth and accuracy.

If a complaint is considered justified, the staff will work with the advertiser and/or agency to seek an appropriate change in the advertising. The emphasis will be on a constructive resolution of the problem. If there is an impasse and the questionable advertising is neither altered nor withdrawn, the complaint will be appealed to the NARB.

To expedite the appeals process, the chairman of the NARB will convene a five-man panel of the board to hear the specific case and reach a decision on behalf of the board. Each panel will include three advertisers, one agency, and one public member.

The decision of a panel will be transmitted to the advertiser at the highest corporate level. If the advertiser refuses to cooperate with the NARB panel or does not agree with the decision of the panel that the advertising is in violation of NARB standards, the chairman of the NARB, after exhausting all procedures, shall inform the appropriate government agency. The letter shall describe the advertising and the questions raised and advise that the NARB file is available for examination upon request. The chairman shall make public the letter and any comments or position statement received from the advertiser.

We believe that these enforcement measures will assure a meaningful and respected effort while recognizing the ultimate jurisdiction of government to exercise its statutory responsibility with respect to such matters. . . .

It has been suggested that the percentage of public representation on the Board should have been larger than 20%. However, it should be acknowledged that the inclusion of public representatives in an industry program of self-regulation is in itself a major step forward. There are, in fact, few—if any—industries or professions that provide for direct public involvement of this nature and extent. The objective is to give the public a voice in an industry program and this has been accomplished.

The quality of the public members selected for the NARB is self-evident—and this is of paramount importance. The question is not the number of public members, but how well this Board performs its responsibilities. We are confident that the program will earn the respect of the public generally, as well as critics based on this performance. It merits the support of all who have an interest in improving the system. The NARB will hold its first organizational meeting next month. And it is hoped that the public will take full advantage of the program.

Earlier I spoke of the importance of local advertising for the small business or retailer in this country. Since this national program of self-regulation will deal with advertising appearing in national media, we believe that machinery should be established to deal with local advertising practices as well.

The AAF and the CBBB are presently developing jointly a blueprint for the establishment of local advertising review boards, initially in those cities where there are local better business bureaus and advertising clubs in a position to administer such programs. We believe that an extension of the national program is essential to complete the circle of concern with respect to the truth and accuracy of all advertising. We will make the blueprint available to the Commission when it is completed.

The AAF is encouraged by the progress that has been made during the past year in the area of advertising responsibility. We are encouraged, too, by the increasing awareness of top management in American business that the public policy questions affecting marketing practices must receive equal consideration with other essential concerns of management and finance. . . .

There is also a greater willingness on the part of business and advertising to listen to the critics—a willingness that should extend to all sides. I would hope that we can continue to find ways to substitute consultation for confrontation on these issues.

If we are going to be constructive, all groups—industry, government, and critic—need to be better informed and have a better understanding of each other's problems and concerns. That should be one of the great values of these proceedings.

As a means of maintaining a continuing dialogue, we suggest that the FTC consider establishing an industry advisory council to assist the Commission on a continuing basis in its consideration of issues such as those being discussed at this hearing. This is a practice followed by other government agencies in dealing with specialized areas of responsibility. Such a procedure could provide the kind of input which the Commission could find of value on broad policy matters. It also would provide a conduit for information and concerns of the Commission to flow back to industry.

3 SUMMARY

From the very first, we have seen that society needs to regulate its mass communication system, including that part we have called the advertising institution. Not only society, but interest groups, and ultimately each individual, can benefit from an appropriate kind and level of public regulation. But what is appropriate? To the witnesses, regulation is appropriate when it strikes a balance between the rights of the individual and those of society.

This means that we cannot maximize the satisfaction of either individual or societal rights; we can only "suboptimize." This applies to all interfaces between an individual and his social environment. Consider, for example, the problem of coping with crime. Most attempts to decrease crime necessarily limit individual freedom and increase government authority. But if we move too far in this direction, we may reach a point where we increase government crime.[1]

What kind of balance is realized in advertising regulation? In the past decades, legislation, regulation, and court decisions have reflected both general trends in the overall relationships of the individual with the state and trends peculiar to advertising. Note, first, that there has been a continuous growth of legislation, and of agencies with regulatory powers, covering more and more of the individuals, as well as the firms' activities. This may ultimately make the economic fabric of society less flexible at a time when technology, with its increasingly fixed costs, is also contributing to rigidity.

[1]S. Kanfer, "Assassin and Skyjackers: History at Random," Time Essay, *Time,* June 12, 1972, p. 20.

In fact, as Mr. Loevinger reminds us, this increase in legislation and regulation may become an additional barrier to entry into the marketplace by new and especially by small firms. Furthermore, as a number of scholars have long observed, interpretations of laws by courts and regulatory agencies have gradually shifted away from a defense of competition and toward a defense of certain types of competitors.[1]

In the regulation of the advertising institution, the most fundamental trend is probably the shift of responsibilities from the buyer to the seller, i.e., from caveat emptor to caveat vendor. Also noticeable is the practically universal adoption by courts of the notion of *implied warranty* as it applies to claims in advertisements.

Another basic trend is the shift from rules that state what a subject cannot do (the "don't's") to rules that state what a subject must do (the "do's"). This implies a shift toward active intervention into the decision making of individuals and firms. To illustrate this trend, we note recent requests that firms submit proof of the claims they make in each ad and that testimonials can be made only by people who are "experts."

As more and more rules apply to the content—rather than to the form—of the information flowing through the institution, the principle of free speech is ultimately being challenged. While we cannot pursue this topic here,[2] we note that our witnesses do not confuse free speech with false advertising. Misstatements of *fact,* they assert, are not (and should not be) protected, but ads whose content involves only opinion should be covered by the free-speech principle. In other words, the witnesses believe that the content of ads should not be regulated except in the case of false information. And they remind us that the diversity of ads from different competitors *and* the consumers' ability to judge and test by their own purchases are both functional ways to regulate the content of ads.

It is interesting that only a few years ago FTC Commissioner Mary Gardiner Jones espoused this view:

> *If the problems posed by the social and cultural impact of advertising on society should,* as I believe is the case *[emphasis added], be analogized to the problem of free speech, the solution of these problems must lie in the same area. We must ensure truth not by regulating content but by promoting as wide a diversity of viewpoints as is possible in this aspect of the media's message.*[3]

Mr. Loevinger's testimony, however, suggests that the FTC has moved in the opposite direction. In his review of the FTC decisions, he argues that the Commission has increasingly taken an activist posture extending beyond pursuit of false ads. Slowly but cumulatively, the FTC has moved toward decisions that unavoidably define what is good or bad for each individual (the "average" individual). On the basis of the material

---

[1] E. T. Grether, *Marketing and Public Policy,* Prentice-Hall, Englewood Cliffs, N.J., 1966.

[2] For an incisive discussion, see J. G. Myers, "Legislative Controls and Freedom of Speech: The Case of Commercial Advertising," *Public Affairs Report,* Institute of Governmental Studies, University of California, Berkeley, August 1972.

[3] From a speech by FTC Commissioner Mary Gardiner Jones to the Association of American Law Schools, San Francisco, December 1969. Cited in J. G. Myers, "Legislative Controls and Freedom of Speech: The Case of Commercial Advertising," *Public Affairs Report,* Institute of Governmental Studies, University of California, Berkeley, August 1972, p. 5.

discussed in Chapter 13, it is impossible to avoid the conclusion that such decisions are based on subjective criteria and that they result in value judgments. These value judgments by powerful federal agencies cannot help but cause changes in the character of society.

Ultimately, the question is whether regulatory agencies should be permitted to take such subjective and activist positions, especially when these are, according to Mr. Loevinger's interpretations, beyond their jurisdiction. As we well know, this question involves not only advertising but many other institutions—from the free press to education and religion.

Beyond the possible legal and moral questions involved in advertising regulation, we also face administrative questions. For example, what priorities should be followed in allocating the scarce resources available to regulatory agencies? A few points can be listed here for consideration.

First, it would appear that the FTC allocates much of its efforts to national advertising. Presumably, this allocation should reflect the distribution of the violations that occur; such allocation makes sense only if most advertising violations take place at the national level. There are, however, almost no systematic data available for determining whether this is the case.

We have only limited evidence about consumer complaints concerning advertising; what we do have shows that their number is relatively small. For example, the FTC itself has released the data shown in Exhibit 15.1. Advertising is the source of complaints in only 5.74 percent of the cases. And, in the analysis of mailbag complaints received by the Office of Consumer Affairs of the federal government, advertising accounted for only 2 percent of the 3,920 complaints received during May 1972.[1]

These isolated statistics suggest that, for purposes of allocating regulatory efforts by *all* concerned agencies, it would be desirable to monitor consumer complaints on a systematic national and statewide basis. The results would suggest whether advertising is, in fact, a major object of consumer complaints.

Second, by looking closely at the nature of the various complaints, we could establish whether the majority of complaints tend to concern local, and especially retail-sponsored, or national, manufacturing-sponsored, advertising. Third, it would be useful to determine whether the complaints tend to involve *members* or *nonmembers* of such organizations as the Association of National Advertisers, the American Association of Advertising Agencies, the Direct Mail Advertising Association, and the like.

To confirm the usefulness of such data for guiding the efforts of public agencies, we need only consider the following. Suppose that the vast majority of complaints refer to local retail firms. Then agencies such as the FTC and the FCC have a basis for rational allocation of their efforts; further, new structural mechanisms would have to be developed, different from those to be used if the majority of complaints concerned national ads. (Apropos of this, note that in recent years local retail firms have continuously increased their use of local TV spots.)

---

[1] *Marketing News,* August 1, 1972, p. 7.

EXHIBIT 15.1
CONSUMER COMPLAINTS, FEDERAL TRADE COMMISSION, 1970

The Federal Trade Commission has analyzed some 8,800 consumer complaints reported in five cities—Boston, Chicago, Los Angeles, Philadelphia, and San Francisco—during six months of 1970. The analysis shows that *national advertising was not significantly involved.* (We have asked if we may see the complaints.)

Six categories accounted for 48% of the total, others being "miscellaneous." The six were:

	%
Failure to deliver merchandise that has been paid for	14.38
Truth-in-lending violations	8.81
Defective work or service	7.42
Inferior merchandise	6.99
False advertising	5.74
Refusal to grant refunds without prior notice such claims would not be honored	4.62

Source: The 4A Newsletter, pp. 2–3, February 16, 1971.

These data would also be extremely important in affecting the direction and success of self-regulation. Suppose, for example, that the vast majority of complaints concerned local ads sponsored by firms who were not members of the associations described in Mr. Bell's testimony. In such cases, the probability of achieving successful self-regulation would be low.

As for the recent attempt by advertisers and agencies to build a mechanism for self-regulation, the following statistics have become available. By August 31, 1972, less than a year after its founding, the National Advertising Division (NAD)—the investigative staff of the National Advertising Review Board (NARB)—has received *or* initiated 337 complaints against national advertising. Of these complaints, 112 were dismissed after the national advertiser provided adequate substantiation in the opinion of the NAD staff. The NAD staff found 72 of the complaints justified and the advertisers agreed to withdraw or modify the ads. As of August 31, 1972, 153 complaints were still under investigation.

In six of the cases dismissed by the NAD, an appeal by the complainants was made to the NARB in accordance with the procedure explained by Mr. Bell. The NARB panel sustained NAD's earlier opinion in four cases. Two complaints, however, were found to be justified. Assured by the advertisers that the challenged ads would be withdrawn, NARB ruled that no further action would be required.[1]

---

[1] H. H. Bell, "Self-Regulation by the Advertising Industry," in S. P. Sethi (ed.), *The Unstable Ground: Corporate Social Policy in a Dynamic Society,* Melville Publishing Co., Los Angeles, Calif., 1974.

Individual consumers accounted for the largest share of the total complaints. Some complaints were the result of internal monitoring of ads by NAD. Surprisingly, relatively few complaints were filed by representatives of consumer organizations. It would be interesting to find out why organizations that are purported to represent consumer interests have not flooded NAD with complaints. Perhaps the NARB and NAD need to advertise themselves—persuasively—to consumer organizations.

As a final note on the subject of self-regulation, let us conclude with a statement by Mr. Gray, one of the witnesses we heard earlier (see Chapter 8, Section 2):

> But we are hopeful that if the job is done well, we will greatly improve the quality of advertising in general, and , I would hope, reduce greatly the number of serious cases that only you can handle. I can't resist adding that this effort by business need not be construed as altruism or the result of massive pangs of conscience. In my opinion, it is pure, unadulterated self-interest. This discipline must be made effective if only to reduce the outrageous discount rate that our customers now put on our advertising messages. We must recognize that those who abuse advertising not only do so at the consumer's expense, but also at the expense of those of us who depend upon advertising to help us conduct our business.[1]

[1] Pp. 10–11 in the original testimony.

Chapter 16

An Epilogue and a Commencement

Toward a Constructive Multilogue

> *The love of liberty is the love of others;*
> *the love of power is the love of ourselves.*
>
> William Hazlitt

As mentioned in the preface, the business sector has only recently joined the debates on advertising in a comprehensive and systematic way. In interpreting the facts and viewpoints of corporate managers, we have not tried to reach conclusions but to stimulate the search for understanding advertising at the micromanagerial and at the macro socioeconomic levels.

The material in this book is only one of the inputs necessary to create the conceptual and empirical foundations that must precede conclusions and action. This book is a taking-off point for future thought, research, and action. The facts, theories, and perspectives presented should lead us beyond taking stock of the status quo. By integrating them with other facts, theories, and perspectives, we shall be in a position to identify the issues and define the parameters of the problems to be resolved, and thus make progress toward satisfying the interests of the many parties involved.

1 THE TESTIMONIES AND COMMENTARIES

To move toward this future work, it is important to appreciate the nature of the testimonies and commentaries. We must especially keep in mind both the range of issues discussed and the limitations of the book's material.

First of all, only the points of view of advertisers and advertising agencies were presented and interpreted. The views of the other parties that participate in advertising activities were often referred to, but somewhat indirectly. Important among these are the mass media, the consumers themselves, and the many critics of advertising. It is thus fair to say that the book's selection and discussion of the issues was, in a sense, biased.

It is also fair to say, however, that none of the salient issues has been left untouched. In a way, it was easy for the witnesses to cover salient issues, because critics have contributed substantially to identifying such issues. As stated in the preface, the uniqueness of the testimonies is that they answer, one by one, the questions raised in the voluminous literature accumulated over decades, if not centuries. On several occasions, furthermore, the testimonies and commentaries posed new questions concerning both concepts and facts.

The consumer's point of view was not present directly. This limitation is shared by all other discussions. Not only business firms but also government agencies and critics of advertising can describe only indirectly what consumers feel, think, and do. There is a noticeable difference, however, in the way the testimonies have brought the consumer into the discussion.

Past and current criticism has attempted to represent the consumer by reference to some idealized prototype that reflects a subjective view (Chapter 11, Section 4). More importantly, legislation and regulation have always assumed, and referred to, the existence of the "average" consumer.[1] And much of the current empirical research (see Chapter 12) also adopts a view in which central tendencies—and thus sameness—in consumer needs and aspirations are assumed; as noted, prevailing econometric studies merely tend to replace verbally stated ideal types of consumers with empirically based "means."

In the testimonies, however, data document that there is no ideal or average consumer in an affluent society; they record the existence of a growing pluralism of consumer types whose needs, motivations, and buying behaviors change over time and across products and brands. These descriptions of the consumer are in tune with

---

[1] See the very useful review of the legal doctrine which determines how legislators, regulators, and courts visualize the consumer as a party in settling issues concerning advertising in G. G. Gerlach, "The Consumer's Mind: A Preliminary Inquiry into the Emerging Problems of Consumer Evidence and the Law," Marketing Science Institute, Cambridge, Mass.; December, 1972.

present-day reality. In fact, we have learned that it is this very pluralism that causes many problems both for management and for public regulation.

The book did not cover in depth the points of view of mass media. Two of the testimonies gave insights into the relationships of advertisers and agencies with mass media (Chapter 12, Section 1) and the commentaries often touched upon the roles of mass media (see, e.g., Chapter 1, Section 3). But more is needed. For example, although there are distinguished studies of individual types of media,[1] we do not have yet attempts to understand mass media in their totality or to study their structural interdependence through time and across countries (see Chapter 11, Section 3.1).

More important, most studies of advertising do not explicitly consider the roles of mass media. This is particularly true of research on advertising's possible effects on prices, profits, and concentration (see Chapter 12). It will be recalled that these are studies at the industry level (i.e., the industry is the unit of analysis); but different industries relate to mass media in different ways and the availability of appropriate media varies enormously from one industry to another. These and other differences may be antecedent variables that explain the varying reliance on mass media advertising by different SIC industries.

Future research on advertising must include mass media roles and points of view because media are at the critical interface of several dynamic factors. As the core of a society's mass communication system, mass media are at the point of confluence not only economic information but also of all other information about social life. As we have seen, the jointness of costs and benefits makes it difficult to disentangle advertising from the flow of other information and to proceed with the study of several important issues.

Mass media are strongly affected by technological innovation—i.e., by the risks and costs implied by new and changing technologies for gathering and distributing information; they face, for example, the possibility that the current distinction between print and broadcast media will become obsolete.[2] Furthermore, located as they are between many different demands for and supplies of information, they are constantly vulnerable to changes in both supply and demand, which are often difficult to predict. Even though mass media managers are in a position to exert considerable social influence—whether through editorials concerning public opinion or decisions as to which ads they will or

---

[1] For a recent example, see R. T. Bower, *Television and the Public,* Holt, Rinehart and Winston, New York, 1973. The most important feature of this study is that its data are to a large degree comparable to previous studies in 1960 and 1940. Similar longitudinal studies of other media are equally desirable (see the discussion in Chapter 11, Section 3.1). See also R. G. Noll, M. J. Peck, and J. J. McGowan, *Economic Aspects of Television Regulation,* The Brookings Institution, Washington, D. C., 1973.

[2] For a nontechnical discussion, see L. Bogart, "Mass Media in the Year 2,000," *Gazette,* vol. 13, no. 3, 1967; W. L. Rivers, "Mass Communication: The Revolutionary Future," American Association of Advertising Agencies, Western Regional Meeting, New York, October 1969; and O. A. Wiio, "System Models of Information," International Communication Association Conference, Montreal, Canada, April 1973.

will not accept—the roles of mass media in the issues discussed in this book have not yet been thoroughly explored.[1]

At least one other point should be kept in mind as plans for the future are made. There were two purposes in restricting this book to the perspectives of advertisers and agencies. First, it will be recalled, there is a need to change the historical imbalance that has given great social visibility to different sets of facts, theories, and perspectives. Second, it is essential to understand the practical and analytical bases of the business view if we wish to compare and integrate it with other views and thus construct the necessary total view of what the problems are. Furthermore, the testimonies and commentaries take as a point of departure the very facts, theories, and perspectives that lend support to a negative view of advertising. Exposure to the business point of view has not deprived the reader of other facts and perspectives. To the contrary, such exposure makes the reader more knowledgeable, providing him with a more balanced understanding of the knowledge available to guide action at the private and public levels.

2 ADVERTISING AS A MANAGERIAL FUNCTION

A modest appreciation of economics and some practical experience are sufficient to understand the micromanagerial roles of advertising. Management is faced on one hand with costs, i.e., demands that can be satisfied by revenues, and on the other, with the need to seek out sources of revenue—and a simple awareness of the practical meaning of affluence can give a good idea of how difficult it is to find buyers and retain their loyalty. This book has illustrated how, in an affluent society, a firm must identify and cater to the wishes of some consumer group large enough to assure the revenues necessary to cover costs.

To satisfy the needs of a consumer group requires more than searching for them. Since needs are generic, to be successful, a firm must find ways to translate them into more concrete desires. A successful firm always searches for latent opportunities and potential trends, and strives to develop them and help them gain momentum.

Many managerial decisions are necessary in order to adapt to the environment and help develop trends favorable to the firm. The entire range of marketing decisions—from the location of plants and distribution centers to the choice of product lines, prices, packaging, and so on—are examples of adaptive decision making. Advertising is a vital component in a firm's attempt to relate to a changing consumer environment, but its relative weight varies from industry to industry, from firm to firm, from brand to brand, and from one marketing and promotional program to another during any fiscal period.

---

[1] This is a difficult task because mass media are a very heterogenous lot. Stresses and complementarities abound between print and broadcast media, and within print as well as within broadcast. Stresses and complementarities also abound within each medium between the editorial and the managerial staffs. And the variations in technology, costs, and public regulations across media are simply mind-boggling. Only a better understanding of the working of this component of the advertising institution will permit us to state more clearly, and thus help resolve, the issues discussed in this book. For some basic research questions concerning mass media, see L. Bogart, "The Management of Mass Media: An Agenda for Research," *Public Opinion Quarterly,* Winter 1973–74.

To the extent that society delegates to a firm the responsibility to operate economically—matching revenues and costs—there is not much that can be said about the management of the advertising function, as long as it respects the law. However, a number of considerations raised in the book go beyond the strict economic efficiency of advertising within a firm. In both Parts 1 and 2 we saw that social and ethical factors often complicate the picture.

What can management do in the future to cope with this complexity? The case of false advertising does not present any difficulty: corporate management should make it very clear to line management that false advertising will not be tolerated. The same should apply to incompetence: for instance, to take a picture of any building and then refer to it as one of the firm's buildings is, at the very least, a senseless lie, and corporate management can certainly make sure that such incidents do not occur.

But there are many other situations in which it is not clear what management can and cannot do. Let us look at a deceptively simple case. Successful firms, we said, are always searching for latent trends in consumer predispositions. It is not surprising that different firms will explore the potential of different trends. If one firm hits the jackpot, many others will rush to follow suit. As in many other diffusion cases, one "discovered" trend may quickly catch on and materialize fully, while another that originally had the same potential remains at the state of opportunity.

This example shows that the behavior of each firm is adaptive in the sense that it reacts to what is acceptable to at least some consumers. However, any trend, once it becomes established, will usually interact with social and cultural values, and may bring about changes in these values. For example, of the many advertising themes explored in the sixties, the nude look had a period of popularity. It is likely that this theme contributed to changes in many sex-related events, and perhaps even to basic changes in society's posture toward sex.

The search for opportunities latent in some segment of the population thus may have effects that go beyond that segment and affect larger parts of society. Of course, this does not apply to advertising alone. These effects may be compared to the effects of decisions by editors and reporters to cover one event rather than another.

There is little that a single firm can do to control such social processes. At best it can exercise judgment. As long as society expects each firm to match costs and revenues in order to survive, it cannot expect any one firm to stop looking for new opportunities nor to ignore what competitors find to be successful in the market.

Management and society may be caught in a potential paradox here. On one hand, society does its best to enforce competition among firms (see, e.g., the increasing body of antitrust laws and rules). That is, it requires firms to be innovative and successful. In so doing, however, management is bound to make choices that may affect social-cultural processes with consequences sometimes unacceptable in terms of current values. It is as if society wants it both ways: innovate but avoid altering the status quo. Furthermore, it is as if society requires each firm to judge which innovation is good for society: here too we observe a conflict with society's current belief that only consumers are to be the judges of what is good for them.

Understanding these emerging conflicts makes it clear that only society can do something to cope with them. For example, well-researched and well-written laws and regulations can offer precious guidance to management in considering the possible social and ethical consequences of decisions that, at the firm level, are in the strictly economic domain. As long as society delegates responsibility for economic efficiency to each firm, it must assume the responsibility to choose and prescribe clearly the framework of values within which each firm can operate (see Chapter 9, Section 4).

And it appears that society now wants to assume the responsibility of choosing goals and priorities through the political system (i.e., legislation and necessarily regulation) rather than through the free interaction of supply and demand in the economic market. In fact, some have suggested that this trend is appearing in all economic activities by firms and consumers.[1]

Although management can do little about these possible social and political trends, it can do a great deal within the domain of strict economic responsibilities. From the early debates concerning labor, management has learned how to deal with decisions that have direct and indirect social and ethical consequences. We may now have reached a historical moment when the advertising function has gone beyond merely attracting a high degree of public awareness; perhaps it may even score a high priority in the public conscience.

If this is happening, corporate management cannot continue to monitor the advertising function only by measuring costs and revenues. Even though it is complex and difficult, advertising research limited to measuring recall and comprehension may no longer be sufficient.[2] Thus, to the extent to which society becomes concerned with the quality of advertising decisions, corporate management must discover new ways to evaluate the social implications of its advertising function.

3 ADVERTISING AS A SOCIOECONOMIC INSTITUTION

The testimonies and commentaries have argued that the debates on advertising concern the entire institution, its structure and function. They have also maintained that the issues can be conceptualized and resolved only by going beyond the simple anthropo-morphic visualization of advertising as *the* advertiser, *the* person who spells out the virtues of a suntan lotion, or *the* jingle that tries to evoke the pleasure of air travel. In Chapter 1, and later in Part 2, we thus raised the level and increased the challenge of our study by developing the outline of a macro approach to advertising.

This outline helped us to appreciate the necessity of studying advertising as an institution. It also helped us put together what is known about the institution and indicated some directions for future work. The awareness of these possibilities is a basis for a constructive multilogue.

---

[1] D. Bell, *The Coming of Post-Industrial Society,* Basic Books, New York, 1973.

[2] See L. Bogart, "Where Does Advertising Research Go From Here?" *Journal of Advertising Research,* March 1969, p. 10.

In some cases, it was possible to identify specific directions for future work. For instance, we proposed a plan to analyse time series that are already available or that require relatively little preparation (see Figure 11.10). We also indicated that it meaningless to study the economic roles of advertising in different industries and in the economy as a whole without considering other channels of communication. And we raised serious doubts about the ability of the current Standard Industrial Classification (SIC) of firms to reflect accurately the variety of decisions involved in advertising, promotion, and marketing.

Beyond the more easily identifiable problems, we were faced with more complex problems and challenges. Some of these deserve concentrated efforts, for understanding them will lead to a better understanding of advertising.

The first problem is the relationship between advertising and the consumer. Even at the micro level, an ad, or a series of ads, is only one of the many inputs that may affect a consumer's psychological state and, perhaps, his purchasing behavior. At the macro level, there is no evidence to suggest that advertising has a greater influence than other inputs on the behavior of all consumers, i.e., on macro consumption behavior. In fact, research suggests that it may have less.

Advertising is only one of society's many institutions: it is literally imbedded in much more basic and powerful institutions such as the family, the school, the church, and the political and legal system. Moreover, advertising operates within the deeply rooted and, in the long run, fundamental characteristics of a society. It shares society's norms, sanctions, and rewards. Undoubtedly, any system of mass communication will have an impact on both social institutions and cultural traits and thus, ultimately, on the members of a society. But, to the best of current behavioral knowledge, it is the institutions and cultural traits that have a far greater impact on advertising *and* on consumers.

Can we test these guesses? Clearly, not yet. The nature and strength of the relationships of advertising with consumers at the macro level are a function of the relationships between consumers and their institutional and cultural environment. Very little is known about these latter relationships: a sociology of consumption has not yet been written. Our search to understand and evaluate the socioeconomic roles of advertising is hampered by this lack of knowledge. For instance, it is impossible to observe and measure whether the advertising institution has any role in the debate over *quality* versus *quantity* in current and future styles of life if the very terms of the debate (quantity, quality, and life style) are not operationally defined, agreed upon, and documented.

The challenge posed by the relationships between advertising and macro consumption behavior is equaled by the challenge emerging from the relationships of the advertising institution with the economy and with the political, religious, and other sectors. We have often stressed the intuitive notion that, as an economy grows in size and complexity, each economic unit—be it a firm, a public agency, or a consumer—will increasingly need an efficient and effective system of mass communication. Some evidence seems to suggest that this is the case and, further, that the advertising system tends to respond to this need rather than to anticipate it (Chapter 11, Section 3.2). But we saw that this evidence must be viewed with caution, since current knowledge of causal and structural relationships is only speculative (Chapter 11, Section 3.3).

Much of our hesitation here is due to the deceptively simple definition of advertising as a subset of the entire communication system. The advertising institution, we said, is the set of all activities undertaken by individuals and organizations that involve the exchange of economic information. We can thus look toward the study of advertising as an entity separated from the entire mass communication system only if we can operationally distinguish between economic and noneconomic information. Undoubtedly this can be done in some cases. But we have consistently faced the dilemma that the distinction is often blurred; in fact it is challenged by both those who favor and those who criticize the institution. We saw not only that it is impossible to distinguish in the absolute whether a bit of information is economic or not, but that any message, once internalized, will acquire total human meanings that cannot be broken down into the neat divisions represented by the departments in a college.

There are further interactions. One is the cost interdependence between the flow of advertising messages and all other messages such as general news or educational programs. And we learned of the current dependence of the free press on the present arrangement. Thus, from the strict economic interdependence of the flows of different types of information we were led to observe that different ideologies interact through a society's mass communication system.

While facing these broad questions, we learned that we must be inventive in separating advertising from the other facets of the communication system. But we also learned that an analysis of advertising is possible only if we start with a strong conceptualization of the entire mass communication system. It is this conceptualization that we most lack.

The difficulties we experience in thinking about and studying advertising at the macro level are probably caused by the fact that applied and basic research have not yet been used to examine one of the key features of modern societies—that is, how these societies develop, and become dependent upon, means of mass communication for all aspects of social life.

If we do not mobilize our energies for the study of this feature, we may risk having an experience similar to the biblical event of the tower of Babel. Even if we manage to avoid this, we may run into an even more unhappy situation. Basic technological changes in the means of mass communication are on the horizon. From the feasibility of two-way communication through mass media to technologies which may essentially obliterate the distinction between mass and nonmass media, society is confronted with questions which, at first glance, seem to imply choices of an economic nature only. But in the long run, these choices and their consequences will inexorably impose narrow restrictions on what each individual and private group can and cannot do. Only if we understand both the need for mass communication systems and the way they develop, can we choose where we ultimately want to be—not only in terms of the kinds of advertising institutions that are desirable but, more importantly, the kinds of overall communication systems that will best serve the next generation with respect to their political, religious, and cultural preferences.

4 MANAGING THE ADVERTISING INSTITUTION

In principle, the mechanism underlying the management of the advertising institution by society is straightforward. The members of society are the stakeholders of the institution. They delegate to *elected* officials (the Congress) the responsibility of selecting the social *goals* the institution should achieve and the *constraints* it must respect. *Legislation* is the vehicle for these selections.

Legislators in turn delegate to *appointed* officials (e.g., the regulatory agencies) the responsibility of selecting the *means* to reach the chosen goals. The vehicle for these selections is *regulation*. Often, regulators are also responsible for policing the implementation of laws and rules. Disagreements between regulators and regulated parties are usually settled by the regulators themselves. The regulated parties, of course, may resort to courts for final judgment.

In practice, things are not so simple. In particular, the separation of responsibilities for choosing goals and means is not as clear as desirable. Legislators often prepare laws that go beyond setting goals—that is, laws prescribe means, that state what one can do or even ought to do. And regulators often tend to influence directly or indirectly the choice of goals by the regulated individual and firms. This mixture of responsibilities is partly unavoidable, for the distinction between goals and means is truly clear only at a philosophical level and is necessarily relative in the dynamics of life. Yet the two must be separated as much as possible: separation of tasks and responsibilities is basic to sound management of both private and public affairs.

Optimal choice of both goals and means depends on managerial expertise. When the criteria and methods used in management decision making are influenced by political ideology, the management of public institutions cannot but suffer. Choice of values and means implies a set of activities with their own requirements; management has its universal features which are independent of the political context in which they operate. From the very decentralized to the very centralized, each political system must recognize that its own survival and welfare depends on sound public management decision making. Here, too, we look with apprehension toward the public management of our advertising institution, for it often seems that public management tends to lose contact with the facts of life—goals and means—and to become dangerously filled with dreams empty of human substance.

As we take stock of what we have learned, we see many problems the solution of which may improve society's management of the advertising institution. Three problem areas, in particular, deserve to be singled out because of their importance in bringing about improvements. They are: national priorities, public regulation, and self-regulation.

4.1 NATIONAL PRIORITIES

There will always be differences between the points of view of an individual or an organization and the "point of view" of society. The history of Western civilizations is essentially a search for a balance between the individual's and the group's interests. This search resembles a pendulum continuously swinging from one extreme to the other, but never coming to a point of rest.

This dynamism must be accepted as a fact of life; we should not try to bring things to a state of rest. However, the interests of society and the individual are best served if we can work toward the elimination of excesses and, above all, sudden and costly changes.

Once we accept that there will always be a stress between the individual and society and that social management can do no more than lessen the amount and cost of this stress, we can appreciate the background to most of the controversy that surrounds advertising. The issues debated simply reflect the lack of understanding of the basic individual-society stress.

A basic shortcoming of modern public management of the individual-society stress is the lack of a clear distinction between the goals society wants to achieve and the methods that it wants to employ to reach them. Without this distinction, much debate simply serves to illustrate the proverb, "We want to eat our cake and have it, too."

A second shortcoming concerns the search for and choice of social goals. Presumably, individuals form a society in the hope that each will be better off—i.e., that the cost to each person for belonging to a group is lower than the benefits he receives from this membership. Thus, in a very general sense, the goal of any society is to make its members "happier."

Happiness is unfortunately not an operational term. Only more concrete goals can be pursued but, at present, the choice of these is a very slow process. More importantly, many of these goals are not clearly stated: they often are as vague as that of happiness. And legislative activities at all levels of government continue to proliferate ill-defined goals.

The consequences of this are easy to forecast. To begin with, legislators themselves lose sense of direction. As proliferating laws accumulate large commitments for many years to come, lawmakers suddenly find, e.g., that 75 percent of the federal fiscal budget for 1974 is beyond managerial reach and modifications; that military spending has decreased to its lowest percentage since 1950 (i.e., 30.2 percent); and that spending for human needs has rapidly increased to 47 percent of the total. Without a sense of historical direction and rational decision making, and with only 25 percent of the total budget available for decisions concerning the future of society, legislators are forced to choose under the duress of the immediate present. The urgency of the present and the fuzziness of the past rule out both systematic inquiries into specific social goals and long-range planning, and, as a result, the ranking of social goals in terms of their desirability and economic feasibility.

Some political scientists argue that this situation guarantees incremental change and is thus desirable. The fact remains, however, that this state of affairs affects the legislators' choices with respect to the advertising institution. One example will suffice. For some time, there have been attempts to create a federal institute devoted to the study of marketing and advertising. The institute's budget would amount to $5 million. Even though this budget is ridiculously small in relation to the tasks involved, it follows from the situation just described that such legislation cannot presently acquire any visibility, and is likely to be pushed aside in favor of more pressing legislation.

We can argue that this manner of selecting social goals, at least at the federal level, is the right one: it assures that only the most important social issues receive attention. But this would imply that the socioeconomic roles of the institution are relatively unimportant and/or that the institution's performance of these roles is relatively accept-able. The latter conclusion is obviously unacceptable to critics and, judging from the amount of time spent on advertising problems, to the FTC staff and commissioners. And the conclusion that the institution is relatively unimportant is clearly unacceptable to all—including the witnesses we have heard and the scholars who have come to see how much modern societies rely on a mass communication system.

The most serious cloud hovering over the study of advertising is the manner in which society ranks its goals at the legislative level. Not only are social goals formulated in too generic terms, but their priorities are neither carefully considered nor spelled out for regulatory agencies' use. Although a number of scholars have been arguing that setting national priorities is a prerequisite for sound public management,[1] there is no evidence that this will happen in the foreseeable future.

It is a managerial truism that failure to specify goals or to rank them will have a negative effect on the choice of means—that is, on the behavior of regulatory commis-sions. Commissions and staffs are faced with either a vacuum of direction or with a series of conflicting goals with no hint of their relative social priority. It is thus unavoidable that the private goals of commissioners and their staffs may tend to influence regulatory choice, whether it be the choice of the issues to be investigated or the rules for settling such issues.

Let us illustrate this point briefly. We saw that, even if the advertising institution were totally useless to both sellers and buyers and made no contribution to the economics of society's mass communication system, its elimination would provide only a minuscule social saving and decrease in the general level of prices. But quantitative smallness does not necessarily mean little importance: facts have different meanings according to the values of the person who judges. Thus, if the staff of the FTC *prefers* to allocate some of its budget to the regulation of advertising rather than to that of monopoly, it is expressing a value judgement as to the importance of a very small potential gain in the level of prices.

Similarly, part of the FTC budget is spent for the regulation of "persuasive" advertising rather than the pursuit of false ads. And funds are spent to investigate how new is "new," and to make the momentous and laborious rulings (1) that a firm can call a product "new" for six months only; (2) that the six months' limitation is suspended during a market test period; and (3) that the six month rule is reinstated if the market test lasts more than six months.[2]

---

[1] See, for example, the literature on social indicators and the work of a national commission appointed by President Johnson in the mid-sixties; the Commission on National Goals appointed during the first administration of President Nixon; the recent series of a yearly publication on setting national priorities in the federal budget by The Brookings Institution; and the work by the National Planning Association (a private group in Washington, D.C.).

[2] Thus, in effect, ruling against longer tests just at the time when more firms find out that longer tests are desirable to decrease the probability of new product failures. And thus creating a potential paradox: product failures in the market represent not only substantial losses to private firms but, ultimately, costs to society since the failure represents misallocation of national resources. In this sense, then, management of the public interest should encourage firms to do more and longer market tests to decrease the risk of wasting society's scarce resources.

And so on with other cases which are not based simply on facts but also on evaluations of these facts. Without a clear direction of national priorities, such evaluations necessarily tend to reflect personal beliefs of what is important for society.

Our witnesses repeatedly pointed out that public management of the advertising institution should not reflect the private preferences of regulatory agencies. Individual regulators may be aware of their appointed rather than elected status and do their best to limit their choice to that of means. And, in cases of genuine disagreement, both parties can resort to courts. But these are only remedial actions. The fundamental problem remains. Unless the legislative process improves, large amounts of time and funds will be spent on arguing about the goals the public management of advertising should pursue in what is the wrong area, i.e., the regulatory rather than the legislative area. And these debates will inexorably confuse the choice of means.

4.2 PUBLIC REGULATION

Since the second half of the last century, the United States has developed a sophisticated approach to the regulation of economic activities—one that is probably more advanced than most others.[1] As the society and its economic system have evolved, several changes have been made, and it is undoubtedly true that many others ought to be made.[2]

The key feature of the current system of public regulation is the *specialization* of regulatory agencies by types of economic activities. For instance, the regulation of railroads is assigned to the Interstate Commerce Commission and that of airlines to the Federal Aviation Agency. From a managerial perspective, this specialization has advantages. Foremost among these is that a regulatory agency can gain the necessary engineering and economic knowledge of what the problems are at the firm and industry levels, and thus learn what action is feasible. Regulators are in the position to know the structure, potential, and limitations of the field to be regulated; thus they acquire knowledge of how to lead a firm and an industry toward a balanced satisfaction of both individual and societal goals.

But this specialization of public agencies suffers also from all the disadvantages inherent in specialization. From a managerial perspective, some disadvantages of specialization are much more basic than others that are more often mentioned. For instance, it is often feared that industry specialization may lead regulators to become too sympathetic to the perspectives and goals of the firms being regulated. When this happens, we are confronted with a failure of men rather than of a system. Similarly, commissioners are appointed and given a large degree of independence from political interference. But this independence can lead to a dangerous insulation from the desires

---

[1] See its evaluation against other systems in the area of regulation of marketing and management decisions by public utilities in F. M. Nicosia, *Tecnica Amministrativa delle Imprese di Servizi Pubblici*, Edizioni Ateneo, Roma, Italy, 1960, Chs. II, III, and IV.

[2] For an overall review of "the government as regulator," see the entire issue of the *Annals* of the American Academy of Political and Social Science, March 1972, edited by M. H. Bernstein.

of those who are regulated and of the consumer. Again, we are faced with failures of men to enact the roles society has assigned to them.

There are structural problems in the system, however, which are becoming increasingly more important and which may be contributing factors to human failures. These problems are inherent in any organizational design stressing specialization. By introducing specialization into the management of social institutions, we gain from deeper expertise in progressively narrower problem areas. But we pay for this gain with an increased loss of the advantages of *coordination.* We lose the ability to see the whole, the interdependencies of the parts, and we find it progressively more difficult to pinpoint responsibility.

To illustrate, specialization in the regulations of means of transportation has made it hard to foresee the consequences of technological changes in the production of cars and trucks and, later, of airplanes. Having failed to take advantage of the complementarity and substitutability among means of transportation, society was forced to give up the enormous investment in capital, equipment, and human skills it had made in the railroads.

In spite of its complexities, the transportation case appears simple when we consider the case of the advertising institution and its public management. We have already stressed several of the economic and social interdependencies of this institution with others. Let us here stress that which concerns the consumer.

Much of our concern with advertising is only a part of a more general concern with the well-being of consumers, which ultimately means of all citizens. As affluence has spread, society has begun to switch its legislative and regulatory emphasis from production problems to consumer problems. The process through which this switch is taking place appears to operate on *ad hoc* principles; it is characterized by responding to problems as they arise rather than by planning.

The net result is that today consumer interests have been compartmentalized into neat little pockets, in a host of laws ranging from the very general to the very specific, and an increasing proliferation of public agencies whose tasks are often unrelated or conflicting. As this has been happening, we have lost sight of the consumer himself in the process. For instance:

> Some 10 years ago a Congressional committee found in a study that nearly 300 different programs were operating to advance consumer interests. These cost taxpayers almost $1 billion anually and employed the services of about 65,000 people.
>
> Another study four years ago found that 39 separate agencies, bureaus and departments were involved in various consumer programs. Then recently, a third study—this one by Mrs. Virginia Knauer, the President's Special Advisor on Consumer Affairs—discovered that the overlapping and duplication of consumer programs made a count almost impossible.
>
> The Wall Street Journal quoted Mrs. Knauer as saying, "I just couldn't believe so many people had their finger in it (consumer programs). It created a bureaucratic mare's nest."[1]

---

[1] In *Questions and Answers for Consumers,* a brochure by the National Association of Manufacturers, New York, n.d., p. 11.

Public management of advertising cannot be improved without a structure that indicates which public office is responsible for each aspect of consumer behavior. Since advertising is only one possible influence on the consumer, it interacts with all others; thus, public decisions on advertising interact with other public decisions concerning the consumer.

We need to develop a matrix in which consumer problems are listed on one axis, public agencies on the second, and specific activities by public agencies on the third. Such a matrix—a familiar tool of management—would make it possible to visualize systematically the presence of interdependencies, and especially of useful and conflicting overlaps as well as gaps to be filled. The creation and assessment of a total picture of current public management of consumer behavior is a fundamental requirement for locating the tasks of the advertising institution and planning its coordination with the management of other consumer problems.

A careful analysis of who does what about which consumer problems cannot be postponed any longer, for the complexity of an affluent and pluralistic society and its related stress on consumer well-being are growing rapidly. It will help to identify existing and, above all, emerging problems.

Consider, for example, a case which is in principle simple: the case of the vitamin and nutritional content in foods. The Department of Agriculture is responsible for assessing the nutritional content of generic food—meats, fruits, produce, etc. The Food and Drug Administration is concerned with how labels on food brands state the nutritional contents, the stress here being on the potential harm different contents may have. Presumably, if nutritional information were to be broadcast, the Federal Communications Commission could be involved: in fact, a precedent has been established in the case of TV advertising of cigarettes. The Consumer Protection Agency would be given the authority to study and intervene in any of the areas assigned to the above three agencies, as well as in other areas. The Federal Trade Commission is also responsible for seeing that labels do not contain false information, and its recent activities suggest that it also deems itself capable of ascertaining whether such information is persuasive. Even though this is a simple sketch, it gives a feeling for the possibilities of conflict and cooperation among public agencies. At present, management of these agencies is bound to react in each case that reveals such conflicts; but a rational blueprint would at least allow the agencies' managers to anticipate them.

Another example dramatizes the need for clarification and coordination. Recall the case of foam plastics introduced into many consumer goods as nonflammable (Chapter 13, Section 4.1). We listed the large number of public and quasi-public agencies responsible for establishing and applying the standards that measure flammability: these agencies allowed such products to be used. A few years after their introduction, courts found the products to be deadly, but the above agencies did nothing about it. And, several years later, in order to file a complaint, the FTC had to build a tortuous case based on the argument that, although the products are *legally* entitled to be described as nonflammable, the firms producing them knew that the current standards were inadequate and that, therefore, the ads were false.

This rather bizarre and inefficient way to protect basic consumer interests is the result of the current proliferation of agencies dealing with the consumer and the lack of a clear map of the interdependencies among such agencies. If not corrected, the situation will worsen and more cases of this type will occur.

Moreover, unsystematic proliferation will insulate public agencies even more from their statutory and moral responsibilities. Public agencies will unavoidably tend to form a social organization of their own, with internal struggles and tacit norms of reciprocal behavior. Managers' energies will gradually be switched away from functional goals and toward the politics necessary to survive within this social group and to deal with the legislative sources of funds.

Unsystematic proliferation of public agencies may not only increase the intricacies of the overall management of consumer interests, but it will also make it impossible for any consumer to exercise his rights and thus provide useful feedback. Consider the case of prescription drugs. As in all cases of advancing technology, a new drug may reveal undesirable or even dangerous side effects. A brief review of the literature indicates that, in such cases, the managers of the pharmaceutical firms have been held responsible for such consequences. But the same review indicates that the managers of the public agencies who developed the standards for firms to satisfy before introducing new drugs, approved the firms' compliance with these standards and, finally, allowed the introduction of the new drugs, have not been called upon by any consumer or consumer organization to respond concerning their decisions. Yet, effective management cannot be achieved without clear rewards and sanctions for the performance of assigned responsibilities.

To sum up, as we look toward the future, the fundamental issues surrounding the public management of the advertising institution are simple to state, but hard to implement in the present circumstances. First, society needs to assess the present system of public management of the entire area of consumer well-being. As for the agencies in charge of advertising, they should be enabled to go beyond just responding to events and issues.

When public agencies are forced merely to react, they will necessarily be seen only as being for or against business. Instead, public management must be given the means to plan well into the future. By identifying and assessing technological and social change, public managers will be able to take a constructive posture, to anticipate problems, and thus to satisfy one of the requirements of management decision making: leadership.

4.3 SELF-REGULATION

A society is an open system and, whatever its political organization, its proper functioning depends not only on the behavior of public managers but also on each individual and each private organization. *Individual* consumers can contribute a great deal to the better performance by the advertising institution. Beyond purchase or nonpurchase decisions, consumers can give direct feedback to both firms and public agencies. This feedback should not be limited to negative information—complaints and the like—for these state only what consumers dislike and not what they would prefer to have.

As a stakeholder of the advertising institution, each consumer has the opportunity to assume the responsibility of active participation. This might mean a high cost to each individual; however, the formation of private groups could decrease individual costs. Active *consumer groups* can effectively communicate emerging problems as well as potential opportunities directly to both firms and public agencies. They can especially help private and public management in dealing with difficult problems created by affluence, in particular, the increasing differentiation and rapid change in people's desires and styles of life. Even though consumer research provides a means for monitoring differentiation and change, additional evidence from consumers themselves would also provide useful feedback. Legislators, public agencies, and also private firms may in the long run find that encouraging the spontaneous formation of consumer groups will produce useful input into the performance of the advertising institution.[1]

Private firms are also stakeholders of the institution. The behavior of *each firm* is as important as the behavior of each public agency, probably even more important in the present context. Self-regulation begins with each firm. Many witnesses, it will be recalled, stressed that self-regulation not only is in the interest of the entire institution, but also helps the private sector and, fundamentally, each firm. To the extent that corporate management believes this, it should be willing to add to its admittedly heavy burden: that of controlling not only the economic but also the qualitative aspects of advertising decisions.[2]

This task is very complex. To illustrate, bringing the qualitative aspects of advertising decisions closer to corporate management would call for changes in the popular organizational structure in which the advertising department does not communicate directly with corporate managers. It would also be necessary to strengthen the current cooperation among the advertiser, its advertising agency, and, often, the law firm (see Chapters 3 and 7).

In addition, remember that most marketing decisions essentially concern information sent to potential consumers, whether it be through the choice of a product design, package design, label, or through the salesman. Thus, studying ways of bringing advertising closer to corporate management makes it apparent that other marketing decisions interact with advertising in the firm's total information program addressed to consumers.

Some firms have realized this and are experimenting with the creation of a consumer affairs office that may or may not report to the marketing department, and may or may not be concerned with the quality of advertising decisions. Though experimental, these attempts signify the realization that the consumer is the target of all information and that self-regulation by advertisers is only a part of self-regulation in its entirety.

As it searches for solutions to organizational stresses, corporate management will face

---

[1] For a thoughtful discussion of this point in the context of the broader problem of *consumer representation*, see M. V. Nadel, *The Politics of Consumer Protection*, Bobbs-Merrill, New York, 1971, *infra*. See also D. A. Aaker and G. S. Day, *Consumerism: Search for the Consumer Interest*, The Free Press, New York, 1974.

[2] The former president of a national TV network has vigorously stressed that the responsibility for what is said in a company's advertising rests directly on the shoulders of management, and nowhere else. See F. Stanton, "Business in the Public Forum," paper delivered to the 1973 Annual Meeting of the American Association of Advertising Agencies, May 18, 1973.

further complexities. Let us mention a few which bear upon the future of a firm's self-regulation with regard to advertising. While advertising is an attempt to communicate with some specific group of potential buyers, any ad usually reaches many who are not its target. While, at the managerial level, this is often justifiable on the basis of cost versus payoffs (this is particularly true for TV advertising; see Chapter 5, Section 3 and Chapter 6, Section 2), it is nevertheless the nontarget persons who may react negatively to this or that ad. Furthermore, many other decisions directly or indirectly imply communication to the general public, even though the messages involved were directed only to special groups—labor, stockholders, etc.

It is beyond the scope of this book to examine these complexities, but it is necessary to take note of them. Foresighted self-regulation of advertising at the firm level calls for a reexamination of corporate management's involvement in the total information process within a firm. It is evident that, as a firm grows in size and complexity, its well-being depends not only on successful communication with specific groups of participants (e.g., labor, consumers, suppliers of capital, and suppliers of equipment) but also on coordination among these specific communications programs and, eventually, coordination of these programs with communications to other publics such as government agencies and the general public.[1]

So far we have looked at the main problems corporate management will face in trying to improve its internal communication processes. Externally, the complexities increase as advertising and other decisions by distributors and retailers are also considered. Essentially, each firm will have to find ways to increase the involvement of distributors and retailers in decisions concerning the qualitative aspects of advertising.

In addition to self-regulation at the firm level, there remains the problem of obtaining *group efforts* at the industry and trade association levels. There have been notable efforts in the past. In the second half of the last century, several private groups felt the need to publish codes of advertising ethics. In this century, the Better Business Bureau was another attempt at the interindustry level to establish behavior codes not only in advertising but also in all relationships between firms and consumers.[2]

In the sixties, economic and social changes have called for additional approaches to group self-regulation. The first results of the most recent interindustry effort were reported earlier (Chapter 15, Section 2): the National Advertising Review Board (NARB) is the most comprehensive effort to date and, for the first time, there are some sanctions incorporated in the mechanism.

[1] For an example of how a specific management question ("What is the best design concerning the content and organizational position of a public relations office and an advertising department?") cannot be resolved without considering the role of corporate management in administering a firm's total communication process, see F. M. Nicosia, "Public Relations: A Managerial Approach," paper presented to the First Asian-American-African Public Relations Conference, Tokyo, Waseda University, April 1959.

[2] In an incisive discussion of self-regulation, La Barbera notes a dilemma: on one hand, federal agencies have at times favored self-regulation; on the other hand, courts and the antitrust division of the Department of Justice have often taken a negative position against it. See P. La Barbera, "Self-Regulation: A Viable Alternative to Government Regulation?," August 1973, Michigan State University, Graduate School of Business, East Lansing, Mich., unpublished manuscript.

Past experience suggests that NARB will succeed only if corporate managers give it full support, including courageous and strict applications of sanctions. Success will also depend on the ability of NARB to extend its jurisdiction to cover local advertising. Finally, the future of advertising as we know it today in the United States will also depend on the ways in which self-regulation is extended to cover many other marketing decisions. All too often consumers' reaction to advertising is based on "minor" but frequent dissatisfactions such as a defective package or a salesman's inappropriate phrase.

Overall, group self-regulation still relies on the input of each firm. The efforts and good-will of a few firms have been sufficient for self-regulation to bear fruit in the past. But if history were to choose advertising as a means to judge the efficacy of private management and entrepreneurship, the good example of a few would not suffice, for the entire class of corporate managers and entrepreneurs would be under scrutiny.

5 DEVELOPING KNOWLEDGE OF FACTS: A NECESSARY CONDITION

Effective public management of the advertising institution will require more information about relationships of costs and benefits and the increasing differentiation of cultural values and aspirations. Neither of these two classes of facts is easily amenable to sound conceptualization and quantification at the moment.

Consider our discussion of the economics of the advertising institution in Chapters 11 and 12. Although we were able to point to some research directions, we learned that even the initial problems of defining, observing, and measuring information and distinguishing it from communication have not been resolved satisfactorily. This is a challenge faced by all disciplines, for the study of any type of information exchange is in its infancy. For instance, although the study of information exchange among a few people in laboratory conditions has been the focus of small group dynamics for decades, what has been learned so far about even the simplest aspects of the process is still ambiguous. In fact, progress in recent years has shown that some of the early empirical "facts" were misleading and need much refinement.[1] Thus, public managers of the advertising institution should not expect that future research will immediately generate useful guidelines and should avoid using early empirical findings to casually support claims about the socioeconomic roles of advertising.

Not only are we not yet ready to describe the working of the institution in relevant ways, but we cannot yet easily identify at the macro level how its members, especially consumers, use it and what they expect from it. Apropos of the consumer, some caveats must be made explicit.

5.1 THE LIMITS OF CONSUMER BEHAVIOR KNOWLEDGE

Throughout Part 1, we saw how the emerging discipline of consumer behavior has been useful to corporate management for planning, implementing, and evaluating the

---

[1] For a careful review of early "knowledge" and the challenging refinements needed, see the mathematical models and empirical results in K. Mackenzie, *A Theory of Group Structures,* Gordon Breach, New York, in press.

advertising business function. We also saw how consumer behavior knowledge can help public agencies manage certain problems of the institution.[1]

Consumer behavior can document to social managers that consumers are not a heterogeneous lot, especially in an affluent society, and that the meaning of information cannot but be subjective. Consumer researchers such as Jacoby, Kassarjian, Myers, Wilkie, and others can help public managers to change their conceptualization of some problems and often obtain meaningful, actionable, empirical findings. Similarly, the work by Aaker, Bucklin, Day, and others can give a nonpopulist foundation to the consumerism notion as it bears on the advertising institution. Further, Bauer, Greyser and, more recently, Barksdale and Pessemier have given some baseline measures of consumers' opinions about the institution.[2]

But as we learn more about what consumer research can do, we must keep in mind its limitations. Although some are hopefully temporary, they are nevertheless real, and must be explained to public managers lest they overestimate the discipline's potential today and then, disappointed, reject it tomorrow. Such events would hamper the removal of limitations that can only be erased by continuous work on the social implications of advertising.

Nothing could be more counterproductive to the discipline's future than the appearance of consumer researchers before congressional hearings and courts, arguing about the pros and cons of different theories and methodologies. (This has, in fact, already happened, for courts have begun to accept survey research data as tentative evidence). While regulatory agencies should be encouraged to make active use of consumer surveys, caution should be emphasized.[3]

Survey research and its applications in marketing, advertising, and consumer research have not yet obtained professional status. Although associations such as the American Association of Public Opinion Research, the American Marketing Association, and Division 23 of the American Psychology Association have developed general codes of ethics, they have taken no active stand on the creation of certification programs. Not even the more modest phases of any survey have been certified.[4]

It is crucial that public managers realize the current limitations of research that

[1] See, e.g., Ch. 13. Recently, the Federal Trade Commission has invited several consumer researchers such as Kassarjian and Wilkie to study the areas in which consumer behavior knowledge may be useful. This is an exciting trend which will bear fruit; for instance, see W. L. Wilkie, "Research on Counter and Corrective Advertising," in S. Divita (ed.), *Advertising and the Public Interest*, American Marketing Association, Chicago, Ill., 1974; and W. L. Wilkie and D. M. Gardner, "The Role of Marketing Research in Public Policy Decision Making" and R. F. Dyer and P. G. Kuehl, "The 'Corrective Advertising' Remedy of the FTC: An Experimental Evaluation," both in *Journal of Marketing*, January 1974.

[2] An exciting and certainly useful research should also be the study of the factors that account for these opinions. Apropos of this, see S. H. Surlin, "The Attitudes of Prejudiced Individuals Toward the Institution of Advertising," *Journal of Advertising*, 1973 (no month given).

[3] Apropos of these, see the many passages in the careful analysis of "evidence" in Gerlach, *op. cit*, and the rich references in footnotes.

[4] Private leadership toward self-regulation is desirable in its own right. Furthermore, it may anticipate problems concerning "public" certification: apropos of this see the current issues in the accounting profession discussed in D. Solomons, "Financial Accounting Standards: Regulation or Self-regulation?" Stanford Lectures in Accounting Series, Graduate School of Business, Stanford, University, 1972 (mimeo).

attempts to conceptualize and measure the consumer at the macro, societal level. This limitation of consumer research is in part due to the discipline's very success at the micromanagerial level. From early *demographics* to recent *psychographics* consumer research has helped advertising managers to realize that the myths of "mass" consumption and "average" consumer do not apply any longer. It has also helped identify different types of Mrs. Joneses—that is, consumer research has shown that people often buy (or do not buy) the same thing for different reasons; that different persons need different information; and so on.[1]

In a nutshell, consumer research has documented the pluralism of consumer decision processes, and thus of the society in which firms operate. While this has been beneficial for optimizing resource utilization by individual firms, it has concurrently deprived us all of a vision of consumers as a whole.

Consumer research can dissect "the consumer" into segments that are relevant to a government agency that wants to reduce foreign travel and increase domestic travel. Or it can provide helpful information to a government agency that wants to encourage consumers who change their own car engine's oil to dispose of it properly, rather than to dump it into the nearest sewer.

But public managers also ask social and economic questions concerning all consumers and, ultimately, society as a whole. For example, in a current publicly sponsored project, the question is: "It has been usually assumed that the wider is the choice of goods offered to the consumer, the better off the consumer will be. Is this empirically correct? What are the trade-offs consumers experience as the variety of goods offered to them increases?" A review of the literature on consumer behavior and in the American Psychological Association information system revealed that no published article contained either empirical data or theoretical concepts bearing upon the question. This can be interpreted as evidence that consumer research has not been previously called upon to answer questions of interest to public managers; at the same time, it suggests the lack of awareness of the power of the consumer in affluent societies.

Similarly, it has been argued that firms, and especially their advertising, are responsible for the trend toward nudity in women's fashion—from the miniskirt to the bikini. Caught in amoral calculations of costs and revenues, each firm has supposedly contributed to the decay of social morality. Yet there are no conceptualizations of this social question from within the micro tradition of consumer research. It can be argued, for instance, that the nudity trend in women's fashion was the result not of moral decay but of technological and other changes. It can even be postulated that the change in fashion might itself have been the cause of changing morality.[2]

The increasing pluralism of affluent societies may, indeed, be the salient fact to cope with. We must perhaps prepare ourselves to accept that affluence ultimately leads to so much decentralization of cultural norms that, at the consumer level, it is relevant to ask

[1] For a thorough documentation of "market segmentation," see R. Frank, W. Massy, and Y. Wind, *Market Segmentation*, Prentice-Hall, Englewood Cliffs, N.J., 1972.

[2] C. Y. Glock and F. M. Nicosia, "The Consumer," in P. F. Lazarsfeld, W. H. Sewell, and W. L. Wilenski (eds.), *The Uses of Sociology*, Basic Books, New York, 1967.

only questions pertaining to specific consumer groups. Perhaps, as affluence spreads to more countries, and as economic and cultural exchange among countries increases, we will have to stop equating a society with its political or geographical boundaries.

Yet there still remains the fact that legislators and regulators are, and will continue to be, concerned with problems that necessarily involve consumers as a total group, and society as a whole, since the most pressing issues facing the advertising institution call for the ability to conceptualize consumers and society as a whole.

5.2 TOWARD A SOCIOLOGY OF CONSUMPTION

Consumer research was in part born as a response to the pressing demands of firms who were experiencing firsthand the coming of affluence and the progressive differentiation in consumer behaviors and motivations. Demand theory from economics and several branches of psychology and social psychology provided the main inputs to help firms understand the differentiated demand for their products. In fact, Glock and Nicosia noted that, throughout the fifties and early sixties, it was micro economists and psychologists who were by far the most active in research into the areas of marketing, advertising, and consumer behavior. They stressed that questions concerning the entire set of consumers in a society had been tackled mainly by macro economists who had to turn themselves into sociologists in order to interpret observations of a strict economic nature.[1] And they concluded with a call to sociologists and others to begin thinking about the need to prepare the foundations for a sociology of consumption.[2]

In the late sixties and early seventies, this need to understand the consumer at the macro, consumption level—i.e., a call for a sociology of consumption—was also increasingly felt by marketing teachers, as reflected in their writing on the social responsibilities of marketing managers and in their efforts to group into books of readings whatever relevant material could be found. Marketing researchers such as Wells, and marketing research firms such as Yankelovich, also began to stress this need. And several of the projects by Greyser, Ray, and others at the Marketing Research Institute have begun to show how the study of the advertising institution must necessarily be related to a better understanding of the macro roles of the consumer at the societal level.

Even today, however, response from the basic disciplines is conspicuously lacking. Apart from the continuing contributions of macro economics, social sciences have focused on partial aspects of the macro roles of consumers: for instance, on leisure, recreation, entertainment, and time budgets. No research is addressed to the totality of consumption behavior in affluent societies. Although the growth of the literature on social indicators signals the need to conceptualize what an affluent society is and may become, the emphasis is still on more traditional topics.

Strange as it may seem, most social science research tends to ignore the new freedom

---

[1] C. Y. Glock and F. M. Nicosia, "Uses of Sociology in Studying 'Consumption' Behavior," *Journal of Marketing,* July 1964.

[2] Glock and Nicosia, "The Consumer," *op. cit.,* and Nicosia and Glock, "Marketing and Affluence," *op. cit.*

and power of consumers to dictate, rather than adapt to, social and economic change. Even the costly change in the measurement of the cost of living by the federal government has been debated on almost every ground except that of its ability to observe, at the social level, what consumers do with their time and income. That is to say, we have ignored the fact that these budget studies could provide us with a very powerful social indicator of what is happening to society.

Only a few established consumer research programs have shown interest in the macro social roles of consumption behavior—e.g., the work by Katona and his associates, among them Morgan, Mueller, and more recently Schmiedeskamp, Strumpel, and Zahn. Trained as a psychologist in the intellectual milieu of Vienna, Katona has worked with macro economists since the late forties and has introduced behavioral elements into the macroeconomic description of the consumer. His systematic attempts to interpret consumer data at the societal level in the sixties[1] and his more recent investigation of how "consumers come to exert a great influence on the rate of growth of the economy" still stand almost alone.[2]

This paucity of interest in the societal meaning of consumption behavior makes current studies of the possible effects of advertising expenditures on consumption expenditures meaningless for basic and applied purposes. We have seen that advertising expenditures cannot be used as a meaningful indicator of the internal structure and external functions of the institution. Now we must add that consumption expenditures alone cannot measure the basic cultural roles of the affluent consumer.[3] Some progress can be made if we begin to ask not only whether the advertising institution affects consumers but also whether the reverse is true. But, when we attempt to do this (see Chapter 11), we quickly discover that new concepts and data are needed regarding the consumer at the societal level.

In short, we cannot pretend to study the socioeconomic roles of advertising, and especially its relationships with the increasingly important roles of consumption behavior, if we do not concentrate our energies on the macro study of the consumer both in affluent and newly developing economies.[4] Sophisticated use of multivariate statistical

---

[1] G. Katona, *The Powerful Consumer,* McGraw-Hill, New York, 1960, and *The Mass Consumption Society,* McGraw-Hill, New York, 1964.

[2] G. Katona, B. Strumpel, and E. Zahn, *Aspirations and Affluence,* McGraw-Hill, New York, 1971, p. 4.

[3] At the very least, the measurement of consumption behavior in affluent societies calls for two additional indicators beyond dollars spent: (a) the kinds of baskets bought by different people, and (b) above all, the allocation of time to different activities by different people. See, e.g., Nicosia and Glock, "Marketing and Affluence," *op. cit.*

[4] The interplay in developing economies between consumers, mass media, and advertising has been pointed out; see, e.g., W. Schramm, *Mass Media and National Development,* Stanford University Press, Stanford, Calif., 1964; and D. Lerner and W. Schramm (eds.), *Communication and Change in Developing Countries,* East-West Center Press, Honolulu, Hawaii, 1967. And it can be argued that the study of such interplays in developing societies can help our search in affluent societies (F. M. Nicosia, "The Role of Consumption in Economic Growth and Social Change," 1966, mimeo). See also the chapters by D. S. Freedman and by A. Lauterback in B. Strumpel, J. N. Morgan, and E. Zahn (eds.), *Human Behavior in Economic Affairs: Essays in Honor of George Katona,* Elsevier, Amsterdam, Holland, 1972.

inference is not sufficient to remedy the fact that current data tend to be empty for our purposes—it may in fact lead us to erroneous conclusions.

The emergence of consumer behavior as a field of study was largely due to the willingness of marketing practitioners and scholars to examine and interpret the possible contributions of demand theory and psychology. It is inevitable that sociology and related disciplines will eventually discover the societal importance of consumption behavior; in the meantime marketing scholars and practitioners may do well to add to the efforts of Zaltman, Smelser, Glock and a few other *bona fide* sociologists in bringing a sociological approach to the study of the consumer and the advertising institution.[1]

5.3 INSTITUTIONAL SUPPORT AND ORGANIZATION

In these concluding pages we have emphasized the need for knowledge of facts concerning social values and the economics of the advertising institution. But we have seen that the relative limitations of consumer behavior knowledge and the lack of a sociology of consumption are major handicaps to improving the management of the institution. Overcoming these handicaps is a tall order.

Just as the federal government was instrumental in instituting censuses of the demographic and economic features of the country, it will again be needed to develop systematic and ongoing databases for recording relevant features of the advertising institution and of the consumer. Many firms would cooperate with such new efforts, as they did in the earlier development of economic and demographic data. New and better measures of changes in the advertising institution and in society would indeed be useful at both corporate and line management levels. Some firms are already actively supporting research by the Marketing Science Institute and/or the program of the Educational Foundation of the American Association of Advertising Agencies. Hopefully, associations such as the Association of National Advertisers and the National Association of Manufacturers will join these efforts and provide the necessary leadership.

Private efforts can be expected to lend support to research of an essentially applied nature. However, the sketch of the problems awaiting us clearly calls for basic research, with its inherent risks. Basic research implies much trial and error, and explorations in many directions where the probable pay-offs cannot even be "guesstimated." Determined and above all *continuous support* by *both* the private and public sectors will be required, for the new and unorthodox can neither be found nor evaluated with a crisis type of approach to the problems discussed.

In addition to a serious and lasting commitment by the private and public sectors, we should search for the new and the unorthodox in two complementary ways. On one hand, some research support should be purposely *decentralized.* The level of competence of the new generation of marketing scholars has increased substantially and so has the ability of many higher educational institutions throughout the country to provide the

---

[1] See F. M. Nicosia and T. H. Witkowsky, "The Need for a Sociology of Consumption," Annual Conference, Association of Consumer Research, Boston, November 1973, mimeo.

right working environment. It is from these "new" institutions that the initial sparks of fundamental rethinking may indeed come. On the other hand, the sheer size and challenge of the task will necessitate coordination and continuity of both theory and administration. This will require that some support should be purposefully *centralized* around individual scholars and programs which have already addressed themselves to the managerial and social questions raised in this book.

Bibliography

Aaker, D. A.: "Deceptive Advertising," Working Paper No. 86, Institute of Business and Economic Research, University of California, Berkeley, Calif., November 1972.

Aaker, D. A., and G. S. Day: *Consumerism: Search for the Consumer Interest,* Free Press, New York, 1974.

Aaker, D. A., and J. G. Myers: *Advertising Management,* Prentice-Hall, Englewood Cliffs, N.J., 1975.

Abbott, J. C.: "Fires Involving Upholstery Materials," *Fire Journal,* published by the National Fire Protection Association, July 1971.

Andreason, A. R.: "Attitudes and Customer Behavior: A Decision Model," Working Paper, Institute of Business and Economic Research, University of California, Berkeley, Calif., 1964.

Arbuckle, J.: *The Role of Mathematical Models in Statistical Models,* MBA thesis, University of California, Berkeley, Calif., June 1970.

Artle, R.: "Urbanization and Economic Growth in Venezuela," reprint from Vol. XXVII Papers, Regional Science Association, n.d.

Artle, R., and C. Avernous: "The Telephone System as a Public Good: Static and Dynamic Aspects," *Bell Journal of Economics and Management Science,* Spring 1973.

Baligh, H., and L. Richards: *Vertical Market Structures,* Allyn & Bacon, Boston, Mass., 1967.

Banks, S.: "Adapting Marketing Strategy to Changes in Business Conditions: Implications for Promotional Programs," unpublished manuscript, National Industrial Conference Board, 18th Annual Marketing Conference, New York, October 1970.

Barton, A. H.: "The Concept of Property-Space in Social Research," in P. F. Lazarsfeld and M. Rosenberg (eds.), *The Language of Social Research,* The Free Press, Glencoe, Ill., 1955.

Bass, F. M.: "Market Structure and Profitability—Analysis of the Appropriateness of Pooling Cross-Sectional Industry Data," Paper No. 424, Purdue University, Lafayette, Ind., October 1973.

Bell, D.: *The Coming of Post-Industrial Society,* Basic Books, New York, 1973.

Bell, H. H.: "Self-regulation by the Advertising Industry," in S. P. Sethi (ed.), *The Unstable Ground: Corporate Social Policy in a Dynamic Society,* Melville Publishing Co., Los Angeles, Calif., 1974.

Bernstein, M. H. (ed.): *Annals,* American Academy of Political and Social Science, March 1972.

Bloch, H.: *Advertising, Competition, and Market Performance,* University of Chicago, Chicago, Ill., 1971.

Bock, B.: *Concentration, Oligopoly, and Profit: Concept vs. Data,* The Conference Board, New York, 1972.

Bogart, L.: "Mass Media in the Year 2000," *Gazette,* vol. 13, no. 3, 1967.

Bogart, L.: "The Management of Mass Media: An Agenda for Research," *Public Opinion Quarterly,* Winter 1973–1974.

Bogart, L.: "Warning: The Surgeon General Has Determined That TV Violence Is Moderately Dangerous to Your Child's Mental Health," *Public Opinion Quarterly,* Winter 1972–1973.

Bogart, L.: "Where Does Advertising Research Go from Here?", *Journal of Advertising Research,* March 1969.

Boulding, K. E.: *Economic Analysis,* Harper and Brothers, New York, 1955.

Bower, R. T.: *Television and the Public,* Holt, Rinehart and Winston, New York, 1973.

Brozen, Y.: "An Ivory Tower View of Advertising," unpublished manuscript, University of Chicago, Chicago, Ill., June 1972.

Bryant, J. E., and W. J. Derrig: *Marketing Potential of the MBA Resume Directory,* MBA thesis, University of California, Berkeley, Calif., June 1972.

Buchen Advertising, Inc.: "Advertising in Recession Periods," New York, 1970.

Bucklin, L. P.: *A Theory of Distribution Channel Structure,* Institute of Business and Economic Research, University of California, Berkeley, Calif., 1966.

Bucklin, L. P.: *Competition and Evolution in the Distributive Trades,* Prentice-Hall, Englewood Cliffs, N.J., 1972.

Bucklin, L. P.: "Consumer Search, Role Enactment, and Market Efficiency," *Journal of Business,* October 1969.

Business Week: June 23, 1973.

Buzzell, R.: "Marketing and Economic Performance: Meaning and Measurement," Marketing Science Institute, Cambridge, Mass., August 1972.

Buzzell, R.: "The Role of Advertising in the Market Mix," Marketing Science Institute, Cambridge, Mass., October 1971.

Clarke, D. G., and J. M. McCann: "Measuring the Cumulative Effects of Advertising: A Reappraisal," Paper No. 410, Institute for Research in the Behavioral, Economic, and Management Sciences, Purdue University, West Lafayette, Ind., May 1973.

Coen, R. J., personal communication.

Developmental Psychology Today, CRM Books, Del Mar, Calif., 1971.

Divita, S. (ed.): *Advertising and the Public Interest,* American Marketing Association, Chicago, Ill., 1974.

Dyer, R. F., and P. G. Kuehl: "The 'Corrective Advertising' Remedy of the FTC: An Experimental Evaluation," *Journal of Marketing,* January 1974.

Economic Report of the President, January 1973, U.S. Government Printing Office, Washington, D.C., 1973.

Emerson, T. I.: "Communication and Freedom of Expression," *Scientific American,* September 1972.

Engel, J. F., D. T. Kollat, and R. D. Blackwell: *Consumer Behavior,* Holt, Rinehart and Winston, New York, 1973.

Ferber, R.: "Consumer Economics from Neo-Classical Times to the Present," Paper No. 100, College of Commerce and Business Administration, University of Illinois, Urbana, Ill., March 1973.

Ferber, R.: "The Maturation of Marketing," *The Marketing News,* August 15, 1972; paper presented in acceptance of the Charles Coolidge Parlin Award.

Fisher, F. M., Z. Griliches, and C. Kaysen: "The Costs of Automobile Model Changes Since 1949," *Journal of Political Economy,* October 1962.

Frank, R., W. Massy, and Y. Wind: *Market Segmentation,* Prentice-Hall, Englewood Cliffs, N.J., 1972.

Freedman, D. S.: in B. Strumpel, J. N. Morgan, and E. Zahn (eds.), *Human Behavior in Economic Affairs: Essays in Honor of George Katona,* Elsevier, Amsterdam, Holland, 1972.

Gerbner, G.: "Communication and Social Environment," *Scientific American,* September 1972.

Gerlach, G. G.: "The Consumer's Mind: A Preliminary Inquiry into the Emerging Problems of Consumer Evidence and the Law," Marketing Science Institute, Cambridge, Mass., December 1972.

Glock, C. Y., and F. M. Nicosia: "The Consumer," in P. F. Lazarsfeld, W. H. Sewell, and W. L. Wilensky (eds.), *The Uses of Sociology,* Basic Books, New York, 1967.

Glock, C. Y., and F. M. Nicosia: "Uses of Sociology in Studying 'Consumption' Behavior," *Journal of Marketing,* July 1964.

Goldberg, M. E., and C. J. Gorn: "An Experimental Approach to the Effects of Television Advertising on Children," in Divita, *op. cit.*

Gould, J.: "Diffusion Processes and Optimal Advertising Policy," in E. S. Phelps, *et al.* (eds.), *Microeconomic Foundations of Employment and Inflation Theory,* Norton, New York, 1970.

Grabowsky, H. G.: "Advertising and Resource Allocation–Discussion," in Divita, *op. cit.*

Grether, E. T.: *Marketing and Public Policy,* Prentice-Hall, Englewood Cliffs, N.J., 1966.

Greyser, S. A.: "Businessmen re Advertising: Yes, But . . . ," *Harvard Business Review,* May–June 1962.

Greyser, S. A., and B. B. Reece: "Advertising Standards and Contents: Executives' Perspective," Working Paper, Marketing Science Institute, Cambridge, Mass., July 1972.

Greyser, S. A., and B. B. Reece: "Businessmen Look Hard at Advertising," *Harvard Business Review,* May–June 1971.

Haire, M.: "Biological Models and Empirical Histories of the Growth of Organization," in M. Haire (ed.), *Modern Organization Theory,* Wiley, New York, 1959.

Hirshleifer, J.: "Where Are We in the Theory of Information?", *American Economic Review,* May 1973.

Holton, R. H.: "Consumer Behavior, Market Imperfections, and Public Policy," in J. W. Markham and G. F. Papanek (eds.), *Industrial Organization and Economic Development,* Houghton Mifflin, Boston, Mass., 1970.

Holton, R. H.: "The Distinctions Between Convenience Goods, Shopping Goods, and Specialty Goods," *Journal of Marketing,* July 1958.

"How to Advertise Out of a Recession," *Printers' Ink,* November 2, 1962, special report.

Howard, J. A.: *Marketing: Executive and Buyer Behavior,* Columbia University Press, New York, 1963.

Howard, J. A.: *Marketing Management, Analysis, and Planning,* Irwin, Homewood, Ill., 1963.

Howard, J. A., and L. E. Ostlund (eds.): *Buyer Behavior: Theoretical and Empirical Foundations,* Alfred Knopf, New York, 1963.

Howard, J. A., and J. Sheth: *The Theory of Buyer Behavior,* Wiley, New York, 1969.

Jones, M. G.: "Social Responsibility: The Regulator's View," in S. P. Sethi (ed.), *The Unstable Ground: Corporate Social Policy in a Dynamic Society,* Melville Publishing Co., Los Angeles, Calif., forthcoming.

Jones, M. G.: Speech to the Association of American Law Schools, San Francisco, December 1969.

Kanfer, S.: "Assassin and Skyjackers: History at Random," Time essay, *Time,* June 12, 1972.

Kassarjian, H. H., and T. S. Robertson (eds.): *Perspectives in Consumer Behavior,* Scott, Foresman & Company, Glenview, Ill., 1968.

Katona, G.: *The Mass Consumption Society,* McGraw-Hill, New York, 1964.

Katona, G.: *The Powerful Consumer,* McGraw-Hill, New York, 1960.

Katona, G., B. Strumpel, and E. Zahn: *Aspirations and Affluence,* McGraw-Hill, New York, 1971.

Katz, E., and P. F. Lazarsfeld: *Personal Influence,* The Free Press, Glencoe, Ill., 1955.

Koback, J. B.: "Business Press Turned the Corner in 1972," *Industrial Marketing,* March 1973.

Kuznets, S.: *Economic Growth of Nations: Total Output and Production Structure,* Harvard University Press, Cambridge, Mass., 1971.

Kuznets, S.: "Modern Economic Growth: Findings and Reflections," *American Economic Review,* June 1973.

Kuznets, S.: *Modern Economic Growth: Rate Structure and Spread,* Yale University Press, New Haven, Conn., 1966.

La Barbera, P.: "Self-Regulation: A Viable Alternative to Government Regulation?", Michigan State University, Graduate School of Business, East Lansing, Mich., August 1973, unpublished manuscript.

Lasker, B.: *Race Attitudes in Children,* Holt, New York, 1929.

Lauterback, A.: in B. Strumpel, N. J. Morgan, and E. Zahn (eds.), *Human Behavior in Economic Affairs: Essays in Honor of George Katona,* Elsevier, Amsterdam, Holland, 1972.

Lazarsfeld, P. F., A. K. Pasanella, and M. Rosenberg (eds.): *Continuities in the Language of Social Research,* The Free Press, New York, 1972.

Lerner, D., and W. Schramm (eds.): *Communication and Change in the Developing Countries,* East-West Center Press, Honolulu, Hawaii, 1967.

Lipstein, B.: "A Mathematical Model of Consumer Behavior," *Journal of Marketing Research,* August 1965.

Luksetich, W. A.: "Some Economic Issues and Policy Implications of Studies on the Competitive Effects of Advertising Expenditures," *Journal of Advertising,* no month given, 1973.

MacKenzie, K. D.: "A Set Theoretic Analysis of Group Interaction," *Psychometrika,* vol. 35, 1970.

Mackenzie, K. D.: *A Theory of Group Structures,* Gordon Breach, New York, 1975.

Mackenzie, K. D., and F. M. Nicosia: "Marketing Systems: Toward Formal Descriptions and Structural Properties," in R. L. King (ed.), *Marketing and the New Science of Planning,* American Marketing Association, Chicago, Ill., 1968.

Marfels, C.: "Some Recent Developments in the Measurement of Business Concentration," Paper No. 7001, Department of Economics, Dalhousie University, Halifax, Canada.

Marketing News, August 1, 1972.

Milgram, I., and R. Lance Shotland: *Television and Anti-Social Behavior,* Academic Press, New York, 1973.

Mitroff, I. I.: "The Myth of Objectivity or Why Science Needs a New Psychology of Science," *Management Science,* June 1972.

Moran, W. T.: "Holding and Switching Strategies," in M. K. Starr (ed.), *Production Management Systems and Synthesis,* Prentice-Hall, Englewood Cliffs, N.J., 1972.

Moran, W. T.: "The Law of Conservation of Advertising Energy," in C. W. King and D. J. Tigert (eds.), *Attitude Research Reaches New Heights,* American Marketing Association, Marketing Research Techniques, Bibliography Series Number 14, Chicago, Ill., n.d.

Moran, W. T.: "Where There Is Choice There Is Value," paper presented to the Annual Scientific Meeting of the Society of Cosmetic Chemists, New York, December 1971, reprinted in *Journal of Advertising Research,* April 1973.

Morgan, J. N.: "A Review of Recent Research on Consumer Behavior," in L. H. Clark (ed.), *Consumer Behavior: Research on Consumer Reactions,* Harper, New York, 1958.

Myers, J. G.: "Legislative Controls and Freedom of Speech: The Case of Commercial Advertising," *Public Affairs Report,* Institute of Governmental Studies, University of California, Berkeley, Calif., August 1972.

Myers, J. G.: *Social Issues in Advertising,* A.A.A.A. Educational Foundation, Inc., New York, 1971.

Nadel, M. V.: *The Politics of Consumer Protection,* Bobbs-Merrill, New York, 1971.

Neisser, U.: *Cognitive Psychology,* Appleton-Century-Crofts, New York, 1969.

Nelson, P.: "Information and Consumer Behavior," *The Journal of Political Economy,* March–April 1970.

Nerlove, M., and F. Waugh: "Advertising Without Supply Control," *Journal of Farm Economics,* November 1961.

Nicosia, F. M.: "Brand Choice: Toward Behavioristic-Behavioral Models," a paper presented to the Symposium on Management Sciences and Behavioral Sciences, sponsored by the University of Chicago and the Institute of Management Science, July 1969.

Nicosia, F. M.: *Consumer Decision Processes: Marketing and Advertising Implications,* Prentice-Hall, Englewood Cliffs, N.J., 1966.

Nicosia, F. M.: "Forecasting Trends in Styling," *Proceedings,* American Statistical Association, Stanford, Calif., August 1960.

Nicosia, F. M.: "Marketing and Alderson's Functionalism," *Journal of Business,* October 1962.

Nicosia, F. M.: "On the Implementation of Panel Designs and Analyses," Consumer Research Program, Survey Research Center, University of California, Berkeley, Calif., December 1972, mimeo.

Nicosia, F. M.: "Panel Designs and Analyses in Marketing," in P. D. Bennett (ed.), *Economic Growth, Competition and World Markets,* American Marketing Association, Chicago, Ill., September 1965.

Nicosia, F. M.: "Public Relations: A Managerial Approach," paper presented to the First Asian-American-African Public Relations Conference, Waseda University, Tokyo, April 1959.

Nicosia, F. M.: "Research in Consumer Behavior: Problems and Perspectives," *Journal of Consumer Affairs,* Summer 1969. Also available in French, *Synopsis,* Janvier–Fevrier 1971, and in Italian, *Studi di Mercata,* Luglio 1972.

Nicosia, F. M.: *Tecnica Amministrativa delle Imprese di Servizi Pubblici,* Edizioni Ateneo, Roma, Italy, 1960.

Nicosia, F. M.: "The Role of Consumption in Economic Growth and Social Change," January 1966, mimeo.

Nicosia, F. M.: "Toward a Model of Consumer Decision Processes," *Proceedings,* American Marketing Association, Chicago, Ill., December 1962.

Nicosia, F. M., and C. Y. Glock: "Marketing and Affluence: A Research Prospectus," in R. L. King (ed.), *Marketing and the New Science of Planning,* American Marketing Association, Chicago, Ill., 1968.

Nicosia, F. M., D. L. MacLachlan, and F. Schreier: *Marketing Research Methods: A Behavioral Approach,* Wadsworth, Belmont, Calif., forthcoming, Ch. 3.

Nicosia, F. M., and B. Rosenberg: "Substantive Modelling in Consumer Attitude Research: Some Practical Uses," in R. I. Haley (ed.), *Attitude Research in Transition,* American Marketing Association, Chicago, Ill., November 1971.

Nicosia, F. M., and Y. Wind: "Social Indicators: Toward a Sociology of Consumption," a paper presented to the International Congress of the Institute of Management Science, April 1972.

Nicosia, F. M., and T. H. Witkowsky: "The Need for a Sociology of Consumption," Annual Conference, Association of Consumer Research, Boston, Mass., November 1973, mimeo.

Noll, R. G., M. J. Peck, and J. J. McGowan: *Economic Aspects of Television Regulation,* The Brookings Institution, Washington, D.C., 1973.

Nonaka, I.: *Organization and Market: Exploratory Study of Centralization vs. Decentralization,* Ph.D. dissertation, Graduate School of Business Administration, University of California, Berkeley, Calif., 1972.

Palda, K.: *The Measurement of Cumulative Advertising Effects,* Prentice-Hall, Englewood Cliffs, N.J., 1964.

Périssé, J.: "L'Homo Economicus Sta Ritornando Ai Menu dell'Età della Pietra?", *Notiziario,* Food Agricultural Organization, Roma, Italy, Luglio 1972.

Peterson, R. D.: "The Advertising Agency Industry: An Analysis of Market Structure Dimensions," abstract in *Western Economic Journal,* September 1971.

Pizzinelli, C.: "La Stampa in Giappone," *Esso Rivista,* Luglio–Ottobre 1970.

Ramond, C.: "Measurement of Sales Effectiveness," in R. Barton (ed.), *Handbook of Advertising Management,* McGraw-Hill, New York, 1970.

Rivers, W. L.: "Mass Communication: The Revolutionary Future," American Association of Advertising Agencies, Western Regional Meeting, New York, October 1969.

Root, H. P.: "Should Product Differentiation Be Restricted?", *Journal of Marketing,* July 1972.

Schmalensee, R.: "Advertising and Economic Welfare," in S. Divita (ed.), *Advertising and the Public Interest,* American Marketing Association, Chicago, Ill., 1974.

Schmalensee, R.: "Brand Loyalty and Barriers to Entry," *Southern Economic Journal,* April 1974.

Schmalensee, R.: *The Economics of Advertising,* North-Holland Publishing Co., Amsterdam, Holland, 1972.

Schramm, W.: *Mass Media and National Development,* Stanford University Press, Stanford, Calif., 1964.

Science (13:1263–64), quoted by J. G. Myers in "The Structure of an Advertising Message," *Journal of Advertising,* Spring 1974.

Simon, J.: *Issues in Economics of Advertising,* University of Illinois Press, Urbana, Ill., 1970.

Solomons, D.: "Financial Accounting Standards: Regulation or Self-Regulation?", Stanford Lectures in Accounting Series, Graduate School of Business, Stanford University, 1972, mimeo.

Stanton, F.: "Business in the Public Forum," paper delivered to the 1973 Annual Meeting of the American Association of Advertising Agencies, May 18, 1973.

Surgeon General's Scientific Advisory Committee on Television and Social Behavior: *Television and Growing Up: The Impact of Televised Violence,* Report to the Surgeon General, U.S. Public Health Service, Washington, D.C., 1972.

Surlin, S. H.: "The Attitudes of Prejudiced Individuals Toward the Institution of Advertising," *Journal of Advertising,* no month given, 1973.

Taylor, L. D., and D. Weiserbs: "Advertising and the Aggregate Consumption Function," *American Economic Review,* September 1972.

Telser, L. G.: "Advertising and Cigarettes," *Journal of Political Economy,* October 1962.

The 4A Newsletter, February 16, 1971.

The National Association of Manufacturers: *Question and Answers for Consumers,* a brochure, n.d.

U.S. Bureau of the Census: "Concentration Ratios in Manufacturing Industry, 1963," Part I, report prepared for the Subcommittee on Antitrust and Monopoly of the Committee on the Judiciary, United States Senate, Washington, D.C., 1966.

U.S. Statistical Abstract 1971: Washington, D.C., 1972.

Valli, C. G.: "Gli Investimenti Pubblicitari in un'Economia in Fase di Sviluppo," *Studi di Mercato,* Numero 1, 1972.

Varaiya, P., and R. Artle: "Locational Implications of Transaction Costs," *The Swedish Journal of Economics,* vol. 74, 1972.

Verdon, W. A., C. R. McConnell, and T. W. Roesler: "Advertising Expenditures as an Economic Stabilizer: 1945–64," *Quarterly Review of Economics and Business,* Summer 1968.

Vernon, J. M.: *Market Structure and Industrial Performance,* Allyn & Bacon, Boston, Mass., 1972.

Vernon, J. M., and M. B. McElroy: "A Note on Estimation in Market Structure-Performance Studies," Marketing Science Institute, Cambridge, Mass., July 1972.

Ward, S., and D. Wackman: "Family and Media Influences on Adolescent Consumer Learning," *American Behavioral Scientist,* January/February 1971.

Wells, W. D.: "Communicating with Children," *Journal of Advertising Research,* June 1965.

Wiio, O. A.: "System Models of Information," International Communication Association, Conference, Montreal, Canada, April 1973.

Wilkie, W. L.: "Research on Counter and Corrective Advertising," in Divita (ed.), *op. cit.*

Wilkie, W. L., and D. M. Gardner: "The Role of Marketing Research in Public Policy Decision Making," *Journal of Marketing,* January 1974.

Wolfe, H. D., J. K. Brown, and G. C. Thompson: *Measuring Advertising Results,* National Industrial Conference Board, New York, 1962.

Zeisel, H.: *Say It With Figures,* Harper, New York, 1957.

Name Index

Subject Index

Advertising comprehends many professions and disciplines; thus, many terms have a multiplicity of meanings. This index, read together with the detailed tables of content for each chapter, should help the reader to cope with the heterogeneity of meanings and to gain access to special topics of interest in the text.